THE HUMAN PROJECT

Readings on the Individual, Society and Culture

THE HUMAN PROJECT

Readings on the Individual, Society and Culture

Edited by

WILLIAM R. HANNA

Humber College of Applied Arts and Technology

CLIVE COCKERTON

Humber College of Applied Arts and Technology

StudyDesk Program

GEORGE BYRNES

Humber College of Applied Arts and Technology

Prentice Hall Canada Inc.,
Scarborough, Ontario

Canadian Cataloguing in Publication Data

Main entry under title:
The human project
ISBN 0-13-207333-1
1. Humanities.   I. Hanna, William R.   II. Cockerton, Clive
AZ221.H85 1996   001.3   C95-931263-3

The human project
Includes computer disk, Humanities studydesk program.
ISBN 0-13-396532-5
1. Humanities   I. Hanna, William R.   II. Cockerton, Clive
AZ221.H85 1996a   001.3   C95-931262-5

Prentice-Hall, Inc., Englewood Cliffs, New Jersey
Prentice-Hall International (UK) Limited, London
Prentice-Hall of Australia, Pty. Limited, Sydney
Prentice-Hall Hispanoamericana, S.A., Mexico City
Prentice-Hall of India Private Limited, New Delhi
Prentice-Hall of Japan, Inc., Tokyo
Simon & Schuster Asia Private Limited, Singapore
Editora Prentice-Hall do Brasil, Ltda., Rio de Janeiro

ISBN: 0-13-207333-1 (Without disk)
ISBN: 0-13-396532-5 (With disk)

Acquisitions Editor: Marjorie Munroe
Developmental Editor: Linda Gorman
Copy Editor: Dianne Broad
Production Editor: Lisa Berland
Production Coordinator: Anita Boyle-Evans
Permissions/Photo Research: Robyn Craig
Cover/Interior Design: Julie Fletcher
Page Layout: Phyllis Seto
Cover Image: Bridgeman/Art Resource, NY
              S0044409   PHD824   Color Transp.
              Friedrich, Caspar David. The Stages of Life. Museum der Bildenden
              Kuenste, Leipzig, Germany.

TABLE OF CONTENTS

UNIT 1:
THE INDIVIDUAL

ISSUE 1: *Why Are We the Way We Are?*

ISSUE 2: *Freedom and Constraint*

UNIT 2:
CHANGE IN THE SOCIAL WORLD

ISSUE 1: *Dynamics of Social Change*

UNIT 5:

ARTS AND CULTURE

PREFACE

The Human Project is an issues-based reader for community colleges, designed to introduce students to Humanities and Social Sciences. It is organized around the fundamental questions asked by a liberal education—questions of social change, politics, science and the arts. The complexity of our world is examined with competing answers to questions such as the following: Are we free or determined? Do we have the sense to co-operate with each other or are we doomed to perpetual conflict? Can science provide solutions to the problems it creates? Students are challenged to grapple with issues that don't have easy answers, to develop the higher level thinking skills that such complex questions require and to acquire a tolerance for the fundamental ambiguities that many of life's basic problems engender. Students who meet this challenge not only become more valuable, flexible and reflective workers and citizens, but they have also started down the path of discovery, making them wiser and more fully rounded individuals.

The text includes a number of features designed to make the book both approachable for students and useful to the instructors. In addition to the inclusion of charts and graphs to give visual examples of ideas and information, there are numerous sidebars that give capsule summaries, highlight important information and direct the student to further reading. Of particular interest is the new "StudyDesk," a computer-based companion guide to the text. Utilizing "hypertext" linking, students are presented with a tutorial on a diskette. This program includes a study guide, review questions, elaborations of points made in the text, etc., allowing students to easily track down explanations or follow their interests. An instructor's manual is also available. This manual identifies the issues presented in each unit, offers suggestions for useful ways to approach these issues, and also provides a comprehensive test bank.

In *The Human Project,* we have endeavoured to present multidimensional issues that encourage students to explore different perspectives and compare theoretical views with their own experience.

While the text doesn't talk down to the student, it remains approachable. The readings have been selected for a cumulative balance of views and, most importantly, for their appeal to students. The perspectives are drawn from various disciplines including psychology, philosophy, sociology, anthropology, political theory, science, medicine and the arts. They are organized into units that begin with the individual and extend to the social, political, physical and cultural realms where the individual operates. This organization, going from the individual *outwards*, allows the student to approach the complexities of the world from familiar ground. Students are encouraged to arrive at an appreciation of the inter-connectedness of things, of how the world is inter-related, by starting with themselves.

The structure of the text and our selections concur with the principles of general education expressed by the College Standards and Accreditation Council of Ontario— principles that are relevant for any college student in the pursuit of a liberal education. To quote from the guiding principles of their document:

> General Education in the colleges shall identify and deal with issues of societal concern in a manner relevant to the lives of students. General education courses shall be structured in such a way as to guide students through the historical context to such issues, their theoretical bases, and application to contemporary life.

The key words "issues of societal concern" and "relevance" have also guided us in our selections. As well, we have been eager to show that contemporary problems have their roots in the past and their solutions in a rich diversity of theoretical perspectives. At least in some measure, the text reflects on the following goals of general education: aesthetic appreciation, civic life, cultural understanding, personal development, understanding society, science, technology, work and the economy. It is only when students become engaged with such issues that real intellectual stretching occurs and they are able to arrive at their own, unique conclusions. We hope that our book, based on classroom experience and inspired by much of the animated debate on general education that has taken place over the last five years, contributes in a real and practical way to the ongoing discussion about what our students need to know to face an ever-changing, complex reality.

We welcome readers' comments, which can be sent by e-mail to

collegeinfo_pubcanada@prenhall.com

The editors would like to thank John Fleming, Marjorie Munroe, Linda Gorman and Lisa Berland at Prentice Hall Canada, as well as Dianne Broad whose efforts as copy editor are much appreciated. Special thanks go to contributing writers who used their understanding of students to translate difficult issues in a way that has relevance to student lives. Above all, we would like to thank all of the instructors who field-tested materials used in this text and all of the students who have responded with such insight and enthusiasm.

The Human Project is available in two versions:
- Text alone (0-13-207333-1)
- Text with "*StudyDesk*" diskette (0-13-396532-5)

INTRODUCTION FOR THE STUDENT

*E*veryone, it seems, wants to be an individual, to be recognized as a unique and special person. Most people also relish the notion of freedom, the idea that they hold the reins, at least some of the time, in determining the course of their lives. Yet, as desirable as individuality and freedom are, very few of us want to live alone. Indeed, most of us need a community of others if we are to live well and flourish. However, the cost of living in a community is usually some sacrifice (in theory anyway) of our individuality and freedom.

Our family expects us to behave in certain ways, our friends demand a code of behaviour, and all the institutions of society, our schools, businesses, churches and government, influence and control our behaviour on many levels. So to live with others is to live with constraint, and yet if we submit to everyone's expectations of us, we run the danger of losing ourselves, our sense of who we are. A natural tension exists in every healthy life and this tension between individual and larger goals doesn't ever finally resolve itself. It is not something you grow out of; it doesn't go away. Just when you're being most dutiful, you can be haunted by the temptation to be wild. Just when you think that indulging your every whim is the answer, the heart responds to a larger call and responds to a need greater than the self.

What do you do with a tension that cannot be resolved, that resists easy answers? You can pretend it doesn't exist and be blown about by the forces of change in an unconscious way. Or you can seek to understand the great tensions and problems of our day and hopefully gain not only awareness but also some influence on how your life evolves.

This book attempts to grapple with some of the difficult problems that confront everyone, from questions of our basic human nature, to social change, to politics, to technology and to arts and culture. This is frequently a dark and complex world, and the modern student needs all the information, all the understanding, all the light he or she can get if they are to find their own way in this world. Grappling with these questions will most probably give your grey cells a good work-out, and thinking skills can be developed that will be useful in all your courses at college and, even more importantly, in your place of work. The possibility of developing your high-level thinking skills through the study of this text is of real and obvious practical bene-fit. But along the way, not in every section or issue, but perhaps in some area, we hope you find some personal revelation and acquire some understanding that is unique to you.

UNIT

1

THE INDIVIDUAL

ISSUE 1:
Why Are We the Way We Are?

ISSUE 2:
Freedom and Constraint

ISSUE
1

WHY ARE WE THE WAY WE ARE?

One of the most revolutionary concepts to grow out of our clinical experience is the growing recognition that the innermost core of man's nature, the deepest layers of his personality, the base of his "animal nature" is positive in nature—is basically socialized, forward-moving, rational and realistic.

Carl Rogers

After all, mind is such an odd predicament for matter to get into. I often marvel how something like hydrogen, the simplest atom, forged in some early chaos of the universe, could lead to us and the gorgeous fever we call consciousness. If a mind is just a few pounds of blood, dream, and electric, how does it manage to contemplate itself, worry about its soul, do time-and-motion studies, admire the shy hooves of a goat, know that it will die, enjoy all the grand and lesser mayhems of the heart? What is mind, that one can be *out of one's*? How can a neuron feel compassion? What is a self? Why did automatic, hand-me-down mammals like our ancestors somehow evolve brains with the ability to consider, imagine, project, compare, abstract, think of the future? If our experience of mind is really just the simmering of an easily alterable chemical stew, then what does it mean to know something, to want something, *to be*? How do you begin with hydrogen and end up with prom dresses, jealousy, chamber music?

Diane Ackerman

PERSONALITY

Jay Haddad

*H*ow much of our personality is learned and how much of our personality is part of our genetic endowment? How much of your personality is changeable and how much is not?

Think about yourself for a minute—would you consider yourself moody? Or shy?

If you feel that you are a moody person, from where does such a trait come? Could it have been genetically passed on to you in the DNA which you inherited from your parents? Is it perhaps an integral part of your body chemistry? Could your "moodiness" be caused by psychological tensions, by anxieties that are stored in your unconscious? Could "moodiness" be a stage you are going through? Or is it a permanent fact of your personality? Will it change? Can it change? You can ponder the same questions with regard to shyness, in fact, to any aggressive or passive behaviours you are aware of as being part of who you are.

As we begin Unit 1, you will see that there are several schools of thought with respect to the nature and origin of personality; at times, the schools are not in conflict with one another but quite often there is a fundamental difference in the way in which the human personality is viewed.

A great deal of conflict often exists in the *basic assumptions* made by each school about the *nature of personality*. Your task, depending on the trait or situation you are attempting to examine, will be to evaluate critically the relative merits of each school's attempt to explain the root causes of human personality.

TRADITIONAL BIOLOGY

The assumption here is that humans have very little choice or free will because our biology determines personality. This "anatomy is destiny" view points to a strong causality between genetic programming and human personality. The view assumes that the 23 chromosomes you inherit from your father and the similar number you inherit from your mother will determine the person you will be. The assumption is a little like Charles Darwin's theory of "natural selection" where strong breeders, that is, people with "good genes," will have strong offspring. Perhaps "good genes" mean that particular gene combinations give some individuals a headstart on a successful life. In short, the biological view assumes humans are controlled by instincts and inborn physical capacities: you are born with your strong points and weak points and there's nothing you can really do about it.

The Traditional Biological School
The traditional biological view assumes humans are controlled by instincts and in-born physical capacities: you are born with your strong points and weak points and there's nothing you can really do about it.

Schools of Thought		
SCHOOLS OF THOUGHT	**MAJOR THINKERS**	**BASIC ASSUMPTIONS ABOUT THE NATURE OF HUMANITY**
Traditional Biological	Biologists	*Human beings have no free will.* Humans are animals whose behaviours are controlled by inherited instincts, in-born physical capacities and individual physical handicaps. Humans are genetically "programmed" at birth.
Psychoanalytic	Freud	*Human beings have no free will.* Humans are not just physical beings, but complex psychological beings, controlled by powerful biological urges from within which are largely unconscious. Humans are in constant conflict between strong sexual and aggressive drives and the controls of conscience and the laws and morals of society.
Behavioural	Watson Skinner Pavlov	*Human beings have no free will.* Humans are infinitely flexible and their behaviours are controlled and shaped by the environment and the effects of its rewards and punishments.
Humanistic Existential	Rogers Maslow	*Human beings have free will.* Humans are humane and caring, motivated from within to grow and develop towards "self-actualization" or the fullest blossoming of their potential.

Issue 1

Be aware that what one person may define as "good genes" may be totally offensive to another person. Because chromosomes may now be technically manipulated and altered by "gene engineers," many unspoken social, ethical, legal, political, racial and gender questions, etc., need to be raised and openly examined.

Some might argue that the biological view absolves the individual from taking any responsibility for behaviour because "I was born this way."

One could also assume that gifted or delinquent or athletic children are exempt from their parents' input because their genetic programming was with them at birth. The parents only carried the genes: the genetic inheritance caused the child's intelligence, delinquency or athletic abilities. This is referred to as the "nature" argument in the *nature vs. nurture* debate. The biological school would assume that personality is basically an inherited phenomenon, and that humans have genes which map out traits like moodiness, shyness, dominance, passivity, and so on.

Sigmund Freud

PSYCHOANALYTIC SCHOOL

Sigmund Freud (1856–1939) devised an interesting way to examine the dynamics of human personality. There are, he assumed, three distinct aspects of human personality:

First, there is the self we think we are, the self which attempts to deal with reality. This Freud called the *ego.* Ego is who we are; it's our awareness of self. It's the person we think we are and the person we display to the outside world. But *ego*, theorized Freud, is never in control of self; *id* comes first!

The *id* is our unconscious, the largest and most important part of personality. The *id* must contain the two biological instincts which govern, dominate and motivate *all* human behaviour—eros and *thanatos. Eros* is referred to as our "life" instinct, but is more generally thought of as the sex, lust, or "pleasure drive." *Thanatos* relates to our "death" instinct but more commonly it is viewed as the human drive toward aggression, hostility and destruction.

As children, the unconscious (*id*) instincts (sex and aggression) surface freely into *ego* or into behavioural action. Children can exhibit anger, rage, destruction and hatred as well as lust, pleasure, arousal and sensuality.

Soon, though, the third aspect of personality emerges: *superego*. *Superego* is, very simply, our conscience; *superego* is our *moral* sense of personality, the part of us that knows (or is supposed to know) right from wrong.

As a person grows up, psychoanalysis assumes, the biological, unconscious, real urges from the *id*, *eros* and *thanatos*, are no longer freely displayed. This is called socialization or internalization which is really the *superego's* attempt to influence *ego* into becoming the personality you are "supposed" to be. As you mature, you also internalize the values and ideals of your society—certainly of your family, your surrounding culture, etc.

(Note that as Freud was developing his concepts, he himself was greatly influenced by his own family history and by the values and pressures of his own society. For this reason, many of his pioneering ideas are often challenged today as being sexist or culturally biased.)

The following is a graphic presentation of the psychoanalytic view of personality:

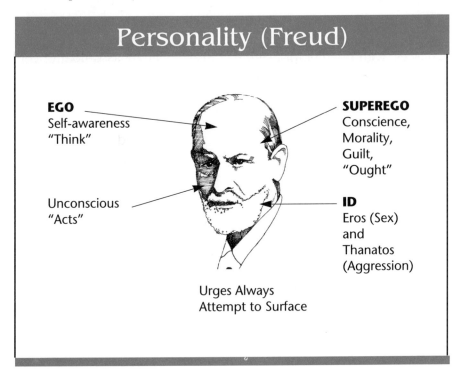

Personality (Freud)

EGO
Self-awareness
"Think"

SUPEREGO
Conscience,
Morality,
Guilt,
"Ought"

Unconscious
"Acts"

ID
Eros (Sex)
and
Thanatos
(Aggression)

Urges Always
Attempt to Surface

The urges or impulses from our unconscious put great pressure on *ego* because *ego* often cannot deal with them or will not deal with them. *Ego's* function is to "think" and *ego* must handle the conflicting demands of *id* and *superego*. *Id* is the primitive, unconscious, childish part of self, saying, "*Do it!* Go for it! I want it!" *Superego*, our moral arbitrator, jumps in and says, "No! Don't do it! It's not right! You know better than that!" *Ego* must weigh the nagging voice of parents and society (morality) against the urges of our unconscious (sex and aggression). Human personality emerges, Freud suggests, by the interactive function between *ego, superego,* and *id.* Too much *ego* repression or denial caused by anxiety or guilt (*superego*) could leave a personality in a disturbed, frustrated or highly dependent state. However, if there is too much *ego* expression, then the *id* surfaces freely, especially if there is insufficient internalization of values by the *superego*. If the *id* is allowed to dominate, one's aggression or delinquency will necessitate society's intervention.

The Freudian School
The assumptions of the Freudian school are simple: in order to gain insight into the causes of personality, one must delve into the world of *id*—the human unconscious which contains all hidden memories, childhood experiences, early life traumas and forbidden fantasies.

The assumptions of the Freudian school are simple: in order to gain insight into the causes of personality, one must delve into the world of *id*—the human unconscious which contains all hidden memories, childhood experiences, early life traumas and forbidden fantasies. Freud and his followers initiated the "talking" cures, intended to give patients insight into their own unconscious minds. Imagine a patient lying on a couch, talking freely of his fears and fantasies, with the therapist sitting at his side, taking notes—and you have the stereotyped beginnings of psychoanalysis. From such talks, from both random and guided conversations, pioneering Freudian psychologists attempted to unlock the unconscious, go deeply into the *id*, and bring to the *ego* an awareness of the causes that may be troubling the patient.

With such knowledge, we can at least begin to understand the complexities of personality.

BEHAVIOURAL SCHOOL

Now we arrive at the "nurture" component of the nature-nurture debate. This school makes three assumptions: behaviour is learned; behaviour is reinforced, and that which is learned can be unlearned and relearned.

Conditioned to play?

This view about personality places the emphasis on the environment and the manner in which you are raised. Your input from your genes is minimal; you can be anything in life, if you are nurtured (rewarded) toward achieving that goal. Star athletes, musicians and academicians, for example, have been nourished and reinforced in their personality development with increased and enriched opportunities. Deprived children, on the other hand, learn low self-esteem and may receive encouragement or a payoff for breaking the rules or breaking the law. Human personality is "shaped," according to behavioural theory.

The cause (*stimulus*) seems unimportant; people emit behaviours, that is, people just do things and don't concern themselves with the "why" (the *cause*) of the behaviour. We are interested in the *payoff!* If whatever you do (and let's not care about "why" you did it) is positively or negatively reinforced, the likelihood of you doing it again *increases*. Similarly, if whatever you do is punished or ignored (no reinforcement), the likelihood of you doing it again *decreases*. This is the *Law of Effect*, the most important equation in all of behavioural science.

The Behavioural School
The behavioural school views behaviours as learned phenomena. Our society merely exerts reinforcers on each individual to shape personality. The assumption here is that delinquent behaviours, addictive behaviours or anti-social behaviours are all learned *inappropriate responses*.

Issue 1

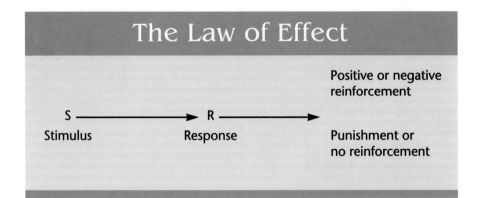

The Law of Effect

Positive or negative
reinforcement

S ——————————→ R ——————————→

Stimulus   Response

Punishment or
no reinforcement

B.F. Skinner

B.F. Skinner (1904–90) in his books and articles (*Walden Two, Beyond Freedom and Dignity,* etc.) attempts to explain the importance of "shaping" behaviours by their consequences. He discusses how personality is relatively neutral and becomes dominant only in the way behaviours are rewarded or not rewarded. For example, a three-year-old child, standing in a checkout line with her mother may ask for some candy two feet away from her. Mother says, "No." The child throws a tantrum, screams, cries and jumps up and down. Mother relents; the child gets the candy and stops crying. The Law of Effect explains what has happened from a behavioural point of view. The response of the child (the tantrum) led to a reward (positive consequences) in that the child received the candy (payoff). Is the tantrum behaviour, according to the Law of Effect, likely to *increase* or *decrease* in this child's personality repertoire?

The behavioural school views behaviours as learned phenomena. Our society merely exerts reinforcers on each individual to shape personality. The assumption here is that delinquent behaviours, addictive behaviours or anti-social behaviours are all *learned inappropriate responses.*

If you assume, as behaviourists do, that anything that is learned can be unlearned and relearned, there is great optimism for changing behaviour (through therapy or intervention techniques). Simply change the reinforcers so that tantrum behaviour (as in the 3-year-old) is no longer rewarded and the child will learn a new behaviour. (Hopefully, a more appropriate behaviour will take its place.) Therapeutically, this is called *behaviour modification,* with no references to "unconscious" impulses or to genetic predispositions at all! One may simply change the behaviour by changing the *consequences* which modify each response.

Issue 1

The important question to ask is not why any person does something inappropriate (Why are some men abusive? Why do some women drink all day? Why is crime increasing among 14-year-olds?)—but rather, in what way is the inappropriate behaviour leading to a payoff? That is, in what way is the behaviour of drinking or sexual abuse being rewarded or reinforced? In what way does crime (anti-social behaviour) lead to payoff in groups of young people today? The Law of Effect, in summary, allows us to examine personality based on behaviour and reinforcers.

HUMANISTIC-EXISTENTIAL SCHOOL

The previous three schools share one important dimension in common: they assume that the individual is *not* in control of self. Your personality, in other words, is motivated by genetic factors of which you are unaware (biological school), or by unconscious forces from the past of which you are unaware (psychoanalytic school), or, finally, by learned, inappropriate social responses of which you are unaware (behavioural school). All of these theories assume a lack of choice or *free will* on the part of the individual. Personality, they emphasize, is *determined* by forces outside of your control!

The humanists assume that we all are fundamentally *free* to make choices at each and every turning point in our lives. We have "free will" irrespective of our biology (genes), our past (unconscious), or our conditioning (Law of Effect). This is the newest of the schools of thought and, because of its emphasis on *choice* and *free will*, probably the most popular theory today.

There is an apparent optimism but a heavy responsibility in assuming that despite your biology, your past or your previous learning, you are free to be whatever you want to be—you are *limitless* in exercising the potential you have within yourself for growth or change! For example, if you were moody or shy as a teenager, you can enjoy the thrill and challenge and excitement of making new choices that will change you. If you were terribly repressed sexually or behaviourally (perhaps due to your parents' hangups), *you* don't have to be—you are free to change (if only you realize it)! If you learned delinquent patterns in your youth and were rewarded for anti-social behaviours, "today is the first day of the rest of your life."

The Humanistic-Existential School
The *humanists* assume that we all are fundamentally *free* to make choices at each and every turning point in our lives. We have "free will" irrespective of our biology (*genes*), our past (*unconscious*), or our conditioning (*Law of Effect*).

Issue 1

Change! Grow! Recognize your incredible potential! The choice is yours!

This tone of optimism for personal growth and change strongly inspired the "School of the '60s," giving rise to the Human Potential Movement. Walk into most bookstores in North America today and you will discover that the majority of modern books on psychology (at least 80% of them) have been influenced by the humanist-existential school. Authors from Rogers to Maslow, Dyer to Buscaglia, Harris to Gordon, clearly support the humanistic message: control is yours, no one else's!

Human personality is capable of changing; humans are motivated from within to grow and develop. This view holds that personality is not static but rather dynamic, always changing. If a person is moody, it is the individual's choice to be moody; the control or responsibility lies with the individual. Thus, "hope springs eternal," for one's past, one's biology and one's learning, are not as important as the present "now" for doing something about yourself, for making choices that will allow you to change and grow.

Abraham Maslow, one of the pioneers of the Human Potential Movement, wrote "the bible" for humanistic psychology (*Toward A Psychology Of Being*). Prior to Maslow, psychological theory was always oriented toward balance (equilibrium, homeostasis); that is, when human needs arise, the individual is in an "unbalanced" state (disequilibrium) and therefore seeks "balance" (homeostasis) by satisfying that need. For example, if your stomach is growling and you are preoccupied with satisfying your hunger needs, then you are in an "unbalanced" (disequilibrium) state. In order for your body to return to homeostasis (balance) you must satisfy your hunger needs by eating.

Abraham Maslow

Maslow, however, rejected this quest for seeking balance in his new psychology (he actually called his humanism the "third force" in contrast to both psychoanalysis and behaviourism). Maslow stated that the "unbalanced" state is the *normal* state. According to Maslow, we are always in a state of "need" (i.e., unbalanced); we are always, therefore, "unbalanced"!

In attempting to seek equilibrium or balance we are not aware of the fact that the satisfaction of one need only leads to the creation of yet another need; it's our needs that are in a continual pattern of change. From this, Maslow developed his famous pyramid where he demonstrated the existence of our needs in a hierarchical manner:

Issue 1

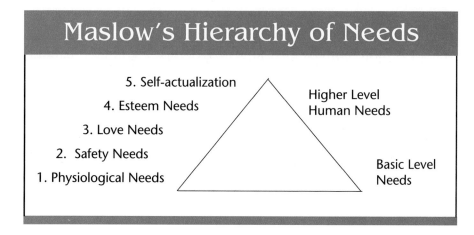

We start off with basic biological needs: hunger, thirst, sex, sleep, elimination. When our basic needs are met, new needs arise—but needs of a higher level. For example, following our basic PHYSIO-LOGICAL needs comes the need for safety and security: having a place to sleep, the security of territoriality and so on. When SAFETY needs are met, LOVE needs arise—our need for bonding, belonging as strong social needs. Following love comes the need for ES-TEEM, the sense of self-worth, the ability to feel good about yourself. Ultimately, our never-ending need is the peak of the hierarchy—the need for SELF-ACTUALIZATION or the fulfilment of all of our human potential. This lofty need obviously never gets fully satisfied; thus, we are in a constant state of evolving, growing, becoming … yet we are always "unbalanced"! One need satisfied simply gives rise to an-other need—perhaps one of a higher level, as the pyramid shows.

Maslow's theory evolved after years of studying "healthy" indi-viduals (as opposed to people who have severe psychological prob-lems). The important thing to remember about Maslow (and humanism) is the fact that he wanted humanistic psychology to be a prescription toward health, toward a better quality of life and to-ward a more complete understanding of the "wholeness" of being human as we seek growth and fulfilment throughout our lifetime.

CONCLUSION

It would sound fairly confusing to lay down the assumptions made by personality theories and discover that they are quite opposite and contradictory!

If the humanists believe that we are essentially "free," while the behaviourists believe that we are essentially "controlled," which school is more correct? Carl Rogers says this is a unique paradox with which we all must live: both schools are correct; we are at the same time helpless souls conditioned and shaped by the reinforcers in our environment AND supreme masters of our own destiny, making free choices throughout every phase of our lives.

Can we understand this paradox? Soren Kierkegaard, a famous Danish philosopher, said: "The paradox is the source of the thinker's passion and the thinker without paradox is like a lover without feeling."

This paradox is uniquely human and allows us to discover the complexity of the human psyche. We *are* influenced, programmed, or controlled by forces totally external to us. Yet, we are also capable at any time of making spontaneous decisions, decisions for which we are wholly responsible.

Psychologists use tests (personality tests with no right or wrong answers) to determine the degree of control that an individual believes he or she may have over his or her own life. There are those individuals that psychologists label "internally controlled" and those categorized as "externally controlled." Internally controlled people believe they are in total command of their lives; they believe that what they do matters and they assume responsibility for their success or failure. Externally controlled individuals feel that they have no real personal control of their lives. It is always the fault of someone else or some other agency when things go wrong. Parents, employers, boyfriends/girlfriends, etc., all make great scapegoats. Their destiny (happiness or unhappiness, success or failure) is perceived to lie in the hands of "others." They feel powerless insofar as they *believe* that what they do has little or no impact on anyone or anything.

Perhaps when viewed from this perspective, our paradox makes more sense. Those individuals who are "internally controlled" clearly fall into the humanist camp, while the "externally controlled" individuals belong in the behaviourist camp. Internally controlled people would probably vote and engage in other activities which would indicate their degree of *perceived* control over their own lives. Externally controlled people, predictably, wouldn't vote and might say: "What difference does my vote make anyway?"

Review

Personality: Four Schools of Thought

This section discusses four reasoned approaches to the question, "Why are we the way we are?"

According to the biological model of human nature associated with 19th-century naturalist Charles Darwin, personality is inherited and cannot be altered through human choice or behaviour. We are determined by heredity, not environment. We must play the cards nature has dealt us because we will pick up no others along the way.

A late 19th- and early 20th-century Viennese doctor named Sigmund Freud revolutionized our perception of human personality by proposing an intricate psychoanalytic model involving components that he called the *ego, id*, and *superego*, which interact with each other to determine personality. The id, our unconscious, is comprised of our pleasure drives (*eros*) and our drives towards aggression,

hostility and destruction (*thanatos*). The superego is our moral sense; the ego is our self-awareness or consciousness which negotiates between demands of the id and the expectations of the superego. According to Freud and the psychoanalytic school, the degree to which the ego and superego repress, alter, or fulfill biological drives determines personality.

The third school of thought is the behavioural school. Behaviourists minimize the role of heredity and heighten the role of environment in determining why we are the way we are. According to the behaviourists, behaviour is learned, is reinforced through positive or negative rewards, and can be changed through conditioning. B.F. Skinner is a major proponent of the behavioural school.

The biological, psychoanalytic, and behavioural schools maintain that we are shaped by

outside forces and we do not possess free will. The fourth and most recent school of thought, known as the humanist-existential school, suggests that we possess free will and the power to change ourselves and the outside world. Humanists contend that we hold all the cards in the game of life and are free to deal them as we wish. The multitude of self-help books and personal growth manuals in bookstores suggests the prevalence of this view in contemporary western society.

These four schools of thought contain many differences, even contradictions. Which one is right? Or does each reflect some part of the whole make-up of personality? Collectively, these four schools of personality theory provide a universe of insight into the dynamic phenomenon of human personality.

Examine the paradox and you will probably find that our attitudes and beliefs are full of contradictions. In this case, perhaps, there is a continuum, ranging from "absolutely no control over my life" to "absolute control over my life." Maybe the behaviourist vs. humanist debate is better understood by first understanding our complex range of perceptions about how much of our lives we *believe* we actually control!

Review

Personality: Four Schools of Thought

Fill in the Blanks

This section discusses four reasoned approaches to the question, "Why are we the way we are?" According to the _____ model of human nature associated with 19th-century naturalists, personality is inherited and cannot be altered through human choice or behaviour. We are determined by heredity, not environment. We must play the cards nature has dealt us because we will pick up no others along the way.

A late 19th- and early 20th-century Viennese doctor named _____ revolutionized our perception of human personality by proposing an intricate model, referred to as the _____ model of personality, involving components which interact to determine personality.

The _____, our unconscious, is comprised of our pleasure drive (_____) and our drive towards aggression, hostility and destruction (_____). The _____ is our moral sense; the _____ is our self-awareness or consciousness, which negotiates between demands of the _____ and the expectations of the _____.

According to this school, the degree to which the _____ and _____ repress, alter, or fulfil biological drives determines personality.

EXERCISE

Remember, your task is to assess the relative impact or importance or merits of each school of thought.

Choose a behaviour and examine the analysis and assumptions made by each school with respect to the causes and treatments of the behaviour. For example, you can look at alcohol addiction and assume—

a. It is *biologically* based, caused by a genetic weakness or predisposition. Alcoholism is not the person's fault, and, therefore, treatment lies in understanding and correcting the biological imbalance. Any "talking" cures (psychoanalysis) would be totally useless and irrelevant to this view.

b. Alcohol addiction is *unconsciously* motivated, caused by misdirected *eros* or *thanatos* energy surfacing to the *ego* in the form of an addiction to drinking. The person is consciously unaware of the cause of this "oral" dependency, and therapy would involve many hours of exposing the unconscious (*id*), that is, of talking out one's feelings, anxieties and early life experiences.

c. Alcohol addiction, to the behaviourist, is a bad habit! It is a behaviour which has obviously been reinforced, in that the behaviour (response) of drinking has led to good things happening (reward). The consequences (reinforcement) of alcohol dependency must be altered so that abstinence leads to reward. Therefore, sessions of behaviour modification might be used to slowly change the reinforcers. (A drastic method of intervention, called "aversive conditioning," was illustrated in the movie, *A Clockwork Orange*.) In short, "bad" behaviours can be unlearned and relearned through appropriate conditioning (reinforcement) methods.

d. The humanist would assume you have chosen alcohol dependency as an escape; this is understandable in a world filled with stress and anxiety. Do you want to change? If you do, you have the power and control within you to make that choice. As one anti-drug campaign put it, "Say NO to drugs!" It's that simple—or is it?

❖

The above theories and examples are presented in an oversimplified and non-technical way. In reality, of course, these theories and therapies do overlap and are more complex. However, we have presented them to you as separate and independent schools to promote analysis, insight and comparison.

Is one theory better than another? Should certain concepts from one theory be married to another theory? Do you yourself have some new clues about personality and human behaviour?

The adventure is to know more about yourself, for such insights often help you to understand how you relate to others, and how you may enrich your own life. Self knowledge, understanding some of the potential causes that make you a personality, also enables you to understand others.

We share with humankind that quality called "personality." It is an exciting, lifetime adventure to discover who we are—and why.

Issue 1

THE CONFLICT WITHIN

Clive Cockerton

*L*ife, for all its rewards, is still for many people a struggle. There are so many choices to get right—the choices of job, partner, children—and the wrong choices can fill our lives with regret. As well, the average day crowds us with so many tasks, errands to do, places to go, responsibilities to take care of, that one has little time for reflection. Yet without reflection, it is very difficult to be clear to ourselves about what we want. Every person, even sane, well-adjusted people, is so full of doubt, contradiction and compromise, that the way forward is confusing. How can we sort ourselves out, how can we understand ourselves better so that we might be happy and lead productive lives? We all want to lead happy and productive lives. But what does that mean? How do you know that the things you do, the relationships you have, are right for you? It is not only thinkers like Plato, Freud and Maslow who address these questions. We all do—to a greater or lesser extent. It is this search for an answer, or a partial answer, that defines our humanity and makes us who we are. These questions, so pressingly contemporary, have haunted reflective minds since the beginning of time.

REASON

Plato (427–347 B.C.) tried to capture the internal conflict so many of us feel when he compared the processes of the soul to the struggle of a charioteer (reason) to control two horses, one vigorous and obedient (spirit), the other aggressive and demanding (appetite). Plato located these three elements of the soul in the body, with reason being located in the brain, spirit in the chest and appetite in the abdomen. Plato never tried to deny the body, but he argued for self-control—for the rule of reason over the urges of the appetites. Reason, with the aid of willpower (spirit), must keep watch and ensure that the bodily urges and pleasure do not become so powerful as to enslave us and turn life upside down. The appetites are waiting to rebel against the rule of reason, and the wise person tries to bring the

Plato

three elements of the soul into harmonious balance through self-mastery and discipline. As Plato writes:

> Only when he has linked these parts together in well-tempered harmony and has made himself one man instead of many, will he be ready to go about whatever he may have to do, whether it be making money and satisfying bodily wants, or business transactions, or the affairs of state.

"Only when he has made himself one man instead of many." In other words, when the contradictions within cease, when the conflict within is wisely resolved according to the guidance of reason. If we don't resolve the conflict and live in harmony, we are always at risk from the rebellion of the darkest desires, "terrible in untamed lawlessness, which reveal themselves in dreams."

More than 2,000 years before Sigmund Freud began his crucial work on dreams, Plato warned of the desires that live within even the most respectable:

> Those [desires] which bestir themselves in dreams, when the gentler part of the soul slumbers and the control of reason is withdrawn; then the wild beast in us, full-fed with meat or drink, becomes rampant and shakes off sleep to go in quest of what will gratify its own instincts. As you know, it will cast away all shame and prudence at such moments and stop at nothing. In fantasy it will not shrink from intercourse with a mother or anyone else, man, god, or brute, or from forbidden food or any deed of blood. In a word, it will go to any length of shamelessness and folly.

If we are to prevent these terrible imaginings from becoming our destiny, we must learn to quieten our potentially raging appetites through moderate use. The answer is not to starve our appetites but to train and domesticate them so that our reason can lead us away from the negative emotions of lust, ambition and greed and towards the positive states of harmony, justice and wisdom.

THE UNCONSCIOUS

Although Plato's wisdom still speaks to us, it is difficult to share his faith in the rule of reason. Owing to the insights of Sigmund Freud, we are too well aware of the overwhelming role of the irrational, the instinctual side of our personality. Our rational side has done much to advance our understanding of the natural world through science and technology, with many benefits for the health and convenience of the modern citizen. But our achievements in this century must stand beside a technologically enhanced savagery that has led to war and genocide. Towards the end of his life Freud worried that thanatos, the biological instinct for aggression, was perhaps the dominant instinct in the id. Our frail, rational egos struggle with powerful urges that resist understanding. In its attempt to negotiate a sensible path, the ego must endure rebuke from the superego. In an image reminiscent of Plato, Freud compared the id to a spirited horse that the rider must struggle to control. But unlike Plato, Freud didn't have much faith in our ability to domesticate the horse, and we are constantly reminded that our victories in taming the beast within are temporary and provisional.

Primarily irrational and instinctual, we remain largely unaware of the conflicts whose origins lie deep in our childhood. However much time and experimental psychology have served to undermine some of the details of Freud's work, it is clear that the shape of our personality has very deep roots and that our relationship with our parents is frequently a troubled thing. Our parents who were prime suppliers of the rules to the superego; our parents who said no more than yes—our parents whom we wished dead; our parents who loved us and whom we love. As children we are dependent on them, yet the struggle to grow up is the struggle to separate from them, to gain independence. Once we stand on our own two feet, we look around for a mate, a companion, and much of our choice is still influenced by our mother and father. How many women unconsciously marry people similar to their fathers, how many men search for the qualities of their mothers? Having found these qualities in a mate, we have the seeds of resentment as well. Because in the choice of our mate, the ultimate act of separation from our parents (we are now starting our own family), we are reminded that we were never really able to break away, our independence day just a temporary breakout, a prison mutiny.

Is there a way out of this cycle of love and resentment? Psychoanalysis has no easy and quick cure, no 12-step program. What it sometimes offers is an opportunity to explore our deepest feelings with a knowledgeable and trustworthy guide. On the analyst's couch ideas and emotions percolate to the surface where they might not be allowed in ordinary life, where they would be self-censored. Through these discussions with the analyst, the patient begins the process of self-discovery and encounters a language and a theoretical structure designed to assist him or her in understanding his or her own life, of bringing the unconscious to the light. But once understanding is achieved, does the conflict within evaporate? Perhaps in some cases it does, but for many the promise of freedom from the traumas and conflicts of our past is largely theoretical and not actual. Still, understanding oneself, even if it doesn't resolve all conflicts, is a major achievement. Many go to their grave with barely a glimmer of insight into their own lives.

FEAR AND GROWTH

Maslow takes a very different tack from Freud and in his studies of healthy, successful people discovered that they tended to integrate the conscious and unconscious sides of their personality. The id and the ego are not so opposed to each other, as there is both less unresolved conflict and more expression of spontaneous impulses. The superego is less punishing, the unconscious more healthy. The rational side finds a place even for irrationality, and accepts the transition from one state to another as healthy and desirable.

When Maslow looks at our natural tendency to growth and self-actualization, he observes that the process is often not a particularly well-prepared plan; we live in the moment, yet growth occurs. We don't so much search for a purpose as find it through a series of experiments with our environment and the people who inhabit it. As Maslow writes:

> ... growth takes place when the next step forward is subjectively more delightful, more joyous, more intrinsically satisfying than the previous gratification.... We don't do it because it is good for us, or because psychologists approve, or because somebody told us to, or because it will make us live longer, or because it is good for the species, or because it will bring external rewards, or because it is logical. We do it for the same reason that we choose one dessert over another.

In other words, because it just feels like the right thing to do. It sounds so natural that we could fall forward into the face of new possibilities without even trying. If this process of growth is so natural and inevitable, however, why do some people seem to grow much more easily than others? What obstacles stand in the way of achieving our potential?

For Maslow, many of us are still deeply conflicted beings. Safety needs cause us to resist the urge to self-actualization; fear of danger, of humiliation prevents us from moving boldly forward and so we cling to the comfort of the familiar. But not without regretting our actions. Every opportunity carries risk. Public speaking contests can be a true high-school horror, and many of us shy away from participation, afraid of humiliation, unsure of our abilities, painfully reminded of past failures. What we need at these moments of self-doubt is a little courage—the courage to find our voice and the wisdom to know that the risks are small. Despite our fears, we wouldn't lose all our friends even if our speech was terrible. So it is with every challenge; with varying degrees of intensity, the conflict between safety and self-actualization needs gallops after every opportunity. Should we let the opportunity slip and be safe or should we go for it and maybe become stronger and wiser for the struggle?

LIVING IN THE PRESENT

For humanists, our life is ultimately of our own making. We are born as biology; we live and write our own biography. The chemical stew of a brain we are born with wants to make something of its pulsing time on earth. It is our responsibility, no one else's. Socrates said that the unexamined life was not worth living and clearly a life without reflection and understanding is impoverished. So too is the un-involved life, the defensive life, the life that at some level seems endured rather than lived, the life that erects barriers between it and the quivering possibilities of the present. Dennis Potter, the English playwright, discovered that he was dying of cancer, and made the following comments in a TV interview:

> We're the one animal that knows we're going to die, and yet we carry on, paying our mortgages, doing our jobs, behaving as though there's eternity and we forget or tend to forget that

life can only be defined in the present tense, it is and it is now. Much as we would like to call back yesterday, and yearn to, we can't. However predictable tomorrow is. Even so, there's the element of the unpredictable. The only thing you know for sure is the present tense, and that nowness becomes so vivid so that in a perverse sort of way, I'm almost serene. I can celebrate life.

Below my window in Ross when I'm working the blossom is out in full. It's a plum tree...it's the whitest, frothiest, blossomest blossom that there ever could be. And things are both more trivial than they ever were and more important than they ever were and the difference doesn't seem to matter. The nowness of everything is absolutely wondrous and if people could see that—there's no way of telling you, you have to experience it.

But the glory of it, the comfort of it, the reassurance... The fact is, that if you see the present tense, boy do you see it! And boy can you celebrate it.

That wondrous sense of life that flows through his remarks on the occasion of his dying calls to us to make much of our time, to feel the force of our own vitality. This perception doesn't banish conflict and doubt and anxiety but puts them in their place, and if we could only hold this perception in the front of our minds, a more authentic, happy life might be possible.

> We almost never think of the present, and when we do, it is only to see what light it throws on our plans for the future.
>
> *Pascal*

ISSUE

2

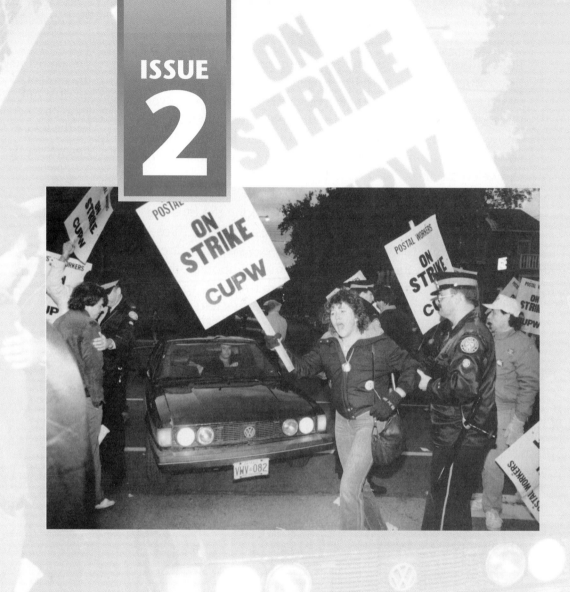

FREEDOM AND CONSTRAINT

Give me a dozen healthy infants, well-formed and my own specified world to bring them up in and I'll guarantee to take any one at random and train him to become any type of specialist I might select—doctor, lawyer, artist, merchant, chief and, yes even beggarman and thief, regardless of the talents, penchants, tendencies, abilities, vocations, and race of his ancestors.

John B. Watson

... if some day they truly discover a formula for all our desires and caprices—that is an explanation of what they depend upon, by what laws they arise, just how they develop, what they are aiming at in one case or another and so on, and so on, that is a real mathematical formula—then, after all, man would most likely at once stop to feel desire, indeed, he will be certain to. For who would want to choose by rule?... for what is a man without desire, without free will and without choice...

Dostoyevsky

I'M A FREAK OF NATURE SO DON'T BLAME MY PARENTS

Jay Haddad

- Dan White, who assassinated San Francisco's mayor George Moscone and city supervisor Harvey Milk, successfully introduced the now-famous "twinkie defence," stating that his penchant for cream-filled twinkies diminished his mental capacity.

- Helmuth Buxbaum's lawyers argued that he murdered his wife due to brain damage, which caused bouts of insanity. The jury disagreed and sent him to jail for life.

- Dr. Langevin (Clarke Institute of Psychiatry) indicates that brain damage from car accidents is increasingly revealing itself among his criminal research subjects; therefore, criminal behaviour may be linked to brain damage.

- English courts have traditionally sympathized with women who committed crimes while suffering from severe premenstrual syndrome and postpartum depression.

- The *Toronto Star's* headline on November 25, 1993, regarding the guilty verdicts of 11-year-olds Jon Venables and Robert Thompson for murdering 2-year-old James Bulger: "Evil Freaks of Nature Get Life for Murdering Tot."

- Dr. George Vaillant (Harvard University) on the discovery of the "addicted brain": it is not important how much a person drinks but rather WHO DRINKS.

- According to Dr. Jerome Kagan (Harvard University), approximately 15% of all children are born with a tendency to shyness, regardless of their upbringing.

- People who are risk-takers have low levels of MAO (monoamine oxidase), a brain enzyme responsible for stimulating behaviour.

- Dr. John Hundleby (Guelph University) says convicts are made, not born; home environment is more crucial than personality in predicting criminality.

- Dr. Pierre Flor-Henry (Alberta Hospital, Edmonton) has found that left hemisphere brain damage is a cause of sexual criminal behaviour; this phenomenon existed in 90 percent of his criminal research subjects.

Nature? Or nurture? How has the pendulum swung with respect to the relative importance of "biology" or "heredity" (nature) and "environment" (nurture) on our developing personality?

NURTURE (ENVIRONMENT)

Fifty years ago, the pendulum had swung firmly to the "nurture" side of the nature-nurture debate, as most behavioural psychologists believed that we could create whatever we wanted simply by enriching the fertile soil under each child, like waving a magic wand. A Wayne Gretzky or Michael Jordan, D.H. Lawrence or Margaret Laurence, Elvis Stojko or Oksana Baiul, was just around the corner, as long as committed parents channelled all the child's energy, direction and labour into the desired activity. Wait a minute, you're thinking—you could become the next Shaquille O'Neal by simply immersing yourself 20 hours a day into the skills and training required for basketball stardom? (Oh, you're not that tall—how about Anfernee Hardaway?)

The notion that success, genius or talent are the product of "ripe" environmental factors suggests that the opposites (failure, simple-mindedness, lack of talent) are equally the product of "deprived" social environments. Therefore, either way, it's to the parents' or caregivers' credit or their fault because they are the ones responsible for creating that important social environment.

The "nurture" school received its greatest edge in the early 1960s as a group of researchers at the University of Wisconsin, led by Dr. Harry Harlow, were about to examine the relationship between "bonding" (psychological affect) and "touch" (maternal affection) on a group of rhesus monkeys. From a strictly behavioural perspective, the researchers wanted to know what influence the deprivation of touch by the mother exerted on the psychological stability (affect) of newborn rhesus monkeys.

One group of monkeys had the infant rhesus monkeys removed from their mothers immediately after birth to separate rooms. A second group of infant rhesus monkeys were removed from their mothers and placed in cages where they could see their mothers, smell their mothers, hear their mothers, but could not touch their mothers (as they were separated by plexiglass barriers).

Scientists were ill-prepared for the results, to say the least! They had thought that "touch," demonstrated by its lack, would be of some measurable significance to the psychological affect of the rhesus monkey. They were shocked to learn that both groups of Harlow monkeys developed the typical affect of either autism (withdrawal) or atavism (aggression).

Obviously, this research had tremendous implications for children who were neglected, left alone too much or simply not cuddled or held. Social rearing ("environment") had a *lot* to do with our psychological health; social policies began to introduce institutional "care-givers" who would routinely and repeatedly hug and cuddle those children who were institutionalized.

A new twist to the Harlow data occurred in the 1970s when pioneering brain research discovered that Harlow's deprived rhesus monkeys actually had developed brain damage.

The Harlow equation is now:

Touch deprivation (maternal deprivation)=
Brain damage (damage to the cerebellum)=
Withdrawal (autism) or aggression (atavism)

Harlow's research suggests that one's physiology (nature, biology) can actually be disrupted by one's life experience (nurture, environment). That disruption can lead to brain damage, which can account for those behaviours that we typically label or associate with aggression in society or withdrawal from society.

Actually, Dr. John Money (Johns Hopkins University) says that the "nature-nurture" equation is, more appropriately, the "nature - critical period - nurture" equation. That is, all developmental tasks must be acquired during the critical periods—that period of time when development has its most profound effect. In the Harlow experiment, rhesus monkeys were deprived of touch during the "critical period" (30–60 days after birth), whereas in humans the critical period for touch is between three to 24 months. We all have critical periods for intelligence, verbal skills, language skills, gender identity, sexual orientation, etc. Sometimes the critical period occurs as a pre-natal influence: thalidomide was believed to be a harmless tranquil-lizing medication prescribed to pregnant women in the 1960s in Canada, England, Germany and Scandinavia. The drug was harm-less if taken *after* the first trimester; however, the effects of the drug were devastating when taken *during* the first trimester in the critical period known as organogenesis (the laying down of all organ path-ways). You can see how the famous Harlow experiment gave "nur-ture" a big nudge as the early life experience of deprivation seemed to lay the groundwork for a personality plagued with problems, dif-ficulties and deficiencies in the Harlow test monkeys. It should be noted that in the "control" group of Harlow rhesus monkeys (i.e., monkeys allowed to grow normally within the colony), no adverse effects were measured, either in behaviour or with respect to brain damage. It's safe to assume that our early life experiences are certainly significant but they are made even more so when they happen to in-tersect with a significant "time" for a developmental task to occur (i.e., critical period).

The significance of "nurture" has, of course, been advanced by the behaviourist school of personality, which you read about in the "Personality" article. We discussed the largest name in operant con-ditioning circles, B. F. Skinner, and his "Law of Effect" that all human behaviour can be understood and/or changed by understanding "payoff" (the system of reward and punishment that follows a re-sponse).

The "nurture" side of the nature-nurture debate has also been greatly advanced by Ivan Pavlov, the Russian physiologist who pio-neered classical conditioning, the notion that personality is influ-enced by the pairing or association of two or more stimulus events, which cause either pain or pleasure in our developing personality. Classical conditioning, for example, would treat alcoholics by pairing alcohol with a substance that induces violent vomiting; the hope is that, in time, the very idea of drinking alcohol will cause revulsion. Similarly, you may be very aroused by the smell of someone's per-fume with whom you are dating; later on, you may smell that fra-grance on someone else and it has a positive effect.

The theory of social learning, advanced by Albert Bandura, is also referred to as modelling or imitative learning. According to Bandura, boys and girls grow up observing their surroundings and learning to imitate the men and women in their lives—in both positive and negative ways. Bandura's experiments involved one group of children watching "violent" cartoons while another group of children watched "non-violent" cartoons. The children were later observed, at play, and those who had observed aggression tended to model or imitate that aggression while children who did not observe any aggression were quite passive and docile at play.

NATURE (HEREDITY, BIOLOGY)

The last twenty years has seen nothing short of an avalanche of scientific evidence pointing us toward a greater understanding that "anatomy is destiny."

We have a heightened understanding of our endocrine system, our prenatal evolution, our DNA mapping and, most particularly, the effects of endogenous and exogenous chemicals and nutrients on the 10 billion neurons that "talk" to each other in the human brain. Dr. Richard Haier (University of California, Irvine) says that "personality may be very much biochemical; and variations in personality are due to variations in brain chemistry."

The first major studies illuminating the powerful effects of "nature" over "nurture" were the twin studies. Hypothetically, an ideal way to study how much of our personality is influenced by heredity versus environment would be to take monozygotic (identical) twins, separate them at birth, have them reared by different families in different parts of the country and reunite them and study them years later. Science found its answer by tracing adoptions of twins from many years ago, who were, indeed, separated at birth and raised by different families. These "identical" twins were reunited and are participating in a rigorous study at the University of Minnesota that began in 1979.

Of course, the nature of monozygotic twins is identical; it is "nurture," therefore, and its influence that is being measured. The University of Minnesota has reunited 75 pairs of monozygotic twins, as well as 50 pairs of dizygotic (fraternal) twins, which share, on average 50 percent of the same genes. These groups of twins were compared with control groups of identical and fraternal twins who were raised in the same home; now the relative importance or impact

Twins marrying twins: studies show that twins share similar taste.

of heredity versus environment on the developing personality could be examined.

The results were startling. More than 350 pairs of twins have gone through six days of extensive testing that scanned their brain waves, monitored their heart rates, measured their skills and asked 15,000 questions designed to reveal their personalities, habits, tastes, values and idiosyncrasies.

Identical (monozygotic) twins are very much alike—personalities, dispositions, habits, abilities, even idiosyncracies—whether they are raised together or not. There is obviously a permanence to nature (heredity) that simply will not change despite environmental forces acting upon us at each moment of our lives. If environment was the main determinant of personality, then identical twins raised in the same home would be expected to show more similarities than would twins who were reared apart. The study actually revealed, however, that the personality differences between the two groups of identical twins were far *smaller* than had been assumed. The personality similarities between the identical twins reared apart are almost as pervasive as they are with identical twins reared together. The researchers found that traits like "traditionalism"—a trait implying conservatism and respect for authority—can be inherited. Other traits most strongly determined by heredity are "leadership," "sense of well-being," "zest for life," "alienation," "vulnerability," "fearfulness" and "risk-seeking." Another highly inherited trait, though one not commonly thought of as part of personality, was the capacity for becoming "rapt" in an aesthetic experience, such as during a concert.

Though the findings point to the strong influence of heredity, the environment still shapes the broad form of personality, even to the degree of fine-tuning it. For example, even though Dr. Jerome Kagan said that approximately 15 percent of all children are born with shyness, the family's influence might make an innately shy child either more timid or less timid; the family would be unlikely to make the child bold.

Dr. Richard Haier studied a group of people who were all very high or very low on one particular personality scale: risk-taking. He conducted thorough examinations of those who were extreme risk-takers and those who were risk-avoidant. Those who were high risk-takers had low levels of monoamine oxidase (MAO) in their brains, whereas those who were risk-avoidant had high levels of MAO in their brains. A brain with high levels of MAO is a brain that is extremely active; however, a brain with low levels of MAO desperately needs strong environmental influences in the form of risk-taking behaviours to activate the brain enzymes.

It has only been 20 years since science discovered that the brain naturally produces endorphins (literally, the morphine within). These endogenous chemicals attach themselves to the opiate receptor sites in the brain; there are opiate receptors in all sensory areas of the brain, as well as in brain parts dealing with emotion. During activities of intense pain and pleasure, it is likely that endorphins "kick in"; in fact, you may have heard the term "a runner's high" as it relates to someone's need to jog. Runners, smokers, exercise buffs, cocaine and alcohol users may all share something in common: addiction.

The way to measure whether an activity or substance is addictive is to remove it and measure the body's withdrawal. Use of drugs like alcohol or heroin deplete the brain's natural opiates, and a dearth of natural opiates means the addict needs to continue using external drugs. Scientists think that perhaps low levels of natural opiates may be a cause of drug abuse rather than a consequence.

Issue 2

Dr. George Vaillant (Harvard University) surprised many people by suggesting that a difficult life was rarely a significant factor in why someone developed alcohol dependence. Also, he found that alcoholics are depressed because they drink; they do not drink because they are depressed. The most significant finding in the difference between alcoholics and non-alcoholics was that most of the men studied who developed alcoholism had alcoholic parents. Further studies (Kansas Medical Centre and Washington University School of Medicine) documented that alcoholic behaviour was not "learned" or "reinforced" but biological in nature. Children of alcoholics had up to three times the risk of developing the disease as did the children of non-alcoholics.

Researchers have identified three specific neurotransmitters: norepinephrine, dopamine and serotonin. These neurotransmitters help to regulate emotion and you can imagine the electrochemical activity with over ten billion neurons in the brain and thousands of neurotransmitter molecules acting on any given neuron.

Norepinephrine:
- found in areas of the brain generating reward and pleasure
- stimulates behaviour and makes us feel good
- low levels predispose people to depression
- tricyclics (antidepressants) work by increasing norepinephrine levels

Dopamine:
- bizarre thoughts and perceptions are related to increased activity of dopamine
- affects complex emotions
- anti-psychotic drugs reduce brain's sensitivity to dopamine neurotransmitters
- sexually stimulates men, but not women

Serotonin:
- inhibits certain neural brain activity
- Wayne State University revealed that brains of suicide victims had distinct serotonin deficiency
- the more deficient the brain of serotonin, the more violent method of suicide

- seems to be sexually exciting for women only
- male power and dominance are linked to high levels of serotonin

It is clear that our understanding of the body's relationship to its biochemistry, with respect to movements and balance, moods and emotions, illnesses and addiction, is in its beginnings.

CONCLUSION

More than ever before in human evolution, it becomes easier and easier to say that "biology is destiny." Certainly environmental factors must always be taken into account, but nature gives us that first boost, our blueprint for so many areas of potential excellence, mediocrity or difficulty. Nurture, our world of experience, helps to modify what nature has given us.

Anyone who has ever coached young people in hockey, ballet or figure skating, knows that "nature" defines everyone's potential. I have witnessed many parents who have made great sacrifices in their quest to turn their young sons, through nurture, into the second coming of Wayne Gretzky. It is often a very sad spectacle to behold, as coaches will quickly tell you that the genetic gift is either there or not there and when it's not there, no amount of reward, punishment, shaping, encouragement or modelling is going to make a significant difference. Wayne Gretzky was born with a genetic gift, an incredible boost from nature, and the environmental factors were present in his development to allow his natural talent to flourish.

Examine, for a moment, the recent tale of Greg Louganis, the greatest diver in the history of the sport. Born with a natural gift (the body type, the sense of balance, the kinesthetic body awareness in space and so on), Louganis was the most successful diver in history. At the Seoul Olympic Games, Louganis won four gold medals, sweeping both the platform and springboard competitions. In his autobiography, *Breaking the Surface*, Louganis revealed his homosexuality and his positive HIV status, and on February 24, 1995, announced that he had AIDS. At that time, he said: "The fact that I was maladjusted, an outcast because of my colour and my sexual orientation, allowed me to pour all of my energy into my one gift: **Diving!**"

Issue 2

Perhaps it's best to conclude with a paradox: we are biologically determined to be at least partly involved in the creation of our environment. Gerald Edelman, in his Theory of Neuronal Group Selection, describes how an individual becomes an active partner with nature in his or her own evolution. A child who is exposed to a nurture that is rich in colour, design and shape in the form of paints, prints, mobiles and toys has those portions of the brain responsible for perceiving colour, design and shape more highly stimulated than other sections of the brain. If the child finds the stimulation pleasurable, the child will then seek out further stimulation of that portion of the brain, thus, in part, creating their own environment. This process continues as the individual grows and evolves. In other words, evolution does not just occur in a whole species over millions of years, but occurs within individuals during their lifetime through the selective stimulation of different parts of the brain. This selection process leads to some parts of the brain being more effectively stimulated than others. Since we seek out pleasing stimulation, we are not just passive receptors of an environment, but creative and active agents of our own destiny. The individual is born with his or her own genetic make-up and certain common values (an appreciation for food, warmth and comfort), but the self, the person, emerges from biology at least partly self-directed.

We are determined by our biology and our environment, yet we remain active in choosing our environments all our lives. With increased awareness of our biology, we will simply possess increased choices over how our lives should be nurtured. Nature gives us the seed, nurture gives us the environment in which the seed will grow; we've all witnessed the same amount of sunlight, soil and water and, yet, the flowers are so different. Ah, the seed! The more insight we have into our genetic make-up, the more options become available to us as we realize how complex and different each of us really is, just as perhaps one flower needed less water and another richer soil and the third more sunlight.

In a world where mass media and advertising try to impose a "sameness" on everyone, we can, with increased awareness of our inherent differences, more easily celebrate those differences.

AM I FREE OR DETERMINED?

Melanie Chaparian

Each of the theories of personality discussed in Issue I takes a stand on the philosophical debate between determinism and libertarianism. On one side of the debate, determinism is the position that all human actions are determined, or caused, by natural and/or environmental forces beyond human control. According to this theory, people do not have any free will. Human beings are like sophisticated computers that can only perform the operations with which they are programmed. Although the traditional biological, psychoanalytic, and behaviourist schools advocate very different theories, they all agree that our personalities and, as a result, our actions are determined by forces outside our control. Thus, these three schools take the determinist side of the debate.

On the other side of the debate, libertarianism is the view that at least some human actions are free. Although many actions may be determined, there are some situations in which people can exercise their free will. Unlike computers, human beings are capable of making real choices between alternative courses of action. Only the humanist-existential school and Edelman's biological theory of personality take the position that people have free will.

AN ARGUMENT FOR DETERMINISM

Determinism may be defended on the basis of the following rather simple argument. Every event in the world occurs because of cause and effect. Like every other event, human actions must be determined by cause and effect as well. If all of our actions are caused, we cannot possess free will because the same action cannot be both caused and free at the same time. Therefore, all human actions are determined, and no human actions are free.

Let's look at this argument in more detail. Few people today question the universality of cause and effect in the natural world. Science teaches us that every natural phenomenon is the effect of a cause or set of causes. Indeed, science assumes a deterministic model of the world. It is the very nature of science to look for the causes of the phenomena it studies. The nature of causality is such that there is an *inevitable* connection between a cause and its effect: if the cause occurs, the effect *must* also occur. For example, if heating water to a temperature of 100°C *determines* the water to turn into steam, then every time water is heated to that temperature it *must* turn into steam. Heating water to 100°C is the *cause* and the water turning into steam is the *effect.* We never entertain the possibility that boiling water, or any other natural phenomena, occurs because of pure chance. Scientists always try to discover the causes of the phenomena they study. Indeed, when they are unable to identify the cause of a particular phenomenon, such as the memory loss suffered by people affected by Alzheimer's Disease, they do not conclude that no cause exists but rather that it simply has not *yet* been discovered.

But the deterministic view is not limited to the natural sciences such as physics, chemistry, biology, and medicine. Determinism is also assumed by the social sciences, such as psychology and sociology, which usually attempt to study and *discover the causes of human behaviour.* A determinist would agree that, although we may believe ourselves to be unique creatures, human beings are just as subject to the world of cause and effect as boiling water and Alzheimer's Disease.

The determinist argues that our distinctive nature only means that the causes which determine our actions are more complex, and therefore harder to discover, than those that cause other events. The *kinds* of causes determining human behaviour depend on the determinist's particular view of human nature. Some point to *nature*, such as hereditary or instinctual forces, as the primary cause of a person's actions. Those who adhere to the traditional biological school of personality, for instance, argue that genetics determines such traits as intelligence, talents, and temperament, which in turn cause an individual's actions. Other determinists argue that a person's behaviour is fundamentally determined by *nurture*, that is, by environmental factors. The behaviourists, for example, point to rewards and punishments as the causes of an individual's actions. Many, if not most, determinists, however, acknowledge that a *combination* of nature and nurture determines a person's actions. A Freudian psychologist, for example, believes that an individual's behaviour is caused by the way the *ego* moderates between drives of the

Issue 2

id, which are determined by instinct or heredity, and the moral demands of the *superego*, which are determined by early childhood environment. Regardless as to the kinds of causes they point to, all determinists agree that all human actions are determined or caused.

No matter how long and hard we may deliberate between different courses of action, the "choice" we finally make has already been decided for us by hereditary and/or environmental causes over which we have no control. This applies to all of our actions, from the most trivial to the most significant.

According to the determinist, an analysis of the motivations of different people reveals the various causes that result in the difference in their behaviour. The determinist is quick to point out that you do not freely choose what interests you. Your interests are determined by your nature, your environment, or, most likely, by a combination of both. For example, you may have a naturally inquisitive mind. This is not an attribute that you freely chose to acquire. Or you may have been raised in a family that constantly debated whether or not people are forced into a life of crime because of social neglect and injustice. You have no more control over your upbringing than you do over your nature. You probably wish to pursue academic success. Why is this important to you? Perhaps your family has always encouraged academic success. Again, the determinist points out that you have no control over the values your family has bred into you. You may be aware that good grades are essential for the new graduate to secure a decent position in today's highly competitive job market. Once again, the determinist points out that you have no control over the increasingly high academic requirements demanded by employers. Nor do you have any control over the high unemployment rates that make today's job market so competitive. *Your* actual motivations for persevering through your homework probably include some of those discussed here as well as a number of others. But whatever they may be, the determinist argues, they reveal that you do not freely choose to study hard.

At this point, you may be convinced that *your* actions are caused by forces outside your control. But how does the determinist explain the actions of other students in your class who socialize at the expense of studying and consequently earn low marks? After all, most of them also come from families that stress academic success, and all of them want good jobs after they graduate. It *seems* that these negligent students are making a free, although foolish, choice.

Things are not always as they first appear. According to the determinist's theory, if your negligent classmates are subject to exactly the same causal forces that determine your behaviour, they would of necessity be studying as hard as you are. The very fact that they sacrifice study time to socialize indicates that their personal histories are very different from yours. Perhaps their families have not so much *encouraged* academic success as relentlessly *pressured* them to do well in school. If so, they may have been determined to rebel by going to all the college parties instead of studying. Just as you have no control over the encouragement you receive, the rebellious students have no control over the pressure they suffer. Other students who neglect their homework may simply not have the maturity required for self-discipline. Having fun may be as important to them, or even more so, than earning good marks or preparing for their future. If so, the determinist points out that a person cannot simply decide to become mature. This is a developmental process that is determined by an individual's nature and upbringing. There is an entire host of other causes that may determine some students to neglect their studies. Whatever these causes may be in any actual case, the determinist argues that negligent students do not freely choose to ignore their homework. Although they may feel guilty that they are not studying, they simply cannot choose to do so. Neither the diligent student nor the negligent student really makes a genuine choice between studying or not studying. The course of action each takes is determined by causes over which neither has any control.

Nor do we have the freedom to make genuine choices concerning even the most important aspects of our lives. Nature or nurture, or both, determine such things as which profession we pursue, who we fall in love with, and how many children we have. According to the theory of determinism, *all* human actions are the effect of causes over which we have no control; consequently, free will is merely an illusion.

Because we usually pride ourselves on our freedom, we may feel reluctant to accept the determinist's conclusion. But this in itself is not a good reason to reject determinism. It would be hard to deny that the deterministic model has helped to advance our knowledge of the natural world in general and the human world in particular. Discovering the cause of an event not only increases our understanding of that phenomenon but also allows us to *predict* and sometimes *control* its future occurrence. If, for example, we know that a virus causes an illness in the human body, we can predict that a person will become ill when infected by that virus, and, moreover, we can control that illness by finding ways to prevent the virus from infecting more people. Or, if we know that a moderate amount of parental pressure causes a student to succeed in school, we can predict that a student subjected to that amount of guidance will earn good grades, and we can control such successes by teaching parents how to provide the proper dose of encouragement. The deterministic model also helps us to make sense out of our personal lives. We are often remarkably successful, for instance, in predicting the actions of our close relatives and friends. If such predictions are not merely lucky guesses, the determinist argues, they must be based on our relatively extensive knowledge of the hereditary and environmental causes that determine the behaviour of those relatives and friends. The fact that we do not *like* the theory of determinism does not negate the wealth of evidence for its accuracy.

JAMES'S CRITIQUE OF DETERMINISM

William James

In his famous lecture entitled "The Dilemma of Determinism," William James, an American philosopher and psychologist who lived from 1842 to 1910, defends libertarianism, the theory that human beings have free will. Before he actually begins his argument for this theory, however, James shows that determinism—its appeal to science notwithstanding—cannot be scientifically demonstrated.

Science cannot really tell us, for example, if the negligent student's background is causing him to rebel. The fact that he does consistently neglect his assigned readings is not in itself conclusive proof that the student is determined to take this course of action. Moreover, *before the fact*—that is, before the student entered college—no one, not even the most learned determinist, could ascertain whether the student's background would lead him to socialize or to study. For instance, it would not have seemed inconceivable to suppose that the excessive family pressure would prompt the student to study harder than any other student. Nor would it have been unreasonable to surmise that this pressure would compel him to overcome his immaturity and set his priorities in a more beneficial way. *Before the fact*, this series of events seems as likely to occur as the events that actually came to pass; thus, James argues, *after the fact,*

Issue 2

there is no way to prove that the student was determined to neglect his studies. The same argument applies to all human actions. James therefore concludes that the determinist cannot prove that all actions are the inevitable effects of prior causes. While this in itself does not disprove determinism, it certainly dispels the myth that determinism has the weight of science on its side, and, furthermore, suggests that libertarianism should at least be reconsidered.

JAMES'S ARGUMENT FOR FREE WILL

Different libertarians disagree among themselves on how far human freedom extends. On one extreme, the existentialists claim that all human actions are free. On the other extreme, some libertarians only argue that actions performed in the face of moral demands are free. In this discussion, we will focus on the views of William James, who defends a relatively moderate version of libertarianism. According to James, we are free whenever we have a genuine choice between at least two possible and desirable courses of action. This does not mean, of course, that we are free to perform any conceivable action whatsoever. Nor does this even mean that we are free to do anything we may desire, for the action that we find most tempting may not be included within the choice before us. All that is required to render an action free is the existence of one other alternative action that it is possible for us to perform.

Essential to James's definition of free will is the existence of *possible actions*; that is, actions which a person is not inevitably determined to do but may perform nonetheless. If an action is the result of free will, then it is, before the fact, merely one of two or more genuinely *possible* alternative actions that the person can *freely choose* to perform; and, after the fact, it is correct to say that the individual *could have acted otherwise* by choosing another alternative. For instance, the negligent student may have freely chosen to spend his time socializing instead of at the library; and even though he made this choice, he could have chosen to study instead. It is the idea of possible actions that puts James in stark opposition to determinism, which states that every action is the *inevitable* effect of a cause.

We have already discussed James's argument that determinism cannot be scientifically demonstrated. He does not attempt, however, to disprove this theory nor to prove libertarianism true. This

Issue 2

"There is nothing more wholesome for us than to find problems that quite transcend our powers."

Charles Pierce

is because he believes determinism and libertarianism to be two alternative theories of reality, neither of which can be objectively proven true or false. Thus, he claims that the best we can do is to examine both theories to see which one offers us the most rational explanation of human behaviour. According to James, a "rational" theory should not only explain objective reality but must account for subjective human experience as well. James's defence of libertarianism consists in the argument that the free will position is more rational in this sense than determinism.

A significant fact of human life is the *feeling of freedom* that we often experience. James argues that any theory of human behaviour must adequately explain this feeling. Unlike determinism, libertarianism conforms to our ordinary experience: we often feel free to choose between alternative courses of action. Of course, the determinist argues that this feeling is merely an illusion because our course of action has already been decided for us by causes beyond our control. But the "illusion" persists in our inner, subjective experience nonetheless. For example, a good student probably *feels* that she or he could have chosen to go to more parties while a negligent student likely *feels* that he or she could have decided to study harder. In his or her practical affairs, even the most staunch determinist probably *feels free* to choose between alternative courses of action. No matter how solidly convinced we may be that determinism offers us a rational account of all natural phenomena and perhaps most human behaviour, we still find it difficult—if not impossible—to *believe* subjectively that we are never free. Thus, determinism requires us to reject as illusory a universal human experience. Libertarianism, on the other hand, acknowledges the feeling of freedom as a natural part of the experience of exerting our free will. According to James, this is a good reason to adopt the free will thesis. While he concedes that determinism is a rational theory of reality from an objective standpoint, James argues that libertarianism is an even more rational position because it can account for our inner, subjective experience of freedom.

Another important fact of human experience that James believes a rational theory must explain are *feelings of regret*. Our dissatisfaction with the world, especially with human behaviour, leads us to regret; that is, to "wish that something might be otherwise." After receiving a poor mark in the course, for instance, the negligent stu-

Issue 2

To Study or To Party

Free Will Re-considered

Suppose you have an examination tomorrow and a friend asks you to forgo studying and spend the evening at a party. Your friend does not urge or threaten or coerce you. You consider the alternatives, and after a moment's thought, decide to give up studying for the night, and go to the party. We would ordinarily say that you are responsible for your decision. We think of such cases as actions in which you are free to decide one way or the other.

Contrast this to a situation in which a headache leads you to lie down and fall asleep on your bed instead of continuing to study. In this case it would not make sense to say that you are free to decide one way or the other about studying. The dispute between advocates of free will and advocates of determinism is basically a dispute whether incidents like the two so cited, which feel so different, are really radically and essentially different when viewed objectively.

Whereas the advocate of free will would perceive these two sorts of acts as essentially different, the determinist would not. The determinist might argue that although you may believe that your decision to stay home to study for the exam was an expression of free choice, nevertheless closer scrutiny would reveal that your behaviour was not really free after all. What you thought was a free choice was really a choice dictated by your desires, which in turn spring from your character, which in its turn is fashioned by the forces of heredity and environment, which are clearly beyond your control.

The central affirmation of determinism is that every event has a cause. By an analysis of the causes of any one of your actions, the determinist would cause your so-called freedom to vanish in a chain of causes that stretches back into the remote recesses of your heredity and environment. Nature and nurture, genes and society—those are the factors that made you what you are and cause you to act the way you do. The notion that you are free is really a misapprehension, an illusion.

Adapted from *An Introduction to Modern Philosophy* by Donald M. Borchert.

dent may *regret* that he chose to spend all his time socializing. And because we regret the actions of others as well as our own, you may also *regret* that he had not studied. The most significant regrets concern the moral sphere. We do not accept as inevitable the senseless murders, rapes, and cases of child abuse we read about in the newspaper; instead, we judge such acts to be bad or immoral to the highest degree and regret that they are part of our world.

A regret implies that something is bad, and "calling a thing bad means … that the thing ought not to be, that something else ought to be in its stead." When we label someone's action immoral, we imply that it should not have been done and that the person should have acted otherwise. For instance, when we proclaim that a murderer

Issue 2

Review

Am I Free or Determined?

This article by Melanie Chaparian explores one of the most basic philosophical dilemmas: does an individual possess free choice or is the path a person walks determined by circumstances beyond his or her control? The author cites the work of the American philosopher/psychologist William James (1842–1910), who espoused the doctrine of "libertarianism." An advocate of free will, James argued that the theory that all human actions are the effects of prior causes cannot be scientifically proven. James also observed that human beings have the capacity for feeling regret, and to regret an action implies an awareness of our ability to create consequences. Since we know we could have acted otherwise, we must assume the existence of free will.

is guilty of the highest moral offence, we mean that he should not have committed homicide and should have instead settled the grievance with his victim in a peaceful, humane manner. Regrets obviously assume the existence of free will. For this reason, libertarianism offers us a better explanation of our regrets than does determinism.

The source of our deepest regrets is the recognition that the world is fraught with immorality. According to determinism, even the most heinous crimes are as much the result of cause and effect as the routine activities we do every day. Knowing the causes of immoral actions does not eliminate our regret that they occur, but it does make our regret merely futile hope. Libertarianism, on the other hand, recognizes immoral actions as the result of free will and, as such, acknowledges that other actions could have been performed instead. Since this applies to future as well as past actions, there exists the possibility that the world—although certainly imperfect—may be made a better and more moral place through free human action. Thus, from the libertarian viewpoint, regrets may virtually be taken at face value—as expressions of our belief that immoral actions *can* be avoided and *should not* take place. This, according to James, renders libertarianism a more rational theory of human existence.

James admits from the outset that his defence consists of the argument that libertarianism is more rational than determinism because it offers a better account of our feelings of freedom and regret. This is not a claim that can be proven objectively, but one that can only be "verified" by consulting our inner, subjective sense. Although James argues that determinism is also incapable of objective demonstration, he acknowledges that determinism appeals to a different kind of rationality, perhaps what we might call a scientific rationality. Even though James finds libertarianism to be more rational than determinism, it remains for each of us to study both theories to see which of the two *we* find to be the most rational.

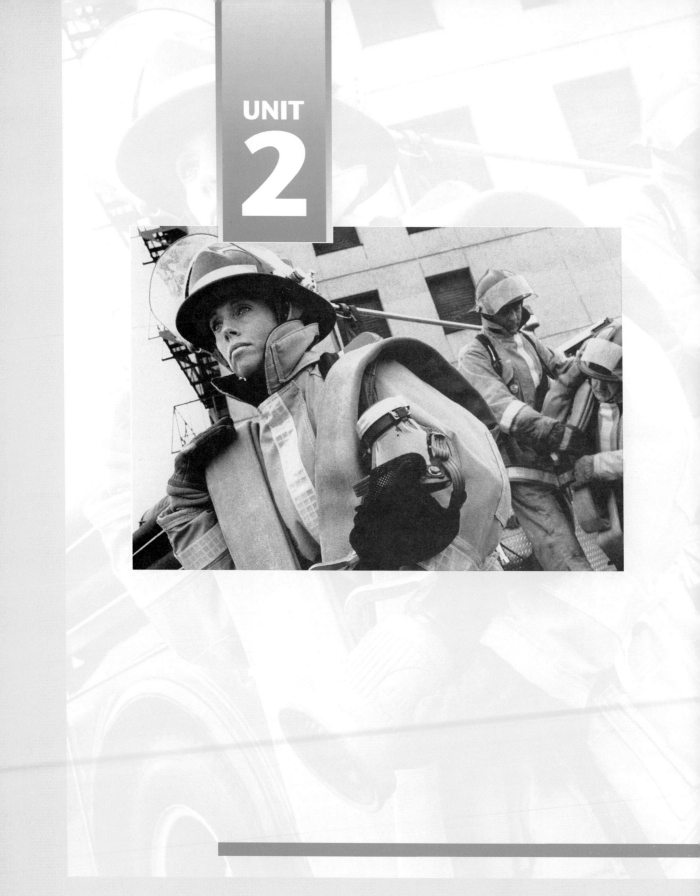

CHANGE IN THE SOCIAL WORLD

ISSUE 1:
Dynamics of Social Change

ISSUE 2:
Public and Private Roles

DYNAMICS OF SOCIAL CHANGE

We make history ourselves, but, in the first place, under very definite antecedents and conditions. Among these the economic ones are ultimately decisive. But the political ones, etc., and indeed even the traditions which haunt human minds also play a part, although not the decisive one ...

Frederick Engels

Though women do not complain of the power of husbands, each complains of her own husband, or the husbands of her friends. It is the same in all other cases of servitude; at least in the commencement of the emancipatory movement. The serfs did not at first complain of the power of the lords, but only of their tyranny.

J.S. Mill

INTRODUCTION

John Steckley

*H*ow do we understand all the new things that are happening to us? Are they progress, as those who market the latest computer bells and whistles tell us? Are they just fashions and fads, like pogs, body-piercing and country meets techno-dance tracks? Or are we headed down the slippery slope of destruction and decay because of changes in the ozone, the federal deficit and the increased use of hockey visors? No one way of seeing changes applies to all cases. Some things will help us in the long run, some will fade fast, and some will be obstacles to overcome. We will understand them best when newness becomes old, and historians, not journalists, tell the story. But how are we to comprehend change as it happens to us today? One way is through a model of change that is almost 150 years old: evolution.

When you see the word "evolution," and the phrase "survival of the fittest," visions of "bigger, stronger, better" dance before your eyes. But that is not what evolution is about, either as a model of biological or social change. It is better described as "survival of the best fit," that is, of that which fits best into a specific set of circumstances. It is exemplified by adaptation to a situation, not long-term improvement. An example will help to illustrate this.

There are two basic colour patterns of the guppies that swim the rivers of Venezuela. In the headwaters high in the hills, the guppies are brightly coloured, with big, flashy dots. There are few predators there to spot and eat them. The most brightly coloured guppies are the ones most likely to attract a mate and reproduce. In the lower waters, the guppies are dull-coloured, with smaller dots. Many predators are there so the ones that are easily seen are soon eaten. Neither colour pattern is "better" in absolute terms, just a better fit into the local environment.

Human societies are a lot like guppy colour patterns. They typically represent good adaptations to unique circumstances. But in the nineteenth century, when Charles Darwin first presented his ideas of evolution, many misinterpreted "survival of the fittest" to mean that only the biggest, strongest and most intelligent would survive, and applied that notion to human groups as if they were separate biological species. They felt that the 10 economically and militarily powerful European and North American nations were in that position because they were better in absolute terms, as societies and as "races." This faulty notion is known as social darwinism. Nineteenth-century scholars documented cultural differences on progress charts. It is like they were saying, "Here we are at the top, the most highly evolved. Our forms of religion, family, commerce, everything, are the best. Anything different is inferior." Today, we say that those ideas are ethnocentric.

The Canadian government had such an ethnocentric attitude towards the potlatch, which is the most important sacred ceremony of Native people such as the Haida (pronounced high-da), Kwakiutl (kwah-kyu-tl), Tlingit and Salish who lived in British Columbia. This ceremony is held for every important event: birth, the receiving of a name, marriage and death. For several days, people give away a great number of gifts collected from the hosts' extended family over a long period of time. They tell, sing, dance and act out the traditional stories that give the people strength. The main performers wear elaborate masks to identify the traditional spirit that they are representing. To the non-Natives in the area, particularly government officials and missionaries, the ceremony seemed bizarre, somewhat frightening, and potentially dangerous. In 1884, it was made illegal. By 1906, this ban on one Native dance ceremony was extended to all such ceremonies. In a trial in the early 1920s, community leaders were arrested, and their masks were confiscated.

This is a classic example of ethnocentrism, the principles that one's own culture sets the standard by which all should be judged. Like sexism, ageism, ableism and other such negative "isms" that we hear about these days, ethnocentrism stems from a simple, foolish notion that difference equals inferiority.

That brings us to the realm of political correctness. How does that fashionable, but not always popular, word fit into an evolutionary picture? Leaving aside the nasty remarks on both sides of the political correctness debate, it is about the "good fit" of recognition and respect for different groups. Take multiculturalism, for example, one area in which political correctness is focused. On one hand, it has a political component that involves legislation that attempts to ensure a "level playing field" or equality between groups.

Issue 1

While discriminatory practices may be reduced in this way, some people question whether you can legislate a change in attitude, make a law that can reduce prejudice. On the other hand, we need to recognize both the different paths that people have taken to become Canadians, and that we share the common path of the country's future. We must also respect both the differences that exist, as well as the common heritage that we have inherited from those who have walked this land or fought for it, one generation or many before our time.

It helps this process to recognize that multiculturalism is not just a modern fad of the last 30 years. Traditionally, our history books reflected a narrow view that only the English and French have contributed significantly to Canadian history. That perspective ignored several basic facts. More than 95 percent of Canadian history is Native history before Europeans settled in Canada. Our Black history also began in the seventeenth century, when the French and English settled here permanently.

Ontario provides a good example of the long roots of multiculturalism. When the French first came to Ontario in the seventeenth century, they encountered people speaking at least five languages, each of which had thousands of speakers and several distinct dialects. The people differed in the foods they ate and the houses they built. The incoming French added another language, cuisine and house style to an already multicultural area.

When my great-great-great-great uncle Alexander Brodie wrote about coming from Scotland in 1835 to live in the Toronto area, he spoke about the many different cultures he encountered: the Gaelic-speaking Irish, thousands of whom would die of cholera on Grosse Isle, where he met them; the Black man who endeared himself to the Scottish children when he gave them maple sugar; the fiddle-playing, dancing French-Canadian raftsmen; and his neighbours, the Germans from Pennsylvania, the Dutch from New York, the Yankees, the English and other new Canadians.

None of this means that multiculturalism is without pain. Change of this nature often hurts. Every culture has its share of ethnocentric people. Between 1300 and 1400 in Southern Ontario, there appears to have been fairly intense warfare between the two main peoples there, until one seemed to have won out. Archaeological sites of that period have revealed heavy palisades of one or even two rows of posts around villages. And there is evidence suggesting cannibalism. In nineteenth-century Ontario, many Irish were told that although a job was available, they need not apply.

You need only listen to a few specific questions concerning multiculturism today to find areas of pain and anger. Is it right to rename and refocus school Christmas celebrations because some newer Canadians are not Christians? Isn't the celebration of Christmas a long-existing and treasured part of our Canadian heritage? Don't people of other countries expect new citizens to respect the long-held, religion-based customs of their countries?

Should Sikhs be permitted to wear their religion-prescribed turbans in the legion, although the official legion policy is not to wear hats out of respect for those who died in the two World Wars? Did they not wear those turbans when they fought on the same side as Canadians during those wars?

CHANGE IN THREE AREAS OF HUMAN LIFE

Much like what happens with animals and plants, human societies also evolve to fit better into a changing environment. Often, for example, a change takes place first in the material area of human life. This includes technology and the relationship to the environment. Then adaptations are made in the social area, that is, in the relationships between genders, or groups based on ethnicity (i.e., language, religion or genetic heritage) or age. For example, about 1000 years ago, Inuit people living on the northern coast of Alaska made a series of technological innovations that drastically altered Inuit society across the Arctic from Alaska to Greenland. Among other things, they invented the kayak, a single-person skin boat that is watertight top and bottom, and is propelled by a paddle that has blades on both ends. The hunters in the kayaks brought another new development—harpoons with floats attached to slow down and help to locate a speared animal. These and other technological changes enabled the Inuit to successfully hunt large bowhead whales, an animal they had not previously hunted. The Inuit social world adapted by expanding in size. Larger groups were necessary both to hunt and to process the whales. More people could live in one house because

Issue 1

they could use whalebones for house frames. With more food in one area, villages could increase in population and in permanence.

Change in either the material or social sphere can also cause adaptations in the intellectual area, which pertains to values, ideas and beliefs. To return to the Inuit, a drastic shift in their material world began in the sixteenth century and increased dramatically until the end of the nineteenth century. European and North American whalers slaughtered thousands of the whales, significantly reducing the number that would swim north to the Arctic Sea. Perhaps it was then, with their social world scattered into fewer, more temporary groups to hunt smaller animals (e.g., seals, walruses, musk oxen and caribou) that were less consistent sources of food, that the Inuit developed a harsh set of values that included the unspoken rule that when food was low, the respected elderly members would not eat, and maybe would walk out into the wilderness, never to be seen alive again.

We can begin to trace similar adaptation patterns following the many material changes taking place in our lives today. How will the family adapt to technological change? Will the VCR compel families to develop new compromising techniques when they go to the video store and try to answer the critical question, "Which movies will we rent?" Will the microwave oven, which allows family members to eat different things at different times cause the family dinner to become a thing of the past? Will the fact that children are often much more competent in working on computers than their parents mean that respect for the "wisdom" of parents will diminish?

Many material, social and intellectual changes are taking place in the world of work. New technology, new relationships between different ethnic groups, women and men, and employers and employees, and new attitudes towards work all are current adaptations, and situations to which individuals must adapt.

Further, there are the adaptations we are making concerning changes in gender roles. Both men and women have worked in Canada in a variety of ways. There is, however, a traditional association of women with children and the home (even if that home is a mobile one), and of men with a workplace (even if it's a trapline or a cod trawler) that is away from home. This isn't necessarily a "bad fit" for the situations that existed in the past. What has tended to not fit so well is that the roles haven't been equally valued, i.e., when men's work away has been paid, women's work at home is not.

Issue 1

During the last 30 some years, much has changed, at least to the extent that women are usually at a workplace away from home now, almost as often as men are. Where might this be headed? An evolutionary model might help here. Evolutionary trends do not keep going in one direction forever. The evolution of the giraffe's neck is a case in point. It continued to get longer and longer, over successive generations, until a point of equilibrium was reached. If it got any longer, it would break. That analogy might work here. Equality of men's and women's roles may happen in terms of equal respect. Men are slowly beginning to do more housework, and women's earnings are approaching the level of men's. However, I suspect there will always be differences in what men and women tend to do. And that might just be a "good fit."

Issue 1

MORE THAN WORDS CAN SAY

Wendy O'Brien-Ewara

*I*n this unit you will be looking at some of the changes that are currently shaping Canadian culture and identity. You will be examining, in particular, the changes in beliefs, values and attitudes that have informed views on multiculturalism, work and gender relations. While each of these forms of change has unique preconditions and repercussions, they share a reliance on language as a means for establishing and maintaining change.

Language is not often a topic for reflection. After all, what can we say about words? Language is usually conceived of in functional terms. That is, it is regarded as a set of tools that everyone has equal access to when attempting to describe the world around them. Consider, for example, the word "date." This word identifies a particular kind of event or activity in which individuals who are attracted to one another engage. When you talk about a "date," an image comes to mind about the kind of event that is at hand. The word is a signifier identifying a particular kind of relationship: a "date" is what is being signified by the word. When you ask someone if he or she would like to go out on a "date," you expect that an image similar to the one produced in your mind when you used this word will be reproduced in the mind of that person and that he or she will respond accordingly. Words simply seem to be means for describing and sharing your experiences, feelings, aspirations and ideas. And language appears to be a storehouse of words the meanings of which are clear, shared in common with others and equally accessible to all. But is language simply the words you use? And do words have the clear meanings that this account of language suggests?

Once again, think about the word "date." Are you sure that you know what it means? When you ask someone on a date, are you always sure that you share a similar image of what kind of activity is being proposed? Do you understand the consequences associated with your invitation? And do you always know how to respond when your offer is accepted or rejected?

If you have asked yourself these questions, you have recognized that language is more than just words. Far from being a neutral tool to describe the world you encounter, language plays a role in structuring and maintaining a particular world view. Implicitly and explicitly, the language you use endorses certain images, social relations and changes in society. It reveals not only the way that you perceive the world, but also the way that you think the world should be perceived. And since language is not value-neutral, you can be held accountable for how you use and interpret language. The role that language plays in constructing the world you encounter can be seen by reflecting on how it is used in everyday situations such as going out on a "date."

Anyone who has ever dated is aware of the role that language plays in constructing social settings and relations. Think about how nervous you become while waiting to go out on a date with someone—particularly when it is your first date. You may really like the person and want him or her to like you too. So what do you do when the person is finally there in front of you? Well, you probably talk a lot. On first dates you tend to talk much more than you will on subsequent outings. Not only do you talk more, but you tend to talk differently. Your style of talking changes. You take on a different tone of voice—you might find that your voice is either a few pitches higher or lower than usual. You tend to laugh more often than usual, sometimes even at comments that you do not find particularly funny. You also take on a different posture. You lean forward more often. You cross your legs. You busy yourself playing with your hair or pulling your shoulders back. You look around and notice that other couples are acting in a similar manner. What are you doing? Why do you engage in such strange behaviour? What do you hope to accomplish? In answering these questions, it is possible to see how language shapes or constructs the world as you see it. But first, we must clarify exactly what language is.

Language is more than just the words you use—it is more than just what you say. Language is a means for communicating with others. When you want to tell someone you are attracted to them, how might you express yourself? Well, you might use words. But sometimes it's hard to find the "right" words to capture the emotion that you are feeling. Sometimes, to express yourself, you rely less on what you are saying than on how you are saying it. That is, sometimes you communicate your thoughts or emotions by using your

"Clearly you send numerous messages to others simply by the position and stance of your body."

tone of voice or the emphasis you place on certain words. What message might you be sending your companion when, for example, you talk slowly in a low tone of voice about the meal you are having or the music that is playing?

At other times you might communicate with your date by means other than words. Sometimes you communicate by using body language. Leaning forward when someone speaks, for example, suggests that you are interested in what they have to say, while sitting back and folding your arms suggests that you are bored or angry. Think about what messages you send when you touch someone's arm, cross your legs, play with your hair or put your hands on your hips. Clearly you send numerous messages to others simply by the position and stance of your body.

Signs and symbols can also be used to communicate. What signs or symbols might be used on a date? While you will probably not have to write on a date, it is important to note that written text is a symbolic means of communication. But it is not the only symbolic means to express your ideas or feelings. For example, fashion—from the clothes you wear to the shoes on your feet—is symbolic. So too is the car you drive or the bus you take. Language is not restricted to words but rather includes all the resources available for communicating meaning to others. But if this is the case, what is it that you communicate when you use language?

When you go on a date you are really on a fact-finding mission. You are interested not only in what your partner says but also in how he or she says it, because language both implicitly and explicitly provides information about the other person. Consider what a person is communicating in the following instances. What would you surmise if your partner sits perfectly still, with his or her arms crossed while music plays loudly in the restaurant? What if the person starts moving his or her head or body to the music? Without using any words, you would know something about the person's likes or dislikes. Now, what if this person told you that he or she thought the music was "beautiful," or "great," or "nice"? Or described it as "groovy," "cool," or "hip," or "funky"? What conclusions might you draw about this person? What might you determine about this person's age, cultural background or education? The language you use reflects your age, gender, cultural background, socio-economic background, education, values, beliefs and biases. When you communicate with others, you reveal yourself not only through the words you use, but also in how you use them. To make this point clear, consider another example. You and your companion see one of your female classmates. Your companion points her out to you and describes her as the "chick" standing by the telephone. What does this word indicate about this person? What if this woman was described as a "broad," a "girl," a "woman" or a "bitch"? What would you conclude about your companion's values and biases?

Unfortunately, the conclusions we draw based on the use of language are not always accurate. This is partly the case because a particular word, gesture or symbol does not always point toward one distinct entity, activity, idea or feeling. Instead, any given piece of language, a word, for example, can point toward any number of possible objects, events, relations or thoughts. Earlier, you were asked to think about how the word "date" can be construed. When hearing this word, some people might think about going to a movie or going out for a meal. Others might perceive a date as having more intimate connotations. For example, a date might be identified with sexual relations. How do you come to understand what this word refers to? How do you know which account of a "date" is accurate? That is, how does language gain its meaning?

In part, the way that you ascribe meanings to words, gestures and symbols reflects the culture in which you live. You tend to use language in the manner that it is used by those around you. Through the various means of socialization, you acquire language. But in the process of this acquisition, you learn more than just that "i" comes before "e" except after "c" and that dating is a kind of activity in which individuals who are attracted to one another partake. Language is one of the means by which you learn your culture. The rules that are developed for structuring what you can say and when you can say it, and the words that you can use to describe your experiences are means by which you learn about society's expectations, about the roles that you are expected to play, about how you are supposed to act and indeed, about what you should think—which moral/political values you should endorse. In the above example, a variety of terms were used to describe a female friend who you see while out on a date. Think about the different values and beliefs that are involved by calling this person a "broad," a "woman," or a "bitch." How is your perception of women shaped by the words that you use in this context? What can and can't you say and think about women if you describe them as "chicks"? How might the use of this word influence how you treat women? Far from being a neutral tool that you use to simply describe the world you encounter, language actively shapes and constructs your world—embedding you in your society and directing what you believe and what you can think.

And language accomplishes these goals in such a manner that you hardly notice its existence. You seem oblivious to its forces. Yet you only need to walk into a bar or restaurant or movie theatre and see so many couples engaged in similar dating behaviour to see how language constructs social settings and relations. The word "date" suggests certain kinds of activities, behaviour and emotions. Language helps to inform you how you should act and what you should expect of others when out on a "date." But if this is the case, how can you explain the different interpretations that individuals might have about what a date entails?

To explain the diverse interpretations that individuals might have of a particular word, gesture or symbol, you must consider that each of us is unique in that we belong to a mixture of cultures, subcultures and communities. Perhaps your parents regard dating as a kind of threat to your personal safety, while your friends consider such outings to be harmless fun. When such conflicting interpretations arise within your own frame of reference, confusion results. You are caught in a web of meanings. If this is the case, how do you know what you mean when you suggest going out on a "date"?

When faced with such conflicts, you usually rely upon individual experience to establish the meaning of the words, gestures and symbols. For while language gains its meaning in the context of the various cultures in which it is used, it is modified in light of individual experiences. Maybe your past dates have involved having a good time engaging in some kind of group activity. For others, the term "date" may remind them of unwanted sexual encounters. Yet for others, the word evokes images of boring evenings spent with uninteresting individuals who only want to talk about themselves. The meanings that you ascribe to particular words, gestures, signs and symbols become personalized over time. Given this, it is easy to see how misunderstandings—misinterpretations of what you mean to say when you ask someone out on a date—can occur. In trying to communicate a message to another person, both of you have your own personalized vision of what the words or body language or signs being expressed mean. Neither of you can be sure what the other person associates with the word "date." You are both trying to determine what messages are being sent, recognizing that it is impossible to pin down the meaning of the terms that you are employing.

To make this point clear, think about how you would interpret your date saying at the end of the evening that he or she "really likes you." Is this a nice way of saying that he or she just wants to be friends—that he or she likes you but does not want to pursue a romantic relationship? Or is this a way of expressing a romantic interest in you? Or is this a means for trying to determine if you would like to pursue a relationship—a means for testing the waters so to speak? Maybe this is a statement of a desire to engage in intimate relations. How do you interpret this statement? And subsequently, how do you respond?

This scenario is further complicated by the fact that language is dynamic, constantly changing to reflect or to help to initiate social change. Sometimes words you are accustomed to change their meaning. Imagine how in various times and places describing your date as "fly" might be interpreted. Or consider how the meaning of the word "gay" has changed over time. Over time language may become outdated or certain words or gestures become trendy. You would rarely greet your date by holding up two fingers and saying "Peace," but in other times and places this would have been the norm. Finally, new words, gestures, signs and symbols are constantly coming into play. Consider that only a few years ago, the term "safe sex" would not have been meaningful. This does not mean that people did not try to protect themselves from sexually transmitted diseases, but rather that until a term was coined to describe this phenomenon, discussions of such practices were not the topic of public discourse. In response to the changing environment in which AIDS and sexually transmitted diseases became an increasing threat to the health and life of individuals, the term "safe sex" was devised in order to allow for the education

lexicon—an inventory of terms

and ultimately the protection of the public. The **lexicon** of words, gestures and symbols associated with dating and with all social practice is continually growing and changing in response to changes in the environment and the attitudes of individuals. Compounded with the idiosyncratic nature of language, these changes and additions to the storehouse of language often result in confusion concerning which words to use and how to interpret the words of others.

labyrinth—maze

Language places you within a **labyrinth** of meanings and misunderstandings. Yet regardless of the complex nature of language usage and interpretation, there are consequences associated with what you say, to whom and under what circumstances. In the example discussed above, by using the loaded statement, "I really like you," your date may lose the opportunity to spend more time with someone whom he or she genuinely enjoys being with. The same holds true in terms of the interpretation of language. In maintaining that the person you are with is trying to brush you off using this statement, you are also limiting your options. Sometimes the consequences associated with your interpretation of language are insignificant. Maybe you miss the opportunity to go out with someone you really like or end up alone on a Saturday night. But other times the outcomes that accompany your interpretation of language are much more serious.

You are held accountable for the words you use and the manner in which you interpret the words of others. This point becomes clear when considering the issue of consent in dating situations. Most of us are familiar with the "no means no" campaign. When an individual, whether male or female, says "no" to a suggestion of sexual relations, you must assume that he or she genuinely means it. That is, you must interpret "no" as meaning "no," not as meaning "try harder," or "I'm playing hard to get," or "I'm too shy to say 'yes.'" A failure to interpret the word "no" in this manner, regardless of the setting or the other messages you perceive that your companion is sending to you, can result in a charge of rape. You can and will be held responsible for the way that you interpret the word "no." But in such instances the onus is also placed upon the speaker to use the word "no" responsibly. That is, the word must be used to signal the genuine desire not to engage in intimate relations. When you use the word "no," you must mean "no." To use this word when you actually mean "maybe" or "I don't know yet," would be irresponsible. You cannot use language without carefully considering the ramifications of what you say and how you interpret the words of others.

This example reveals how language is socially constructed. Language reflects the time and place in which you live. As such, it provides you with opportunities and stumbling blocks with regard to what you can say, how you can say it, and when it should be said.

Language embeds you in a social setting, imparting cultural expectations and roles for which you will be held accountable. The examples discussed reveal how language is far from being simply a means for describing the world around you. Language helps to construct the world around you. It is a means through which information is acquired about the individuals whom you encounter and about the cultures in which you participate. That is, it is a means by which social standards and expectations are learned. Since language is thus laden with values and open to diverse interpretations, issues of accountability inevitably arise. You are responsible for both what you say and what you believe others are saying. As such, language provides you with opportunities and with stumbling blocks as you try to determine what you should say, how you should say it, and when it should be said. This becomes evident whether you look at how language structures dating or job interviews or your evaluation of politicians. Language encompasses more than words can say. And as a result, communication becomes both a reward and a challenge.

nores subst
yond forma
suring that
interviewed
candidate s
clearly refle

FORMA
EQUAL

The argum
state shoulc
tecting min
assumptior
Several twe
ity requires
sible with a
equality rec
vide citizen
beings.

The Ro
that Black n
an example
cess. Some
tions argue
that is more
have reque
dominantly
riculum.

MULTI

Much of the
tween those
stantive eq
substantive
into accoun
portunity. F

MULTICULTURALISM AND EQUITY

Greg Narbey

*C*anadians live in a society that is formally committed to multiculturalism in our laws and public policy. Generally, this commitment means that not only are people of different racial, ethnic and cultural backgrounds welcomed in Canada, but also that once here, newcomers are not expected to conform to the dominant culture, nor can they be discriminated against for continuing to value and practise their cultural and religious customs.

In recent years, this policy of multiculturalism has come under attack on two fronts. Some people argue that a policy of multiculturalism concentrates too much on what makes us different, on what divides us, and not enough on what we share in common as Canadians. Others argue that multiculturalism represents only superficial support for cultural minority groups, while permitting the continued exclusion of these groups from the institutions of power in Canadian society. Multiculturalism, it is charged, encourages people of different ethnic and racial backgrounds to open restaurants and continue certain artistic pursuits (dance, music, etc.) while at the same time failing to promote equitable access to power, education, housing and jobs.

These two views deeply conflict, with one group believing that multiculturalism already goes too far in emphasizing differences, while the other group believes that it doesn't go far enough in promoting the fair and full sharing of power. Many people find it difficult to accommodate the changing reality of Canada, and it is not unusual for individuals to have difficulty adjusting when confronted with difference in their world. Multiculturalism is an attempt to smooth the transition by reassuring the diverse groups that they will be treated with respect. Equity law is an attempt to insist that we progress through this adjustment with fairness.

The debate over multiculturalism is complicated by two fundamentally different conceptions of equality. One view is sometimes

INDIVIDUAL RIGHTS AND GROUP RIGHTS

It has been commonly regarded by those who favour formal equality that laws that protect individuals from unfair interference by the state, or society, (sometimes called rights), can only recognize and protect individuals (they support individual rights). For example, the state has a responsibility not to interfere with whom you associate provided you do not intend to harm others. Additionally, no matter how offensive other people may find your ideas or religion, the state has an obligation not to interfere with your right to practise your religion, or exercise your right to free speech (again as long as there is no harm to others). This approach to rights has emphasized the separation between the individual and society.

Those who support substantive equality often support group rights. They argue that all human beings develop and thrive within communities and groups and therefore the state has an obligation to extend protection and recognition to those groups and communities where they are in danger of being overwhelmed by larger groups or a majority culture. This approach recognizes that people are discriminated against because of the groups they are associated with, i.e., discrimination against a Muslim individual occurs because he or she is part of a larger community of Muslims. According to this view, minority groups and cultures have a right to protection and recognition, collectively, from the state, in order to protect their basic rights.

cause you must leave work before sundown on Friday," may claim to be applying equal standards in hiring, but in fact has excluded any person (in this case, an orthodox Jew) whose religion requires observance of the Sabbath beginning Friday at sundown. Supporters of substantive equality claim that formal equality (treating everyone the same) may require some people to abandon religious beliefs, for example, in order to be "just like everyone else." In this respect, they claim that the formal equality is only really equal for those of the dominant culture.

Supporters of substantive equality often charge that formal equality can lead to *systemic racism*. Systemic racism occurs when an institution discriminates against individuals and groups of people without a formal policy of discrimination being in place. An example of systemic racism is a high school Canadian history course that only recognizes the historical contributions to the development of Canada made by Canadians of European origin while neglecting the contributions of Canadians of other racial or cultural backgrounds. When a group of people is ignored in this manner, the effect can be similar to being directly discriminated against.

Recognizing the different conceptions of equality put forward by those debating multiculturalism does not eliminate the debate. Indeed, Quebec takes a fundamentally different position on this issue. While those who have been educated in an English-speaking school in Quebec may choose to enrol their children in an English- or French-speaking school, newcomers to Quebec must send their children to a French-speaking school. The choice that is open to some Quebecois is not available to everyone (a denial of formal equality). In their defence, many Quebecois view multiculturalism as an attack on the "two founding nations" theory of Canada, undermining the French-Canadian culture's unique position by making it one of many partners, rather than an equal partner, in the construction of Canadian life. Subsequently many Quebecois argue that recognition of Quebec culture necessitates the unequal treatment of minority cultures within Quebec.

However, while people may be discriminated against because of racial or cultural identities, they are also more than the sum of those identities. That is, the identity of individuals is not wholly determined by their membership in a group. In addition to being black, a person may be a woman, a parent, a member of a political party, a lawyer. People are multi-dimensional, and our efforts to protect one aspect of their lives (their membership in a group) should not undermine their wholistic rights to formal equality. Briefly stated, formal equality protects the rights of the whole individual, rather than just one aspect of their character. For example, some Muslim organizations recently requested the establishment of an Islamic judicial system in Ontario for settling civil disputes, including divorce. This recognition of difference (substantive equality) would mean that a person's religious identity would be considered more fundamental to their character (self) than any other element of their self (i.e., gender, sexual orientation, career, etc.). Formal equality guarantees equal treatment for the whole individual, not just specific elements of a person's identity. Formal equality recognizes that people are more than just the sum of their parts.

Recognizing the different conceptions of equality put forward enables us to move past strongly enculturated responses, based often on opinion, and ask questions about the underlying claims being made by the contending parties. Trying to understand which conception of equality is being appealed to and why gives us the opportunity to reason about the validity of a claim.

Issue 1

The RCMP has chosen to integrate new traditions with the old.

Take as an example the argument that was touched off recently when a Canadian Legion Hall prohibited the entry of Sikhs unless they removed their turbans. Those who defended the Legion's argument often invoked a conception of equality close to formal equality, i.e., they argued that regardless of class, rank, racial or cultural background, everyone had to remove their hats and headwear. They claimed that there was no discrimination against the Sikhs because they were not being requested to do anything differently from anyone else.

Those who argued that the Sikhs were discriminated against generally appealed to substantive equality (recognizing difference) in their arguments. They argued that the rule disallowing headwear in the Legion Hall was formulated at a time, and in a culture, in which most headwear was worn for reasons of fashion. Thus, insisting on

Issue 1

removing hats was in part to assure a minimum sign of respect for the dead, of putting vanity aside. Those who appealed to substantive equality claimed that equating headwear worn for religious reasons with hats worn for fashion reasons was to overlook a fundamental difference. Equality in this case would require recognizing the different purposes of the head coverings and the rule requiring no hats be amended to exempt headwear worn for religious reasons. Indeed, it would have been disrespectful to the dead for a religious Sikh to have removed his turban.

This is a rather straightforward illustration of how this debate can be conducted at the level of fundamental claims about equality rather than at the level of name calling. These conceptions of equality are not always reconcilable. Nevertheless, as a society we consider both of them to be true at different times. Much of the underlying disagreement about multiculturalism is about which version of equality should take priority over the other. There are no easily applicable rules for deciding this question. In a democratic society, these competing conceptions of equality will be discussed in the news media, public forums, political rallies and classrooms.

However, to discuss the underlying claims being made in the debate enables us to understand the reasons for disagreement. To give someone you disagree with a reason for your position is to recognize them as someone worth talking to. It is a sign of respect. On the other hand, to call someone a name, or tell them, "This is the way we do it around here because we can, or because we like it that way," is to treat them as less than worthy partners in a discussion. The debate about multiculturalism, while it is sometimes difficult to recognize, is a discussion about what it means to treat people equally, and what we as individuals and communities have a right to expect from our fellow citizens in terms of equal treatment.

"I'M NOT RACIST BUT..."

Neil Bissoondath

Someone recently said that racism is as Canadian as maple syrup. I have no argument with that. History provides us with ample proof. But, for proper perspective, let us remember that it is also as American as apple pie, as French as croissants, as Jamaican as ackee, as Indian as aloo, as Chinese as chow mein, as …. Well, there's an entire menu to be written. This is not by way of excusing it. Murder and rape, too, are international, multicultural, as innate to the darker side of the human experience. But we must be careful that the inevitable rage evoked does not blind us to the larger context.

The word "racism" is a discomforting one: It is so vulnerable to manipulation. We can, if we so wish, apply it to any incident involving people of different colour. And therein lies the danger. During the heat of altercations, we seize, as terms of abuse, on whatever is most obvious about the other person. It is, often, a question of unfortunate convenience. A woman, because of her sex, easily becomes a female dog or an intimate part of her anatomy. A large person might be dubbed "a stupid ox," a small person "a' little" whatever. And so a black might become "a nigger," a white "a honky," an Asian "a paki," a Chinese "a chink," an Italian "a wop," a French-Canadian "a frog."

There is nothing pleasant about these terms; they assault every decent sensibility. Even so, I once met someone who, in a stunning surge of naivete, used them as simple descriptives and not as terms of racial abuse. She was horrified to learn the truth. While this may have been an extreme case, the point is that the use of such patently abusive words may not always indicate racial or cultural distaste. They may indicate ignorance or stupidity or insensitivity, but pure racial hatred—such as the Nazis held for Jews, or the Ku Klux Klan for blacks—is a thankfully rare commodity.

Ignorance, not the wilful kind but that which comes from lack of experience, is often indicated by that wonderful phrase, "I'm not racist but…." I think of the mover, a friendly man, who said, "I'm not racist, but the Chinese are the worst drivers on the road." He was convinced this was so because the shape of their eyes, as far as he could surmise, denied them peripheral vision.

Or the oil company executive, an equally warm and friendly man, who, looking for an apartment in Toronto, rejected buildings with East Indian tenants not because of their race—he was telling me this, after all—but because he was given to understand that cockroaches were symbols of good luck in their culture and that, when they moved into a new home, friends came by with gift-wrapped roaches.

Neither of these men thought of himself as racist, and I believe they were not, deep down. (The oil company executive made it clear he would not hesitate to have me as a neighbour; my East Indian descent was of no consequence to him, my horror of cockroaches was.) Yet their comments, so innocently delivered, would open them to the accusation, justifiably so if this were all one knew about them. But it is a charge which would undoubtedly be wounding to them. It is difficult to recognize one's own misconceptions.

True racism is based, more often than not, on wilful ignorance, and an acceptance of—and comfort with—stereotypes. We like to think, in this country, that our multicultural mosaic will help nudge us into a greater openness. But multiculturalism as we know it indulges in stereotype, depends on it for a dash of colour and the flash of dance. It fails to address the most basic questions people have about each other: Do those men doing the Dragon Dance really all belong to secret criminal societies? Do those women dressed in saris really coddle cockroaches for luck? Do those people in dreadlocks all smoke marijuana and live on welfare? Such questions do not seem to be the concern of the government's multicultural programs, superficial and exhibitionistic as they have become.

So the struggle against stereotype, the basis of all racism, becomes a purely personal one. We must beware of the impressions we create. A friend of mine once commented that, from talking to West Indians, she has the impression that their one great cultural contribution to the world is in the oft-repeated boast that "We (unlike everyone else) know how to party."

There are dangers, too, in community response. We must be wary of the self-appointed activists who seem to pop up in the media at every given opportunity spouting the rhetoric of retribution, min-

Issue 1

ing distress for personal, political and professional gain. We must be sceptical about those who depend on conflict for their sense of self, the non-whites who need to feel themselves victims of racism, the whites who need to feel themselves purveyors of it. And we must be sure that, in addressing the problem, we do not end up creating it. Does the Miss Black Canada Beauty Contest still exist? I hope not. Not only do I find beauty contests offensive, but a racially segregated one even more so. What would the public reaction be, I wonder, if every year CTV broadcast the Miss White Canada Beauty Pageant? We give community-service awards only to blacks: Would we be comfortable with such awards only for whites? In Quebec, there are The Association of Black Nurses, The Association of Black Artists, The Congress of Black Jurists. Play tit for tat: The Association of White Nurses, White Artists, White Jurists: visions of apartheid. Let us be frank, racism for one is racism for others.

Finally, and perhaps most important, let us beware of abusing the word itself.

FATHER TELLS WHAT IT'S LIKE FOR BLACK KIDS IN METRO

Philip Mascoll

*T*he gas station clerk's eyes widen and he stares past me at the door.

Myself and the two others in the Kennedy Road and Steeles Avenue East gas station in Scarborough turn slowly, now frightened, wanting to see what it is that has caused this man to practically pee himself.

There are two young men—boys—dressed in what most teenagers wear in winter, tuques, a jacket with a hood, and those impossibly baggy jeans that cling precariously to their backsides.

And by now they're standing with packets of potato chips in the line waiting to pay. They are black kids.

They paid for the chips and left. I watched them walk off to the bus stop on Kennedy Road. They didn't rob the guy, but he thought they would.

Imagine if he had a gun. What would he have done to these children? Children who he clearly assumed were criminals because they were black.

There are blacks who commit crimes, and a disproportionate number of blacks who commit crimes. Having dealt with crime on a daily basis as those of us who report it do, you would have to be a blind, partisan fool not to see this.

But there is now a collective feeling among police and public—even among black people—that all young black people, particularly males, may be criminals.

And because of this attitude on the street, in schools, in stores, everywhere, black children are being treated with a suspicion bordering on open hostility.

Sure, there are blacks and black kids with "an attitude." If you were treated like a criminal, like a fool, like a no-account, no-good-use clown, day in, day out, you'd have "an attitude," too.

I wonder if those who complain about the "attitude" have ever had a teacher tell your black child that he and the other black children have to be the floor sweepers during a kindergarten game of McDonald's.

How do you explain when that child asks why he always has to be the sweeper while the white and Chinese kids get to be the manager and supervisors and clerks?

How do you handle it when you question a high school teacher's surprise that you, the child's father, are speaking to him on the telephone and get the reply "usually with you people we speak to the mother."

How do you handle it when a dentist tells you the cost of dental work and you say go ahead and her reply is "that's a lot of money, what are you doing? Dealing drugs?" That crack of course is dismissed as "a joke" and you are being "too sensitive" when you say you find it rude.

How would you handle this one?

I was in Woodside Square in Scarborough to buy luggage with one of my two sons. He went into the shop ahead of me, and I came in, prepared to buy some $400 worth of luggage for a trip to Jamaica.

He wanted a pouch, a $44 pouch, and as I spoke to the downright unfriendly Oriental woman clerk—whose attitude changed as she realized I really could buy the luggage—her eyes never left my child, who was thumbing through the pouches. I realized she had not connected him with me.

When I asked her what was the matter, this woman who could barely speak English, said, "They steal."

I wonder if Metro police Chief Bill McCormack or police association head Art Lymer has ever had a 16-year-old child come in near to tears, saying a police officer had just swung his cruiser across the sidewalk in front of him and of three friends and asked them for "identification." And that was at the top of the street where his family owns a very expensive house.

I wonder if either has ever been told, in front of his wife and children, by a Metro police officer, young enough to be his child, not to "give me any lip."

Has McCormack or Lymer ever felt the rush of fright when a police officer at a radar trap approaches you and then puts his hand on his gun when you try to take out the wallet with the driver's licence he has demanded—not asked for—demanded. That hand-on-the-gun incident on Birchmount Road was with three small children in the back seat, clutching balloons and in paper hats, on the way home from a birthday party at McDonald's.

Clearly this is the way that all holdup men make their escape. The balloons, children and party hats are just another trick of the terrible Jamaicans.

Has McCormack ever been shuffled into a "second check" line at Pearson International Airport to be grilled about drugs, because he was on a flight from Jamaica? The person that happened to was a deputy chief of the Jamaican police who was landing in Canada to be a guest of the Metro police for three weeks.

Have McCormack or Toronto Mayor June Rowlands ever had a child embarrassed and frustrated at being called asshole and nigger and coon in front of his girlfriend?

Have they ever had a police officer appear at their door after their 15-year-old child and another—a white child—get into a fight on a basketball court?

No one denies that white child's parents right to call police. What is wrong, in any country, in any language, is for a police officer to refuse to explain to a naturally concerned parent what he wishes to see her child for; for him to say "mind your own business" when she insists.

It was wrong, wrong, wrong, for that white York Region police officer to raise his voice to shout at the mother and father; to threaten the 15-year-old black child with arrest, without finding out who was wrong; to call the boy's father "idiot," to assume the child was the aggressor without hearing the full story.

He was wrong, indefensibly wrong for not apologizing when a white parent brought his child and several others who were present at the fight to say the black kid was defending himself from a larger bully. Not only did he not apologize, but he stormed off, throwing back over his shoulder, "You people should be charged for wasting time."

On Wednesday afternoon in the midst of the hunt for the four suspects in the Just Desserts slaying, Metro officers stopped a TTC bus at the corner of Birchmount Road and Finch Avenue East and dragged out a tall black kid, who by all accounts looked like one of the suspects.

Not one black person who was there had a problem with the police doing their job.

There was probably not one black parent in Metro Toronto who has not prayed since last week Tuesday that the police would quickly apprehend the person or persons who caused the death of a 23-year-old innocent who was having coffee and cake. Just like the whites and every other race, I certainly was. My friends and relatives were.

But I suspect, they, like me, had one more reason than a white parent to utter that prayer.

When our children are out of the home they face twin dangers—other children with guns and a police force that may hassle or harm them. And then there are the shopkeepers or gas station attendants who could hit the holdup alarm when the kids were buying gas or a candy bar.

I do not, and hopefully nor do other black parents, suffer collective guilt because the suspects in that robbery were black.

I will not take responsibility for that——and every other crime in which the suspects or perpetrators happen to be black—until Lymer or McCormack or Rowlands and all white people are burdened with collective responsibility and collective guilt for every white criminal.

CHANGE, LAW AND THE WORKPLACE

Kathy Casey

*C*ompared to twenty-five years ago, today many more women, visible minorities, disabled and Native Canadians can be found in offices, schools, industries and medical centres. These workers are qualified for their positions and work productively at their jobs. However, some feel disadvantaged, that they are not receiving equal treatment in the workplace. Others are discriminated against and harassed, even though it is public policy that every person is free and equal in dignity and rights and can expect to live and work in an environment that is exempt from discrimination and harassment.

In order to understand why people are treated differently and, in some cases, unfairly, let's examine what discrimination and harassment are and review how the legislation in Ontario attempts to prevent unfair treatment and remedy the effects.

Now, *discrimination* is a tricky word. Sometimes, definitions of the term are devised to accelerate the interests of those people who claim they are being discriminated against. However, at its simplest level, discrimination merely means making a choice, and making choices is an essential part of everyday life for individuals and organizations. These choices are governed by many factors including attitudes, traditions and rules. When these factors have the effect of limiting the opportunities of certain groups of people because of their sex and colour, for example, then the problem of discrimination arises.

When our different treatment of people is based on stereotypical perceptions rather than real characteristics, then we are illegally discriminating. For instance, some women are not hired or promoted to senior management positions because of the attitude that women have family obligations and therefore won't make good senior managers. As well, some blacks are not hired or promoted because of the attitude that blacks are lazy and won't make good employees. Ultimately, illegal discrimination is based on prejudiced attitudes about people that result in unfair treatment of people.

Discrimination may also be defined as an action or behaviour that attaches exaggerated importance to physical differences between people. When we assume that people have certain characteristics because of their skin colour, disability or sex and then treat them unfavourably, we have created a situation of illegal discrimination.

Harassment may be defined as repeated vexatious or distressing conduct or behaviour that is known or ought to be known as unacceptable and unwanted. Harassment takes many forms: for example, sexual, racial, gender, age and ethno-cultural. However, what is important to note is that all forms of harassment are uninvited and unwelcome. Furthermore, harassment is a form of discrimination. It occurs because people have internalized the stereotypes and prejudices that exist in our society.

Unwelcome touches are more than embarrassing

Harassment is based in the abuse of power—real or perceived. It is generally carried out by members of a dominant group against members of a minority group. Incidents of harassment tend to be repeated and to grow in intensity. Victims often say nothing because of fear or embarrassment. The person doing the harassing then feels a distorted sense of power and continues his or her demeaning treatment of others. It is important to note that, because people often accept the stereotypes and prejudices of the dominant culture, a person can harass another person or group of people of the same gender, race or ethno-cultural background as himself or herself.

Despite public policy, there are many indications that racial and sexual harassment are on the increase today. Signs and buttons presenting "Keep Canada White" have been displayed in public. Also,

Issue 1

anti-female slogans have been heard on some post-secondary campuses in opposition to women studying in non-traditional programs.

Acts of discrimination and harassment are illegal in Ontario. All persons in the province are protected under the *Ontario Human Rights Code*. First enacted in 1962 as a consolidation of various anti-discrimination provisions, the *Code* provides, among other matters, that every person has a right to freedom from discrimination and harassment in a number of areas and various different grounds. The areas are services, goods, facilities, accommodation, contracts, employment and membership in associations and trade unions. The grounds are race, ancestry, colour, ethnic origin, citizenship, creed, sex, handicap, age (18–65), marital and family status, receipt of public assistance, record of offences and sexual orientation. For example, you cannot be denied accommodation because of your colour, denied education because of your handicap, or denied employment because of your religion (creed). As well, according to the legislation, you cannot be the object of harassment which could consist of slurs, jokes, stares, isolated treatment and/or suggestive touching or remarks.

If you think that you have been discriminated against or harassed by someone in your workplace, then there are a number of procedures to follow. If you work in a unionized environment, you can speak to your union representative. Alternatively, or as well, you can file a complaint internally through the Human Resource Department in your company or externally with the Ontario Human Rights Commission.

Another type of legislation in Ontario has come about because of the historical undervaluation of the work that women workers do. It is the *Pay Equity Act*. Historically, men and women have tended to do different work, and the work that is performed by women has not been paid as well. This undervaluation has resulted in a wage gap: the difference between the average earnings of men and women. Currently, the wage gap in Ontario means that women earn 30.4 percent less than men.

A lot of the mistaken ideas about the role of women in the workplace and the worth of their work are based on the assumption that women are secondary workers. Some believe that women's contribution to the economy is less important than that made by men and that women don't really need employment income. Moreover, a lot

Harassment
Harassment may be defined as repeated vexatious or distressing conduct or behaviour that is known or ought to be known as unacceptable and unwanted. Harassment is based in the abuse of power: real or perceived. It is generally carried out by members of a dominant group against members of a minority group.

Issue 1

of the jobs available to women are secondary jobs—part-time, temporary, dead-end and poorly paid.

This idea of secondary workers and secondary jobs—secondary, meaning less important—has caused some people to undervalue the work that women do. This is one of the main factors contributing to the wage gap. Though the wage gap stems from a number of reasons (such as differences in education, differences in experience, prejudice, job ghettos and hours worked), a third of the wage gap exists because of the myth that the work women do is of less value.

To bridge the wage gap, *Pay Equity* was enacted as of January 1, 1988. The Act requires an employer to pay men and women the same wage for work that is different but of equal value. Pay equity is not to be confused with "equal pay for equal work" which means that if a woman is doing the same job as a man she will be paid the same wage.

Pay equity compares different jobs to see if the jobs are of equal value to the employer. Although the jobs may be different, their contents may be similar and therefore comparable.

To compare jobs, the criteria used are skill, effort, responsibility and working conditions. The *Pay Equity Act* requires employers to compare female job classes to male job classes using the four criteria. When it is found that the female and male job classes are of the same value, yet the female jobs are paid less, compensation in the female job class must be improved. Both men and women within the underpaid female-dominated jobs will receive adjustment.

If you currently work in a female-dominated job class (one in which 60 percent or more of the members are women), and if you are interested in seeing how your position has been compared, your employer is required upon request to show you the evaluation method used. If you are concerned that you are not being paid fairly, you can ask the Pay Equity Commission for assistance.

The *Ontario Human Rights Code* is an example of legislation that has been enacted to prevent unfair treatment of all workers in the province. The *Pay Equity Act* is an example of legislation to remedy past discriminatory treatment of all workers in female-dominated job classes. Another example of legislation that has been enacted to remedy past discrimination within a company is *Employment Equity* legislation. This law came into effect in September 1995 and affects

Issue 1

the Ontario provincial government. In March 1996, all municipalities, universities, colleges, school boards, hospitals and large private firms will have to abide by *Employment Equity* legislation. By September 1996, smaller firms will have to file equity plans detailing how they will achieve equitable representation in their workforce. Employment equity is a planning process adopted by an employer to examine how women, the disabled, visible minorities and Native persons are recruited, hired, trained, promoted and represented within an organization. It seeks to identify and eliminate illegal discrimination in a company's process and policies and tries to remedy the effects of past illegal discrimination. These remedies may include programs aimed at changing representation within and across occupational groups so that target group members are appropriately represented throughout the workplace. Canadian and Ontario laws specifically require that programs designed to change the effects of past discriminatory behaviour are not in themselves discriminatory.

Some people are concerned that remedies such as selective hiring are discriminatory. They use the term "reverse discrimination" when criticizing organizations that have chosen to offer jobs to qualified people from one of the designated groups. For example, for the next few years, only women will be qualified to apply for positions at the Ontario College of Art and Ryerson University. By having such a program, an employer is broadcasting that certain groups are unfairly represented within that organization and that, for a short term, only qualified members of those groups will be hired. Once the organization determines that there is fair representation within its workforce, then all persons who apply for positions will be considered. It is important to realize that these programs are short term, justified only as long as the inequalities exist. Their sole purpose is to counter the long-term effects of past discrimination.

Change is difficult for every generation. We hear that we are losing what has been important, that other areas will also change, that we must adjust and learn new ways when we are already comfortable with what we know. However, change is the norm of the human condition. We must confront the paradox. While we are always seeking new knowledge and new ways of being, we resist change. However stubborn our resistance may be, one thing is evident. The workplace has changed from what it was just a short time ago, and not only the government but also individual employers have responded to that change in a variety of ways. New legislation and

Issue 1

The Value of Household Labour

Much work, time and energy is invested in the maintenance of the household (cleaning, laundry, cooking, repairs, shopping) and in the care and nurturing of household members.

new programs have been created in response to the multicultural, multinational, dual gender workplace that we now have. Examining our own behaviour in an attempt to understand and change, rather than to defend, allows us a new perspective on a changing environment, a perspective that will allow us to accept how others differ, to respect those differences, and to value ourselves and others as unique individuals who have a worthwhile contribution. As a result, we all grow in our understanding of ourselves and each other, an understanding that will increase our ability to live and work together in harmony.

Research shows that the majority of work in the home is done by women, even in households where both the woman and the man are working outside the home.

Obviously, this is an arena for much negotiation, debate and change in coming years.

Issue 1

SEX, STATISTICS AND WAGES

Globe & Mail Editorial, January 21, 1993

Give the Canadian media some credit: they didn't make as much of a hash of this story as they usually do. The subject is the much ballyhooed "wage gap" between men and women, documented annually by Statistics Canada, and eagerly lapped up by the nation's newspapers and television news shows. Faint praise is in order this year, however, because three ingredients that are essential to understanding the wage difference—education, hours worked and marriage—receive at least passing mention in some of last week's coverage.

It was reported that women's wages rose to 69.6 per cent of men's in 1991, from 67.6 per cent the year before. But what does that mean? For starters, it does not mean, despite the **obfuscatory** efforts of those who ought to know better, that women are being paid nearly one-third less to do the same jobs. A recent ad campaign by the Ontario Women's Directorate, for example, asked Toronto bus and subway passengers, "How much would they pay a man to do your job?" The slogan, and the text that followed, suggested to female readers that, by the simple virtue of being a male, a man at their firm is being paid one-third more to do precisely the same job. He isn't. Sex discrimination in wages—paying a man with the same qualifications more than a woman to fill exactly the same position—is against the law, and has been ever since Bob Rae was in short pants.

obfuscatory—intentionally confusing

Statscan's numbers are, of course, an average of millions of Canadians, with different ages, levels of and types of education, skills, years of work experience and jobs. An average focusing solely on gender tends to obscure the degree to which all sorts of other factors come into play. (Keep in mind also that the following statistics refer to full-time workers only.)

One would expect that, since society's attitudes towards women's work and education have changed relatively recently, the difference in average wages would be least among the young. And that is precisely what one finds. The hypothetical full-time working woman over age 55 earned 63.6 per cent of the income of her male counterpart in the same age bracket, while her granddaughter, aged 15 to 24, earned an average of 86.4 per cent as much as a man in the same age group.

Crunch the numbers a bit further, and other interesting facts pop up. Education, for one thing, matters. Women with a university degree earned more, not less, than men with lower levels of education. When one considers that a majority of those enrolled in Canadian universities are female (55.3 percent of full- and part-time university students are women) it's hard to imagine a future in which the wage difference will not continue to narrow.

But there is already almost no wage gap between single men and single women. In 1991, single women's average earnings were 91.1 per cent of those of their male counterparts. For some women, there was even less of a difference. Data compiled by Statistics Canada at The Globe and Mail's request show that the income of single women age 35 to 44 was 94.5 per cent of that earned by men of the same age. And looking only at the most educated members of that age group, single females with a university degree—women actually made six per cent more money than single, 35 to 44 year-old, university-educated men. (In fairness, the margin of error in Statscan's survey is large, so these last two percentages could be off by these several points.)

All of these numbers refer, of course, to full-time workers. But not all full-time workers work the same number of hours. On average, men work more than women: 40.4 hours vs. 35.2 hours a week. In other words, the average man works 12.9 per cent longer, explaining a large part of the wage gap.

But the biggest factor is marriage. The earnings of single women, single men and married women working full-time are roughly comparable. But the earnings of the average married man rise above those of everyone else. That is the only real "wage gap." Whether or not it is a problem is a subject worthy of discussion. Its existence suggests that, as one would expect, married men and women choose certain career and life paths, different from those chosen by singles. But why is it that many married women work only part-time, or adopt less time-consuming (and less well-paying) full-time careers? Are they forced to by their husbands? By circumstance? By entrenched social attitudes? Do many, for a whole variety of unquantifiable reasons, freely choose this path, thinking it best for their families?

In the debate that ought to take place around this issue, answering these questions would be a good place to start.

A Response to the Globe and Mail Editorial

Are Women's Salaries Behind Men's?

The *Globe and Mail* made extended editorial comment on the fact that, as reported by Statistics Canada, the earnings gap between women and men closed slightly in 1991. Readers should not be misled into believing that the position of women in the labour market is improving significantly, even relative to that of men ("Sex, Statistics And Wages"—editorial, Jan. 21). It is true, as Statistics Canada reported, that the earnings of full-time, full-year women workers in 1991 were 69.6 per cent of the earnings of men working full-time, full-year, up from 67.6 per cent in 1990.

This mainly reflects the fact that the loss of full-time, full-year jobs in 1991 disproportionately took place in manufacturing and construction, sectors where relatively well-paid jobs are held disproportionately by men.

Most importantly, it should have been noted that just 51 per cent of working women are employed on a full-time, full-year basis, compared to 68 per cent of working men. For the 49 per cent of women working on less than a full-time, full-year basis, Statistics Canada reported that average earnings fell by 6 per cent from 1990 to 1991 (more than the 5.1 per cent fall for the 32 per cent of men who did not work full-time, full-year). The important fact that wages fell significantly for the 49 per cent of women who did not work on a full-time, full-year basis was prominently reported by Statistics Canada in the summary of the publication from which the "closing of the earnings gap" story was extracted. It was generally ignored by the media. Why? It is true that many women "choose" not to work on a full-time, full-year basis, though this choice is shaped by the fact that, in the absence of a national childcare system, women bear a disproportionate burden of family responsibilities. Exclusion from full-time, full-year jobs is not, however, just a matter of choice. Between one-fifth and one-third of part-time women workers regularly report to Statistics Canada that they work part-time only because they cannot find a full-time job.

It is important to understand that the overall deterioration in the labour market in the recession has affected women in specific ways. Women have not suffered quite as much as men from massive industrial layoffs, but hundreds of thousands of women have been marginalized through unemployment and underemployment, and earnings have clearly fallen for almost half of the women in the labour market. It takes a rather perverse perspective to interpret all this as a step toward equality. We are, of course, very far from equality. The Statistics Canada study shows that just 3.7 per cent of women earned more than $50,000 in 1991, compared to 15.7 per cent of men. At the other end of the spectrum, 37 per cent of women earned less than $10,000, compared to 23.9 per cent of men.

Nancy Riche, Executive Vice President, Canadian Labour Congress, Ottawa. Reproduced from the *Globe and Mail*.

PUBLIC AND PRIVATE ROLES

It is understood that in a developed society *needs* are not only quantitative: the need for consumer goods; but also qualitative: the need for a free and many-sided development of human facilities, the need for information, for communication, the need to be free not only from exploitation but from oppression and alienation in work and leisure.

A. Gorz

THE END OF THE JOB

William Bridges

*E*very morning's newspaper carries another story of new job losses. We hear the recession has been over for quite a while, but the percentage of workers who are jobless has not fallen as after previous recessions. The Clinton administration is trying to create jobs, but critics claim some of its new taxes and regulations will destroy jobs. We are told the only way to protect our jobs is to increase our productivity, but then we discover that reengineering, using self-managed teams, flattening our organizations, and turning routine work over to computers always make many jobs redundant.

We used to read predictions that by 2000 everyone would work 30-hour weeks, and the rest would be leisure. But as we approach 2000 it seems more likely that half of us will be working 60-hour weeks and the rest of us will be unemployed.

What's wrong?

It is not that the President or his critics don't care what happens to us, or that organizations that asked for our loyalty and grew because of our efforts have double-crossed us. The fault does not lie even with that dread monster, overseas competition, which has been blamed for everything from unemployment to falling living standards.

It's a shame these things are not the culprits, for if they were our task would be simpler. The reality we face is much more troubling, for what is disappearing is not just a certain number of jobs—or jobs in certain industries or jobs in some part of the country or even jobs in America as a whole. What is disappearing is the very thing itself: the job. That much sought after, much maligned social entity, a job, is vanishing like a species that has outlived its evolutionary time.

A century from now Americans will look back and marvel that we couldn't see more clearly what was happening. They will remark how fixated we were on this game of musical jobs in which, month after month, new waves of people had to drop out. They will sympathize with the suffering we were going through but will comment that it came from trying to play the game by the old rules.

The modern world is on the verge of another huge leap in creativity and productivity, but the job is not going to be part of tomorrow's economic reality. There still is and will always be enormous amounts of work to do, but it is not going to be contained in the familiar envelopes we call jobs. In fact, many organizations are today well along the path toward being "de-jobbed."

The job is a social artifact, though it is so deeply embedded in our consciousness that most of us have forgotten its artificiality or the fact that most societies since the beginning of time have done just fine without jobs. The job is an idea that emerged early in the 19th century to package the work that needed doing in the growing factories and bureaucracies of the industrializing nations. Before people had jobs, they worked just as hard but on shifting clusters of tasks, in a variety of locations, on a schedule set by the sun and the weather and the needs of the day. The modern job was a startling new idea— and to many, an unpleasant and perhaps socially dangerous one. Critics claimed it was an unnatural and even inhuman way to work. They believed most people wouldn't be able to live with its demands. It is ironic that what started as a controversial concept ended up becoming the ultimate **orthodoxy**—and that we're hooked on jobs.

orthodoxy—traditional belief

Now the world of work is changing again: The conditions that created jobs 200 years ago—mass-production and the large organization—are disappearing. Technology enables us to automate the production line, where all those job holders used to do their repetitive tasks. Instead of long production runs where the same thing has to be done again and again, we are increasingly customizing production. Big firms, where most of the good jobs used to be, are unbundling activities and farming them out to little firms, which have created or taken over profitable **niches**. Public services are starting to be privatized, and government bureaucracy, the ultimate **bastion** of job security, is being thinned. With the disappearance of the conditions that created jobs, we are losing the need to package work in that way. No wonder jobs are disappearing.

niches—small corner of the market
bastion—stronghold

To an extent that few people have recognized, our organizational world is no longer a pattern of jobs, the way a honeycomb is a pattern of those little hexagonal pockets of honey. In place of jobs, there are part-time and temporary work situations. That change is symptomatic of a deeper change that is subtle but more profound.

Issue 2

The deeper change is this: Today's organization is rapidly being transformed from a structure built out of jobs into a field of work needing to be done.

Jobs are artificial units superimposed on this field. They are patches of responsibility that, together, are supposed to cover the work that needs to be done. His job is to take care of this, hers is to take care of that, and yours is to take care of the other things. Together you usually get the work done, though there are always scraps and pieces of work that don't quite fall into anyone's job description, and over time job responsibilities have to be adjusted and new jobs added to keep getting everything done.

discrepancies—inconsistencies

When the economy was changing much more slowly, the **discrepancies** between the job matrix and the work field could be forgotten. If new technology opened up a new area in the work field, new jobs could be created to cover the new work that needed doing. If a new market opened up, new jobs could be created to serve it. If a new law or judicial ruling required an organization to do something different, new jobs could be created to take care of the situation.

But in a fast-moving economy, jobs are rigid solutions to an elastic problem. We can rewrite a person's job description occasionally, but not every week. When the work that needs doing changes constantly, we cannot afford the inflexibility that the job brings with it. Further, at a time when competitive organizations must reduce head count, jobs—those boxes on the organization chart, with regular duties, hours and salaries—encourage hiring. They do this by cutting work up into "turfs," which in turn require more turfs (and more hiring) whenever a new area opens up. They encourage additional hiring by giving managers a level of power **commensurate** with the number of turf areas for which they are responsible: The more areas, the more power. Jobs also discourage accountability because they reward people not for getting the necessary work done but for "doing their jobs."

commensurate—appropriate for

Jobs are no longer socially adaptive. That is why they are going the way of the dinosaur.

Organizations, like individuals, will have trouble shifting their expectations and habits to fit the new post-job world. Some will try to get by with job cuts, reducing the number of hands and heads that do the work but leaving in place the old idea that work must be packaged into jobs. Not surprisingly, such organizations find that removing job holders leaves holes in the job field and that less work gets done as a result. An American Management Association survey of companies that had made "major staff cuts" between 1987 and 1992 found that, despite the reduced labour costs, less than half improved their operating earnings—while one in four saw earnings drop. More ominously, said the AMA's report, "These figures were even worse for companies that undertook a second or third round of downsizing." Many companies that fail to get their expected result within the first round of cuts simply repeat the process.

Other companies cut jobs and use temps to fill in the spaces or build in staffing flexibility. Tomorrow's organization certainly must turn a significant part of its work over to a **contingent** work force that can grow and shrink and reshape itself as its situation demands. But note that even the most creative work design begs the question of how unready most organizations are to manage this work force of temps, part-timers, consultants, and contract workers effectively. A large manufacturer that used office temps extensively found that the temporaries on the clerical staff, lacking loyalty to the organization, had leaked details of the company plan for union negotiations to the union that represented the manufacturing employees. A worker at another company, a condom maker, found that "every time you'd get a big batch of new [temp factory workers], you'd start finding more holes in the condoms."

contingent—dependent upon conditions

Other companies couple job cuts with reorganization. This makes more sense, since it recognizes that you can't just take pieces out of a system and expect it to keep working well. But while the goal may be more defensible, the process causes so much distress and disruption that the change meant to strengthen the company often ends up weakening it. That is because such changes force people to switch jobs, a process that undermines the three qualities that Michael Beer and his Harvard colleagues have identified as the source of competitive advantage: competence, coordination, and commitment. People are moved to unfamiliar jobs (competence declines), they are working in new teams, for new bosses, and with new customers (coordination declines), and they are demoralized by their new insecurity and the loss of co-worker friends (commitment declines).

Issue 2

TQM—Total Quality Management

Still other companies seize on one of the cure-alls of the day—empowerment, flattening the organization, self-directed teams, **TQM**, reengineering, flex-time, telecommuting, job sharing—and hope it will do the trick. Any of these efforts can improve the organization, but all are compromised by the fact that everyone has a job. For as long as people are expending their energies on doing their jobs, they aren't going to be focused on the customer, or be self-managers, or be empowerable. They won't be able to capitalize on the possibilities of empowerment, automation, or anything else.

The answer is to create the post-job organization. It is ironic that most organizations need employees to stop acting like job holders, yet they know only how to hire, pay, communicate with, and manage job holders. Most organizations also maintain policies, strategies, training programs, and structures meant to enable employees to be more successful in their job activities. In fact, a wave of job-free workers intent on doing what needs to be done rather than on doing their jobs would wreck most traditional organizations. Just as individuals need to rethink their assumptions and strategies, organizations too will have to rethink almost everything they do.

Look at the characteristics of the post-job organization. The first is that it hires the right people. That sounds obvious, but it means something quite different in an organization that is no longer job-based than it does where one is hiring to fill slots. To begin with, you must find people who can work well without the cue system of job descriptions. At Ideo, America's largest industrial design firm, in Palo Alto, no one has a title or a boss. The head of marketing there, Tom Kelly, leaves no doubt about the importance of hiring: "If you hire the right people—if you've got the right fit—then everything will take care of itself."

Even the right people will produce poor results if organized in the old way. Yes, complex hierarchies are out and the flattened organization is in, but not because that is fashionable. Rather, the post-job employee's necessary vendor-mindedness—thinking of himself or herself as an independent business—just doesn't mix with hierarchy. The post-job employee is going to need a much more flexible organization than most can easily find today. How to create this flexibility? Organizations using such workers most successfully are finding a number of approaches effective.

Project participants *not* job-holders.

Common to many is a reliance on project teams. The project-based organization is not a new idea; 25 years ago Melvin Anshen wrote in the *Harvard Business Review* that traditionally structured organizations were inherently designed to maintain the status quo rather than to respond to the changing demands of the market. But, he noted, "the single organization pattern that is free from this built-in bias [toward maintaining the **status quo** is the project cluster." Since those words were written, companies like EDS, Intel, and Microsoft have used the project as their essential building block—though "block" is far too fixed and rigid a term to describe the way projects are actually used.

status quo—the present situation

Study a fast-moving organization like Intel and you'll see a person hired and likely assigned to a project. It changes over time, and the person's responsibilities and tasks change with it. Then the person is assigned to another project (well before the first project is finished), and then maybe to still another. These additional projects, which also evolve, require working under several team leaders, keeping different schedules, being in various places, and performing a number of different tasks. Hierarchy **implodes**, not because someone theorizes that it should but because under these conditions it

implodes—collapses upon itself

Issue 2

cannot be maintained. Several workers on such teams that Tom Peters interviewed used the same phrase: "We report to each other."

In such a situation people no longer take their cue from a job description or a supervisor's instructions. Signals come from the changing demands of the project. Workers learn to focus their individual efforts and collective resources on the work that needs doing, changing as that changes. Managers lose their "jobs," too, for their value can be defined only by how they facilitate the work of the project teams or how they contribute to it as a member.

No good word exists for the place that an individual fills in this kind of organization: It isn't a "job"; "position" sounds too fixed; "role" sounds too unitary. Whatever it is, it is changing and multiple. It is a package of capabilities, drawn upon variously in different project-based situations. Anything that stands in the way of rapid regrouping has to go.

Some of what it takes to run the organization moving beyond jobs is part of the environment: The databases and the networking technology, for example, that make it possible for a delocalized operation to function effectively. Such technology, one of the forces transforming organizations and de-jobbing the workplace, is part of the emerging organizational **infrastructure**. It was out there waiting to be utilized.

infrastructure—underlying structure

Not so with the social and cultural infrastructure for this kind of work world. Far less developed, not yet widely embraced, and lagging behind the technical, these **nascent** infrastructures threaten to undermine the new work world. You cannot run a post-job organization the same way you ran the organization when it was job-based. Policies on work hours, for example, won't be the same. Compensation plans will have to change. New training programs will be needed. A different kind of communication is essential. Careers have to be reconceptualized, and career-development has to be reinvented. New redeployment mechanisms become necessary. And the whole idea and practice of "management" need to be re-created from scratch.

nascent—emerging

Many organizations have experimented with flex-time, job sharing and telecommuting, but the disappearance of jobs puts all these into a new context. Standardized work hours and places, and the equation of one person and one job, were products of mass production and the government bureaucracies occasioned by it. They were wholly irrelevant to the pre-job world and would have been burdensome checks on productivity. Take job sharing. Work was usually shared in arrangements that varied with the demands of the situation. Only when work was divided up into activity packages and distributed one to a person in the form of jobs did anyone imagine that anything but talent, proximity, strength, and availability would determine who did what and when. Of course once you have divided up the common task into jobs, then anyone whose other responsibilities, physical capabilities, or financial needs make a "whole job" unappealing or unworkable will suggest job sharing.

But if jobs disappear, there is no longer any reason to treat these eight-hour chunks of effort as the building blocks from which the organizational structure is assembled. Not that job sharing will be permitted in the post-job organization—much more than that: The issue disappears. Naturally work will be shared. People working on more than one project are already dividing their job into several pieces. If you spend four hours doing A, two doing B, and two doing C; and if Dave spends two hours doing A, two doing B, and four doing C—then you are all job sharing already. What will the post-job policy be on job sharing? It will be to put the old policy in the Policy Museum as an artifact of a bygone age and get on with doing the work that needs doing.

The same thing will happen to policies on flex-time and telecommuting. These matters will be governed partly by the demands of the work and partly by other economic factors, which can include the cost of office space, the availability of technological linkages between delocalized co-workers, and such **idiosyncratic** matters as the parties' family responsibilities, commuting conditions, and whether they work better early in the day or late. Self-employed workers always take all these matters into account, and so will post-job workers.

idiosyncratic—individual or non-conforming

How about policies on leaves of absence, vacations, and retirement? Leaves from what? Vacations from what? Retirement from what? The post-job worker will be far more likely to be hired for a project or a fixed length of time than a job holder is today. Working and leisure are no longer governed by the calculus of constant employment. Without the job, time off from work becomes something not taken out of job time but something taken during the interims be-

Issue 2

tween assignments or between project contracts. And retirement? As ever more people become businesses in themselves, retirement will become an individual matter that has less to do with organizational policy and more to do with individual circumstances and desires.

If self-employment is any guide, the de-jobbed worker will likely be a stern taskmaster. This worker is losing with the job a definition of what is enough—of what constitutes a day's work and entitles one to go home satisfied. Add the fact that the de-jobbed worker will be scheduling his or her own employment and trying, like any independent professional, to make hay while the sun shines. The result is that de-jobbed workers will have to learn to pace themselves. For the organization, leave policies, vacation policies, and retirement policies will become relatively insignificant.

untrammelled—unre-stricted

Still not quite clear is what the post-job manager will have to do. Everyone agrees that tomorrow's worker, **untrammelled** by old constraints of hierarchy and job boundaries, will be far more independent and self-directed than today's. Will such a worker even need managing in anything like the accepted sense of the word? Michael Hammer, the consultant who has done most to advance reengineering, leaves no doubt where he stands: "Middle management as we currently know it will simply disappear." Three-quarters of middle managers will vanish, he says, many returning to the "real work" they did before they were promoted into management, with the remainder filling a role that "will change almost beyond recognition." How? "To oversimplify, there will be two main flavours of [new style] managers: process managers and employee coaches. Process managers will oversee, end to end, a reengineered process, such as order fulfilment of product development. Their skills (will need to be those of) performance management and work redesign. Employee coaches will support and nurture employees—much as senior managers do in corporate America today."

It is not too much to say that we have reached the point where we must talk about the end of management. The reason is that the manager was created only a little more than a century ago to oversee and direct the work of people who held jobs. Before that, there were masters and gang bosses and commanders and overseers, but there were no managers. People were led, but whatever management existed was self-management. That is what we are returning to—with a crucial difference. The old self-management was taking care of yourself while you followed the leader. The new self-man-

Issue 2

agement is acting toward the business at hand as if you had an ownership stake in it.

This means that tomorrow's executive, coordinator, facilitator, or whatever we choose to call the non-manager will have to provide people with direct access to information that was once the domain of decision-makers. Tomorrow's employees and contractors will have to understand the whys and wherefores of the organization's strategy far better than today's do; they will have to understand the organization's problems, weaknesses, and challenges realistically. The de-jobbed worker will need to be much clearer on the organization's vision and values than the job-based worker needed to be. In a job-based environment, you just do your job. In a de-jobbed environment, you do what needs to be done to honour and realize the organization's vision and values.

Specifically, companies that have already begun to employ de-jobbed workers effectively seem to share at least four traits: (1) They encourage rank-and-file employees to make the kind of operating decision that used to be reserved for managers. (2) They give people the information that they need to make such decisions—information that used to be given only to managers. (3) They give employees lots of training to create the kind of understanding of business and financial issues that no one but an owner or an executive used to be concerned with. (4) They give people a stake in the fruits of their labour—a share of company profits.

The organization that wants to move down the path toward the post-job future must answer several key questions:

- Is work being done by the right people?
- Are the core tasks—requiring and protecting the special competencies of the organization—being done in-house, and are other tasks being given to vendors or subcontractors, temps or term hires, or to the customers themselves?
- Are the people who do the work in each of those categories chosen in such a way that their desires, abilities, temperaments, and assets are matched with the demands of the task?
- Is everyone involved—not just the core employees—given the business information they need to understand their part in the larger task? Do they have the understanding needed to think like business people?

Issue 2

- Does the way people are organized and managed help them complete their assignments, or does it tie them to outmoded expectations and job-based assumptions?

Too often new ways of doing things are viewed as add-ons: "If we ever get a spare moment around here, let's flatten the organization chart!" That's a big mistake, of course. Part of the reason there is so little time is that most of today's organizations are trying to use outmoded and underpowered organizational forms to do tomorrow's work. They insert an empowerment program here and a new profit-sharing plan there and then announce that those things aren't so great after all because profits are still falling. Such organizations won't have better results until they do two things. First, get rid of jobs. Second, redesign the organization to get the best out of a de-jobbed worker. A big task, sure. But like any evolutionary challenge, it will separate the survivors from the extinct.

SEVEN RULES TO BREAK IN A DE-JOBBED WORLD

Most of us still play under the old rules of jobs and careers. In examining your own attitudes, watch out for these old rules — and replace them when you find them.

Don't leave a job when good jobs are so hard to get.

Remember: The same thing that makes other jobs scarce makes your present job only a temporary expedient. It too is going to disappear. This is no argument to make ill-considered moves, just a challenge to the rule you are depending on. It is dangerous.

The best jobs go to the people with the best qualifications.

This rule is a half-truth because it fails to acknowledge that the whole idea of qualification is changing. The old qualifications included degrees or other formal certification, length of experience in a similar job, and recommendations. Today most recommendations are known to be hot air and tail-covering platitudes. Experience is more likely to produce a repetition of the past than the kind of new approaches that today's conditions demand. And there often isn't any degree or certification in the activity that today's organization needs. The new qualifications are that you really want to do the work (desire), that you are good at what the work requires (ability), that you fit that kind of situation (temperament), and that you have whatever other resources the work requires (assets). Those so-called D.A.T.A. are the only qualifications that matter in a rapidly changing work world.

Getting into the right business assures a secure future.

The Dustin Hoffman character in *The Graduate* was told to get into plastics. Today it might be computers or biotechnology. But designating any field would be bad advice because while parts of the economy are surely destined to expand, no part of the economy is immune from de-jobbing.

Don't try to change careers after 40.

The world of jobs is full of age discrimination, but that's the world you are leaving. There is far less age discrimination in the world of You & Co. Vendors get paid what they can show they are worth. Those age-related bugaboos, health insurance and pension contributions, are things you are going to take care of yourself, so they aren't a factor the way they were when you were looking for a job.

It doesn't matter what you want. It's what "they" want that counts.

Most of us were raised on this one. Maturity was a matter of tempering our wants and conforming to what someone with more influence or resources (like IBM or the state department of education) wanted of us. But today it doesn't matter nearly as much as it used to what an organization wants. The power has moved elsewhere; the only "they" that matters much anymore is customers. Since what you want is an important part of your D.A.T.A. — that is, of your qualifications — you'd better pay attention to it.

You have to be a salesman to get ahead today.

Another half-truth. The old-style salesman who could sell anything is as much at risk as any other job holder. Far better off is the person with a clear product that she or he believes in. The truth element in the idea is that people will need the ability to conduct **quid pro quo transactions** involving not the old-line salesman's gift of gab but a clear understanding of why someone needs what one has and the ability to make the case effectively. Many people who do that well have no experience or interest in sales as a field.

quid pro quo transactions—equal exchanges

Issue 2

If you have responsibilities — people dependent on you — you can't leave the world of jobs.

This rule misidentifies the risk. If you have responsibilities, it is more important for you to look ahead and develop the kind of career that has a life expectancy beyond the end of the year. Risky and responsible have been redefined: The good job, once the definition of responsibility, is now a very risky business, and the old kind of freelance activity that was once risky is now in tune with the future and is becoming the choice of many people who want to act responsibly.

ON THE MEANING OF WORK

Mitchell Lerner

*T*here's a story told about a young man who brings the ruler of a peaceful kingdom a secret method of making bread without labour. At first everyone, ruler included, is delighted because it seems that hunger will be gone and the need to work will vanish. Then, painfully, reality sets in. What will people do with time on their hands? The king orders the young man killed. "The devil," as the saying goes, "makes work for idle hands." As the king belatedly understands, work is a necessity, an inescapable part of the human condition.

No civilization can survive without work. But what is the nature of this activity that by necessity is part of your life and mine? This essay presents several interpretations of work from ancient to modern times.[1]

One of the earliest interpretations goes back to the Judaeo-Christian roots of western civilization to the first story in Genesis. Eve having eaten from the fruit persuades Adam to do the same and together they are banished from paradise to "a life of toil and sweat of the brow." This kind of work means drudgery, repetition, punishment and suffering.

> Accursed be the soil because of you.
> With suffering shall you get your food from it.
> Everyday of your life
> It shall yield you thorns and thistles and you shall eat wild plants.
> With sweat on your face shall you eat your bread
> Until you return to the soil
> As you were taken from it.
> For dust you are
> And to dust you shall return.

---

[1] In these considerations I have been generally influenced by Hannah Arendt's discussion of work. I am also indebted to some theological interpretations and to some concepts of Peter Berger.

In this fundamental Judaeo-Christian understanding of work, humankind did not deserve the gift of paradise, the gift of a complete world. We got instead an incomplete world—filled with necessity and condition. To survive, we must work. It is not a very pleasant role we have to play since according to this view work is a punishment.

At face value this interpretation of work as punishment is intolerable. Every religion has a work ethic because few can imagine work without some reward. We view work as a mixed blessing—something people love to hate, but can't see doing without. Therefore, we redefine work in both religious and secular philosophies so that work offers something positive. So, this early view gets modified.

Rational moral thought does just that. It holds that our expulsion from paradise and the subsequent necessity of work has a reason: to develop moral character. We attach certain values to work. Work keeps us out of trouble. It reduces the wastefulness of idleness. Work challenges us to use our talents and abilities, and helps develop personality. It is said to reduce self-centredness and arrogance, moderating the excessive lifestyle in favour of the modest one.

Work separates the authentic from the image. Think of two bike riders on the street: same racing gear, same bikes, same clothes. You cannot tell one from the other. Only in the race is the true racer distinguished from the hopeful novice. Without exception, the real thing, not the appearance, shows through work.

So, in rational moral thought, the Fall from paradise becomes advantageous since work fosters positive qualities in us: generosity, because by working we give; faith and good will because we hope without knowing that the fruit of our labours will be good. In fact, work mirrors our human condition. We strive in the face of the unknowable, we seek means to great ends, we are forever impatient with the pace of our progress. Ultimately, work is a supreme test for all of us. Through work we succeed or fail; become great or small; are judged to be worthy or petty, good or bad, high or low.

The trouble is, though, that this profound and ennobling view of work doesn't fit easily into our modern experience, so we must look further. This brings us to our next interpretation.

Issue 2

LABOUR OR WORK?

Hannah Arendt, the influential modern philosopher, wrote much about the meaning of work in her book *The Human Condition*. She suggested that our understanding of work goes back as far as the ancient Greeks. Greek culture distinguished between craftsmen, those who made things, and labourers, those who worked with their bodies. In ancient Greek society, slaves and women laboured, performing menial tasks. Labouring was in Aristotle's description "the meanest, because the body is most deteriorated."

Arendt points out that this distinction between work and labour exists in many languages. In French it is *travailler* and *ouvrer*, and in German it is *arbeiten* and *werken*. The German word *arbeit* originally referred to farm labourers. In English, the word *labour* connotes a sense of drudgery and suffering as found in the biblical story of Man's Fall, while the word *work* connotes effort that is directed toward the accomplishment of making something. So we get phrases like "the works of Shakespeare, Beethoven, and the Beatles" and by contrast the "labours of Hercules" that involved back-breaking physical tasks.

This distinction between "work" and "labour" helps us to think about what we will be doing the rest of our lives. Will we be labouring, which suggests a kind of slavery? Or working, which suggests a more meaningful connection to the activity and the possibility of producing something? For the most part, we share with the ancient Greeks the feeling that physical labour is a menial occupation holding little status in society because labour leaves little trace behind.

So, working is making something that stays. For us and our friends in ancient Greece, where modern civilization was born, work holds status because it means leaving a trace of your existence, a "body of work." On the other hand, labourers, who make neither a complete thing nor leave any notable contribution to humankind, are relegated to the periphery of society. In the last century, labourers sought to correct this flaw in the scheme of things by organizing into collective political units. As a result of the labour movement, the status of labourers was raised, both intellectually and socially. This was something the ancient Greeks never accomplished.

Issue 2

For the ancient Greeks the highest form of work allowed for as much leisure time as possible for the pursuit of philosophy and virtue. In our day, the labourer is equally entitled to leisure, protection, dignity and an OHIP number, while the philosophers, and some craftsmen, are often relegated to the unemployment lines.

Wisdom is best pursued when food, shelter and other basic human needs are met, even though, according to some, we gain much wisdom from scrambling to meet our basic needs of survival. In ancient Greece, where the pursuit of wisdom became an ideal, only twenty percent of the eligible population could participate in politics, philosophy and pure thought, while eighty percent had to work.

Our next interpretation of work demonstrates that wisdom derives not from the luxury of philosophy but from the experience of the common labourer.

KARL MARX ON WORK

Karl Marx, the 19th-century socialist philosopher, had much to say about this question. Marx believed that industrialization turned labour into a product to be bought and sold in the marketplace. He called it labour power. And every individual had about the same share. As the factories of the industrial revolution churned out more and more product, more and more labour was required. People abandoned the land because increased agricultural efficiency freed them to move to cities where a better life was possible. People moved from being generalists, capable of many things, to being specialists, capable of one or a few things only.

When people sell their labour, they are exchanging an essential part of themselves for money. And this process of trading labour for a wage leads to measuring self by the wage, not by ability. Even people who define themselves as workers rather than labourers are not immune. On the industrial assembly line, in the steel or textile mills, in many human spheres, work became increasingly subdivided into limited operations performed by separate workers. While this maximized productivity, it minimized craftsmanship. Workers became increasingly adept at repetitive tasks as the various aspects of the work became disconnected.

It's difficult to find meaning in repetitious work.

When work is divided into component parts—we call this the *division of labour*—the individual worker finds it increasingly difficult to improve through work. He or she therefore seeks self improvement elsewhere. Aware of a growing split between public and private roles, the worker may attempt to integrate the two, with some success. However, the division of labour ultimately requires a division of self. And the modern struggle becomes one of composing one's identity.

For example, a doctor's social identity is distinct from his or her private self which is found at home. The patients know nothing of that doctor's private life. The sphere of work is geographically and socially separate from the private sphere where the "real person" is known.

So, fragmenting the production of a thing into isolated tasks has consequences beyond the workplace. The worker in a sweater factory who only sews labels day in and day out, may feel detached from the product, from the manufacturing process, and from himself as an individual capable of more than repetitive tasks. This detachment is called *alienation*. And it is not restricted to the assembly line but is a social fact found in middle-class occupations as well. We have assembly-line education, medicine and law where teachers, doctors and lawyers are so specialized that they are attached to small parts of the overall process.

Issue 2

WAGE LABOUR

Karl Marx, the 19th-century socialist philosopher, believed that industrialization turned labour into a product to be bought and sold on the marketplace. When people sell their labour, they are exchanging an essential part of themselves for money.

Alienated work leaves no trace of our presence as individuals. The industrial division of labour redefined workers as labourers because they no longer make a whole thing but a part of it. This notion of "alienated work," of being fragmented into parts in the process of production, and in ourselves, has been the negative side of work since the industrial revolution.

Marx wrote his ideas in the 1800s when working conditions were absolutely intolerable, when owners of mines would hire children because they were small enough to dig coal in the smallest seams and workers died early in life from breathing metal dust in cutlery factories. His ideas have never gone away. The long sweaty hours in unhealthy conditions that characterized the working environment of the past can still be found in the developing countries.

"MODERN" WORK

Work remains a constant but the kinds of work change with the times. Today, we need to be seduced to work by a illusory guarantee of security, fulfilment and advancement. The promise of "making it" is deceptive because it doesn't remove the necessity for having to work, but only sweetens it. Winning the lottery doesn't mean you no longer have to work. "Making it" refers to having it all now; and even though it is a culturally esteemed value, it is not the same goal as "making something." It is ironic but people who focus on making something often end up having really made it.

Today many occupations seem to offer more freedom from having to labour to meet our basic daily needs. Machines take the place of manual labour. Motors replace the strain of lifting and pulling. Workers operate and monitor machines that do everything from cutting metal to stitching leather. In an explosion of technological change, photography, telephones, radio, television, nuclear power, rubber and plastics, medicine, and computers redefine lifestyles at a pace never before experienced, leaving little time to reflect and plan.

Alienation is still a reality in the modern world. And along with it comes the challenge of finding meaning in work.

THE MEANING OF WORK

Finally, whether work implies suffering and drudgery, or leaving a trace of your existence, or if work means alienation, the work you choose is probably the most important decision you will make. There is something irrevocable about that choice. Your lifestyle gradually envelopes and defines you and you become whatever occupation you have chosen: technician, accountant, housewife, teacher, nurse, farmer, truck driver, writer. The work we do folds us into various known and unknown quantities: measurable players in the game of life. It is inevitable; even if we remain idle, we are defined.

To many of us, ultimately, work means maturity. It helps us to identify and accept ourselves: to teach us our limits and possibilities on the testing ground. It is not enough to be a "good person," or a "promising individual." Work, in the final analysis, defines a person, clearly and mercilessly, for all the world to see. As the humanists say, we have some control over the circumstances of our lives—we have some choice of occupation, of deed. In the end, our lives are measured by what we accomplish and leave to memory. We all strive, secretly and openly, to make a difference, to make our existence worthwhile for others to benefit from. So the challenge laid down to Adam and Eve, to the ancient Greeks, and to us is the same—to make something of value when nothing of value is possible without engaging the human condition, without modifying the world; that work is the ultimate pain and pleasure of life, both necessary and desirable.

Issue 2

German Workers Like Time, Americans the Cash

Daniel Benjamin and Tony Horwitz

*A*ngie Clark and Andreas Drauschke work comparable jobs for comparable pay at department stores in Berlin and suburban Washington. But there is no comparison when it comes to the hours they put in.

Mr. Drauschke's job calls for a 37-hour week with six weeks annual leave. His store closes for the weekend at 2 p.m. on Saturday and stays open one evening each week—a new service in Germany that Mr. Drauschke detests. "I can't understand that people go shopping at night in America," said the 29-year-old supervisor of the auto, motorcycle and bicycle division at Karstadt, Germany's largest department store chain. "Logically speaking, why should someone need to buy a bicycle at 8:30 p.m.?"

Mrs. Clark works at least 44 hours a week, including evening shifts and frequent Saturdays and Sundays. She often brings paperwork home with her, spends her days off scouting the competition and never takes more than a week off at a time. "If I took any more, I'd feel like I was losing control," said the senior merchandising manager at J.C. Penney in Springfield, Va.

The 50-year-old Mrs. Clark was born in Germany but feels like an alien when she visits her native land. "Germans put leisure first and work second," she said. "In America it's the other way around."

While Americans often marvel at German industriousness, a comparison of actual workloads explodes such national stereotypes.

In manufacturing, for instance, the weekly U.S. average is 37.7 hours and rising; in Germany it is 30 hours and has fallen steadily over recent decades. All German workers are guaranteed by law a minimum of five weeks annual holiday.

A day spent at a German and a U.S. department store also shows a wide gulf in the two countries' work ethic, at least as measured by attitudes toward time. The Germans fiercely resist any incursions on their leisure hours while many Penney employees work second jobs and rack up 60 hours a week.

But long and irregular hours come at a price. Staff turnover at the German store is negligible; at Penney it is 40 per cent a year.

Germans serve apprenticeships of two to three years and know their wares inside out. Workers at Penney receive training of two to three days. And it is economic necessity, more than any devotion to work for its own sake, that appears to motivate most of the U.S. employees.

"First it's the need and then it's the greed," said Sylvia Johnson, who sells full time at Penney and works another 15 to 20 hours a week doing data entry at a computer firm.

The two jobs helped her put one child through medical school and another through college.

Now 51, Mrs. Johnson said she doesn't need to work so hard—but still does. "My husband and I have a comfortable home and three cars," she said. "But I guess you always feel like you want something more as a reward for all the hard work you've done."

Mr. Drauschke has a much different view: Work hard when you're on the job and get out as fast as you can. A passionate gardener with a wife and young child, he comes in 20 minutes earlier than the rest of his staff but otherwise has no interest in working beyond the 37 hours his contract requires, even if it means more money. "Free time can't be paid for," he said.

The desire to keep hours short is an obsession in Germany—and a constant mission of its powerful unions. When Germany introduced Thursday-night shopping in 1989, retail workers went on strike. And Mr. Drauschke finds it hard to staff the extra two hours on Thursdays, even though the late shift is rewarded an hour less overall on the job. "My wife is opposed to my coming home late," one worker told him when asked if he would work until 8:30 on a coming Thursday.

Mr. Drauschke, like other Germans, also finds the American habit of taking a second job inconceivable. "I already get home at 7. When should I work?" he asked. As for vacations, it is illegal for Germans to work at other jobs during holidays, a time that "is strictly for recovering," Mr. Drauschke explained, adding: "If we had these con-

Issue 2

ditions like in America, you would have to think hard if you wanted to go on in this line of work."

At Penney, the workday of Mrs. Clark begins at 8 a.m. when she rides a service elevator to her windowless office off a stock room. Though the store doesn't open until 10 a.m., she feels she needs the extra time to check floor displays and schedules. Most of the sales staff clock in at about 9 a.m. to set up registers and restock shelves— a sharp contrast to Karstadt, where salespeople come in just moments before the shop opens.

Penney salespeople, all of whom are non-union, take the requirements of their jobs for granted and respond with astonishment when told of German conditions, which include strong job security, an extra month's pay as a bonus every year and generous maternity and paternity leave, with parents' jobs protected for up to three years.

"You're kidding, aren't you?" saleswoman Shannon Cappiella asked. "Six weeks holiday? No Sunday shifts? No way."

Checking her schedule for the coming week, she found she would be working Thursday and Friday nights and Saturday until 5 p.m. That left several nights and all of Sunday free—free, that is, to work her second job as a receptionist at a hair salon. She will earn about $300 for her 60-hour week. "Just enough to pay the bills," she said. As for leisure, the 21-year-old adds: "Most nights I just veg in front of the TV. I'm too tired to do much else."

Her manager, Mrs. Clark, said that a quarter to a third of the sales staff typically hold second jobs. Some try to supplement their pay at Penney by working on commission, though they only earn extra if they reach a certain level of sales, called "making the draw."

And the staffers are busier than five years ago, before the recession, when Mrs. Clark had 38 salespeople instead of the current 28.

The Penney staff also is largely self-taught, apart from brief training that mainly focuses on how to work the registers.

"Why train someone who may leave in three or four months?" Mrs. Clark said.

"It's a waste of time."

At Karstadt, by contrast, workers serve long apprenticeships, spending three days a week working in the store and two days in school on a variety of subjects from bookkeeping to "product information." Mr. Drauschke's three years of training, and the 13 years he has spent at the same store, allow him to discourse at length, for example, on the various types of nylon available in motorcycle jackets.

His top staffer in the bicycle department is a racer and triathlete who has been selling bikes and accessories for 17 years. The 16 staffers in his department have all been there at least five years, and half have been there for 10.

This stability carries with it a degree of immobility. Mr. Drauschke doesn't want to enter senior management because it could mean transferring outside Berlin or spending time on the road, away from his family. So he feels there is only one job advancement open to him in the Berlin store's tight hierarchy: department head.

But drinking beer with a colleague in a back office after the last customer had left at 6:30, Mr. Drauschke said he's content with the status he has achieved at age 29 and the $2,365 he earns each month, plus sales bonuses and holiday pay. "There is a feeling of being sated," he said.

Mrs. Clark's day ends differently. At 5:30, half an hour after she's supposed to leave, she still hasn't finished choosing bathmats to order for the coming year. So she scoops a thick file from her desk to take home. "Another exciting Friday night," she joked. "Two hours of paperwork, some TV and bed."

Mrs. Clark, who is separated from her husband and has three grown children, said her schedule doesn't leave much time for fun, apart from visits with grandchildren and friends. Last year, while recuperating from surgery, she even had an assistant bring her paperwork to do in bed.

Still, she wouldn't have it any other way. One day, perhaps, she will become assistant store manager. In the meantime, there are last year's sales figures to beat, and the bonus to her $32,000 salary that comes with such success.

"Selling more is what we're all here for," she said, touring the sales floor one last time and stopping to help several customers. "I just don't feel right if I don't do a little extra."

Issue 2

BEING AND BECOMING

Earl G. Reidy

Who am I? What am I? These fundamental questions are commonly asked by people throughout the world many times during their lives. They are complex questions related to who and what we are as individuals and as part of groups. There are no simple answers. Each of us is unique, the result of a combination of many experiences and conditions, some learned, other influenced by our biology. In the natural and social sciences, the issue has often been over-simplified as a question of "nature" or "nurture." Frequently, today, those terms which relate to how we become who and what we are have been replaced by "essentialism" (the result of our nature or biology) and "social constructionism" (the result of social forces strongly influencing the construction of our identities), although the argument remains fundamentally the same.

Relatively early in our lives we begin to recognize, from urges within ourselves (our biology) and from external social forces (our family, peer group, the media, etc.), that our sexuality is a powerful force that helps to define our self concept, one which, as young people, we often find difficult to understand and manage. What we are usually unaware of is the degree to which social institutions play a crucial role in conditioning our biological urges and fashioning them into socially acceptable sexual behaviours which are always framed in a heterosexual context. In other words, we are taught through social influences by the family, the school, religion, the media, political, economic and other institutions to become erotically and affectionally attracted to persons of the opposite sex. There is a great deal of debate within the social scientific community about the extent to which our sexuality is the result of deliberate social engineering.

Until recently, there has been an almost unexamined assumption that human beings are naturally attracted (a result of our biology) sexually to persons of the opposite sex. Cross-cultural and cross-species studies have seriously challenged those assumptions. For example, Gilbert Herdt, an anthropologist studying a group he identifies as the Sambia in New Guinea, has documented social practices where all Sambian men are actively involved throughout their lives in what we would classify as same-sex (homosexual) behaviours which are socially acceptable and even necessary for the maintenance and survival of their society. A number of other studies illustrate similar situations in other societies and among our closest non-human, primate relatives.

Others have suggested that our sexual and affectional selves are the result of biology; that our sexuality is programmed either fully or largely by genetic factors. For example, a recent and highly controversial study by Simon Levay, an American pathologist, suggests that there may be some differences in brain size between gay and nongay men. It is important to note, though, that Levay himself does not make any claims that this can be generalized to the total population. This, though, if proven, would indicate that we are "born with" certain potentials over which, as individuals, we have no control.

Sexual orientation, regardless of our gender, is a critical and complex part of who and what we are. To whom we are sexually and emotionally attracted is not a static one-time decision which we consciously make, although it may appear so. Most of us accept, without question, our society's assumption of heterosexuality. Some of us don't. A number of women and men throughout the world and throughout time have recognized that their sexual, affectional and erotic desires lean toward persons of the same sex either for a lifetime or for varying periods of their life. The sexual identities available to us in Western culture include heterosexual (opposite sex), gay (male same-sex), lesbian (female same-sex) and bisexual (attraction to both sexes). It is important to note, though, that while a sexual/affectional identity is crucial in a person's life, it should not be the only criteria by which we evaluate ourselves or other people. We are all multidimensional.

It is unclear whether the process of self-definition is the same for all people even within a single culture. For example, a number of factors such as gender, social class, racial and ethnic group, and age, influence how we recognize, develop, accept or deny sexual and affectional feelings and desires.

Another difficulty in assessing our sexual and affectional identities is tied in with learning our gender roles. The social presentation of a male identity in Western culture, for example, often includes

Issue 2

Support groups help end a
feeling of isolation.

behaviours which deny males the opportunity to express emotional
and affectional ties toward each other. Our culture tends not to do that
to women as much; they are often encouraged to express their emotions. It has been suggested that this restriction is placed on males as
a result of "patriarchal" (male dominated and controlled) social institutions which set up strict expectations of masculine behaviour as
a means of defending and reinforcing male privilege and power.
Such a defensive position produces very strong and negative attitudes towards males who may display any behaviours which are
considered to be feminine, and thus weak. This, many feminist theorists tell us, supports the status-quo, male power arrangement and
keeps women subservient and males "in line." George Smith, a sociologist at the Ontario Institute for Studies in Education, says that one
of the most important ways that North American society maintains a
strict interpretation of masculinity is through what he calls the "ideology of fag." Perhaps you can recall using the term "fag" or hearing

Issue 2

others use it. It is a powerful heterosexist[1] and homophobic[2] weapon used to force males to conform to the dominant interpretation of acceptable masculinity. When a male begins to recognize that he is sexually and affectionally attracted to other males, he quickly realizes that he must hide this from others because he becomes vulnerable to physical and verbal abuse. This form of self-protection is often referred to as being "in the closet." Women also report that they experience homophobic verbal and physical abuse which calls their femininity and sexual identities into question. The female equivalents of "fag" include "lezzie" or "dyke," derogatory and hurtful terms which are also used to reinforce male power since, according to patriarchal notions, women are supposed to seek and find their identity only in relation to males.

When does a person begin to recognize that they may not "fit" the expected heterosexual norm? That is a very difficult question to answer, since each person's development is so unique. However, it is important that we distinguish between same-sex feelings and a gay or lesbian identity. The Kinsey studies on male and female sexual behaviour, although flawed, are the most comprehensive and important pieces of research we have regarding the sexual behaviour of North American men and women. Kinsey and his researchers found that a number of men and women may have erotic or affectional feelings for people of the same sex for short or long periods of their lives, but never develop or assume a gay or lesbian identity.[3] Laud Humphreys, an American sociologist, discovered that many men who firmly identify as "straight" often participated in impersonal, same-sex behaviours. These findings reinforce the idea that how humans construct their sexual identities is very complex.

---

[1] Heterosexism is usually defined as the assumption that everybody is heterosexual, and if they aren't, they should be.

[2] Homophobia is defined as an irrational hatred or fear of gay men and lesbians. Homophobia, as both a condition and a practice is, like sexism and racism, often well entrenched in social institutions and can be used to justify verbal and physical violence against lesbians and gay men.

[3] Results of a 1993 American study of American males, reported in *Time Magazine*, disputes the Kinsey findings. That survey, by the Batelle Human Affairs Research Centres in Seattle, Washington, noted that only 2.3% of the sample reported having sex with men in the past 10 years. The study has been widely criticized as being methodologically unsound. No figures were reported for females.

Issue 2

Current research indicates that recognition of a gay, lesbian or bisexual identity depends on a number of factors. My own studies of gay, male community college students regarding the development of their sexual identities confirm reports that males tend to realize earlier than females that their primary attraction is to persons of the same sex. Males report that they often knew about their difference during their elementary school years, but generally did not know what it meant nor even what to call it. Many of them said that since such feelings preceded any social knowledge of a gay identity, they believe they were "born that way." Females, on the other hand, report recognizing their lesbianism much later, sometimes after they had married and produced children.

Early recognition of a gay or lesbian state often produces, especially for young people, a great deal of confusion and pain as they

The *Ontario Human Rights Code* prohibits all types of discrimination against people on the basis of sexual orientation.

Know Your Rights

Sexual Orientation and the *Human Rights Code*

The *Ontario Human Rights Code* prohibits discrimination on the basis of sexual orientation in services, goods and facilities; accommodation; employment; contracts; and vocational associations. This means that a person cannot be treated unequally in these areas because he or she is gay, lesbian, heterosexual or bisexual, for example.

The *Code* prohibits all types of unequal treatment, from the denial of a job, service or accommodation to comments, displays and jokes which may make an individual uncomfortable, because of his/her sexual orientation.

- If you were denied a service or treated unequally by a store, restaurant, theatre, club, government agency, school, hospital, dentist's or doctor's office or other provider of services, goods and facilities because of your sexual orientation...

- If you were denied employment or treated unequally in your place of work because of your sexual orientation...

- If you were denied accommodation or treated unequally by your landlord because of your sexual orientation...

contact your local office of the Ontario Human Rights Commission. You may be able to file a complaint.

Issue 2

begin to experience the negative, social response to gay and lesbian people which results in stigmatized status. These youths feel isolated because they don't know others like themselves and there are few visible role models to help them construct their sense of self as a lesbian or gay person. Most feel that they cannot turn to their families, friends, schools or other social groups for help. A 19-year-old male college student reported that when he told his mother he was gay, she told him, "I wish I had never given you birth."

Studies of Canadian and American gay and lesbian youths indicate that many of them consider, attempt or commit suicide as a result of extremely negative social pressures. A fortunate few, mostly those who grow up in big cities, may have access to gay and lesbian support groups, but many young people have to struggle, mostly alone, without the benefit of accurate information, to construct, deconstruct (as they get access to more information) and then reconstruct their identities, sometimes many times over. Among the many questions the youthful gay male or lesbian must grapple with, in addition to other concerns of growing up, are, am I gay or lesbian; what is a gay or lesbian, what is it like to be gay or lesbian; how does my gender identity as a male or female "fit into" being gay or lesbian, am I a bad person; what will this mean to my life, my relationships and my future; can I live with this identity? For gay males, the fear of HIV disease must also be confronted. This growth process can be made even more difficult as a result of religious, racial and ethnic group membership. Some gays and lesbians have been abused or rejected by their families, in extreme cases being declared actually dead, as a result of religious beliefs or because of attitudes which their families or other members of their racial/ethnic communities have brought with them from other cultures or social groups.

It is crucial to understand that a sexual identity is not just about sexuality; it becomes part of the person's core, inner-being and helps to structure how they see themselves and their relationships with the rest of social world. Identities also differ for men and women. Once people work through the painful and difficult process of accepting their sexual identity, they need to integrate it with other aspects of their personality. This is the coming-out state which results from social interaction. Most major cities in the world have gay and lesbian communities which offer a variety of support services including groups for young gays and lesbians. It is within these communities that people begin to learn that they are not alone, that there are role models available to help in constructing their identity. Coming out is not a one-time event; it can be never-ending. There are parents, other family members, friends, business associates to tell or not tell. Gays and lesbians have to learn how to structure and live their partner relationships outside the social construction of marriage and how to explain their partner when they are asked to participate in social events and family gatherings. It can get very complicated.

For young men and women who identify as bisexuals, their lives become even more problematic. Drawn sexually and emotionally to people of both sexes, they are often misunderstood and shunned by the lesbian, gay and heterosexual communities.

Conditions for lesbians and gays in North America, and in some European countries, have improved significantly in recent years. This has largely been the result of political activities by lesbian and gay groups. In Canada, there is now federal and provincial legislation prohibiting discrimination; many union contracts contain anti-discrimination clauses; and almost every employment category—including the military and many religions—is now open to lesbians and gays. Popular culture, including literature, film and television, is now beginning to portray lesbians and gay men more positively, thus informing the public, helping to reduce negative and harmful stereotypes and producing more realistic role models for isolated youth. However, there still is resistance to providing accurate information to young people, especially in schools.

Unfortunately, it has also been necessary for police departments in some Canadian and American cities to develop "hate crime" units because of continuing violence, often referred to as "gay bashing," against lesbians and gay men who become scapegoats for others' insecurities. Systemic homophobia, often combined with sexism and racism, continues to be a problem for North American societies.

CONCLUSION

In the development of "who we are," some men and women must come face-to-face with the recognition that they don't fit taken-for-granted expectations of a major part of their personality—their sexual identity. The process of "becoming" a sexual person, whether straight, bisexual, gay or lesbian is complex and may involve both bi-

Issue 2

ology and social learning acting in complicated and, as yet, largely unknown ways. For those who do recognize they do not fit the assumed heterosexual pattern, the development of their self-concept, their very identity as a person, frequently becomes, because of hostile social responses, extremely difficult and painful. More accurate and available information, support from family, friends and social institutions—especially schools—and greater social intolerance of homophobic verbal and physical abuse would make their lives far less problematic. Society must seriously question whether it can afford the incredibly high personal and social costs of prejudice and discrimination whether directed against racial, ethnic or sexual minorities.

Issue 2

THE GENDER DANCE: LEARNING THE NEW STEPS

Wendy O'Brien-Ewara

Walk into any bookstore and look in the psychology section and you will find row upon row of self-help books. There are books which will help you find the right mate, keep your mate happy and survive your mate's death. With titles such as *Dances with Intimacy, Women Who Love Too Much*, and *Necessary Losses*, these books claim to improve your self-image, your sex life, and your communication skills. They promise to resolve your supermom complex, your Marilyn dilemma or Peter Pan syndrome. Why do such books line shelf after shelf in bookstores and libraries? Why do such titles continually top bestseller lists?

In what follows, I argue that the popularity of self-help books reflects the changing nature of gender relations. As traditional sex roles have eroded in response to the dissolution of belief in inherent sex differences, it is no longer clear what roles men and women ought to play. Nor is it clear how they ought to interact with one another. Self-help books address these issues, providing answers to questions about the nature of masculinity and femininity and offering guidance on how to structure and conduct interpersonal relationships. However, I caution readers to carefully evaluate the advice such books furnish. Understanding what it means to be male and female in the 1990s requires critical reflection on the assumptions we make about gender roles, on the nature of sexuality, on the value we place on our physiology and on quick and easy remedies for resolving our gender troubles.

Every day we are bombarded with images of what it means to be male and female in contemporary society. They are relayed to us on television programs as diverse as *Designing Women* and *Home Improvement*, in advertisements for everything from cleaning products to cars, and in magazine articles bringing up topics like the perfect breast and the hottest careers. Such messages are also conveyed to us in the laws enforced by a particular province or country, in religious creeds and in cultural traditions. However, the images presented before us often are inconsistent. Men are encouraged to be sensitive and caring, and at the same time tough and independent. Women are portrayed in some mediums as self-sufficient and career oriented, while in others they are depicted as happy homemakers. Given that these ideals are incompatible, how should we determine what characteristics to admire or what kind of interpersonal relationships to emulate? What can we reasonably expect from ourselves and our potential partners? Self-help books are designed to assist us in answering these questions.

That there is a need for such literature should not be surprising. Only thirty to forty years ago ideals of gender roles were much more clearly defined. Quite simply, women stayed home and men went to work: the private realm was the domain of women while men governed the public arena. This division of labour was justified according to inherent sex differences. Women did not simply develop their culinary and parenting skills; they were born with such abilities. By nature women had an aptitude for housework and, as they were more emotional and thus more irrational, they were best suited for staying at home and caring for the family. If they did work, women could only perform jobs which were viewed as extensions of their "wifely" or "motherly" roles; they could be nurses or teachers. And these pastimes were not expected to interfere with the fulfilment of their familial duties. After working all day, there were still children to be cared for, meals to prepare and a home to keep clean.

Men likewise were born with certain innate qualities. They were born rational and ready to deal with the intricacies of public life. Men didn't succumb to their emotions or passions and as such they were better equipped to handle power and mechanics. Their duty was to "bring home the bacon." Responsibility for the financial support of the family was placed squarely upon their shoulders. They had neither the time nor the aptitude for dealing with children or doing housework. Yet they were the "king of their castle;" they "ruled the roost." As women were the weaker sex, they required men's guidance and protection. In return, men expected to be treated with due respect: their superiority in both judgement and action was to be met with deference.

During this era, we might buy a self-help book to help us get rid of nasty stains, improve our manners, or help us tune up our car. But we would not buy a book to help us determine what qual-

Despite confusion around gender roles, moments of clarity do occur.

ities, attitudes and actions were appropriately masculine and feminine. The images of men and women endorsed through various mediums were uniform. In an attempt to discourage women who had worked in various jobs during the war from continuing to participate in the public realm, a unified effort was made to have women return to their "proper place"—to once again be happy homemakers. As such, the messages transmitted from television, advertisements, the state and the church were homogeneous. Although not all men and women ascribed to these ideals, they knew what qualities defined a "good" woman and distinguished her from a "good" man. This consistency was furthered by a veil of silence which prohibited discussions of sex and sexuality. Good "girls" and responsible men simply did not talk about their bodies or about their intimate relations. Questions about how men and women were to interact and about the nature of femininity and masculinity were not raised in the realm of public discourse. Somehow everyone just knew the answers to such questions. Consequently, there was neither a forum nor a perceived "appropriate" need for self-help books focusing on gender roles and personal relationships.

Such is not the case for us in the 1990s. Over the past thirty years dramatic changes have taken place in our ideals about what roles men and women should play and about what constitutes a "good" relationship. It is no longer apparent that sex differences are inherent. Few women would stand for being told that by nature they are irrational, emotional, and inferior to men. And how many men would agree that by nature they do not have the capacities necessary to be a primary caregiver? Differences in the attitudes, aptitudes and behaviour of men and women are viewed as the consequence of not only physiology, but also of socialization and enculturation. Consider the problems this introduced into gender relations. Gone was the theoretical basis for uniform images and ideals about masculinity and femininity. With the dissolution of belief in sex differences came the need to question the roles traditionally ascribed to each sex. This provided new opportunities and new obstacles. Public discussions of gender issues led to the advocation of diverse accounts of what men and women are and should be like and about how their relationships should be structured. The need to sort through these alternatives gave rise to the kind of self-help books that today line our bookstore and library shelves.

Until recently, books of this kind primarily have been written for women. With titles such as *Why Women Worry* and *Why Do I Feel Like I'm Nothing Without a Man*, self-help books have responded to the difficult choices women have had to make regarding careers, marriage and family. Consider, for example, the repercussions of women entering the work force on their expectations about education and employment options, marital status, childbearing, and child rearing. With the expansion of career options came the need to determine what kind of profession to pursue. Should she become a lawyer, a construction worker or a homemaker? In addition to changing social values, the financial independence of working outside the home gave many women the option of marrying later in life or of not marrying at all. Reproductive technologies have given women some measure of control over when, where and if they will have children. Moreover, choosing to have children no longer necessarily required women to abandon their jobs. Indeed, this has resulted in the birth of the daycare industry. In light of the possibilities which changing social circumstances have afforded women, there are no longer any clear-cut expectations about women's place in society and about what qualities and characteristics "good" women exhibit. Self-help books are designed to assist readers sort through these difficult issues.

The same is true for men. The recent upsurge of the Men's Movement has led to the expansion of the market in men's self-help

Issue 2

books. *Iron John* and *Fire in the Belly* are just two bestsellers that question what it means to be masculine in contemporary society. Rejecting the roles men have traditionally been required to fill, these books explore the options which men have when it comes to careers, family and personal development. Not wanting to be the stoic master-of-all nor wanting to feel that they must be sensitive, caring homemakers, an attempt is made to understand men's nature based upon ancient rituals and the notion of brotherhood. These books try to understand what men are like outside the limitations placed upon them by references to sex differences.

With both sexes trying to define for themselves what it means to be male and female, confusion about interpersonal relationships can only be expected. Titles such as *Men: A Translation for Women, When Love Goes Wrong*, and *The Modern Man's Guide to Modern Women* line bookstore shelves. When the need to marry was alleviated and equality between the sexes became the goal for many, the traditional ideal of what good relationships entailed broke down. No longer willing to divide responsibilities according to the public/private distinction, it became necessary to negotiate what roles each partner will play both in the workforce and in the household. In spite of being paid only 69.6% of their male counterparts' wages, of facing sexual harassment, and of continually bumping into an artificial **glass ceiling**, women are entering the workforce in increasing numbers. Couples must now deal with the stress and strain of two careers. Furthermore, as women rise through occupational hierarchies, it is possible for them to make more money and have more prestige than their male partners. Consider how such social changes have upended the roles traditionally ascribed to men and women.

glass ceiling—invisible barrier to advancement.

Expectations have likewise changed with regard to the division of labour within the home. It is no longer given that women will stay home and care for their children. Nor is it the case that they are willing to work full time and take full responsibility for housekeeping and child rearing. Decisions must be made about who should wash the laundry, care for the children, tune up the car and fill out the tax forms. As noted earlier, there is no consensus on what duties each sex ought to undertake. This is the case not only in the kitchen but also in the bedroom. There are no clear cut rules about who should make the first move, when it's appropriate to initiate sexual relations, and when or if one should marry. Amidst all these arbitrations, is it any wonder that we would look to books to help us sort out gender relations?

Self-help books have played an important role in bringing issues concerning gender and interpersonal relationships into the realm of public discourse. By exploring the repercussions of the breakdown of stereotypes, these books have made possible discussions about sexuality, abuse and harassment. They have increased our awareness and tried to guide us through the myriad of alternative accounts of what it means to be male and female in the 1990s. And for this such books should be praised. However, the advice they offer needs to be carefully evaluated.

Too often books in this genre provide pat answers to complex questions. Personal experiences vary greatly yet they provide the basis for determining what we think are appropriate gender roles and relations. Our ideals about men and woman are influenced by societal norms, cultural traditions and familial standards. How can self-help books contend with such diversities? Another problem with such texts is that although they often sound convincing, they cannot offer any final solutions to our gender troubles. As noted earlier, there are conflicting messages from a variety of sources about what men and women in the 1990s ought to be like. There are no standard formulas that can be applied to sort through this fluctuating mass of information. Note that resolutions to various dilemmas differ from text to text. How then should we choose which book to read? Which solution, which book is most reliable? Furthermore, gender relations continue to evolve as new pressures are placed upon them. Consider how our understanding of relationships must change in order to come to grips with AIDS, date rape, and the backlash to feminism. Is it possible for self-help books to adequately account for how such factors will influence gender roles and relationships? And can they forecast what influences will precipitate future change?

There are no short cuts in trying to understand and define one's gender role, if indeed there is such a role. And there are no ways to side step careful consideration of the nature of interpersonal relationships. We need to begin by becoming aware of the presuppositions we have about gender roles. What roles have we been socialized to believe are appropriate for men and women? Questions also need to be asked about how we define and give expression to our sexuality. From where do the ideals and the presumptions which interlay our understandings of femininity and masculinity arise? How do these ideals mould our attitudes towards our physiology? Finally, we must investigate how value has been attributed to activities and attitudes which are deemed masculine and feminine. Only once we have addressed these kinds of questions can we begin to sort through the complexities of our gender relations, for such considerations frame the way we perceive and respond to changes in our ideals about men and women and about relationships. While self-help books can bring our attention to specific problems and dilemmas, they lack the theoretical depth necessary to address these broader issues. So while it may be tempting to try to resolve your problems with your partner and come to have reasonable expectations of yourself by referring to *Women Who Love Too Much* or to *Why Men Are The Way They Are*, be forewarned. It is only through critical reflection that we can begin to understand what it means to be male and female in the 1990s.

CONFLICT AND COOPERATION

ISSUE 1:
The Individual and the
Collective

ISSUE 2:
Relations between Collectives

ISSUE

1

The Individual and the Collective

No man is an island entire of itself; every man is a piece of the continent, a part of the main. If a clod be washed away by the sea, Europe is the less, as well as if a promontory were, as well as if a manor of thy friend's or thine own were. Any man's death diminishes me, because I am involved in mankind, and therefore never send to know for whom the bell tolls; it tolls for thee.

John Donne

One always bakes the most delicate cakes
Two is the really superb masseur
Three sets your hair with exceptional flair
Four's brandy goes to the Emperor
Five knows each trick of advanced rhetoric
Six bred a beautiful brand-new rose
Seven can cook every dish in the book
And eight cuts you flawlessly elegant clothes
Do you think those eight would be happy
if each of them could climb so high
and no higher
before banging their heads on equality
if each could be only a small link
in a long and heavy chain
Do you still think it's possible
to unite mankind...

Marquis de Sade in the play Marat-Sade *by Peter Weiss, adapted by Adrian Mitchell*

POLITICS IN THE LIFE OF THE INDIVIDUAL

Morton Ritts

POLITICS

As we saw in the previous unit, we live in a time of unprecedented change. Technology, demographics and the clash between old and new values are just some of the things that cause change. But so is something we haven't paid much attention to yet—politics. Whether we care or not, politics matters. Political decisions affect jobs, taxes, social policy, immigration and other current issues. Politics helps to define our society's notions of freedom, law and justice.

Politics isn't something that happens only at election time. Politics occurs when students protest higher tuition fees, business groups lobby for free trade, unions go on strike, women and minorities fight for employment equity, and governments act—or don't act.

In its broadest sense, politics refers to the complex relations among various members and groups in society. There is politics between you and your boss, you and your parents, you and your teachers, you and your boy- or girlfriend. Politics is about power—competing for it, sharing it, imposing it. We want power not simply because we want things our own way. We want power because it gives us the feeling that we have some control over our lives, that we are free.

Obviously certain individuals and groups in society are more powerful than others. What is the basis of this power? Does "might make right," as the Renaissance political theorist Niccolo Machiavelli argued? Does sex, race, wealth, intelligence, status or tradition? Or moral or religious authority? Or a commitment to ethical principles? In some way, these are all factors in determining how much or how little power people have.

GOVERNMENT

Simply put, government is the mechanism that regulates power relations and the rights and duties of citizens and their rulers. According to the Greek philosopher Aristotle, there are basically three kinds of government: autocracy or government by one person; oligarchy or government by the few; and democracy or government by the many. Everything else—from monarchy to aristocracy or military rule—is an example of one of these three basic forms.

Whatever the case may be, some individuals and groups have more rights than others. And this in turn, as we've already suggested, depends to a large extent on a society's notions of freedom, law and justice. Later we'll examine how political thinkers like Thomas Hobbes, John Locke, John Stuart Mill and Karl Marx thought about these issues, and how reformers like Mahatma Gandhi, Martin Luther King and Malcolm X acted on them.

Whatever our political philosophy, however, we must acknowledge the role that government plays in our daily lives. Consider a government's monetary and fiscal policies, which affect everything from inflation to interest rates—in other words, everything from your ability to find a job, to your ability to borrow money to start a business, or to buy a house or car.

At the same time, consider the degree to which a government is involved in economic and social matters. Those who argue for more state intervention claim that government investment in areas such as education, health care and transportation is vital for the national interest. They argue that government regulation is also necessary to ensure that businesses don't pollute the environment, treat employees unfairly or take advantage of consumers.

On the other hand, those who adopt a "laissez-faire," or hands-off approach, believe that government involvement in social and economic matters should be minimal and that it is best to allow the "market" to regulate itself.

Another important question about government is constitutional. How should power be divided among central, regional and local governments? Over the past 30 years in Canada, an extraordinary amount of energy has been devoted to the question of federal-provincial re-

Issue 1

lations. Compared to other countries, Canada is already very decentralized, and many people who objected to the Meech Lake and Charlottetown agreements did so because they feared that these agreements would further weaken the federal government's power.

LIBERAL DEMOCRACY

Of all forms of government, democracy (in theory at least) encourages the greatest redistribution of power and the greatest amount of change. In Canada and the United States, women, visible minorities, the disabled, aboriginals, environmentalists, gays and lesbians—all the groups we talked about in Unit 2—have been in the forefront of such controversial political issues as employment equity, human rights, land claims and same-sex benefits.

Of course, this kind of freedom to challenge the status quo and to fight for political change doesn't exist in every society. Freedom of speech and individual rights are values that we associate with liberal democracy. You don't have to look beyond the nearest headline or newscast to see that most of the time most governments around the world suppress human rights, crush dissent and persecute minorities.

THE END JUSTIFIES THE MEANS: MACHIAVELLI

When governments act this way, we often aren't surprised: we've almost grown up with the conviction that self-interest is what politics is all about. One influential political theorist who believed this was Niccolo Machiavelli (1469–1527), whose famous book, *The Prince*, is a shrewd and cynical analysis of human nature and power politics. It tells would-be leaders how to obtain power and keep it, how to play rivals off against each other, and how to conduct foreign policy.

For Machiavelli, individual freedom and justice are not as important as the stability that a strong leader must provide, which alone legitimizes his rule. In domestic affairs, the prince rules by fear rather than love and eliminates his opponents by whatever means necessary. Most important, the successful leader is a master of deceit and **dissimulation**, who appears to be virtuous when in fact he's most ruth-

dissimulation—concealment

Issue 1

less. According to Machiavelli, the prince is guided by the conviction that "might makes right," and that the end justifies the means.

This is equally true, Machiavelli argued, in the prince's handling of international relations: right or wrong, the interests of his country come first. The prince realizes that he has no friends, only interests. He does what is best for him, not what is right by others. Thus, when a sovereign power uses chemical or nuclear weapons in war, or when it refuses to make an issue of a trading partner's poor human rights record in peacetime, it is following a policy of "realpolitik," where the only principle that matters is self-interest—anything that furthers it is good, anything that restricts it is bad.

Because many of us, consciously or otherwise, seem to accept Machiavellian self-interest as the norm in politics, we tend not to have a very high opinion of those who practise it. And too often their actions fail to shock us: patronage, corruption, dirty tricks, broken promises, slush funds, sex scandals—the dirty laundry list of unsavoury political practices, even in a liberal democracy, can turn us off any interest in politics at all.

THE DANGERS OF APATHY

Many political theorists argue that such apathy is dangerous, however. Whether we vote or not, politics affects us in large and small ways. It determines the programs we watch on TV and the music we hear on the radio—because decisions about Canadian content are political decisions. It determines whether there is room for us at college or a job when we're finished—because education and employment policy decisions are political. So are decisions about how much money comes off our paycheques, what social programs our taxes will fund and which regions of the country will get them.

But apathy is only one response to the frustration that we may feel about how we are governed. Another, and opposite, reaction is to become politically engaged, like the groups mentioned earlier in this article. Such activism may even take the form of new political parties, like Reform or the Bloc, which capitalize on public discontent.

Of course, political activity isn't always legal or peaceful. The Los Angeles riots in the aftermath of the first Rodney King verdict were a spontaneous and violent expression of rage against the L.A.

Issue 1

police and state authorities. In Quebec, the tense stand-off at Oka was the result of years of frustration by the Mohawks against all levels of Canadian government.

The ultimate reaction to an insensitive and/or unjust government is revolution. This occurs when governments lose touch with people and efforts at legal and peaceful reform have failed to produce a satisfactory redistribution of power. The consensus that has bound people together breaks down, and a new social arrangement is needed. The violent overthrow of the existing order is seen as the only way to make this happen.

THE SOCIAL CONTRACT

Many of you may be familiar with the film *The Road Warrior* or the novel *Lord of the Flies*. In these and similar works, we're presented with a vision of the world in which law and order, morality and peace have broken down—the end of what political philsophers call "civil society." In such apocalyptic, or end-of-the-world visions, life is ruled by naked power—by selfishness, fear, superstition, mistrust, brute force. Without the guiding authority of tradition, laws and institutions, without consensus, society descends into anarchy.

For this reason, no political philosopher would argue that we should trade society for the raw state of nature—not even the great French social philosopher Jean-Jacques Rousseau (1712–1778), whose writings contrast the natural goodness of people with the largely destructive impact of social institutions. But while Rousseau denounced his own artificial, class-ridden society with the famous words, "Man was born free, and everywhere he is in chains," he nevertheless understood that we are first and foremost social beings. We are united, he argued, by the arrangement that we make with each other to surrender at least some of our desires in exchange for at least some of our needs. Rousseau, Thomas Hobbes and John Locke called this arrangement "the social contract."

For them, the social contract is an act of collective faith. Its effectiveness depends on our ability to obtain a satisfactory balance between what we want and what we're prepared to give up to get it. The social contract breaks down when people believe they're surrendering too much or not getting enough in return. Or when they lose the trust that binds them to others and to a government that may be incompetent, unfair or tyrannical.

In the absence of effective government, then, the social contract crumbles and no one has any security. Freedom, laws, justice, and human rights are ignored, replaced by the social chaos of Bosnia and Rwanda. We need government to maintain the social contract, and we need the social contract if we want to survive.

WHAT KIND OF GOVERNMENT IS MOST DESIRABLE?

The answer to this question depends on a number of things, but mainly what people believe to be the purpose of government. Is it to maintain peace and stability at any price (totalitarianism)? To promote a particular set of religious beliefs (theocracy)? To promote the interests of an elite, land-owning class (aristocracy)? To preserve the rule of a king or queen (monarchy)? Or to guarantee freedom, rights, law and justice, which we have said are the underlying principles of liberal democracy?

Our definition of the most desirable form of government may depend on more than what we believe to be government's purpose. It may depend on some of the most fundamental questions that we ask about human nature. Are people good or bad? Are they ruled by reason or emotion? Which people are best suited to make decisions? How much freedom should ordinary people have? Are we motivated by self-interest or a desire to help others?

By the time we reach college, we have no doubt asked at least some of these questions to try to determine what kind of relationship ought to exist between ourselves and others in society, what we are willing to give up to fulfil our part of the social contract and what we expect in return.

Political philosophers since the time of Plato have tried to describe which arrangements they believe will make society function most effectively. And they often begin by trying to identify what motivates the social contract in the first place. Thomas Hobbes (1588–1679), for example, argued that it was fear.

Thomas Hobbes

Issue 1

THE FEAR FACTOR

Hobbes lived through a tumultuous period in English history where civil war had torn his country apart, and where law, order and security had broken down. The war reinforced Hobbes' pessimistic view of human nature. People, he believed, were naturally aggressive, violent and competitive, dominated by their emotions and instincts, or by what Freud would later call "the id."

Because they lived in a constant state of fear, people's first impulse was to overpower others before being overpowered themselves. Hobbes describes this state of nature before the social contract as a situation in which "every man is enemy to every man" and "life is nasty, brutish and short."

Imagine that all laws in your city have been suspended for 24 hours and that the police are on strike. Is this the time to fly to Vancouver for a holiday? Or would you stay home with a shotgun and make sure that no one tried to grab your property? According to Hobbes, fear would keep you at home. What's more, he argued, fear would keep you from trying to grab your neighbour's property—because your neighbour also has a shotgun.

According to Hobbes, fear is our salvation and is the great equalizer. It plays the supremely useful role of keeping you and your neighbour honest: you resist your impulse to steal your neighbour's new television and she gives up her desire to steal your new stereo. The fact that you both own shotguns helps the situation.

It makes sense to surrender the desire to attack your neighbour because he has likewise given up his desire to rob you. Mutual fear, which keeps you both honest, is the basis of a social contract that lets you sleep nights. And the job of government, or what Hobbes called "the sovereign," is to make sure that the social contract doesn't become "unstuck." If it does, you and your neighbour had better get used to insomnia.

In other words, Hobbes says that we may indeed be creatures of greed and passion who are driven by a desire to dominate and control. But we're also reasonable creatures who realize that our interests are better served within a framework of law, morality, peace and security than in a state of violence and anarchy. Fear motivates us to agree to the social contract and to accept the power of government to enforce it.

How much power should the sovereign, or governing authority, have over us? Hobbes believed that whether the sovereign is autocratic, oligarchic or democratic, it should have absolute power to do its job well. That might mean giving up not only some of our desires but also some of our rights—such as freedom of speech, the right to assembly and anything else that could threaten political and social stability. But, like Freud, Hobbes believed that such stability came at a price, although unlike Freud he thought the price was rarely too high.

As a political conservative who had little faith in the capacity of people to govern themselves well, Hobbes personally favoured autocracy as the most desirable form of government, believing that a single ruler could act far more efficiently than any government requiring the support of a fickle electorate and the unpredictable mechanics of democracy.

THE NATURAL RIGHTS FACTOR

John Locke

But it is precisely a belief in the unpredictable mechanics of democracy that leads other political theorists to argue that something other than fear motivates us to become party to the social contract. For example, another English philosopher, John Locke (1632–1704), argued that natural rights form the basis of consent between ourselves and the rest of society.

Like Hobbes, Locke lived in a time of great social and political upheaval when the belief in an absolute monarch who ruled by divine right was being challenged and power was being transferred from the king to the people in the form of parliamentary democracy. Locke fully supported these radical changes. He differed from Hobbes in that he had an optimistic view of human nature and of people's ability to make intelligent, right-minded choices about the kind of society they wanted.

Locke believed that all people are born free, equal, rational and moral. He also believed that we have certain God-given natural rights of life, liberty and property, which form the basis of the social con-

Issue 1

tract and which it is the chief purpose of government to protect. To do so, it must be given the power to resolve conflicts and restrain violent and criminal acts. If the government fails to do its job properly, the people have the right to overthrow it—violently if necessary.

Locke's ideas on natural rights had an influence that extended well beyond the development of liberal democracy in England. They also helped to shape the thinking of the leaders of the American Revolution in their fight for independence. Indeed, Locke's theory that natural rights form the basis of the social contract is the **ideology** of liberal democracies everywhere, particularly in the United States where individual rights are paramount. The core of these rights, Locke argued, is private property.

ideology—system of beliefs

But what exactly is private property? And why is it the defining feature of that economic system we call capitalism? Private property is more than the piece of land we own, or the house we live in. It is, Locke says, whatever "we mix with our labour." It includes "the labour of (our) body and the work of (our) hands." It is also the fruits of our labour—the products we make and the goods we buy. They belong to us because we've earned them.

For Locke, private property is important because it defines the boundaries of individual freedom. Within those boundaries, the individual has the right to do as he or she wishes and the state has no right to intrude. This principle may seem obvious to us, to the point where we take it for granted. But it wasn't always the case, certainly not before Locke's time, when land defined wealth and most of the land was owned by a relatively small aristocratic elite or the sovereign.

Locke believed in extending the right of private ownership beyond the privileged few. In doing so, he also endorsed the right to privacy itself, a mainstay of a free and open society. Twenty-five years ago, Prime Minister Pierre Trudeau echoed Locke's view when he proclaimed, "The state has no business in the bedrooms of the nation." In the privacy of our own homes, Trudeau meant, the state has no business defining what is acceptable or unacceptable sexual behaviour between consenting adults.

(Locke, of course, could never have anticipated how the rapid growth of technology in the latter part of the twentieth century has made us more vulnerable than ever to invasions of privacy. The "information highway" allows governments, corporations and individuals to gain access to our bank accounts, medical records, political affiliations and other forms of highly personal information. Despite the warnings of the federally appointed Privacy Commissioner, we are becoming an increasingly closely monitored society.)

Meanwhile, as industrial capitalism in western Europe and North America developed, Locke's notion of ownership and private property was expanded to include the tools, machines, factories, transportation systems, capital and human resources that made further accumulation of property possible. But clearly not everyone benefitted under such a system, and the freedom, rights, laws and justice that protected the privileged minority class did not extend to the masses.

So where Locke saw private property as the basis of freedom, socialist thinkers like Karl Marx saw it as the basis of exploitation. And where Locke argued that property was the basis of privacy, Marx replied that it was the basis of inhumanity. According to Marx, private ownership created an intolerable conflict between the "haves" and "have-nots." The only way to eliminate this conflict was to eliminate private property.

THE CLASS CONFLICT FACTOR

Born in Germany and living much of his life in exile, Karl Marx (1818–1883) analysed the great divide between the weath and power of the owner/capitalist class and the workers or proletariat. Rejecting Locke's view of the sanctity of individual ownership, Marx called for a revolution to redistribute social, economic and political power. According to Marx, history showed that it was not fear or consent about God-given natural rights that defined the nature of our relationship to society. It was class conflict—between rich and poor, haves and have-nots, the powerful and the powerless. To resolve this conflict and re-organize the social order in a way that guaranteed true freedom, rights and justice, it was necessary to abolish private property.

Karl Marx

Marx disagreed with those historians and political philosophers who contend that our innate human nature predisposes us to one kind of society or another. According to Marx, it is the other way round: the kind of society we live in determines our consciousness,

Issue 1

or how we act and think. If people are selfish and greedy, the reason has little to do with human nature and much to do with social conditions.

As proof, Marx turned to capitalism. Throughout industrialized Europe, Marx saw men, women and children working long hours in unsafe mines and factories for wages that were a fraction of what their labour entitled them to. They had no pensions, health insurance or safety protection. They had no collective agreements, job security or social safety net. Capitalism, Marx argued, really offered only two choices: be a loser or a winner, exploit others or be exploited yourself.

In the article on "The Meaning of Work" in Unit 2, we discussed Marx's belief that this "survival of the fittest" mentality was the very essence of industrial capitalism. The division of labour and alienation that turned workers into products, into property belonging to someone else, destroyed the human spirit and caused untold suffering. If life is "a war of all against all," as Hobbes said, it is not human nature that causes this war but a society based on class conflict.

Marx did not look to government or the church to change this situation. In his view government, religion, media, the education system—all the institutions of capitalist society—served the interests of the owners who controlled them and kept the workers in their place. Marx was especially critical of the role played by organized religion ("the opiate of the people"), which, he said, made people passive and accepting of their misery in this life by promising them rewards in the next.

But there is no afterlife, Marx argued, only this one. And he looked to the proletariat to lead the revolution that would destroy class conflict and alter the course of world history: "Workers of the world unite!" he wrote in *The Communist Manifesto*, adding with an unmistakable reference to Rousseau, "You have nothing to lose but your chains!"

Marx's view of history led him to reason that just as slavery had given way to feudalism, and feudalism to capitalism, so too capitalism would inevitably lead to socialism. Under socialism, ownership of the means of production would be collective, not private. Under socialism, the welfare of people would come before profit, and everyone would share in society's resources and wealth—"from each according to his abilities, to each according to his needs." Beyond socialism lay the "classless society" of communism, the promised land where, according to Marx, the state itself would "wither away."

Marx's influence on the twentieth century is undeniable. Until the collapse of the Soviet Union, over a third of the world's population claimed to be living under some form of communism. But whether Marx would have been happy with those who have practised what he preached is highly unlikely. Communist revolutions in Europe, Asia, Latin America and Africa have resulted in nothing like the free, classless and just societies that Marx envisioned.

Nevertheless, Marx's socialist ideals have had a profound impact on capitalism itself. Today free schooling to age 16, government loans and scholarships after that, universal health care and progressive taxation policies are characteristic of many capitalist societies. So too is a more enlightened approach to work and the workplace, as we saw in the previous unit. And so is the belief in a mixed economy of public and private ownership. Ironically, Marx's legacy may have been to help renew the very capitalist system that he was so certain was doomed.

THE HAPPINESS FACTOR

For John Stuart Mill (1806–1879), yet another English political theorist, the purpose of life was the pursuit of happiness. And this, not fear or class conflict, is the guiding principle of human action. According to Mill's "utilitarian" philosophy, (derived from Jeremy Bentham (1748–1832)), actions are good if they promote the greatest happiness for the greatest number of people. But this position doesn't include just any kind of happiness. Mills argued that some types of happiness are better than others; as he said, it is better to be a human being dissatisfied than a pig satisfied. In other words, it is better to aspire to all that humans can be than to simply satisfy individual pleasures. Mill believed that a society that valued rights, laws and justice was the best guarantee of both individual and collective happiness.

John Stuart Mill

In what kind of society can happiness best be achieved? A society, Mill argued, liberal enough to allow individuals maximum freedom to do whatever they wanted, as long as their actions don't harm

Issue 1

others. Because he believed that people are basically decent and by nature are rational, co-operative and sensitive to the needs of others, Mill trusted people's ability to choose what they thought best for themselves. And what is "best," of course, is whatever makes people happy.

Mill argued that the primary job of government was to preserve individual rights and freedoms. He rejected the libertarian notion that government should simply stand back and let people fend for themselves. He advocated instead the classical liberal idea of government intervention—not to tell people what to do or to curtail their liberty—but rather to provide the means for them to make choices through enlightened education, progressive laws and a fair justice system.

As we have already suggested, Mill believed that once government had made the advantages of liberal democracy available to all, it should restrain an individual's actions only when they harmed or interfered with the actions, interests or liberty of others. But some of us may have problems with what is referred to as the "harm principle." For example, how can we be sure when you smoke that I, a non-smoker, am not harmed? You can argue that you'll take responsiblity if you get lung cancer. But your second-hand smoke can give me lung cancer too. So where does your right to smoke end and my right to clean air begin?

You might also argue that the government has no right to enforce measures of individual choice like whether you wear a seat-belt. You may say you'll take your chances in your own car, thank you very much. But if you go through the windshield, whose tax dollars will help to pay for your rehabilitation—assuming you survive?

And then, of course, there's the issue of freedom of speech. Does free speech mean that you have the right to say things that could threaten the interests, rights and even physical well-being of certain racial, religious or other groups?

Mill's "harm principle" does not deal fully with problems resulting from the impact that an individual's actions may have on others (abortion is an even more troubling example). However, Mill did anticipate objections to his utilitarian principle of "the greatest happiness for the greatest number."

Issue 1

You may recall that in Unit 2 we noted how the ideas, customs, laws, privileges and opportunities that bring happiness to the greatest number in society can sometimes bring misery to minorities. Mill acknowledged the potential dangers of this "tyranny of the majority." He believed, therefore, that a democratic society should not only be liberal (i.e., promote individual rights), but should also be representative and pluralistic (i.e., safeguard minority rights).

Unlike Marx, Mill did not call for the demise of capitalism. Nor did he view history as a class conflict between owners and workers, haves and have-nots. The issue for Mill was the conflict between individual freedom and government control. Mill believed strongly that in this struggle the balance of power should rest with the individual because the purpose of government was to serve the people, not the other way round.

THEORISTS AND ACTIVISTS

The line between political theory and political activism is often an artificial one. Karl Marx, for example, believed a philosopher's role wasn't only to try to understand history, but to change it. So in addition to his more theoretical writings, he wrote and edited newspaper articles and took part in numerous political activities. For his part, John Stuart Mill served as a member of parliament and busied himself in a variety of progressive social causes.

Nevertheless, just as we've emphasized the theoretical side of Hobbes, Locke, Marx and Mill, so we will now stress the activist side of Mahatma Gandhi, Martin Luther King and Malcolm X, leaders who have left us a significant body of work that outlines the theory behind their actions.

"SOUL FORCE"

Marx argued that social change could only come about as a result of revolutionary economic change. Mill, on the other hand, believed that social change was the result of enlightened political reform. Like Mill, Mahatma Gandhi (1869–1948) was also a reformer. But he be-

Issue 1

Gandhi

lieved that social change was the result of spiritual change—a transformation of the soul that would be the basis of a new and truly just social order.

This revolutionary idea was embodied in Gandhi's criticism of the Hindu caste system, which separated people into various classes from Brahmin at the upper end to the Untouchables at the lower. Rejecting his own high-caste background, Gandhi sought to eliminate the enormous social divisions created by such a hierarchy and replace them with a classless society (similar to Marx's) that affirmed the brotherhood and sisterhood of all.

Gandhi had a very benign view of human nature, believing that people are good, the world is ultimately just and that peaceful political change is eminently possible. According to Gandhi, real and lasting change was achieved not through violence but through the Hindu principle of "ahimsa," or non-violence. Gandhi believed that "ahimsa" was a universal spiritual force within all humans that could be awakened by example.

The way to awaken the conscience of one's oppressor was through non-violent acts of civil disobedience that Gandhi called "satyagraha"—"soul force" as opposed to "body force." This turning of the other cheek wasn't some masochistic invitation to be beaten by the police or army during strikes, mass demonstrations or marches. Instead, satyagraha was a way to change an enemy's hatred to love, his or her resistance to acceptance.

Despite his charismatic leadership and his great victory in gaining Indian independence from Britain in 1948, Gandhi's non-violent politics of liberation has its critics. Theorists who side with Darwin, Freud or Hobbes think Gandhi's views of human nature and political change are naive and simplistic. Moreover, they argue that while non-violence may have been successful in the struggle against British colonialism, it would have been useless against the radical evil of Nazi Germany. Gandhi's harshest critics believed him to be an impractical and even dangerous idealist.

"WE ARE ALL CREATED EQUAL"

But Gandhi has had his supporters—social reformers inspired by his spirituality and the philosophy of satyagraha. One man who was strongly influenced by Gandhi was the American civil rights leader, Martin Luther King Jr. (1929-1968). Like Gandhi, King believed in the innate goodness of human nature, that "we are all God's children," and that the universe is a moral and just place.

One of the great public speakers in American history, King was a Baptist minister from the American south steeped in the prophetic tradition of the Bible, which he saw as a narrative of liberation and deliverance. King's Jesus was a social activist who championed the rights of the poor and downtrodden. It wasn't difficult for King to identify with Gandhi's struggle against the bondage of colonialism. After all, the United States was a country that claimed to be a beacon of freedom and equality, but a hundred years after the Civil War, black Americans had a long way to go before they could enjoy the "liberty, equality and freedom" that the Constitution promised everyone.

Like Marx, King saw the struggle between haves and have-nots as the defining feature of history. But unlike Marx, for whom religion was an oppressive institution, King saw religion as a liberating force that led to social and political change. He believed that white America was ultimately a just society but, like Gandhi, disagreed with Marx's ideology of violent revolution. Violence, he argued, led only to more violence. It could never form the basis of a viable social contract.

King believed it was possible to achieve his goal of an integrated society by changing people's hearts and minds. Reform the spirit, he preached, and you will reform the attitudes and laws that bar blacks from being part of the American Dream. Few leaders in the world today dare to talk about issues like rights and freedom in a spiritual context. King did, and succeeded in raising the debate over justice to a level of moral significance not seen in American political culture since the time of Lincoln.

In his famous "Letter" from Birmingham Jail, where he was briefly imprisoned for breaking a local ordinance against political demonstrations, King pointed out that there were two kinds of laws: just and unjust. Just laws were those that uplifted the human spirit. People have a legal and moral obligation to obey them. Unjust laws, on the other hand, were those that degraded the human spirit—laws that prohibited blacks from using "whites only" washrooms and restaurants, or denied them the same opportunities as whites for employment, housing and education. According to King, we have a moral responsibility to actively disobey unjust laws.

Issue 1

His argument has profound implications for human behaviour. For example, if more people had acted like Oscar Schindler and resisted the laws and official directives that sent millions to the Nazi death camps in World War II, they could have changed the course of history. King's moral universe of civil disobedience based on principle exists in direct contrast to that of Machiavelli, where expedience and self-interest reign supreme.

But for King, as we've said, civil disobedience had to be non-violent. Like Gandhi, he had no doubt that soul force was stronger than physical force, loving one's enemy the only way to truly humanize and change him. Throughout the late 1950s and 1960s, King helped to organize countless voter registration drives, freedom rides, sit-ins, marches, and rallies involving thousands of black and white Americans who were often harassed, threatened, beaten, arrested and killed for their efforts.

In the end, the civil rights movement stirred the conscience of America and the world. Landmark civil rights legislation was introduced in 1965 and King won the Nobel Peace Prize. But he paid dearly. He was assassinated in 1968. Like Moses, he led his long-suffering people to the Promised Land, and, like Moses, he didn't live to enter.

"BY ANY MEANS NECESSARY"

Martin Luther King promoted non-violence as the means to reform an unjust society because, like Gandhi, he believed in the fundamental decency of human nature and in a world where, in the end, good triumphs over evil. But just as Gandhi had his critics, so did King. And since his death some of their voices seem to speak more loudly to black Americans than his.

In the United States today, for example, the Nation of Islam has a powerful following among those African-Americans who argue that racial integration can't work, that the separation of black and white races is both desirable and necessary, and that blacks must reconnect with their African roots. If such views sound surprising in light of King's reputation, it is important to remember that even at the height of the civil rights movement's popularity, King was only one of several major African-American leaders, who didn't always agree on ideology or strategy. One of King's major rivals for the loyalty of black Americans was Malcolm X (1925–1965).

Malcolm X's critical analysis of white American society and his prescription for change differed radically from King's. Malcolm X came into contact with the ideas of the Nation of Islam while in prison. Subsequently, he changed his surname from "Little" to "X" to indicate that, as the descendant of slaves, he'd been stripped of his ancestral identity.

Once out of prison, he soon became chief spokesman for the Nation of Islam and its founder, Elijah Muhammad. In brilliant speeches that were inflammatory and confrontational, Malcolm X condemned white people as "blue-eyed devils" who could never be trusted. He rejected Christianity as a racist, oppressive, "white man's religion" that didn't speak to the true black identity, which was African. King and other black Christians had "sold out," Malcolm X said.

The philosophy of the Nation of Islam stressed the need for black pride, independence, discipline and power. These could be achieved if African-Americans challenged whites on their own terms by developing their own banks and businesses, their own churches and schools, their own social and cultural support systems. Only through "black power" would African-Americans gain the freedom, justice and equality that was their right.

For the Nation of Islam, black power meant separation, not integration. Black Muslims also disagreed with King's philosophy of non-violence, Self-preservation "by any means necessary" was justified, Malcolm X said. This meant fighting back, not turning the other cheek.

In 1964, Malcolm X went to Mecca in Saudi Arabia, the spiritual capital of Islam. There he met Moslems of all races and nations worshipping together in peace, equality and dignity. The experience moved him to reject racial hatred as a liberation strategy. He began to view the struggle against oppression in universal terms, not exclusively African-American.

After returning to the United States, he broke with Elijah Muhammad and the Nation of Islam, becoming an orthodox Sunni Muslim who believed that the social order should embrace all peoples. It was while preaching this new message of hope and solidarity that he was gunned down on February 21, 1965. He was 40 years old.

SUMMARY

In this article we've attempted to explain how politics, or the power relations between individuals and groups, creates change. At the same time, we described government as the system of mechanisms and institutions that regulates these social and economic power relations.

The relationship between the individual and the collective has been the common thread throughout our discussion. Each person accommodates the collective when we surrender certain individual impulses and desires in return for benefits that guarantee our survival and ultimately promote our self-interest.

Thomas Hobbes believed that fear was the motivating factor behind the social contract, while John Locke argued that it came out of our mutual recognition of natural rights, particularly the right of private property that was the foundation of the capitalist system. For his part, Karl Marx argued that under capitalism the social order was defined by class conflict, where owners exploited their workers and the strong dominated the weak.

John Stuart Mill, meanwhile, believed in the possibility of major social reform. He argued that people were motivated to participate in the social order by the utilitarian principle of happiness. This principle was the key to a progressive liberal society that would guarantee rights, laws and justice to everyone.

Even libertarians and anarchists agree on the need for some government at least to regulate the social arrangement. What form of government can do this best? We have said that any answer has to first address the question of government's purpose. And our answer to this question, in turn, depends largely on some of our fundamental beliefs about human nature. Are people good or bad? Who is best suited to make decisions? How much freedom should people have?

Political philosophers, politicians and reformers deal with these and other questions in their efforts to define or change society. Hobbes, for example, believed in the need for a strong and absolute sovereign to limit individual action because he thought that people were driven by passions that easily turned destructive. Locke and Mill, on the other hand, believed that sovereign power should be vested in a parliamentary democracy that protects and extends our rights and interests.

As we have seen, Marx repudiated parliamentary democracy as nothing more than a tool of capitalism to create "false consciousness"—i.e., people only think they have rights and freedoms but these are, in effect, carefully managed by the owners of the means of production who control government, finance, the media, religion and the other institutions of society. According to Marx, the social contract is a fraud. Only when capitalism is overthrown can we enjoy non-exploitative social relations.

Mahatma Gandhi, Martin Luther King and Malcolm X believed society needed to be re-organized to right the wrongs of colonial and racial oppression. Gandhi and King tried to reform their respective societies through acts of non-violent civil disobedience, while Malcolm X first justified violence and black power before his Islamic faith led him to consider the struggle for justice in more universal terms.

To know politics is to know how power operates and how government and society function. If we choose to be ignorant of power, we choose to yield control of our lives to others. Politics is not just about politicians or political philosophers or reformers. It's about the interaction of forces that make things happen in a society. It is about what happens far away—Nelson Mandela becoming president of South Africa, children being butchered in civil wars; and what happens at home—NAFTA, the Bloc Quebecois, employment equity, political correctness.

People who understand how such issues are played out have the power to change their lives in ways that offer them real choice and real freedom. As consumers in an entertainment-driven culture that plays up the inane and plays down the serious, it's in our self-interest to take politics—all politics—seriously.

Issue 1

I HAVE A DREAM...

Dr. Martin Luther King, Jr.

Martin Luther King

I am happy to join with you today in what will go down in history as the greatest demonstration for freedom in the history of our nation.

Five score years ago, a great American, in whose symbolic shadow we stand today, signed the Emancipation Proclamation. This momentous decree came as a great beacon light of hope to millions of Negro slaves, who had been seared in the flames of withering injustice. It came as a joyous daybreak to end the long night of their captivity.

But one hundred years later the Negro still is not free. One hundred years later the life of the Negro is still sadly crippled by the manacles of segregation and the chains of discrimination.

One hundred years later the Negro lives on a lonely island of poverty in the midst of a vast ocean of material prosperity. One hundred years later, the Negro is still languishing in the corners of American society and finds himself an exile in his own land. So we have come here today to dramatize a shameful condition.

In a sense we have come to our nation's capital to cash a cheque. When the architects of our great republic wrote the magnificent words of the Constitution and the Declaration of Independence, they were signing a promissory note to which every American was to fall heir.

This note was a promise that all men, yes, black men as well as white men, would be guaranteed the inalienable rights of life, liberty, and the pursuit of happiness.

It is obvious today that America has defaulted on this promissory note in so far as her citizens of color are concerned. Instead of honouring this sacred obligation, America has given the Negro people a bad cheque, a cheque which has come back marked "insufficient funds."

But we refuse to believe that the bank of justice is bankrupt. We refuse to believe that there are insufficient funds in the great vaults of opportunity of this nation. So we have come to cash this cheque, a cheque that will give us upon demand the riches of freedom and the security of justice.

We have also come to this hallowed spot to remind America of the fierce urgency of now. This is no time to engage in the luxury of cooling off or to take the tranquillizing drug of gradualism.

Now is the time to make real the promise of democracy.

Now is the time to rise from the dark and desolate valley of segregation to the sunlit path of racial justice.

Now is the time to lift our nation from the quicksands of racial injustice to the solid rock of brotherhood.

Now is the time to make justice a reality to all of God's children.

It would be fatal for the nation to overlook the urgency of the moment. This sweltering summer of the Negro's legitimate discontent will not pass until there is an invigorating autumn of freedom and equality. Nineteen sixty-three is not an end but a beginning. Those who hope that the Negro need to blow off steam and will now be content, will have a rude awakening if the nation returns to business as usual.

There will be neither rest nor tranquillity in America until the Negro is granted his citizenship rights. The whirlwinds of revolt will continue to shake the foundations of our nation until the bright day of justice emerges.

But there is something that I must say to my people who stand on the warm threshold which leads into the palace of justice. In the process of gaining our rightful place we must not be guilty of wrongful deeds.

Let us not seek to satisfy our thirst for freedom by drinking from the cup of bitterness and hatred.

We must forever conduct our struggle on the high plane of dignity and discipline. We must not allow our creative protest to degenerate into physical violence.

Again and again we must rise to the majestic heights of meeting physical force with soul force. The marvellous new militancy which has engulfed the Negro community must not lead us to a distrust of all white people, for many of our white brothers, evidenced by their presence here today, have come to realize that their destiny is tied up with our destiny and their freedom is inextricably bound to our freedom.

We cannot walk alone.

Dr. Martin Luther King Jr.

The World House

Some years ago a famous novelist died. Among his papers was found a list of suggested plots for future stories, the most prominently underscored being this one: "A widely separated family inherits a house in which they have to live together." This is the great new problem of mankind. We have inherited a large house, a great "world house" in which we have to live together—black and white, Easterner and Westerner, Gentile and Jew, Catholic and Protestant, Moslem and Hindu—a family unduly separated in ideas, culture and interest, who, because we can never again live apart, must learn somehow to live with each other in peace.

One of the great liabilities of history is that all too many people fail to remain awake through great periods of social change. Every society has its protectors of the status quo and its fraternities of the indifferent who are notorious for sleeping through revolutions. But today our very survival depends on our ability to stay awake, to adjust to new ideas, to remain vigilant and to face the challenge of change. The large house in which we live demands that we transform this world-wide neighbourhood into a world-wide brotherhood. Together we must learn to live as brothers or together we will be forced to perish as fools.

Issue 1

As we walk, we must make the pledge that we shall always march ahead. We cannot turn back. There are those who are asking the devotees of civil rights, "When will you be satisfied?"

We can never be satisfied as long as the Negro is the victim of the unspeakable horrors of police brutality.

We can never be satisfied as long as our bodies, heavy with the fatigue of travel, cannot gain lodging in the motels of the highways and the hotels of the cities.

We cannot be satisfied as long as the colored person's basic mobility is from a smaller ghetto to a larger one.

We can never be satisfied as long as our children are stripped of their selfhood and robbed of their dignity by signs stating "For White Only."

We cannot be satisfied as long as the Negro in Mississippi cannot vote and a Negro in New York believes he has nothing for which to vote.

No, no we are not satisfied and we will not be satisfied until justice rolls down like waters and righteousness like a mighty stream.

I am not unmindful that some of you have come here out of great trials and tribulations. Some of you have come fresh from narrow jail cells. Some of you have come from areas where your quest for freedom left you battered by the storms of persecutions and staggered by the winds of police brutality.

You have been the veterans of creative suffering. Continue to work with the faith that unearned suffering is redemptive.

Go back to Mississippi, go back to Alabama, go back to South Carolina, go back to Georgia, go back to Louisiana, go back to the slums and ghettos of our northern cities, knowing that somehow this situation can and will be changed.

Let us not wallow in the valley of despair. I say to you today, my friends, so even though we face the difficulties of today and tomorrow....

... I still have a dream. It is a dream deeply rooted in the American dream.

I have a dream that one day this nation will rise up and live out the true meaning of its creed. We hold these truths to be self-evident that all men are created equal.

Issue 1

I have a dream that one day out in the red hills of Georgia the sons of former slaves and the sons of former slave owners will be able to sit down together at the table of brotherhood.

I have a dream that one day even the state of Mississippi, a state sweltering with the heat of injustice, sweltering with the heat of oppression, will be transformed into an oasis of freedom and justice.

I have a dream that my four little children will one day live in a nation where they will not be judged by the color of their skin but by the content of their character.

I have a dream today.

I have a dream that one day down in Alabama, with its vicious racists, with its governor having his lips dripping with the words of interposition and nullification; one day right there in Alabama little black boys and black girls will be able to join hands with little white boys and white girls as sisters and brothers.

I have a dream today.

I have a dream that one day every valley shall be exalted, and every hill and mountain shall be made low, the rough places will be made plane and the crooked places will be made straight, and the glory of the Lord shall be revealed and all flesh shall see it together.

This is our hope. This is the faith that I will go back to the South with. With this faith we will be able to hew out of the mountain of despair a stone of hope.

With this faith we will be able to work together, to pray together, to struggle together, to go to jail together, to stand up for freedom together, knowing that we will be free one day. With this faith we will be able to transform the jangling discourse of our nation into a beautiful symphony of brotherhood.

This will be the day when all of God's children will be able to sing with new meaning "My country 'tis of thee, sweet land of liberty, of thee I sing. Land where my fathers died, land of the Pilgrim's pride, from every mountainside, let freedom ring!"

And if America is to be a great nation, this must become true. So, let freedom ring from the prodigious hilltops of New Hampshire. Let freedom ring from the mighty mountains of New York.

Let freedom ring from the heightening Alleghenies of Pennsylvania.

Issue 1

Let freedom ring from the snow-capped Rockies of Colorado.

Let freedom ring from the curvaceous slopes of California.

But not only that, let freedom ring from Stone Mountain of Georgia.

Let freedom ring from Lookout Mountain in Tennessee.

Let freedom ring from every hill and molehill of Mississippi, from every mountainside.

Let freedom ring and when this happens, when we allow freedom to ring, when we let it ring from every village and every hamlet, from every state and every city, we will be able to speed up that day when all of God's children, black men and white men, Jews and Gentiles, Protestants and Catholics, will be able to join hands and sing in the words of the old Negro spiritual, "Free at last, free at last. Thank God Almighty, we are free at last."

Delivered at the Lincoln Memorial, Wednesday, August 28, 1963.

The View of Malcolm

Malcolm X

Malcolm X

Malcolm X was born Malcolm Little in Omaha, Nebraska. He was assassinated in 1965. His life has recently been portrayed in the film Malcolm X.

While in prison, Malcolm X joined the Nation of Islam. He took on the surname "X" to signify that, like most descendants of the slaves forcibly brought to the United States from Africa, he had lost his ancestral name. He joined the Nation of Islam in prison and became a devoted follower of the Islamic religion. The Nation of Islam maintained that the solution for black people in the United

Issue 1

in the United States was complete separation for blacks.

Malcolm X's views underwent a radical change in 1964. During a series of religious trips to Mecca and the newly independent African states, he encountered good people of all races. His views began to change accordingly. He came to the conclusion that he had yet to discover true Islam. He came to regard not all whites as racists, and saw the struggle of black people as part of a wider freedom struggle. He established his own religious group and a political organization, the Organization for Afro-American Unity.

Along with Martin Luther King, Malcolm X symbolized the civil rights movement in the United States during the 1960s.

Before Going to Mecca

"No *sane* black man really wants integration! No *sane* white man really wants integration. No sane black man really believes that the white man ever will give the black man anything more than token integration. No! The Honorable Elijah Muhammad teaches that for the black man in America the only solution is complete *separation* from the white man!" *The Autobiography of Malcolm X*, p.248.

"And this is one thing that whites—whether you call yourselves liberals or conservatives or racists or whatever else you might choose to be—one thing that you have to realize is, where the black community is concerned, although the large majority you come in contact with may impress you as being moderate and patient and loving and long-suffering and all that kind of stuff, the minority who you consider to be Muslims or nationalists happen to be made of the type of ingredient that can easily spark the black community. This should be understood. Because to me a powder keg is nothing without a fuse." *Malcolm X Speaks*, p.48.

After Going to Mecca

"Never have I witnessed such sincere hospitality and the overwhelming spirit of true brotherhood as is practiced by people of all colors and races here in this Ancient Holy Land, the home of Abraham, Muhammad, and all the other prophets of the Holy Scriptures. For the past week, I have been utterly speechless and spellbound by the graciousness I see displayed all around me by people of *all colors*." *The Autobiography of Malcolm X*, p.344.

"My pilgrimage broadened my scope. It blessed me with a new insight. In two weeks in the Holy Land, I saw what I never had seen in thirty-nine years here in America. I saw all *races*, all *colors*,—blue-eyed blonds to black-skinned Africans—in *true* brotherhood! In unity! Living as one! Worshipping as one! No segregationists—no liberals; they would not have known how to interpret the meaning of those words.

"In the past, yes, I have made sweeping indictments of *all* white people. I never will be guilty of that again—as I know now that some white people *are* truly sincere, that some truly are capable of being brotherly toward a black man. The true Islam has shown me that a blanket indictment of all white people is as wrong as when whites make blanket indictments against blacks.

"Yes, I have been convinced that some American whites do want to help cure the rampant racism which is on the path to *destroying* this country!" *The Autobiography of Malcolm X*, p.366.

THE GREAT LAW OF PEACE

John Steckley

As we have seen in Morton Ritts' "Politics in the Life of the Individual," Aristotle tells us that there are three basic forms of government, based fundamentally on how many people actually govern the society: one, a few, or many. One of these forms, democracy, can be called "government by the many." We can subdivide democracy into two types: **majoritarian** and **consensus**. In majoritarian democracy, "majority rules." Whichever candidate receives the most votes gets elected. Whichever party has the most elected candidates gets to form the government. In a referendum, whichever alternative—either "yes" or "no"—is chosen by most people becomes the decision of the people. For example, if three friends want to go to a rock bar one night and a fourth "votes" to go to a country bar, the group will not be line dancing that night.

In consensus democracy, everyone has a say and must agree with the decision before it can be acted upon. One form of consensus democracy is when a jury must be unanimous in its verdict. As has happened in some famous cases, it can take a long time to reach a decision in this way. However, it is one way of perhaps avoiding the danger in majoritarian democracy that J. S. Mill saw: tyranny of the majority—where the majority acts like a tyrant or dictator—which, at its worst is a version of Machiavelli's "might makes right." That is, do what we do or suffer the consequences.

In this article, we will look at the Great Law of Peace, the founding story and principles of the Confederacy of the Iroquois. Iroquois society differed from the societies in which the other political philosophers and activists described in the Ritts' article lived. The private property that John Locke attached so much significance to was only of secondary importance to the Iroquois. The most valuable property was non-material—names, songs, stories, dances, spirit guardians, respect and medicinal knowledge—and most of that property was neither privately nor publicly owned. It belonged to the clan. These clans would not fit into the category of classes that Karl Marx saw in the societies he described, as they were fundamentally equal, all possessing roughly the same amount and kind of property, all providing leaders or sachems. While some lineages or family lines had the advantage of being responsible for providing the sachems, a person from any lineage could become a Pine Tree Chief.

Further, it should be noted that the Great Law of Peace should not be considered to be just a set of rules. Like the work of Gandhi and Martin Luther King, it has a strong spiritual component. Similar to Gandhi's "soul force," the spiritual purity and strength of the Peacemaker and of Hiawatha were tested throughout the story, which is an integral part of the Great Law of Peace. Without them, there would have been little respect for the political goals that it set out.

We hear and read so much about "great political philosophers" who developed their ideas far away from Canada that we are surprised to learn that an influential political thinker lived and developed his revolutionary ideas in Ontario. He is known as the Peacemaker, his set of ideas, the *Kayanerenkowa* or the Great Law of Peace. He grew up on the north shore of Lake Ontario, near the current Mohawk community of Tyendinaga. Exactly when he lived is uncertain; estimates range from 100 to 1350 A.D. He may have been a member of the Huron-Wendat nation, who were living in the area at the time.

The Great Law of Peace is both a set of ideas and the story of how the ideas developed and came to be accepted. It brought together five warring nations, known now in English as the Mohawk, Oneida, Onondaga, Cayuga and Seneca. These five linguistically and culturally related peoples lived in villages in what is now New York State. The uniting of these peoples is termed *Rotinohsoni* in Mohawk, which means "They Build or Extend A House." It is referred to in English as the Confederacy of the Iroquois. It incorporates five key elements of traditional Native governance:

1. *Consensus democracy*—the notion that to make a decision on an issue, *everyone* must be in agreement (i.e., a consensus), rather than having the majority automatically imposing its will on a minority;

2. *Leader as speaker of consensus*—the idea that the leader or "chief" does not make decisions, but merely states the consensus that the people meeting in council have reached;

3. *Council of equals*—the notion that people who meet in council do so as equals, with no one having the power to give commands to the others;

4. *Separation of leaders of war and peace*—the notion that those who lead or speak consensus in matters of peace should not be those who lead or speak consensus in matters of war;

5. *Impeachment*—the notion that there should be a quick and efficient means of deposing a leader as soon as that person loses the respect of the people.

THE STORY

The political part of the story begins with the Peacemaker crossing Lake Ontario to the country of the Mohawk, the easternmost of the five nations. Once there, he convinced a man known in English as Hiawatha that the Iroquois-speaking people should not fight among themselves, but should join together in one confederacy or union of nations. Gradually the Peacemaker's ideas were heard by all five peoples, and acceptance of his wisdom grew, sometimes through tests of the Peacemaker's spiritual purity and strength.

The last and most difficult nation to win over was the Onondaga, which was geographically the middle nation, whose leader, Thadodaha, was the most powerful and feared man in the five nations. To win over Thadodaha, the Onondaga were given the title of Fire Keepers, the ones who held the council meetings in their country, and were given the greatest number of representatives in the council. Further, Thadodaha, and those who later were to bear that name, would be the leader to speak the consensus of the Confederacy, which was a great honour.

THE SACHEMS

The council of the Iroquois Confederacy was made up of fifty leaders, known in English as sachems. They were divided among the five nations in the following way:

Onondaga 14
Cayuga   10
Mohawk   9
Oneida   9
Seneca   8

Issue 1

Clans were very important to the Iroquois Confederacy. Each clan owned a set of names, including those of the sachems. The three clans of the Mohawk, for example, each owned three of the Mohawk sachem names. Within each clan, lineages or family lines usually supplied the adult men with sachem names. The person who designated the sachem, and who could depose him, was the Clan Matron. She was usually an older woman who was considered wise enough to perceive and speak the consensus of the entire clan.

What would lead to the sachem being deposed? He would be deposed if he acted according to his own interests rather than those of his clan and nation, or if he lost the respect of the people for other reasons. Since the Iroquois nations were matrilineal, that is, they determined kinship along the female line, women had the authority to depose a sachem. Children would belong to their mother's clan, not their father's. Why was clan membership determined this way? Some writers connect this with the fact that Iroquois women were traditionally the farmers—the main food providers. By growing corn, beans and squash, they produced most of the food. They were the (corn) breadwinners. They also decided how food was distributed.

HISTORICAL EXAMPLE

Tekarihogen ("Affair or Matter Split in Two") is a Mohawk sachem name, the first named in council. It belongs to the Turtle clan. A man with the English name Seth held this title during the second half of the eighteenth century. When he died, the name was passed on to his sister's son, since he belonged to the same lineage and clan. Around 1780, that man's sister, Catherine, then the Clan Matron of the Turtle clan, named his successor upon his death, which was her son, Henry. When he died in 1830, she bestowed the title on her son, John, a child from her marriage to the famous Mohawk leader Joseph Brant (after whom Brantford is named). When John died, Catherine put her daughter's son into the position. The name Tekarihogen still exists and is still respected today.

PINE TREE CHIEFS

If you did not belong to an appropriate lineage, you could not become a sachem. However, there was a basic equality of lineages because a man of exceptional ability could become a Pine Tree Chief. This term is used for someone who was not officially part of the council of sachems, but who could have tremendous influence on it, depending on the respect with which his ideas were held. John Brant (Tyendinaga) is an example of a Pine Tree Chief. He led some 2,000 Iroquois to Canada after fighting against the Americans in the American Revolution during the 1770s and 1780s.

WAR CHIEFS

War chiefs could not be sachems. If a sachem went on a raid, he would have to do so as an "ordinary citizen." War chiefs had their own councils, which met separately from the sachems or "peace chiefs." Compare this division with the modern alternative. In the Canadian and American systems of government, the decision to go to war is made by politicians who will not actually fight, although younger people who are not politicians will. In the Iroquois system, the people who made that decision were involved with the fighting that they initiated.

COUNCIL MEETINGS

In the council house of the sachems, the Senecas, Onondaga and Mohawk who would sit on one side of the fire were called "older siblings" (i.e., a term that referred to both brothers and sisters). On the other side of the fire were the "younger siblings," the Cayuga and the Oneida. The traditional manner of dealing with issues was as follows: the Onondaga leader, Thadodaha, would state the issue. He would then pass it to the Mohawk to discuss. When the Mohawk had arrived at a consensus decision, the consensus would be passed to the Seneca. They would arrive at their own consensus and return the issue to the Mohawk, who would pass both opinions "across the fire" to the Oneida. The issue would move in this way from the Oneida to the Cayuga, back to the Oneida and then "across the fire" back to the Mohawk. The Mohawk would then pass the issue, complete with all the opinions decided upon by all the nations, to the Onondaga, who would consider what had been said and then arrive at their own decision.

Issue 1

At this stage, the Onondaga could do one of three things. First, if all the nations had arrived at the same consensus, Thadodaha would announce or speak the decision. Second, if the Onondaga disagreed with the consensus decision, which they could do only if that decision represented a serious breach of established custom or public policy, they could send the issue through the entire process again. Third, if the nations disagreed, an Onondaga sachem, *Hononwiyehti*, the Wampum Keeper, would suggest a compromise. This compromise would then be discussed by the five nations in the same manner as the initial issue.

INFLUENCE OF THE GREAT LAW OF PEACE

For most of the seventeenth and eighteenth centuries, the Iroquois were an imposing military and political force in the Great Lakes area. During the latter half of the eighteenth century, Iroquois leaders, such as the great Seneca orator Red Jacket, influenced American political thinkers such as Thomas Paine, Thomas Jefferson and Benjamin Franklin. They learned from the Iroquois Confederacy how a group of separate nations or states could be stronger if they united as one. The American Constitution reflects some of the ideas that these men learned from the Iroquois. For example, members of the United States Congress cannot go to war without resigning their seats. Likewise, military officers must at least temporarily resign their commission before running for office. Another Iroquois concept—removing discredited holders of public office—is known as the impeachment process. All elected positions, including that of the President, are subject to impeachment. Canadians are sometimes envious of that particular American/Iroquois political feature.

In Canada, we have Mohawk communities in Ontario and Quebec, an Oneida community in Ontario, and a mixed group (mostly Mohawk, Onondaga and Cayuga) at Six Nations, near Brantford. The sixth nation is the Tuscarora, who were invited into the Confederacy when the Americans drove them out of their ancestral home early in the eighteenth century.

The sachem had official authority in Canada until 1924. At that time, the federal government arbitrarily decreed that the Confederacy was neither "modern" nor "democratic" enough to continue to exist. Perhaps the Confederacy's opposition to federal policies had something to do with that. The federal government then removed the sachem from office, changed the locks on the council doors, and made the Iroquois vote in their leaders by majority vote. The result was division within the Iroquois communities that still persists.

Now, as First Nations across Canada are looking for models of self-government, they look to the ideas contained within the Great Law of Peace. Canadians of all origins could learn a great deal as well.

THE UNKNOWN CITIZEN

W.H. Auden

(To JS/07/M/378
This Marble Monument
Is Erected by the State)

He was found by the Bureau of Statistics to be
One against whom there was no official complaint,
And all the reports on his conduct agree
That, in the modern sense of an old-fashioned word, he was a saint,
For in everything he did he served the Greater Community.
Except for the War till the day he retired
He worked in a factory and never got fired,
But satisfied his employers, Fudge Motors Inc.
Yet he wasn't a scab or odd in his views,
For his Union reports that he paid his dues,
(Our report on his Union shows it was sound)
And our Social Psychology workers found
That he was popular with his mates and liked to drink.
The Press are convinced that he bought a paper every day
And that his reactions to advertisements were normal in every way.

Policies taken out in his name prove that he was fully insured,
And his Health-card shows he was once in hospital but left it cured.
Both Producers Research and High-Grade Living declare
He was fully sensible to the advantages of the Instalment Plan
And had everything necessary to the Modern Man,
A phonograph, a radio, a car and a frigidaire.
Our researchers into Public Opinion are content
That he held the proper opinions for the time of year;
When there was peace, he was for peace; when there was war, he
went.
He was married and added five children to the population,
Which our Eugenist says was the right number for a parent of his
generation,
And our teachers report that he never interfered with their education.
Was he free? Was he happy? The question is absurd:
Had anything been wrong, we should certainly have heard.

Review

The Unknown Citizen by W.H. Auden

The "Unknown Citizen" in Auden's poem of the same name does not seem like a particularly noble hero, does he? In fact, his primary quality is that he has managed to keep himself entirely out of trouble.

A competent worker and a good consumer, he led a statistically "normal" life—neither complaining nor arousing complaints from others. He had few positive attributes to speak of. He was just a small voiceless cog in a big machine. What kind of state might erect a marble monument to honour a person like that?

In many respects, this state has much in common with contemporary Western society, especially the America of several decades ago, when the poem was written. It is a nation of automobiles, phonographs, radios, refrigerators, unions, factories—and a highly compartmentalized government bureaucracy that pervasively keeps a close (and not entirely innocent) watch on its citizens.

This poem is an ironic view of a society that sees itself as an ideal place to live, a Utopia, but one that is actually highly intolerant of individuality and free expression. The Unknown Citizen complacently accepts the status quo (and the irony) without protest. Now a monument has been erected to remember his name—even as that name is forgotten for all time.

RELATIONS BETWEEN COLLECTIVES

Out of timber so crooked as that from which man is made nothing entirely straight can be built.

Immanuel Kant

The worst sin towards our fellow creatures is not to hate them, but to be indifferent to them; that's the essence of inhumanity.

G.B. Shaw

A COSMOPOLITAN AMONG THE TRUE BELIEVERS

Michael Ignatieff

*A*nyone whose father was born in Russia, whose mother was born in England, who was educated in America, and whose working life has been spent in Canada, Great Britain, and France cannot be expected to be much of an ethnic nationalist. For many years, I believed that the tide was running in favour of cosmopolitans like me. There seemed to be so many of us, for one thing. There were at least a dozen world cities—gigantic, multi-ethnic melting pots that provided a home for expatriates, exiles, migrants, and transients of all kinds. For the urban professional populations of these major cities, a post-national state of mind was simply taken for granted. People in these places did not bother about the passports of the people they worked or lived with; they did not care about the country-of-origin label on the goods they bought. They simply assumed that in constructing their own way of life they would borrow from the customs of every nation they happened to admire.

This cosmopolitan ethic is not in itself altogether new. We have lived with a global economy since 1700, and many of the world's major cities have been global **entrepots** for centuries. But in 1989 we entered the first era of global cosmopolitanism in which there was no framework for imperial order. For two hundred years prior, the global expansion of capitalism was shaped by the territorial ambitions and policing authority of a succession of imperial powers—the British, French, German, Austro-Hungarian, and Russian empires of the nineteenth and early twentieth centuries and the Soviet and American joint **imperium** after the Second World War.

America may still be a superpower, but it is not an imperial power: its authority is exercised in the defense of exclusively national interest, not in the maintenance of an imperial system of global order. As a result, large sections of Africa, Eastern Europe, Soviet Asia, Latin America, and the Near East no longer come within any clearly defined sphere of imperial or great-power influence. This means that huge sections of the world's population have won the

entrepots—trading centre

imperium—rule

"right of self-determination" on the cruellest possible terms: they have simply been left to fend for themselves. Small wonder, then, that, unrestrained by stronger hands, they have set upon one another for that final settling of scores so long deferred by presence of empire.

With **blithe** lightness of mind, we had assumed that the world was moving irrevocably beyond nationalism, beyond tribalism, beyond the provincial confines of the identities inscribed in our passports, toward a global market culture that was to be our new home. In retrospect, we were whistling in the dark. The key narrative of the new world order is the disintegration of nation-states into ethnic civil war; the key architects of that order are warlords. The repressed has returned, and its name is nationalism.

blithe—carefree

Everywhere I've been, nationalism is most violent where the group you are defining yourself against most closely resembles you. A rational explanation of conflict would predict the reverse to be the case. To outsiders at least, Ulstermen look and sound like Irishmen, just as Serbs look and sound like Croats—yet the very similarity is what pushed them to define themselves as polar opposites. Since Cain and Abel, we have known that hatred between brothers is more ferocious than hatred between strangers. We say tritely that this is so because hatred is a form of love turned against itself. Or that we hate most deeply what we recognize as kin. Or that violence is

Civil war: "Since Cain and Abel, we have known that hatred between brothers is more ferocious than hatred between strangers."

Issue 2

the theory of the narcissism of minor difference—refers to the theory that the more minor the distinction between two groups, the more important such difference becomes to those obsessed with self-identity

the ultimate denial of an affiliation we cannot bear. None of this will do. There are puzzles that no theory of nationalism, no **theory of the narcissism of minor difference**, can resolve. After you have been to the wastelands of the new world order, particularly to those fields of graves marked with numberless wooden crosses, you feel stunned into silence by a deficit of moral explanation.

In his 1959 essay "What Does Coming to Terms with the Past Mean?" Theodor Adomo says, in passing, "Nationalism no longer quite believes in itself." Everywhere I went, there was a bewildering insincerity and inauthenticity to nationalist rhetoric, as if the people who mouthed nationalist slogans were aware, somewhere inside, of the implausibility of their own words. Serbs who, in one breath, would tell you that all Croats were Ustashe beasts would, in the next, recall the happy days when they lived with them in peace. In this divided consciousness, the plane of abstract fantasy and the plane of direct experience were never allowed to intersect.

Nationalism is a form of speech that shouts, not merely so that it will be heard but so that it will believe itself. It is almost as if the quotient of crude historical fiction, violent moral exaggeration, ludicrous caricature of the enemy is in direct proportion to the degree to which the speaker is himself aware that it is all really a pack of lies. But this insincerity may be a functional requirement of a language that is burdened with the task of insisting upon such a high volume of untruths. The nationalist vision of an ethnically pure state, for example, has the task of convincing ordinary people to disregard stubbornly adverse sociological realities, like the fact that most societies are not and have never been ethnically pure. That such fantasies do take hold of large numbers of people is a testament to the deep longing people have to escape the stubborn realities of life.

Nationalism, in this interpretation, is a language of fantasy and escape. In many cases—Serbia is a flagrant example—nationalist politics is a full-scale, collective escape from the realities of social backwardness. Instead of facing up to the reality of being a poor, primitive, third-rate economy on the periphery of Europe, it is infinitely more attractive to listen to speeches about the heroic and tragic destiny of Serbia and to fantasize about the final defeat of her historic enemies. Nationalist rhetoric rewrites and re-creates the real world, turning it into a delusional realism of noble causes, tragic sacrifice, and cruel necessity.

Issue 2

Yet there is a further element to add to the picture. As all of us can see on our television screens, most nationalist violence is perpetrated by a small minority of males between the ages of eighteen and twenty-five. Some are psychopaths, but most are perfectly sane. Until I had spent some time at the checkpoints of the new world order, until I had encountered my quotient of young males intoxicated by the power of the guns on their hips, I had not understood how deeply pleasurable it is, for some, to have the power of life and death in their hands. It is a characteristic liberal error to suppose that everyone hates and fears violence. I met lots of young men who loved the ruins, loved the destruction, loved the power that came from the barrels of their guns.

Perhaps liberals have not understood the force of male resentment that has accumulated through centuries of gradual European pacification. Liberals have not reckoned with the male loathing of peace and domesticity or with the anger of young males at the modern state's confiscation of their weapons. One of the hidden explanations behind nationalist revolts is that they tap into this deep substratum of male resentment at the civility and order of the modern state. It seems obvious that, for many, the state's order is the order of the father and nationalism is the rebellion of the sons. How else are we to account for the staggering **gratuitousness** and bestiality of nationalist violence, its constant overstepping of the bounds of either military logic or legitimate self-defense, unless we leave some room in our account for the possibility that nationalism exists to warrant and legitimize the sons' 'vengeance against the father.'

gratuitousness—unjustified nature

My journeys have also made me rethink the nature of belonging. Any expatriate is bound to have moments of wishing for a more complete national belonging. But I have been to places where belonging is so strong, so intense, that I now recoil from it in fear. The rational core of such fear is that there is a deep connection between violence and belonging. The more strongly you feel the bonds of belonging to your own group, the more hostile, the more violent will your feelings be toward outsiders. When nationalists claim that national belonging is the overridingly important form of all belonging, they mean that there is no other form of belonging—to your family, work, or friends—that is secure if you do not have a nation to protect you. Without a nation's protection, everything that an individual values can be rendered worthless. Belonging, in this view,

Issue 2

is first and foremost protection from violence. Where you belong is where you are safe; where you are safe is where you belong. You can't have this intensity of belonging without violence, because belonging of this intensity moulds the individual conscience: if a nation gives people a reason to sacrifice themselves, it also gives them a reason to kill.

Throughout my travels, I kept remembering the scene in Romeo and Juliet in which Juliet whispers to herself on the balcony in her nightgown, unaware that Romeo is in the shadows listening. She is struggling to understand what it means for her, a Capulet, to fall in love with a Montague. Suddenly she exclaims,

> 'Tis but thy name that is my enemy;
> Thou art thyself though, not a Montague.
> What's Montague? It is nor hand, nor foot,
> Nor arm, nor face, nor any other part
> Belonging to a man. O, be some other name!
> What's in a name?

On the front lines in Bosnia, in the housing projects of Loyalist and Republican Belfast, in all the places where the tribal gangsters—the Montagues and Capulets of our day—are enforcing the laws of ethnic loyalty, there are Juliets and Romeos who still cry out, "Oh, let me not be a Croatian, Serbian, Bosnian, Catholic, or Protestant. Let me be only myself."

But such people are an embattled minority. The world is run not by skeptics and ironists but by gunmen and true believers, and the new world they are bequeathing to the next century already seems a more violent and desperate place than I could ever have imagined. If I had supposed, as the Cold War came to an end, that the new world might be ruled by philosophers and poets, it was because I believed, foolishly, that the precarious civility and order of the states in which I live must be what all people rationally desire. Now I am not so sure. I began my journey as a liberal, and I end as one, but I cannot help thinking that liberal civilization—the rule of laws, not men, of argument in place of force, of compromise in place of violence—runs deeply against the human grain, and is achieved and sustained only by the most unremitting struggle against human nature. The liberal virtues—tolerance, compromise, reason—remain as valuable as ever, but they cannot be preached to those who are mad with fear or mad with vengeance. In any case, preaching always

Issue 2

rings hollow. We must be prepared to defend these virtues by force, and the failure of the sated, cosmopolitan nations to do so has left the hungry nations sick with contempt for us.

Between the hungry barrier of incomprehension, there is an impassable barrier of incomprehension. I've lived all my life in **sated** nation-states, in places that have no outstanding border disputes, are no longer ruled by foreigners or oppressors, where citizens are masters in their own house. Sated people can afford to be cosmopolitan; sated people can afford the luxury of condescending to the passions of the hungry. But among the Crimean Tatars, the Kurds, and the Cree, I met the hungry ones, peoples whose very survival will remain at risk until they achieve self-determination, whether in their own nation-state or in someone else's.

sated—satisfied

What's wrong with the world is not nationalism itself. Every people must have a home, every such hunger must be assuaged. What's wrong is the kind of nation, the kind of home that nationalists want to create and the means they use to seek their ends. Wherever I went, I found a struggle going on between those who still believe that a nation should be a home to all—and that race, colour, religion, and creed should be no bar to belonging—and those who want their nation to be home only to their own. It's the battle between the civic and the ethnic nation. I know which side I'm on. I also know which side, right now, is winning.

Issue 2

THE FUTURE OF SOVEREIGNTY

Toby Fletcher

Much of our every day life is guided by widely accepted, but unwritten rules of conduct called manners. For instance, many of us try to get a cup of coffee in the cafeteria before that first class in the morning. Although we may be late, we will line up and wait patiently, as long as it's clear that we are served in the order we arrived. But that quiet patience can quickly turn to anger as we see a late arrival butt into the line ahead of us. Why? What rule or tradition or custom has been broken? There is no sign which states "Line up or else." Who said a bunch of strangers are supposed to line up? Why do we feel this deep sense of injustice, even outrage, when someone is rude or impolite?

Our favourite teachers are often the ones who clearly describe a reasonable set of rules governing how classes will be managed and especially how course work will be evaluated. If the rules are clear, fair, and consistently applied, we usually accept the results of those rules. If it is clear how a paper is to be marked, we usually accept the grade we get because it is clear how the grade was determined. We keenly feel a sense of injustice if we get an unjustified low grade and we often feel a sense of being devalued if we get an unjustified high grade. Teachers and students are happier with clear and fair rules in the classroom.

The principles of proper manners and academic regulations can be generalized from the relationships among individuals to the interactions among nation states. The peoples and nations of the world have been merging more and more into an interdependent global society. Advances in technology have improved communications around the world to the point where "spaceship earth" is a concept most people can readily accept. Supersonic jet travel, live rock concerts played and televised simultaneously on two continents, instantaneous transfers of hugh sums of money from Hong Kong to London to New York to Los Angeles to Tokyo, timely news and information reports from anywhere to anywhere—all of these technological applications have clarified that we live on a small, finite planet. Countries rely on each other for trade and economic stability, for security and peace, and for help and friendship when disasters strike. Unfortunately, world politics have not kept pace with world problems. Only forty years ago, the world and its resources seemed limitless, inexhaustible, yet we had just developed the means to annihilate it. Commenting on the nuclear bomb, Albert Einstein said: "It has changed everything except our way of thinking, and so we drift toward unparalleled catastrophe." We are technically quick and politically slow, with the result that our technology has far exceeded our social and spiritual development.

Our biggest problem is that while the world has become a finite, integrated whole, we continue to think that all political power should be kept at the level of the nation. Global politics are still dominated by a view of the world that prevailed before growth and technology made us so interdependent. In this view, the world is an aggregate of sovereign nations having neither rights nor obligations toward each other. Sovereign-nation thinking relies on "might makes right" and divides the world into East and West, North and South, "us" and "them." People are citizens of the country to which they owe their highest loyalty. We support two standards for humanity— we look after the welfare of our own citizens, but disclaim any political or ethical responsibility for the plight of people in other countries. Just as sovereign-nation thinking sets up boundaries to compassion and responsibility, so it sets up barriers to cooperation around the vital interests which all people, all nations have in common. An intolerable irony: each nation trying to put its immediate interests ahead of the overall interests of the world worsens the global crisis and no one's interests are truly served. Everyone who has a television has seen the images of starving children in Ethiopia. We know there is a problem of properly distributing the food we produce to ensure that everyone is fed. Last year, the world's military expenditures totalled $1,000 billion spent to buy weapons to hurt others and protect ourselves. Imagine potential changes, if even half of those dollars went to help feed the hungry or to improve agricultural methods and technology.

Millions of young people have been killed or maimed in over 150 wars fought since 1945. We are poisoning our air, our water and destroying our habitats. Our situation begs us to change, begs us to rethink our assumptions, to go beyond the sovereign-nation system to conceive a new world order.

Issue 2

Humans are social and cooperative. We are born into groups, nurtured by groups, socialized by groups, and very early on in our lives we begin to influence, create, and develop groups. We form groups for many reasons: to protect ourselves, to gather food, to teach the young, to have fun, to solve problems, to do things. We form families, clans, tribes, churches, nations, provinces, states, countries, empires, dynasties, teams, associations, leagues, companies, corporations, and conglomerates.

If we want the nations and peoples of the world to live together as a peaceful, interactive community, then we need some form of government. Most people, even those who don't like government, accept that to be able to live together socially, we must have a way to make decisions and take action on matters affecting the community as a whole. Many people resent government for being restrictive, cumbersome, and expensive, yet ignore the freedoms and benefits provided.

More and more now we are confronted by problems that threaten all humans, problems which transcend city and state boundaries, problems which require national governments to cooperate and collaborate—two activities which many governments are reluctant to do.

Canadian values of regionalism, interdependence, multiculturalism, and national problem-solving could provide the foundation for a global political framework. Newfoundland, Quebec, Ontario, and British Columbia are very different and distinct components of Canada. Disputes among them are settled at conferences, in the courts, or in their legislatures. It is extremely unlikely that citizens of one province would actually go to war against citizens of another province. It is not that there is no conflict; it is that the conflict is appropriately managed.

Federalism is a system of government in which a number of states form a union but remain independent (or sovereign) in their internal affairs. A federal government can be weak or strong, depending on how responsibilities are divided between central authority and the component states.

The United States of America is an example of a strong central government with fifty relatively weak states. The European Union is an excellent example of fifteen sovereign, diverse states joining together to form a remarkably effective and powerful federal union. Canada's federal system lies somewhere in between.

Countries have associated with each other for a variety of reasons:

1. *geographic*, such as the Organization of American States (OAS), the Organization for African Unity, the Pacific Rim, the Arctic Nations;
2. *colonial*, e.g., the Commonwealth, the Francophonie;
3. *military*, e.g., the North Atlantic Treaty Organization (NATO);
4. *political*, e.g., the Western democracies, the Communist Bloc, the nonaligned countries;
5. *religious*, e.g., Arab League;
6. *economic*, e.g., the Organization of Petroleum Exporting Countries (OPEC), the Group of Seven, the European Union (EU).

Economic partnerships seem to be the most enduring, egalitarian, and effective. Countries seem to be much more willing to surrender certain sovereignty rights for economic gain. The best example of this exchange of sovereignty for economic gain is the European Union. The European Union has become a single market of 340 million highly educated, sophisticated consumers. The EU comprises fifteen remarkable nations: Austria, Belgium, Britain, Denmark, Finland, France, Germany, Greece, Ireland, Italy, Luxembourg, Netherlands, Portugal, Spain, and Sweden. Remarkable because of their ethnic, cultural, political, and historical diversity. Many of these countries have been at war with each other and are still intensely nationalistic, yet they will share a common currency and passport; they will recognize common patents and professional designations; citizens can live, work and move freely anywhere within the community. These countries have established a democratically elected parliament to pass legislation to deal with common problems—for example, their environmental challenges. But each country retains a distinct identity and internal control over social policies, language, culture, and internal security. Together, they are the strongest economic union in the world. Each member nation has sacrificed some sovereignty to the centre of European power, Brussels. But this surrender has nothing to do with altruism or high-minded idealism, but

Issue 2

everything to do with a practical re-definition of self-interest, involving a redrawing of the boundaries of identification to include not only a sense of being French or German or Italian but also a sense of being a member of a united Europe. With this membership comes, of course, much greater clout in the world.

But even with this greater clout, the EU has not been able to do much to stop the savage wars and ethnic rivalry that have torn Yugoslavia apart. At the same time as many countries wish to put aside old grievances and integrate into larger units such as the EU, NAFTA and the Pacific Rim, it is also apparent that many people do not seem to be able to surrender old hatreds. This ethnic nationalism threatens the peace of vast areas, and may yet prove to be a stumbling block to creating a working model of "harmonious diversity."

The EU may not yet speak with a united political voice capable of imposing order on other nations, but its economic achievements have been a magnet that pulls other countries into wanting to join. With the remarkable changes that have taken place in Eastern and Central Europe since the collapse of the Berlin Wall, the EU may well expand to include the former East Bloc economies and provide "associate" status to the newly emerging Baltic nations. The

Review

The Future of Sovereignty

The principles that govern good behaviour among individuals should also be applied to govern the conduct among modern states, Toby Fletcher writes in this essay.

Technological changes have advanced communications and travel so rapidly that it is possible to perceive the world not just as a conglomeration of nations but as a unified "spaceship earth." In this modern world, Fletcher writes, the concept of "nationhood" is old and divisive; people need to put the global agenda ahead of nationalistic goals.

The author proposes that nations should invest in agricultural technology, not weapons, and co-operate to find fair solutions to a host of global problems such as food shortages and starvation, pollution, exploitation of resources and war. As there is government on the municipal, provincial, and federal levels, so too the nations of the earth ought jointly to establish a world government.

According to Fletcher, the global government would be composed of a democratic legislature and a justice system, and impose sanctions against transgressors of international law. A global police force would also be necessary to enforce compliance.

Issue 2

economic incentive has compelled nations to rid themselves of outmoded political organizations and search for new ones.

The success of the EU means that the relative power of the U.S. is declining, although the U.S. still retains enormous economic strength and will remain powerful throughout the 90s. The contest between the old "superpowers" is over but that does not mean that we do not face many multi-lateral, global concerns for which we need global cooperation:

- reducing armed conflict
- managing population growth
- reducing defence budgets
- distributing food
- reducing debt
- disposing of hazardous waste
- protecting the environment
- establishing human rights
- accommodating refugees.

To face these problems, we need world institutions. Although we are a long way from a federated world community of nations, we do have a number of global organizations, e.g., The United Nations, The World Court, The World Bank, The International Monetary Fund (IMF). The U.N. is constantly criticized for being weak and ineffective, yet its strength is in being a forum for even the weakest nation to voice its concerns. The U.N. has survived since 1945 precisely because it relies on consensus, the lowest common denominator, and the single veto. From tribe to feudal kingdom to nation-state, from town to city to metropolitan area, there has been an historical trend to ever larger social groupings. When we transcend sovereign-nation thinking, we become citizens of the world. Global interdependence requires new definitions of who we are and what constitutes self-interest. It may be possible to think of ourselves belonging to a larger unit than a country. Our personal and national interests may best be served through a more sophisticated, cooperative and collaborative relationship among nations.

World federation will not be cheaper nor necessarily more efficient as a bureaucracy, but if we create a world order in which every individual and every nation assumes certain global responsibilities in exchange for certain guaranteed rights, then world federation will be more effective in dealing with our global challenges. Strong economically based associations of nations would reduce the need for elaborate defense systems and free up huge amounts of money which could be used to eliminate hunger and promote health and education. Open, unrestricted communications and news services would reduce totalitarian oppression and provide the opportunity for global human rights.

Minimal world governance means establishing at the global level the principles and institutions we already recognize as fundamental to our social order at the civic, provincial, and national levels. These include:

1. a democratic legislature to develop a body of world law setting out basic rights and obligations;
2. a system of world courts for interpreting those laws in cases of dispute;
3. a set of sanctions to motivate compliance with the laws; and
4. a recognized, fully resourced and effective global police force.

These principles are familiar to everyone and are as relevant on a global scale as on a local one. International trading partnerships, associations, and communities seem to be the best way of establishing collaborative, productive relationships among nations. Clear, just rules of international behaviour are simply our best hope for a peaceful, prosperous future.

ON INHUMANITY

Mitchell Lerner

THE PROBLEM

Ever since Cain raised his hand against his brother Abel, the Earth has witnessed inhumanity, brutality and indifference. Even as I write this essay, newspaper stories and photos convey painful images of the latest atrocity—the Rwandan civil war. In this fight between the Hutu and the Tutsi, the blood of hundreds of thousands of men, women and children has been spilled. More than a million refugees have fled to neighbouring areas, where many are dying of disease.

A million refugees here ... ethnic cleansing there ... the imagery of human tragedy marks both the present and the past. How do we as individuals make sense of distant suffering and death on a massive scale? How do we comprehend what is happening in Rwanda today, Bosnia yesterday, and other places 50 and 80 years ago? How do we think about the magnitude of human evil? Can thinking about what it means to be human ensure our survival?

In this essay, we address the very difficult concepts of genocide, dehumanization and the banality of evil.

GENOCIDE

The term "genocide" comes from the Greek word *genos*, meaning people, and the Latin word, *cide*, referring to killing. Raphael Lemkin coined the term in 1944 to describe the attempt to destroy a nation or an ethnic group either by killing them or by depriving them of the ability to live and procreate. In 1948, the United Nations resolved that genocide means an intent to destroy, in whole or in part, a national, ethnic, racial or religious group:

a)   by killing members of the group;

b)   by causing serious bodily or mental harm to members of the group;

c)   by deliberately inflicting on the group conditions of life calculated to bring about its physical destruction, in whole or in part;

> "Thinking is the ... work of a species that bears responsibility for its own survival ... to carry on thinking [is] the authority by which we survive in human form."
>
> Hannah Arendt
> *Life of the Mind*

d)   by imposing measures intended to prevent births within the group;

e)   by forcibly transferring children of the group to another group.

Over the years, genocide has come to mean a form of one-sided mass killing in which a state or another authority intends to destroy a group, as that group and membership in it are defined by the perpetrator.[1]

This definition is important in several ways. First, it acknowledges that there is no reciprocity in genocide: it is not a war, although it may and often does occur in the midst of war, hiding in the **machinations** of war.

machinations—hostile manoeuvres

Second, genocide means that all group members are targets, regardless of individual characteristics. Einstein and Freud were Jews and, as such, didn't have the right to exist in the Nazi universe. Not long ago, the Soviets and the Americans pointed weapons of mass destruction at each other, putting humanity at great risk. The enormous power of nuclear weapons makes possible the indiscriminate destruction of entire national groups, and allows us to conceive of the enemy as an entire people.

Third, those who attempt genocide regard specific populations as dispensable. The notion that entire groups of people are disposable demeans the value of human life and negates all the spiritual, religious, and cultural aspirations of the species.

The indiscriminate destruction of an entire people is genocidal, and the genocidal illusion is that we can become more pure by eradicating those who are different from ourselves. Genocide is the worst outcome of labelling and stereotyping. Blinded by prejudice, we cannot see or hear the other as they are. This, then, is the genocidal mentality—irrational, merciless, making no exceptions.

This century's first instance of genocide occurred in 1915, when the ruling government of the Ottoman empire, the Young Turks, attempted to create a new order for their state. Their ideology of Pan-Turanianism required that all of Turkey be of one religion: Muslim. The government of Enver and Talaat perceived the several million

---

[1] *Genocide Watch.* Helen Fein, Ed., Yale, 1992.

Issue 2

Armenians who lived in the eastern Ottoman Empire as a threat, and secretly declared them as undesirable and expendable. The Turkish Armenians were a cultured, civilized, creative, educated people who had expected to receive some form of sovereignty within the Ottoman empire.

Instead, hiding behind the smokescreen of World War I, the Turkish government implemented a bureaucratic system to destroy the Armenians. After allying with Germany, the Turkish military invaded Armenian population centres, conducted deportations, and brutally slaughtered approximately 1.5 million Armenians. To this day, the Turkish government denies the extent of the killings, and keeps many of its documents sealed to investigators. Armenians around the world and others continue to urge political leaders to acknowledge the genocide that prefigured and predated the Nazi Holocaust by some 20 years. They contend that the present Turkish government, by not acknowledging the destruction of a people, is attempting to dispense with historical fact the way its predecessors dispensed with Armenian souls.

❖

Since 1945, at least 22 documented examples fit within the definition of genocide. The estimated number of deaths, between three

Inmates at a Nazi concentration camp.

and nine million people, does not include the 1.5 million Armenians or the six million Jews who died in the Nazi Holocaust.

"The most painful question of genocide," write authors Chalk and Jonassohn, "is, How is it possible for people to kill other people on such a massive scale? The answer seems to be that it is not possible. At least not as long as the potential victims are perceived as people. We have no evidence that genocide was ever performed on a group of equals. The victims must not only *not* be equals, but also clearly defined as something less than fully human."[2]

When European pioneers haphazardly slaughtered North American aboriginals, when the Khmer Rouge campaigned to slaughter the urban population of Cambodia, when white slave traders ripped apart black families on the Ivory Coast, when the Hutu macheted the Tutsi, what must these individuals have been thinking? What understanding of another human being must go on in the head of a person who is shredding, burning, stabbing or enslaving human beings?

Chalk and Jonassohn raise an important and essential point. It is *not* possible for genocide to occur unless the perpetrator regards all members of the target group as less than human. The victims must be dehumanized. Since dehumanization is a process that happens over time, it contains enough warnings that it can be stopped.

DEHUMANIZATION

Hitler's "Final Solution," the Nazi's clinical term for mass murder, involved the systematic slaughter of six million Jews. It was designed to eliminate an entire people by using the efficient mechanisms of an industrial culture. The Holocaust took place in the midst of a culture that was rich in art, music, philosophy and science. The term *Holocaust* is reserved for this particular tragedy of the twentieth century, which was the ultimate ideological genocide. It refers to the period from January 1933, when Hitler seized power on a platform of racial purity and superiority, to May 1945, when the Nazi regime dissolved.

---

[2] *The History and Sociology of Genocide.* Frank Chalk and Kurt Jonassohn. Yale, 1990.

German statistics indicate that 5.8 million Jews were murdered. The recognized figure of non-Jewish civilians murdered is six million, including Gypsies, Serbs, Polish intelligentsia, resistance fighters, German opponents of Nazism, homosexuals, Jehovah's Witnesses, habitual criminals and the disabled.

European Jewish culture was destroyed, along with a host of other "less-than-humans." German technical specialists engineered mass-murder camps, known as concentration camps, and built special killing apparatus. In these devices, which included gas chambers, crematoria and burial pits, the destruction of a people transpired. Hundreds of thousands of Nazis actively participated in the ghettoizing, deportation and mass killings of the Jews, which went on for six years. Fathers, mothers, grandparents and 1.5 million children were sent up in flames.

Like all genocides, dehumanization was a necessary precondition of the Holocaust. Dehumanization involves fear of the other. Like the body's immune system, which attacks foreign elements, the mind seems to attack foreign ideas and ways before it can understand them. The process of dehumanization, of deconstructing another, is a way of asserting one's own identity. But being unlike the other does not empower you to deny those others their existence. The essence of civilization—the essence of a social contract—is the acknowledgment of shared basic rights. And none is more fundamental than that of existence. Dehumanization, then, is the process by which we devalue the other and soon remove their right to exist.

Possessed of a long militaristic, patriotic, nationalistic history, the Germans felt humiliated by their loss in World War I and by the excessive demands of the post-war Treaty of Versailles. By **promulgating** theories that the Germans belonged to a "master race," the Nazis redefined dehumanization and made it into a high art. The fiercely proud and **narcissistic** tendencies in German culture were exploited to the hilt by the Nazi propaganda machine. The Germans scapegoated and stereotyped their targetted group, the Jews, as inferiors and a national threat, and instituted laws to curtail their rights. The long history of anti-Semitism in Europe simplified the process.

promulgating—promoting

narcissistic—self-obsessed

The Nazi illusion of grandeur and perfection threatens our understanding of civilization, as formulated from ancient times. Civilization does not mean that some are superior and some inferior, or that some are masters and others are slaves. Civilization de-

Issue 2

mands that we accept others as part of a broader human community; that others are different, not less than; that others are strange, not threatening. Civilization, like marriage, requires compromise. But for Hitler, his thugs, and the passive European population, there was no compromise.

banality—trite predictability

THE BANALITY OF EVIL

We told them not to be afraid, we wouldn't do anything to them, they should just stand in front of the wall. But it was taken for granted among us that they should be killed. So when somebody said, 'Shoot,' I swung around and pulled the trigger, three times, on automatic fire. I remember the little girl with the red dress hiding behind her granny.

One sunny morning in June 1992, Borislav Herak and two other Serb nationalist soldiers gunned down a Muslim family found hiding in a basement. Later, from a jail cell, he described many crimes he had committed to a reporter from the *New York Times*. "(H)is account was offered in a matter-of-fact manner, and always with a keen attention to detail. As he shifted between one killing and another, and between rapes, the young Serb gave the names of many of his victims. He described where they were killed, what they were wearing, and what they said immediately before they died."

What does a soldier think of as he carries out the genocidal policies of his government? The soldier quoted above, like many others, seemed to be obeying orders and following the crowd, with the rules around him laid down by the circumstances of war. Where was his conscience? Why do so few people involved in genocide recognize their own ability to take a moral stand and oppose evil? The soldiers doing the hacking in Rwanda, the rape in Bosnia, the slaughter of "non-desirables" anywhere, go against conscience by participating in thoughtlessness as much as they participate in genocide.

The philosopher Hannah Arendt, whose studies of totalitarianism remain central for all scholarship on this topic, has made a simple but startling observation: there is no great demon who acts as a mastermind behind evil. Evil comes out of the hearts of ordinary people who prefer to obey rather than think. This, then, is the banality of evil. Destruction arises not from some demonic vision but from ordinary thoughtlessness, indifference and silence. Some argue that historical precedents, economic conditions or cultural conflict cause people to be seduced by what appear to be passionate but simplistic solutions. And while it may be easier to get swept away by the crowd, we need courage to stand up against it.

SOME CONCLUSIONS

Many follow the crowd, while a few say "No." Even in a world of horror there are some who act according to their conscience, such as, the righteous people of Le Chambon sur Lignes, France, who saved 5,000 Jewish lives during World War II.

For you and me, genocidal events may seem to defy ordinary language and cause us to disbelieve the truth. They may seem so irrational and incredible that we may prefer to ignore, doubt or deny the documented facts. The numbing effect of the incomprehensible may inhibit the very thoughtfulness that we need in order to resist. As hard as it is to do, we should not let the experience of the unthinkable overwhelm our ability to fasten to the truth.

All the testimonies of survivors; all the elaborate words, ideas and structures of scholars attempting to frame the subject; all the memoirs written to recall the slain and condemn the injustice—all these are words in a vocabulary of responsibility to the human family. We owe it to the victims of genocide, to each other, and to our children to respond with thoughtfulness, conscience and spirit.

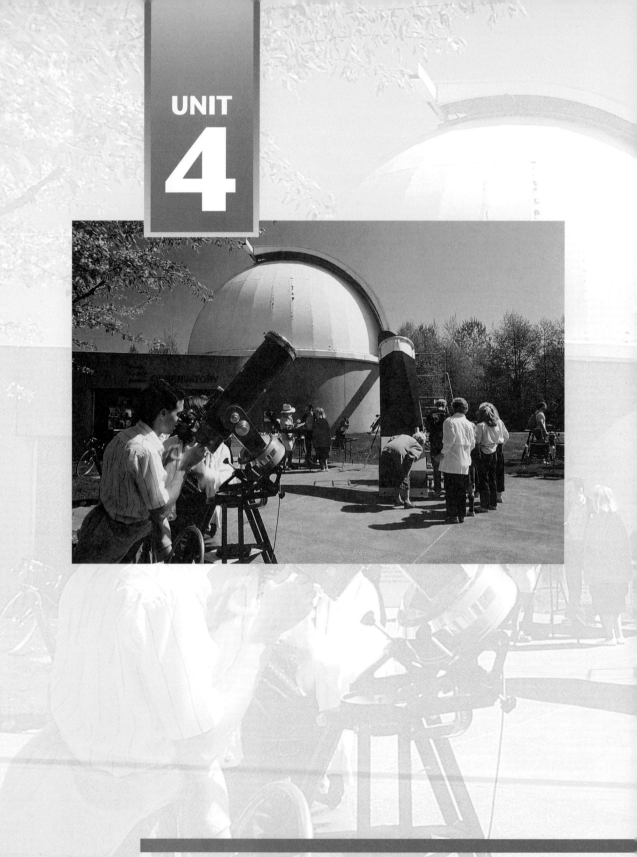

PERCEPTIONS OF THE NATURAL WORLD

ISSUE 1:
Science and the Natural World

ISSUE 2:
The Illusion of Certainty

SCIENCE AND THE NATURAL WORLD

It seems to me that those sciences are vain and full of error which do not spring from experiment, the source of all certainty.

Leonardo da Vinci

I cannot believe that God plays dice with the cosmos.

Albert Einstein

THE PATH OF SCIENTIFIC DEVELOPMENT

Tom Olien

*T*he three primary activities involved in scientific development are (1) observing; (2) structuring the information; and (3) discovering or creating an underlying mechanism.

Inherent in each activity is a relentless (or an on-going) process of reflection, checking equipment, correcting observations, updating technique, confirming speculation and questioning theory. The result is the process shown in the chart on the next page. This process parallels the steps of the scientific method, the discipline of curiosity used by individual scientists.

Observing

Scientific activity starts with observation. Initially, observations were limited to the five human senses. We now live in a world with powerful extensions to our primary senses. A simple set of binoculars drastically changes our ability to identify a bird in the woods or to see the stars and planets with a clarity that the most astute astronomer of four hundred years ago could not imagine.

Many instruments measure features of the universe that go beyond our senses. A voltameter measures electrical potential, a feature of an electric circuit unseen by human eyes except in the high values that produce a dangerous shock. A compass can detect the direction of the earth's "invisible" magnetic field, while other instruments measure its strength. The Herculean forces between the rock faces of sliding continental plates can now be measured, as can the temperatures of outer space or the heat in the core of a nuclear reactor. Today, in most industrialized countries there is a significant industry associated with the development, manufacture, sales and operation of scientific instrumentation.

Every area of scientific observation requires a unique "objectivity." Scientific "objectivity" should allow one to "see" what is really there and not what one hopes to "see." The ability to achieve this ulti-

The Path of Scientific Development

The Process

OBSERVING:

- Instrumentation that extends our senses
- skill in specific techniques
- patience and "objectivity"

STRUCTURING AND USING THE INFORMATION

- patterns and laws
- applied mathematical tools of analysis
- empirical rules for design and extension

DISCOVERING/CREATING AN UNDERLYING MECHANISM

- a creative leap beyond reasoning
- a simple, elegant unifying principle
- constantly creating new possibilities and being tested against new observations

mate abstract objectivity is at best tainted by human frailty and at worst perverted by the massive personal, social, economic or ideological consequences of the impact of a given observation. In spite of these complications, the process of scientific observation usually converges to the point where all competent observers agree that they "see" the same thing in the same set of circumstances.

Structuring the Information

Once a body of data has been accumulated from reliable observation, the next task is to attempt to make some sense and order out of the data. Science assumes that every action follows some pattern, usually some cause and effect connection. Sometimes the connections are fairly simple and obvious. Two of you may just manage to push a stalled car out of an intersection, but six of you could move it much more easily and quickly. The connection between force and motion is fairly obvious.

The Development of Science

The three primary activities involved in scientific development are:
(1) observing;
(2) structuring the information; and
(3) discovering or creating an underlying mechanism.

Issue 1

The search for patterns or laws is a long-term goal of science. The methods include cataloguing samples, making diagrams, lists and graphs. Statistical analysis and other powerful mathematical tools are also used. The details of a discovery may be tucked away in seemingly random data or "noise." Finding patterns in such circumstances is not unlike the capacity of the human ear to pick out a faint cry for help in the midst of the roar of a hurricane.

At this stage of observation we may have some very useful rules for how things work, but we do not know why they work as they do. There is no obvious fundamental mechanism, only rules, often very complex and arbitrary ones connecting certain facts and events. There is still a need for a unifying principle to simplify and make sense of the regulations.

Discovering or Creating an Underlying Mechanism

The discovery of grand themes and fundamental theories is the crowning achievement of the creative human mind in the arena of science. The theories of universal gravitation, relativity, evolution, continental drift and the role of DNA in genetics are examples of underlying mechanisms.

These themes did not emerge from reason alone. Like an artist, scientists must step beyond the structured data and rules. Typically a person or a group makes an educated guess, an intuitive leap, that opens a new possibility and a new way of thinking. The genius of the process of science is that it doesn't stop with a good guess, but sets to testing it thoroughly. The creative guesses that were wrong have long since disappeared leaving us only the heroic tales and legacies of the ones that worked.

A fundamental theory (such as gravity) is often simple. It is seen as an elegant and aesthetically pleasing unifying principle. Looking back, most people would say it is obvious; it looks so right and natural. From examples in celestial mechanics, genetics and neurology we can see how these three stages develop.

THE PATH TO AN UNDERLYING MECHANISM IN CELESTIAL MECHANICS

Global navigation in the fifteenth century revived interest in the stars and planets. Little change had been made to the Ptolemaic system of the universe from second-century Rome. The Ptolemaic theory held that the earth was the center of the universe and that the earth was at rest with no rotation or motion. The sun, the stars and the planets rotated around the earth. The system was adequate for the needs of the time (it worked as a system of navigation) but was very complex.

Nicholas Copernicus (1473–1543)

Copernicus suggested that the system would be simpler if we treated the sun as the centre of the system of planets and rotated the earth daily to allow for the rising and setting of the sun and moon and stars. It seems obvious now, but was not in the context of his time. Religious dogma and our own ego demanded that we see ourselves and our earth as the pinnacle of God's Creation, and thus the centre of it all. But the simplicity and elegance of the Copernican suggestion was convincing and encouraged a new wave of thinking.

Galileo made use of the newly developed optical lenses to make a telescope. His observations of the rotation of the sun and of moons revolving around the planet Jupiter did much to challenge the dogma that had kept a static world view dominant for so many centuries. He was also instrumental in developing the experimental method and theories of terrestrial mechanics that would be vital for the next leap.

Galileo (1564–1642)

In the meantime, Tycho Brahe, a Danish astronomer, had made meticulous observations of the heavens. His observations were extensive and some one hundred times more accurate than previous observations, pushing the very limits of accuracy of the unaided eye. Johann Kepler, a German mathematician and astronomer, applied his skills to this new accurate data to develop the three laws of planetary motion. These laws correctly described and predicted the motion of the earth, moon and planets about the sun, but lacked any explanation of why they should be so.

Issue 1

The Path of Scientific Development

Celestial Mechanics

OBSERVING

- **Copernicus** (1473–1543): an idea—earth not the centre.

- **Tycho Brahe** (1546–1601): an observatory—new precision of information about planets.

- **Galileo** (1564–1642): used telescope to observe rotation of sun and the revolution of the moons of Jupiter.

STRUCTURING AND USING THE INFORMATION

- **Kepler** (1571–1630): develops three laws of planetary motion. (1) the orbits of the planets around the sun are elliptical, with the sun at one focus; (2) the line drawn from the sun to a planet sweeps out equal areas in equal times; (3) the square of the period of the planet is proportional to the cube of the radius.

DISCOVERING/CREATING AN UNDERLYING MECHANISM

- **Newton** (1642–1727): the law of universal gravitation. All objects in the universe attract each other. The force increases with the product of their masses and decreases with their distance apart.

$$F = \frac{Gm_1m_2}{r^2}$$

Isaac Newton (1642–1727)

Issue 1

The explanation came from the leap made by Isaac Newton. Galileo had described the action of gravity for earthbound objects such as stones and cannon balls. The leap that Newton made was to ask if gravity actually extended to the moon. Again, it may seem obvious, but it represented radical new thinking at the time, and only a few decades earlier would have been ruled out as heresy by both church and science. Newton calculated and found it worked for the moon. In fact, it worked for all the planets, with the sun as the gravitational centre of the solar system. Kepler's laws could then be deduced as a consequence of universal gravitation rather than as a separate set of rules for our planetary system.

The mechanism of universal gravitation could be applied to all objects on the surface of the earth and beyond. It explained the pattern of the tides and allowed for accurate predictions, such as the date of return of Halley's comet and the existence of the planet Neptune, finally observed in 1846.

THE PATH TO AN UNDERLYING MECHANISM IN GENETICS

Genetics presents a current example of the path of scientific development. Mendel is credited as the father of genetics based on his systematic observation and explanation of the patterns of genetic inheritance. The physical location of the "inheritance material" was found in the chromosomes. These appear under a microscope as

The Path of Scientific Development

Genetics

IDEA—organisms "inherit" characteristics of the parent

OBSERVING

- **Mendel** (1822–1884)—observed the inheritance pattern in peas

STRUCTURING AND USING THE INFORMATION

- introduced the basic form of the laws of genetics
- many people use the laws of genetics to improve grains and livestock and to understand and control some genetic diseases

DISCOVERING/CREATING AN UNDERLYING MECHANISM

- **Watson and Crick**—the DNA molecule reveals the code that governs all genetics

Issue 1

small sausage-like objects within the nucleus of the cells of an organism. But there are a small number of chromosomes and a very large number of genetic features for even the simplest organism. The gene is the package of information coded for a particular characteristic. The sense of what form this "gene" could take was unknown.

Black box—a term scientists use to describe a situation in which we know essentially what something does, but we don't yet comprehend how it operates (like machinery covered up by a black box).

For over half a century increasingly complex rules of genetics were developed and applied to improvements of grains and livestock and to understanding of hereditary diseases. But the gene itself remained a mystery. The fundamental mechanism driving genetics was an illusory black box with many patterns of input and output understood, many more not understood and the action within the black box unknown. It was the study of nucleic acids, culminating in the illumination of the structure of the DNA molecule by Watson and Crick in 1953, that opened the black box and caused the revolution in genetics. Just as mechanical engineers, armed with the foundations of mechanics, generated the industrial revolution in a previous era, now genetic engineers equipped with an understanding of the fundamental genetic structure are developing tools and techniques that can systematically control the features of plants, animals and human beings. The implications are exciting and frightening but with the basic mechanism understood there is no turning back the exploration.

THE PATH TO AN UNDERLYING MECHANISM IN NEUROLOGY

Neurology is the study of the nervous system and encompasses many domains of study: anatomy, physiology of the neuron, psychology, psychiatry, neural pathology. Each area has many rules and laws that can be used to predict actions in response to specific causes or stimuli. The drug *curare* was used by South American Natives on poisoned arrows. We now know that this drug blocks the transmission of nerve impulses to muscles and thus leads to paralysis. Our clear understanding of its action allows us to use curare in controlled ways during major surgery to avoid muscle reflex. Psychiatry has used electro-shock and drugs to control certain extreme psychiatric illnesses and has models of the actions of the brain that suggest why these methods are effective.

Issue 1

The Path of Scientific Development

Neurology

IDEA—the basis of perception and consciousness is associated with the electrical activity of the brain

OBSERVING

- **Eccles**—physiology of individual neurons - the action potential
- **Sherrington**—physiology of nerve sequences involved in reflexes

STRUCTURING AND USING THE INFORMATION

- **Penfield**—memory triggered at specific sites within the brain
- **Edelman**—groups of neurons form the basis of perception

DISCOVERING/CREATING AN UNDERLYING MECHANISM

- no single simple process is able to present itself as the fundamental operating mechanism of the brain

But the field of neurology is full of seeming contradictions. Wilder Penfield in working with epileptic patients was able to stimulate specific points in the brain and have memories brought to consciousness. Thus, specific memories seem to be located in a specific place in the brain. But it is also known that brain injuries to these areas do not necessarily remove the memory, but rather it seems to be stored like a hologram within a large domain of the brain.

In spite of all we know about the brain, all the rules and patterns we have sorted out so far, we do not have a clue about the fundamental mechanism of the brain. From the neck up we are wrapped in mystery. And so we stumble along, making the best we can with the rules we have obtained so far, and looking enthusias-

Issue 1

tically to the time we will break-through to a clear view of this most intriguing of all fundamental mechanisms.

THE ILLUSION OF FUNDAMENTAL MECHANISMS

The illusion that the power of a few fundamental mechanisms holds out to us is that we will be able to explain the universe fully. But again we are forced to let in newer and grander theories that reject previous notions or treat previous theories as a subset of a larger picture.

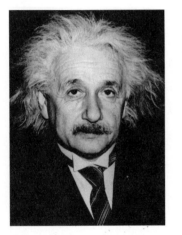

Albert Einstein

Only a century ago it was suggested that the physics of the day could explain all basic physical phenomena. Within twenty years, the discovery of features within the atom itself and the observance of activities taking place at close to the speed of light showed that classical mechanics and electromagnetism did not apply at the atomic level or at very high speeds. Einstein's Special Theory of Relativity thus superseded Newtonian Mechanics, not making it wrong, but limiting it to objects of ordinary size and speeds. Fundamental mechanisms still beg the question of why they are there in the first place. Newton's law of universal gravitation does not really explain what gravity is but just how it acts.

An even more subtle illusion is hidden in the almost religious belief that the methods of science will answer all life's questions and eventually allow for a more stable and satisfying life on the planet. Many of the noted physicists of the twentieth century were essentially mystics. They allowed the possibility of a dimension to human life experience that was not accessible by the methods of their science. That doesn't mean they invoked God or some outside mystical force to explain the problems of their science. But neither did they expect science to explain the mystical elements of their unique life experience. Science seeks only to illuminate the mechanisms of repeatable phenomena in all domains of our universe. As for ultimate questions about the meaning of life, science may provide clues but no answers.

Issue 1

THE MATTER MYTH

Paul Davies

Scientists are really quite nice people. Unfortunately science, and its practitioners, have a rather bad public image. Partly this stems from the problems of sinister science—weapons of mass destruction, polluting technology, unethical medicine, and so on. But there is a deeper reason for the widespread antipathy. It is connected with the underlying philosophy of science itself.

For three hundred years science has been dominated by extremely **mechanistic** thinking. According to this view of the world, all physical systems are regarded as basically machines. Whether we are talking about the solar system, the planet's ecology or the behaviour of a human being, the machine image is usually seized upon as the appropriate **paradigm**. By studying the components of these machines, scientists aim to understand how they work. Central to this philosophy is the belief that complicated physical systems are merely the sum of their parts, so that understanding the parts serves to explain the whole. This is known as reductionism, and has been popular for two and a half millennia, since the Greek philosopher Democritus proclaimed that the world consisted of nothing but atoms moving in a void.

mechanistic—machine-like

paradigm—framework or model

The dominance of the mechanistic view of nature has provoked a sharp backlash from nonscientists, who regard science as a threatening and alienating activity. Not only does it rob the universe of its essential mystery, it seems to reduce people to mere automata, and nature to a set of mathematical rules. The scientist is portrayed as power-crazy, seeking to gain control over nature through the manipulation of these "machines."

During the last few years, however, mechanistic thinking has attracted some bitter criticism from within the scientific community itself. This is largely a result of advances in the physical sciences, such as chaos theory and information technology, that paint a very different picture of physical reality. To understand these significant developments, it is first necessary to know something of the history of the ideas involved.

... secrecy strikes at the very root of what science is, and what it is for. It is not possible to be a scientist unless you believe that it is good to learn. It is not good to be a scientist, and it is not possible, unless you think that it is of the highest value to share your knowledge, to share it with anyone who is interested. It is not possible to be a scientist unless you believe that the knowledge of the world, and the power which this gives, is a thing which is of intrinsic value to humanity, and are willing to take the consequences.

J. Robert Oppenheimer

Esoteric—intended or understood by only a small group.

The triumph of mechanistic thought was achieved in the early nineteenth century, with an astonishing statement by the French mathematician Pierre Laplace. (It was Laplace who responded to Napoleon's famous query about the role of God in nature with the dismissive phrase, "I have no need of this hypothesis.") Imagine, wrote Laplace, a superbeing who could know the exact state of the universe in complete detail at some instant of time. Assuming the superbeing is capable of unlimited computing power, it could use this knowledge to calculate the entire future of the universe, and also infer its past, in every intricate detail.

Laplace arrived at his startling conclusion by appealing to the laws of mechanics formulated over a century before by Isaac Newton. The form of these laws is such that, given the position and motion of a particle of matter at some initial moment, its future motion is uniquely determined, and therefore computable, at least in principle. This unswerving faith in determinism—the belief that the future is contained in the present, and so can be figured out from a careful analysis of the present—underlies a key element of the scientific enterprise, which is prediction. The power of prediction is immense: astronomers can predict future eclipses, artillery officers can predict the point of impact of a shell, and so on.

Newton's own image of the universe was that of a gigantic precision clockwork mechanism, with each material body faithfully conforming to eternal mathematical laws. Laplace extended this idea to encompass every atom in the universe. He concluded that if each tiny particle was locked in the deterministic embrace of a vast and lumbering cosmic clockwork, then everything that ever happened, that is happening now, and that ever will happen, is fixed since time immemorial by Newton's laws. The entire cosmos, he was convinced, slavishly follows a preordained pathway of evolution to a unique destiny already written into its component parts.

Esoteric though they may seem, such topics were not confined to the rarefied strata of philosophical debate. It was from the doctrine of mechanistic thought so starkly expressed by Laplace that the European Industrial Revolution sprang. The view that the world is a machine ruled by mathematical certainty encouraged the belief that nature could be controlled and manipulated by understanding the laws of mechanics. And by focusing on the mechanistic aspect of physical systems, the Victorian industrialists elevated the value of

Milky Way: gigantic clockwork mechanism or living organism?

material substance. Mechanistic thinking led inevitably to materialistic thinking: matter was all. Real value was that which attached to material stuff. Thus wealth was measured in bars of gold, tons of coal or acres of land.

The legacy of materialism and mechanism still permeate our society. The machine image is everywhere: the political machine, the economic machine, the weather machine. Even life itself has been mechanized. Richard Dawkins, the eloquent biologist, likes to refer to people as "gene machines." In the 1930s the Oxford philosopher

Gilbert Ryle coined the phrase "the ghost in the machine" to reflect our impression that we possess nonmaterial minds that infuse our mechanistic bodies with the spark of free will. But generations of psychologists have sought to exorcise that unruly ghost. The title of a recent British television documentary about behaviour says it all: it was called *The Mind Machine.*

I have little doubt that much of the alienation and demoralization that people feel in our so-called scientific age stems from the bleak sterility of mechanistic thought. How often does one hear the plaintive cry: "We can do nothing, we are only cogs in a machine!"?

But how secure is the mechanistic paradigm? Physics, the science from which the philosophies of mechanism and materialism have sprung, has undergone some convulsive transformations in the past few decades. Einstein's theory of relativity undermined Newton's picture of space and time, while quantum mechanics has dramatically affected our view of the nature of matter. No longer can atoms be viewed as tiny billiard balls with well-defined locations and paths in space. The emerging picture of the microcosms is an Alice-in-Wonderland realm populated by fleeting, **nebulous** entities and ghostly patterns of pulsating energy. Crucially, quantum physics has uncovered a world that is fundamentally indeterministic and unpredictable. Newton's precision clockwork has been exposed as a myth: matter is inherently rebellious and nonconformist.

nebulous—vague

More recently, the theory of chaos and the study of physical systems capable of spontaneous self-organization have reinforced the new perspective of nature. Far from being imprisoned in a predestined pattern of change, the universe possesses a genuine openness, freedom to explore alternative pathways of evolution. In some ways the physical world more closely resembles a living organism than a machine. It is ironical that just as biologists are busy reducing life to a mechanism, so physicists are going the opposite way. Curiously the image of the universe as a living organism was common in many ancient cultures, but was cast aside by the ascendancy of physical science. Now that softer view of nature is in the process of being recaptured. History is turning full circle.

Physicists have come to recognize that inert, clodlike matter can, under the right circumstances, almost take on a life of its own. Certain physical and chemical systems have been discovered that display uncanny qualities of cooperation, or organize themselves sponta-

Issue 1

neously and unpredictably into complex forms. These systems are still subject to physical laws, but laws that permit a more flexible and innovative type of behaviour than the old mechanistic view of nature ever suggested.

Gone are the days when matter and energy were the hard currencies of physical theory. The new physics emphasizes instead the key role of concepts like information flow, complexity and organization in the behaviour of physical systems. Physicists no longer regard the world as merely a collection of particles being pushed and pulled by forces. They also perceive an elaborate network of creative activity. Reductionism has little place in this picture, for complex, chaotic or self-organizing systems are clearly more than the sum of their parts.

It is a perspective that has penetrated the new **cosmology** too. The evidence suggests that the universe was born in a state of almost total featurelessness, and has progressed, step by step, into the elaborate system we see today. The staggering richness and diversity of physical forms and structures that adorn the cosmos were not implanted at the outset but have emerged, spontaneously, in a long and complex sequence of creative, self-organizing processes.

cosmology—the study of the universe

This sweeping new view of nature will undoubtedly have profound implications for the way we view ourselves, and our relationship to the universe we inhabit. It is already being reflected in the manner that science impacts on the world's economy. The old material-based industries—mining, primary production, heavy engineering—are everywhere in decline. The wealth-creating industries of the future are systems-based and information-based. Today's so-called material scientists concern themselves with creating new structures on a molecular scale to produce "smart matter"—systems with novel qualities to perform tasks we never dreamt of. ... The indicators are clear: in the twenty-first century real power will lie with those nations and institutions that control and manipulate information, not material resources.

The death of materialism will mean some painful adjustments in the decades ahead, but it also offers an exhilarating challenge. Mechanistic thought has undoubtedly had a stifling effect on the human spirit. Liberation from this centuries-old straitjacket will enable human beings to reintegrate themselves into the physical world of which they are a part.

Issue 1

It has been fashionable among scientists to suppose that mind is just an incidental and insignificant quirk of evolutionary fate, a meaningless accident in an ocean of blind and purposeless forces. As we move to embrace twenty-first century science, consciousness will come to be seen as a fundamental property of a generally creative cosmos. No longer will human beings feel marginalized—even trivialised—when set against the awesome outworking of cosmic forces. We live in a universe that has the emergence of conscious organisms written into its laws at the most basic level. There is no ghost in the machine, not because the ghost is dead, but because there is no machine.

THE ILLUSION OF CERTAINTY

What men really want is not knowledge but certainty.

Bertrand Russell

Science cannot solve the ultimate mystery of Nature. And it is because in the last analysis we ourselves are part of the mystery we are trying to solve.

Max Plank

HUMAN REPRODUCTION AND THE LIMITATIONS OF SCIENCE

Brian Doyle

*T*he headline reads "Women trade eggs in try for baby." The article describes how a private clinic in Toronto had arranged for women who were unable to afford in vitro fertilization to give their eggs to couples who needed them. In exchange, the couple who received the eggs would pay for the woman's in vitro treatment. The thought of selling human eggs horrified some people, while others argued that it was simple economics; that is the way a "laissez-faire" market works. There is always a buyer for every seller.

The controversy surrounding the new reproductive technologies (NRTs) illustrates the difficulties we face at the frontiers of science. What principles should be used to regulate NRTs? Should society play a role in what is usually a personal decision made by an individual or couple?

NRTs are of enormous benefit to infertile couples (couples who have tried unsuccessfully to conceive for two years). The reasons for infertility are many, but may include damage to the woman's reproductive organs or an extremely low sperm count for the man. Thousands of women around the world have been able to have children because of NRTs. Before we can deal with the issues and questions surrounding NRTs, it is useful to review some of the recent developments in NRTs.

WHAT ARE THE NRTs?

Artificial or Therapeutic Insemination

Artificial insemination is used for couples when the man's sperm cannot fertilize the egg and for women who want to have a child without a man. This process involves placing the man's sperm into the woman's upper vagina using a tube or syringe.

The couple may choose to use donated sperm, if the man's sperm is not viable or if he carries a genetic defect. The donated sperm may come from a sperm bank or from a specific individual.

In Vitro Fertilization

Normally when a woman's egg is released from her ovary, it travels down the fallopian tube to her uterus. If it is fertilized along the way, it will become attached to the uterus wall and start to develop. However, if the tube between the ovary and uterus is damaged, the egg may not make it to the uterus. In this situation, the couple may consider in vitro fertilization. This medical procedure involves a number of steps. First, several eggs are taken from the woman's ovaries. These eggs are placed in a petri dish and given nutrients to keep them healthy. Then the man's sperm is placed on the petri dish and the eggs are fertilized. The fertilized eggs are carefully monitored for two to three days and then several are placed inside the woman's uterus. This is called embryo transfer.

Surrogacy

If a woman cannot have the embryo transferred into her own uterus or does not want to be pregnant, she might make an agreement with a surrogate to bear her child. The embryo is transferred into this woman's uterus, where it will develop until the surrogate mother gives birth to the child. The child is then "returned" to the genetic mother.

Egg Donation

Sometimes a woman cannot produce a viable egg that can be fertilized and develop. This inability may be due to damage to her reproductive system. In this situation she may receive an egg from a donor—sometimes her sister or another woman who is willing to donate an egg.

Pre-Implantation Diagnosis

This new technique allows the physician to check the embryos for genetic defects before implanting them in a woman's uterus. Genetically defective embryos can then be screened out.

Issue 2

Prenatal Diagnosis

To some extent it is now possible to determine the genetic "health" of the fetus before it is born. This often involves screening the genes of the potential parents to determine whether either parent is a "carrier" of a disease-linked gene that may be passed on to the child. For example, a couple undergoing genetic screening may find that they are both carriers for **Tay-Sachs disease**. Further tests can determine whether a fetus has the disease. Although there are thousands of genetically linked diseases, only some are detectable.

Tay-Sachs disease: a genetically linked enzyme deficiency resulting in nervous system damage and early death.

Of course, all these technologies have ethical implications. To sort out this new and complicated area, the federal government formed the Royal Commission on the New Reproductive Technologies in 1989. The Commission investigated NRTs and consulted Canadians about their concerns. In their final report, they took a practical approach to the ethical issues surrounding the NRTs, identifying seven guiding principles.

High tech comes to the aid of parents-to-be.

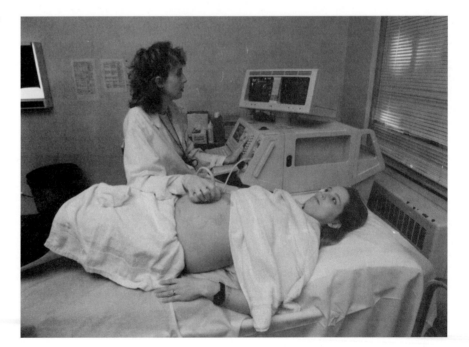

GUIDING PRINCIPLES

1. Individual Autonomy

People should be free to choose how they want to live their own lives, as long as they do not harm others. This principle implies that people have control over their own bodies. For example, a person who is receiving treatment must consent to that treatment and be informed of the different treatments available.

This simple and straightforward principle limits society's ability to interfere with the individual. However, some examples reveal problems with even this simple guideline. Should we allow individuals to use the prenatal diagnostic techniques to determine the sex of the fetus? Some couples may use this information to select the sex of their children, aborting the fetus if it is not the sex that they desire. Some people have argued that a woman has the right to know all available information about the fetus and has the right to abort that fetus if she chooses. However, some prenatal clinics no longer reveal the sex of the fetus to expectant mothers because of concern over sex selection and abortion.

Is sex selection widespread in Canada? Apparently not. The Commission found that just over 70 percent of those people considering having children did not express a preference for a girl or boy.

2. Appropriate Use of Resources

The members of a society must decide how they will use their resources to satisfy the needs of that society. One must weigh the costs of a new technical procedure against the benefits that it will provide. Technologies that have little benefit to society should not be funded, while we need to fund technologies that do provide benefits. For example, the NRTs were developed to help infertile couples have children. Many people have argued that too much time and money have been spent on developing the technology to deal with the problem of infertility and not enough on determining the causes and working on the prevention of infertility. Sexually transmitted diseases, smoking, workplace and environmental pollution, drug and alcohol abuse and poor nutrition are all factors linked to reduced fertility or infertility. Perhaps more money should be spent on programs that address these practical problems, and less on the expensive but glamorous process of developing and providing reproductive technologies.

Issue 2

3. Non-Commercialization of Reproduction Technologies

For many people, human life has value that cannot be measured in dollars. For them, the buying or selling of human embryos or fetuses or fetal tissue is unacceptable. Nevertheless, for others, a woman should have the right to do what she wants with her body, which may include selling her eggs. Similarly, a man has the right to do the same with his sperm.

Why shouldn't a woman be allowed to sell her eggs? If the government attempts to stop her, wouldn't it be restricting her freedom? Perhaps, but Dr. Anne Boetzkes, a professor of ethics at McMaster University, suggests that we need to examine carefully how this situation will affect other women in society. She argues that the sale of eggs turns the reproductive aspect of life into a commodity, reducing it to the status of any other consumer item, and reinforcing the view of women as reproductive vessels. Other critics of the commercialization of NRTs point to the case of Mary Beth Whitehead. In New Jersey in 1984, Mary Beth Whitehead agreed to be the surrogate mother for Elizabeth and William Stern's child. Ms. Whitehead was impregnated by artificial insemination with Mr. Stern's sperm. After "Baby M" was born, Ms. Whitehead decided to keep the child and the Sterns took her to court to gain custody of the child. Many people were disturbed by the terms of the contract between Ms. Whitehead and the Sterns. The contract indicated that Ms. Whitehead would receive $10,000 if the pregnancy resulted in a healthy infant. She would receive only $1,000 if the child was stillborn and the Sterns had the right, according to the contract, to demand that Ms. Whitehead have an abortion if the prenatal testing indicated that there was something wrong with the fetus.

4. The Principle of Equality

This principle suggests that each person deserves an equal amount of respect and concern as human beings. Any activity associated with the NRTs must be measured against this principle. For example, do buying and selling human eggs violate this principle of equality? Dr. Boetzkes suggests:

> Is a transaction like that going to set back the interests of the disadvantaged? Is it going to lead to the exploitation of the disadvantaged? So if somebody is so poor that they're looking for ways to make money and one way they're offered is to

sell reproductive services. What's wrong with that? Well, what it means is that someone who is already disadvantaged because they're poor is then going to have to compromise over their human dignity in order to get ahead…in order to improve their situation. And a member of the group who is already well advantaged is going to take advantage of that situation…

This principle also infers that we should all have equal access to these new reproductive technologies. Our ideas of what constitutes a family are changing and NRTs will influence this process. Single women may choose to have and raise a child without a male partner. For lesbian couples, NRTs present an opportunity to have children of their own if they use artificial insemination. And for gay male couples who wish to enter an agreement with a surrogate mother, NRTs provide an opportunity to raise children who are biologically their own sons or daughters.

Some individuals view the use of NRTs as an attack on the traditional family. They argue that many single mothers live in poverty and that allowing single women access to artificial insemination procedures will simply increase the number of poor mothers in society and that the lack of a male role model may lead to difficulties as the child grows up. Others argue that a gay couple could not provide a balance of role models.

5. Respect for Human Life

This principle indicates that human life deserves respect at all stages of development. Some groups argue that although the fetus may be created by humans and is living tissue, it is not necessarily a human being. Others disagree, arguing that we become a human being at the moment of conception and therefore no one, including our mother, has the right to end our life. For many people, these two extremes are unacceptable. At what stage of fetal development does the fetus become a human being and possess rights and protections? In March 1991, the Supreme Court of Canada ruled that a fetus is not a person until it has completely left its mother's body. Groups such as Real Women and Canadian Physicians for Life point out that the ruling means that premature babies born 24 weeks after conception have all the rights of Canadian law, but that a full-term fetus (40 weeks), about to be delivered, does not.

Although as a society we have not reached a consensus on when we become human beings, most individuals would agree with the Royal Commission report when it states, "While the law does not treat embryos and fetuses as full members of the community, they are loosely connected to the community in virtue of both their genesis and their future," and therefore must be treated with respect and dignity.

What actions are disrespectful to human life? Fetal tissue is used in a variety of medical and research procedures. It is used in the study of diseases, in the development of new drugs and the education of health professionals. This worries some individuals as they are concerned that these uses of fetal tissue may cause people to view the fetus as a commodity. For example, studies suggest that patients with Parkinson's and Alzheimer's disease can be helped by transplantation of fetal brain tissue. Some people have worried that women may become pregnant so that aging parents suffering from diseases such as Parkinson's could use the fetal tissue. Others fear that women may be subjected to unnecessary abortions to supply fetal tissue for research.

Supporters of fetal tissue research argue that these situations could be avoided with careful monitoring and that fetal tissue research has provided remarkable benefits to society. For example, many vaccines, including the polio vaccine, were developed using fetal tissue.

What may become a dilemma for parents is their ability to control not only the quantity of children they have, but also the quality of the children they have. This situation may develop as prenatal and pre-implantation diagnostic techniques improve. By identifying severe disabilities at or before the fetal stage and terminating the pregnancy, are we reducing human suffering, both for the individual who would have had the disability and the parents who would care for that individual?

Joseph Fletcher believes we are. In his book, *The Ethics of Genetic Control*, he describes the creation of children without the use of quality control as "sexual roulette." He writes that, "we ought to protect our families from the emotional and material burden of such diseased individuals and from the misery of their simply existing (not living) in a nearby 'warehouse' or public institution." Fletcher provides an example of a man with hemophilia. Men who suffer from this disease have difficulty forming scabs when they are cut.

In severe cases the person may bleed to death if he is cut and cannot get to a hospital. The disease is caused by a gene and is sex-linked; a father who is a carrier will pass it on to his daughter but not his sons. His daughters will not get the disease but will pass it on to their children. Fletcher argues that it is the "moral responsibility" of this man to ensure that he has only male children, aborting any female embryos that would carry the gene. "Choosing high quality fetuses and rejecting low quality ones is not tragedy; sad, but not agonizing."

Many groups, particularly people with disabilities, strongly disagree with Fletcher's point of view. They point to the tremendous contributions made by people who happen to have genetic disabilities. By what criteria should the "quality" of the fetus be judged?

There are also concerns over who has access to this genetic background information. Insurance company executives have indicated that it should be included in any medical history forms that are submitted by individuals who are applying for health insurance. In Ontario, where health care is paid for by our taxes, it is unlikely that any health services will be denied to a person. But in the future, will parents feel pressure to abort abnormal fetuses that, if born, will be costly for taxpayers to care for and educate?

6. Protection of the Vulnerable

This principle indicates that individuals who cannot look out for their own welfare should receive special consideration. Should these special considerations be extended to include children who may be born through NRTs? Some groups have argued that society has an interest in protecting NRT offspring from unsuitable parents. However, except for the circumstances of the birth, NRT children are the same as other children and deserve society's support and protection.

7. Accountability

Finally, we as members of society are responsible for the control and regulation of the new reproductive technologies. These guiding principles were offered by the Commission to help all of us in sorting out the dilemmas we face because of NRTs. These technologies are progressing at a fast rate, and each new stage brings new ethical concerns. These concerns are important to all of us, not just the scientific community. Clearly, we have both the right and the obligation to participate in the debate over the new reproductive technologies.

Issue 2

LIMITS OF THE POSSIBLE

Douglas Shenson

Cardiac intensive-care units are paradoxes. They are filled with the tools to delay dying but they keep the language of death at a distance. As an intern, I worked in such a place: a small, brightly lit area, partitioned into eight cubicles and filled with an overwhelming array of electronic equipment. Watching the nurses fit a patient into one of the cubicles was like watching an astronaut slip into a space capsule, engulfed and diminished by the machinery. But such thoughts did not immediately occur to me. My job was to work hard, attend to my patients, and leave the deeper problems of philosophy for later. Those were my priorities on the first day of my intensive-care rotation.

It was also the day we admitted a man I'll call Mr. Strap to the hospital. He came to us with an extraordinary long and complicated history of heart ailments: three attacks, one bypass operation, and one heart-valve replacement. Now he had returned, complaining of chest pain—brought in by the paramedics when his wife suspected he was having another heart attack.

I met him in the emergency room. He was sitting up on a gurney, breathing slowly through an oxygen mask; he wore a patient's pajama top, but had on his trousers, shoes and socks. Like a minotaur, I would later kid him, neither man nor patient.

In his late seventies, Mr. Strap had the false robustness of a chronic smoker, and tired, apprehensive eyes. He spoke with the anxiousness and impatience of one who has met too many doctors, each seeking an understanding of his illness, which he himself had not yet found.

We talked about his previous hospitalization, his medications, his smoking. I examined him carefully, and told him I would be taking care of any day-to-day problems in consultation with more senior physicians. I communicated with that combination of signs doctors use when brought to a patient by crisis: the well-chosen word, the reassuring touch, the articulation of friendship, all mixed to support a sense of self, which, in parallel with his heart might also be collapsing.

It was not possible to assess how sick he was simply from his symptoms, I told him. It would be the laboratory that would indicate whether he had suffered another heart attack.

"I don't need a lab to tell me my chest hurts," he snapped, "I'm telling you, I'm having another bad one."

His family doctor soon arrived to evaluate his condition. After speaking at length to Mr. and Mrs. Strap, he moved away so we could discuss our initial therapeutic approach. I wrote the orders for Mr. Strap's medication and the family doctor rejoined the couple—only to be interrupted by the paging operator. Shortly, with a harried, fraternal look, he left for another patient.

I introduced myself to Mrs. Strap, who scrutinized me as we talked about the next steps in her husband's hospitalization. She spoke quietly, bracing herself for the unwanted intimacy inescapable in such encounters. We covered what must have been familiar material. I ordered medication and said he needs sleep now—that morning would be a better time to visit.

She turned to squeeze his hand and utter a few words before leaving; there was talk between them only of the magazines and family snapshots she would bring in—the soothing vocabulary of ordinary life, which she used instinctively to reduce their fright.

When she had left, he looked at me again.

"A kid like you really knows what he's doing?"

I smiled and assured him I had my medical school debt to prove it. Eventually he relaxed, and through the verbal jockeying I made myself a doctor in his eyes, as his disease had made him a patient in mine.

We came to know each other slowly. I was at first preoccupied with exploring his illness through the conventional prisms of medicine: evaluating the results of his blood tests and analyzing subtle changes in his X-rays and electrocardiograms. Every morning I checked his blood pressure, listened to his heart and lungs and watched for changes. I would in all likelihood be the first to detect it if he started to deteriorate.

Initially, the news was good: he had not had another heart attack. Yet the bouts of chest pain continued, only sometimes relieved by tablets of nitroglycerin. There were also episodes of difficulty in breathing. I was called repeatedly in the early hours to help him through these times. At one point, I found him struggling, sitting up in his darkened cubicle, neighboured by sleeping cardiac patients, a look of terrible fear in his eyes, nearly drowning as fluid seeped back in his lungs—the burden of a heart unable to pump blood through his arteries. An injection of medicine promised to bring back his breath to retrieve him from the disarray of his panic. As moments passed and the drug worked its way, I calmed him with explanations of how his heart was contracting more easily, of how his blood pressure was returning to normal, plying him softly with the reassurances of science, words in a kind of medical lullaby.

Soon it was over and we spoke again, like victorious confederates, conspiring now to exploit the coming day: there would be his wife's visit, family gossip, and reports of his young grandson's Little League accomplishments (there was greatness in this natural outfielder—he just knew it!). Before long, his energy dissipated and he fell asleep.

In time, we became chums. He seemed to depend on me more and more as his drug regimen was adjusted and readjusted. When a conference was called between his cardiologist and his family physician, he naively turned for my opinion first. With halting success, the team tried new approaches, investing him with our own sense of the possible. He clung fiercely to my medical powers, to my expert knowledge, to my white coat.

"You'll see me through, Doc. You're a magician," he would say.

Perhaps I could—my pride swelled and I told him that, with the right medicines, he'd soon be feeling much better. But by believing in the power I became a magician who had eaten his own rabbit; swallowing the illusion was simply the last possible trick, and nothing was left up my sleeve. The chest pain continued, **exacerbated** by his dread of each coming night and the fear of a body over which he had lost control.

exacerbated—made worse

More specialists met to consider therapies. Experimental drugs were proposed and other diagnostic tests were performed. As he was too old for a heart transplant and had already undergone extensive surgery, we searched for a successful pharmacologic approach. The cardiologist began his analysis by drawing graphs of a normal cardiac output: the contractility of muscles, the size and internal pressures of the heart chambers, the rates of cardiac contrac-

Issue 2

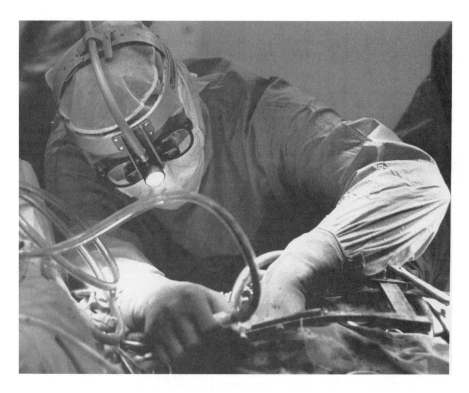

"We had persuaded ourselves that his sick heart was simply a pump in disrepair."

tions, all playing their parts. Then, superimposed upon these orderly studies, he drew in the distortions of Mr. Strap's cardiovascular machinery. Our goal was to find the ways to get it running properly again.

But as we concentrated on the mechanics, we became captives of our own metaphors. We had persuaded ourselves that his sick heart was simply a pump in disrepair, and had forgotten that his body, despite our exertions, would tell its own story. When his wife visited, she saw things we did not: his wilting posture, the altered resolution in his voice, a different look in his face.

"Just do what you can," she said.

Her conversation had a premature sadness in it, coming—I thought then—from her lack of knowledge rather than her wisdom. She, better than we, understood the **evanescent** source of his deterioration.

evanescent—fading

As we turned more toward our pharmacopoeia, I watched his faith in the scientific arsenal ebb. And as the algorithms of the medical textbooks that guided our decisions failed him, so did the roles

Issue 2

Review

Limits of the Possible

This article, which originally appeared in the *New York Times*, is about an interning doctor's first days in a cardiac intensive-care ward. In particular, it is about the nature of the relationship that develops between himself as "doctor" and the elderly, seriously ill "patient," named Mr. Strap.

At first, Mr. Strap responds well to various forms of treatment, and increasingly regards the novice medicine man as a kind of magician, seemingly able to correct any health problems with pills and machinery.

Over the next few days, the patient survives one medical crisis after another, and his faith in medical science grows. However, his wife seems to understand, even before the doctors, that her husband is dying and their reassurance that medicine can save him is their illusion.

Mr. Strap's condition deteriorates and the doctor-patient relationship is transformed; the doctor becomes "a young man watching an old man die" as he realizes the limitations of the discipline of medical science.

that went with them. Our relationship transformed itself again—I went subtly from doctor and saviour to friend and son. It was as if he had forgiven me for something he had known all along I could not do.

In this transformation our customary discourse dissolved with the inability of the machinery and the drugs to fulfill their promise. Each layer of formality faded away, and the two of us were left surrounded and unhindered by the equipment, simply as witnesses to a repeating, timeless process: a young man watching an old man die. And this teaching hospital, with its complex hierarchy and its ambitious science, became in that moment merely a place where young men and women, with titles of maturity and profession, oversee the dying of their elders.

Soon our conversations were punctuated by the empty dance of doctors confronting terminal illness. The pace of these activities quickened, and I worked to manipulate his failing blood pressure and improve his breathing. But Mr. Strap's death occurred while I was not in the hospital, and he seemed to leave me without transition. His last breath and heartbeat were caught immediately by the intensive-care nurse, and I was told that a long and energetic cardiac arrest code was performed on an unresponsive patient. I must have looked as though I was going to cry when they told me, because the resident on duty placed his hand on my shoulder and said it would be different next time. I wasn't sure.

Issue 2

ACID RAIN

Michael Badyk

Acid rain is a term that is now in common use by us all, including most of the people involved in the study of this problem, such as biologists, ecologists and chemists. In reality, the problem includes not only acid rain but also acid snow, acid fog, acid dew, acid frost and dry fallout that occurs on perfectly sunny days. It is reaching the earth all day, all year and all over the planet.

The source of this problem is the technology that we have used over the last few hundred years. Acid rain is not new to the last 20 or so years. There is some evidence from illustrations made from carved wooden stamps and also from paintings originating in Germany in the late 1700s that suggest that acid has been damaging trees for some time. The main aspects of our technology that have contributed to these acids are: first, the refining and burning of fossil fuels (including the production of petrochemical-based materials

Acid Rain
Acid rain is a term that is now in common use. In reality, the problem includes not only acid rain but also acid snow, acid fog, acid dew, acid frost and dry fallout that occurs on perfectly sunny days.

Can science repair the damage?

such as plastics); and, second, the refining and manufacture of metals.

Our global economy is tied to these activities. Our technology often is measured by what we can produce from metal or plastic, and by using power contained in the carbon of the fossil fuels we can accomplish fantastic things. The burning of coal over the last few hundred years greatly improved life for all humanity, and the more recent use of oil and gasoline has changed our society forever. Automobiles and aircraft that we really can't do without any longer are perfect examples of the application of these technologies. The use of metal and the acquisition of the means to do things with it is woven through our past. It can be seen in such terms as the "Bronze Age" and the "Iron Age," used as labels for time periods based on the metallic achievements of the times. These two terms are used to denote our increasing sophistication in the application of technology over time.

IMPURITY AS A NORMAL STATE

There is one aspect of the fossil fuels and metals that is not evident to most people—what we pull from the ground to use is seldom pure. Sulphur is commonly contained in coal, oil and natural gas. There are exceptions of course. In Pennsylvania, some of the oil is so pure that you could take it out of the ground and pour it right into your car. Normally, though, if you tried this with most crude oil, you would destroy the engine. The purer the oil or coal or natural gas is, the more its value increases. The less pure is known as dirty coal, or sour gas, and there are many different types of oil quality. Something like iron or nickel doesn't occur very often in purities that would allow us to use it directly out of the ground. Again, there are some exceptions. On the south shore of Lake Superior in what is now the State of Michigan there are deposits of copper that are almost pure. The aboriginal peoples who inhabited the area discovered it and were able to fashion useful items from it (which were traded all over the Great Lakes region). Again, normally what we get is the metal contained in something called an ore. Iron ore, for example, has lots of iron but also impurities, including other metals, silica, and most likely sulphur.

BY-PRODUCTS: THE RESULT WHEN IMPURITY CHANGES TO PURITY

These impurities are removed by refining. Most of the sulphur can be removed from the fossil fuels by chemical treatment. One of the common sights around a petrochemical refinery is a flame. This flame is fuelled by the sulphur waste being burned off. The same thing is true with natural gas. Further, more often than not, we don't even try to remove the impurities from coal—we just burn it as is. The product of this burning is a chemical compound known as sulphur dioxide.

An oxide is produced when a substance reacts with oxygen in the atmosphere to form a compound. Iron oxide, which we call rust, is a simple example. Sulphur dioxide denotes that there are two oxygen molecules linked with one sulphur molecule. When we turn on our automobiles we burn the gasoline and any sulphur that still may be in it, once again producing sulphur dioxide. We purify metals by heating them to liquefy the solid ore. We can then separate the part we want. The only thing wrong with this procedure is that the sulphur in the ore burns off rather than liquefying. And once again, this produces sulphur dioxides that enter the air. And, unfortunately it isn't just sulphur dioxides. There are oxides of nitrogen contained in there, too. There is also a range of other materials released into the atmosphere. They might not necessarily form acids, but their production goes hand in hand with acidic materials.

Basically, anywhere on earth where we refine fossil fuels or purify metals, we will be creating pollutants. You could look at the Tar Sands project in Alberta, the iron factories of Hamilton, the metal refining of Rouyn and Noranda in Quebec for Canadian examples. Everywhere that you can find an automobile you can find another source of pollutants.

From a chemical standpoint, the problem is that sulphur dioxide combines with water to form an acid. Nitrous oxides do the same thing. The water can be in a cloud (where the compounds of sulphur and nitrogen combine with the water) and then subsequently fall to earth. Or, the compounds can fall in a dry form (dry fallout), and when they encounter water they form an acid just as easily as the acids form in the clouds.

Issue 2

ACIDS AND BASES

Acids carry the connotation of something harmful. However, we use acids quite often in our everyday lives. Lemon juice is an acid, and so is vinegar. Coffee and tea are acids. We also use acids to power batteries, thus creating the term "battery acid."

Almost everyone knows that acids are reactive—in other words they act upon whatever they come in contact with to form a new substance, which obviously alters the old substance permanently. That is, if an acid is poured on an object, then something is going to happen (e.g., if you pour acid on your hand and your hand dissolves). But there is a range of substances that are reactive that are not called acids; they are known as alkaloids or bases or antacids (the opposite of acids). This would include such things as hydrogen peroxide and ammonia.

Acid Rain

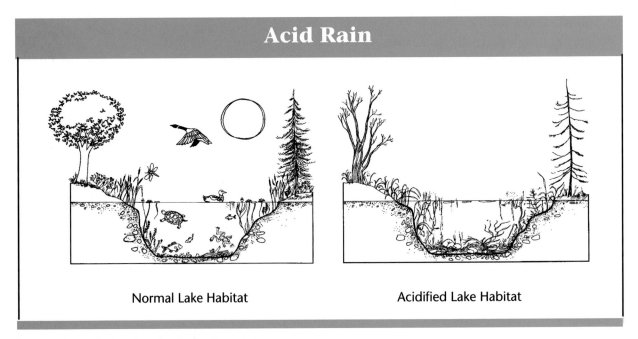

Normal Lake Habitat   Acidified Lake Habitat

The Life and Death of a Lake Ecosystem
To support normal aquatic life, a lake habitat must have a balanced food chain and allow for normal reproductive cycles.

When acid is introduced to the ecosystem, either through acidic rainfall or runoff from acidic snowpack, the influx of acid may alter the lake's overall pH, creating a more acidic environment. Also, acidic runoff can release heavy metals—highly toxic for many aquatic species—from rocks and soil. Sensitive organisms may be wiped out and resistant life forms are weakened as their food supplies are affected.

Issue 2

There are two substances that make things reactive. For acids it is hydrogen ions (H), and for bases it is hydroxides (OH). If you combine the two of them in equal strengths and quantities you end up with something un-reactive that is very familiar: H_2O (water). Pure water is said to be neutral. If this is true, then we can use it as a means of comparing the other substances that may be acidic or basic.

In order to make comparisons between substances, chemists have devised a scale knows as the *pH*, or *potential hydrogen scale*. It has values that run from 0 for a strongly acidic, to 7 for the pure water, and finally to 14 for those that are strongly alkaline. Vinegar would have a value of about 3.1 and ammonia would have a value around 11. Lemon juice comes in at around 2.2 and battery acid is about 1.8. You might ask how we can drink lemon juice with a *Ph* value not too far from battery acid when we know what would happen to us if we drank the battery acid. The way in which the *Ph* scale has been constructed is on a logarithmic basis. That implies that, for example, if the *Ph* value went from 5 to 4, then the actual acidity of the substance increases 10 times. So the difference of 0.4 *Ph* units between lemon juice and battery acid is very significant.

THE NEUTRALIZING PROCESS

If acids can be so damaging, how can we get rid of them? To neutralize the acids a base of equal strength would have to be added. If you have ever had a bitter cup of tea or coffee you would normally add milk or cream to it to reduce the bitterness. The bitterness comes from the acids that are contained in the beverage. The milk or cream contains a reasonable amount of calcium carbonate, which is the base. By combining the two of them, you approach the neutral value. If you have ever had an acidic stomach, then you have probably taken an antacid such as Rolaids or Tums, which contain calcium carbonate, just like the milk.

THE BUFFERING CAPACITY OF ROCK

Lakes, rivers and the soil have a built-in neutralizer, similar to Rolaids. This usually comes from the type of rock that the body of water or

Normal Lake Habitat
- Fish prey on insects and provide food for certain birds.
- Fish eggs hatch in the normal way.
- Insects provide food for fish and amphibians. Hunting birds, such as the osprey, live on fish.
- Frogs feed on insects.
- Trees are supported by local soil.

Acidified Lake Habitat
- Acid influx and heavy metal poisoning can kill sensitive fish, such as rainbow trout and salmon.
- Fish eggs can be destroyed or deformed by environmental changes. Certain insects, such as the whirligig beetle reproduce in an uncontrolled manner. They are resistant to acidification and their main predators are fewer.
- Birds must seek fish in other lakes. Frogs die in heavily acidic habitats.
- Acidic soil can damage or even kill certain trees.

the soil sits upon. This ability to neutralize an acid is referred to as the *buffering capacity*. This capacity is extremely variable on both a global and local basis. In southern Ontario the rock is mostly limestone, which is high in calcium carbonate. A lake that sits on this limestone will be able to neutralize a good deal of acid that falls into it because the soft and easily dissolved rock will enrich the water with minerals. The exact opposite is true of the area in central and northern Ontario, which is dominated by the type of rock known as the Canadian Shield. It is very different from the limestone. It is infinitely harder and is usually lacking in calcium carbonate. In fact, it is so hard that very few minerals ever dissolve into the water. This makes the buffering capacity very low. Unfortunately, both areas receive precipitation that has to be considered acidic.

Normal precipitation has a value between 5.5 and 7.0 on the *Ph* scale. Ontario quite regularly receives precipitation with values around 4. While the lakes in southern Ontario are still in good condition, and the soil and the vegetation seem to be reasonably good, on the Canadian Shield it is a very different story. Some of the trees seem to be dying and some of the lakes are dead.

What Makes a Lake Live

The death of the lakes is really what has attracted public attention. You have to understand how a lake lives before you can understand how it dies.

To make a lake you first of all need water. Then you need some sort of basin to put it in. That is a start, but it still doesn't make it suitable for life. You need certain dissolved minerals to feed the plants (mineral nutrients) and you also need sunlight and warm temperatures over a reasonable period of time. These variables mean that there can be many types of lakes and also a great variety in both the amount and type of life that a lake will have.

Just from this you could probably tell that a lake on the limestone of southern Ontario will potentially have more life in it than a lake on the Canadian Shield, based on the amount of dissolved minerals and the latitude. You might have noticed this on your own. The lakes of the tourism area of the Canadian Shield are noted for their clarity, while most lakes on the limestone turn into green soup

Can we save our lakes from becoming wet deserts?

by the end of the summer. The presence of all those mineral nutrients will feed a wide variety of aquatic plants. The plants in turn will feed a variety of plant-eaters (herbivores) and subsequently a variety of meat-eaters (carnivores). This interconnection is known as the food chain. The water and minerals of the lake make life possible for a wealth of plants and animals both in and around the lakes.

THE DEATH OF A LAKE: HOW "WET DESERTS" ARE CREATED

Acid affects the lakes in a number of ways. The first thing that happens is that the mineral nutrients that would normally feed the plants are used up in the neutralization of the acid. This, of course, implies that less is available for the plants, so the number of plants in the lakes decreases. This then lessens the herbivore and the carnivore population which affects the animal life directly. The acid in their systems forces dramatic chemical changes, the most insidious of which is that the animals' reproductive organs are slowly destroyed. This means that the existing animals are the last of their kind in the lake—they will not produce offspring. The overall effect on the lake

Issue 2

is that life slowly winds down. It is a slow, gradual fade to oblivion over 20 years or even longer. The strangest thing is that the water looks to be in perfect health. It is absolutely crystal clear. That extreme clarity is achieved because there are no algae or bacteria or anything in there that would cloud the water—it has been called a "wet desert." Perhaps that is why we have not reacted to it until recently—the water is clear so it has to be healthy.

That is the scientific, objective, quantified assessment of this problem. We used chemistry, geology, geography and biology to assess the acidification of our lakes. You may not have understood all of the technical information, but you will understand the implication. Canada is dominated by the Canadian Shield geology. We have millions of lakes on this type of rock and they are all potentially threatened.

HUMAN LOSSES: WHERE SCIENCE ENDS

Science is able to illustrate the chemical and biological loss. However, it is unable to illustrate the losses to humanity. These losses are many and varied.

Psychological Losses

It is not possible to list these losses in any sort of hierarchy, or order of importance; that is up to the individual person to determine. But let us look at some of them. There is definitely a psychological loss. It is very common for people, even those in urban areas, to think that there are or should be areas on this planet where the hand of humanity has not reached. It is stressful to think that there are many remote lakes that are dead. Killarney Provincial Park, south-west of Sudbury, is officially designated as a wilderness park and is often called the "Crown Jewel" of the province's parks. It has magnificent high ridges of startling white quartzite rock, almost pure silica, and on a bright day it gives the illusion of snow on top of these high rounded ridges. These high ridges look down on brilliant blue lakes, but most of the lakes are dead. One can describe this but it is difficult to convey the profound feeling one gets when standing beside this clear lake knowing that it is dead. Or, what it feels like to cup your hand and drink some water from the lake and taste aluminum that has been pulled out of the rock by the acidic water. That impact is far greater than reading that there are so many parts per million of aluminum in the water or that the *Ph* is at a certain level. It is a profound sense that something is dreadfully and painfully wrong.

Social Losses

There is a social loss here as well. The native people of the area are now living with lakes that are not in the same condition as they were for thousands of years. We might not be able to appreciate this. The ridges of Killarney are holy places to these first peoples and are regarded as a source of great spiritual power. Natives today still seek the solitude and power emanating from nature in these ridges. To be on a ridge top and look down on a lake and know that it is now dead must be unbelievably sad to them. Or possibly it is maddening. Someone not from their culture can identify with their anguish and anger.

In non-Native society there is a loss as well. The people that would go to the north, the wilderness, and the solitude, are now faced with an altered world. We can't escape the hand of humanity even in the Canadian north. That hand is there in the lakes in which we fish, on which we canoe, in which we swim and by which we live. It may never be the same. Throughout this text, we have discussed the fact that societies do change, but are we prepared to see our world and that of Native peoples change so dramatically in this way?

Economic Losses

An economic loss is present here as well. Many of the communities of the north owe their existence to the recreation that occurs on the lakes around them. The small community of Killarney just outside of the park is a perfect example. Although it is not evident as yet, it is inevitable that people will stop coming to an area where all the lakes are poisoned and polluted. The loss of tourism dollars will lead to the end of the community, a fact already appreciated by the people of the north. Their livelihood could disappear very soon. Their economic well-being will fall into our hands through unemployment insurance and welfare payments. We may even have to pay to have water brought into the community because the residents can no longer

Issue 2

drink it. Acidic water can dissolve the copper in the plumbing of homes and businesses and poison people with copper sulphate, which can affect their liver and kidneys. Once again, the rest of society will have to pay for the health care costs to these victims of acid rain pollution. As our taxes will probably have to be increased to pay for all this, the standard of living of all Canadians will be directly affected.

Cultural Loss

In one sense, the greatest loss is a cultural one. The one thing that is deeply engrained in the Canadian mind is a sense that this great and untouched wilderness is just over the next hill. The sense of wilderness turns up in our art. Musicians such as Gordon Lightfoot, CANO, and Bruce Cockburn have composed lyrics and ideas based on these images. Writes such as Farley Mowatt, Pierre Berton and Gabriel Roy craft pictures of wilderness which once read are never forgotten.

Probably the most distinctive appreciation of this wilderness is the paintings of the Group of Seven. The abstract landscapes of these artists are part of the Canadian identity. They are found in all of our museums and art galleries, and many of them are found as reproductions in our homes. They are part of our culture, and they are painted at Killarney. There is an A.Y. Jackson Lake in the park; there is also an O.S.A. Lake, standing for the Ontario Society of Artists which is the official working name for the Group of Seven. Most of us have seen paintings of the Killarney area in their art and not even known it. They depict rugged hills and lone gnarled pine trees. They are almost a stereotype of what the north should be. And those lakes in those paintings are now dead. We, as Canadians, have lost something here.

THE ROLE OF THE SUBJECTIVE SELF

We may now be at the limits of what science can do. It is not to say that we should abandon the science; it is just that science needs to be motivated by a profound sense of humanity and human emotion. To solve the problem of these dead lakes will take human emotion more than it will take a scientific solution. We will have to become concerned or angry enough to become involved with the solution. Science can supply us with the tools, but our emotions and our feelings will be a vital part of the solution. It might require a deep involvement in our economic or political system to say to the people in charge that the losses that have been detailed in this short essay are no longer acceptable, and those prepared to sacrifice our environment in the name of profit or science or both should be stopped.

Adding more science is not the answer. Science is sometimes seen as a way of automatically solving the problem that it has created. This is a false sense of security. It has been suggested that we could dump concentrated calcium carbonate, lime, in the lakes and then restock them with plants and fish, but this is only a band-aid solution that looks at the symptoms but not the cure. We have to look at ourselves. We are the cause because of our demand for energy and consumer products. That demand has to change before the problem can be solved.

Ultimately our lives depend on the solution. If the food chains of our planet, both on land and in the water, fail, then the life-support system for us will also have failed. Are we, as a technically advanced society, prepared to die by our own hand? We can't ignore what we have done to this planet. We have to be aware of all this because "all this" is us—we are dependent on the whole variety of plants and animals that exist here. The tool we have in science is very powerful. With this power comes great responsibility. One can only hope we are responsible enough to make the right decision.

Our life depends on it.

ARTS AND CULTURE

ISSUE 1:
The Role of the Arts

ISSUE 2:
Objective vs. Subjective
Responses to Art

ISSUE

1

THE ROLE OF THE ARTS

The purpose of art is the lifelong construction of a state of wonder.

Glenn Gould

As an artist, one is not a citizen of society. An artist is bound to explore every aspect of human experience, the darkest corners—not necessarily—but if that is where one is led, that's where one must go. You cannot worry about what the structure of your own particular segment of society considers bad behaviour, good behaviour; good exploration, bad exploration. So, at the time you're being an artist, you're not a citizen. You don't have the social responsibility of a citizen. You have, in fact, no social responsibility whatsoever.

David Cronenberg

PORTRAIT OF THE ARTS

Morton Ritts

*I*n this unit we examine the role of the arts. Sometimes it's harder to say what art is than what it isn't. Art, for example, isn't science. As we saw in the previous unit, science is factual and **propositional**. It tries to provide knowledge that is objective and clear, with verifiable observations based on a rigorous method of enquiry.

propositional—tested using formal propositions

Art, on the other hand, tends to be ambiguous and problematic. It is both factual and fictional. Indeed, on one level, narrative arts like literature and film proclaim themselves to be not "true" at all, to be "made-up." How can something that's made up be true? And yet, we know from our own experience that when we read certain novels or see certain films we're struck by just how "true to life" they are.

There is a profound paradox here. Characters in novels and films who are invented, who are fictions, often reveal more about human nature than real people. Fiction, in other words, has the capacity to provide us with greater insight to truth than truth. But fiction is just another kind of truth. All art is.

Of course, psychology and biology also provide us with truth. But their focus is always general, while art portrays the particular. In Unit 1, for example, we came across Freud's famous "oedipal complex." As a psychological theory, the oedipal complex is universal and abstract. But in his novel *Sons and Lovers*, D.H. Lawrence gives this theory specific, concrete form by creating a rich and complex character whose intense, troubled relationship with his mother dominates his life.

For another example compare the description of anxiety and fear in a psychology textbook with how these same emotions are depicted in a novel or film. The textbook account is analytical, factual. This is fine, but such an account doesn't convey to us what anxiety and fear "feel" like. A well-written novel or well-made film does, however, by locating these emotions in actions that compel our interest. This difference between fact and fiction is the difference between science and the arts. Science and the social sciences "tell" whereas the arts "show."

We've said that the arts "show" by giving us knowledge of he particular. As the *Sons and Lovers* example suggests, we come to know an important universal relationship (mothers and sons) in the depiction of a specific relationship.

The arts "show" by way of creativity, discipline, expressiveness. They give form to our experience. Sometimes the result is indirect, as in expressionist painting. Sometimes it's brutally direct, as in *The Killing Fields*, a powerful film about the genocide that occurred in Cambodia in the 1970s. Different as they are, both examples represent some important aspect of truth.

ART AND SOCIETY

One thing we can say for certain is that artists work in a social context. On the walls of the vast cathedral-like caves at Lascaux in southwestern France, our palaeolithic ancestors painted picture-stories of their communal hunts. These extraordinary images bind us to our own prehistoric beginnings some 20,000 years ago. At the same time, they're a good example of one of the underlying impulses behind art—the impulse to leave our mark, to say we were here.

In his essay in this book, "On the Meaning of Work", Mitchell Lerner makes much the same point. But is there a difference between work and art? Yes and no. No doubt, what a good painter or a writer produces is always the result of hard work. But if all art is work, the opposite—that all work is art—is not true. This is because most of us work to please someone else while most artists work primarily to please themselves. In this sense, the more a job allows you to please yourself the closer you are to being an artist.

Most of us don't have this luxury. If we work in a factory, in an office or retail store, or in a school, our individual needs count for less than those of the company or our clients. Certainly we can find fulfilment in our work, but never at the expense of the group. While enlightened employers try to create the conditions for a balance between our individual interests and those of the company, this isn't often possible.

So in this way art is different from work. Unlike work, art, in western culture at least, stresses the primacy of the individual. In this tradition, even performing artists, like musicians, actors and

"...performing artists, like musicians, actors and dancers, have a healthy regard for their own uniqueness."

dancers have a healthy regard for their own uniqueness. They may be part of a team, but some will always insist on shining more brightly than others—on being "stars."

Throughout history, societies have often objected to the idea of artists as individuals, arguing that their first loyalty is not to themselves but to the state. This was the case in the former Soviet Union, and is still the case in China. Even in democracies like Canada and the U.S., books, magazines, paintings, photographs and films are

Issue 1

censored because they are deemed in some way a threat to society for reasons of obscenity, libel or blasphemy.

The Greek philosopher Plato would have heartily endorsed such censorship. For him, art was at best a distraction, at worst a danger. He believed it was difficult enough to know reality. Art only made it harder—instead of showing things as they were, it offered distorted representations of those things. Drama, poetry, painting gave us a kind of secret second-hand version of life, he argued. They served no constructive purpose.

According to Plato, only the study of science, philosophy or history enlightened us because these disciplines appealed to the mind, to our rational selves. Drama, poetry, music, the visual arts appealed to our senses, our irrational and emotional selves. In doing so, they not only distorted reality, they threatened the security and well-being of the state because they tended to mislead, confuse and excite people.

THE NEED TO IMAGINE

Just as art differs from philosophy, science and history, writers, actors, dancers and other artists differ from philosophers, scientists and historians. Like them, artists attempt to impose their own sense of order on the random flow of life around them. But as we've already seen, their method is different—artists work with their senses, with feeling and intuition, with metaphor and imagination.

In his play, *A Midsummer Night's Dream*, William Shakespeare compared artists (poets) to lovers and lunatics. What connects them, he suggests, is precisely this power of the imagination:

> And, as imagination bodies forth,
> The form of things unknown, the poet's pen
> Turns them to shapes, and gives to airy nothing
> A local habitation and a name.

The artist, then, is someone whose imagination makes the unknown known, the invisible visible and the unconscious conscious—which is very close to the therapeutic process of Freudian psychoanalysis. Art itself is a way of exploring the mysteries of the human condition, not in the linear fashion of scientific enquiry but in the associative, circular manner of therapy. "We shed our sicknesses in books," D.H. Lawrence wrote. Art, he meant, heals.

That's perhaps one reason why people feel the need to write, paint, play an instrument or sing. Another reason, we've suggested, is the desire to leave some sign, some evidence of our existence. As children we seek even the most trivial kind of immortality, nothing more sometimes than carving our initials into the trunk of a tree or printing our name in the fresh concrete of a sidewalk.

The humanistic psychologist Abraham Maslow offers still another way of looking at the desire to create. We may recall that in his hierarchy of needs, Maslow speculates that physical survival is basic. Someone who lacks the requirements for physiological well being, including food and shelter, isn't much interested in writing novels or painting landscapes.

But once these basic needs are satisfied, we often ask ourselves, "What more is there to life?" What's more, Maslow says, are the higher level needs for love, esteem and, above all, self-actualization. More than most people, artists are obsessed by the need to self-actualize, to be the best they can at whatever they are. A tale about two modern painters, Amadeo Modigliani and Chaim Soutine, illustrates this point.

Modigliani and Soutine were friends who shared a studio in a small garret in Paris at the turn of the century. They were almost stereotypes of the starving artist, deprived of material comforts but endowed with rich and productive imaginations.

One day, the story goes, they bought a chicken at the local butcher shop, as the subject for a "still life." They hung it from the rafters in their studio and set up their easels. In the midst of their preparation, however, it occurred to them that they hadn't had a decent meal in weeks. They'd spent their last francs on a chicken, but incredibly—foolishly, it seemed at that moment—they were intending to paint it, not eat it.

Maslow might explain their dilemma this way: If the two friends cooked the chicken, they'd satisfy their basic survival needs but not their need for art. On the other hand, if they painted the chicken, they'd satisfy their need for self-actualization, but might starve to death in the process. What to do? In fact, they arrived at one of those inspired compromises that are the mark of true genius—they painted very quickly (while the chicken was still fresh).

Issue 1

The story is a good example of the struggle between the demands of life and those of art. Someone once asked the great artist Picasso whether, if his house caught fire, he'd rescue his cat first or his paintings. He answered his cat. Picasso's point was that artists draw their inspiration from life. Without life there can be no art.

ART REDRAWS THE BOUNDARIES OF OUR LIVES

As much as artists deal with the world of imagination and subjective perception, their messages of pain or celebration correspond in some way to life outside them, to the common experiences of humanity. When we see a film or hear a song that absorbs us, we feel this connection too. The artist redraws and enlarges the boundaries of our emotional and intellectual landscape.

At their best, the books and films and music that mean most to us tell us stories in provocative new ways. Since the beginning, the human species has always felt compelled to tell stories. There are the hunting pictures in the caves at Lascaux. There was remarkable poetry, music and painting in the Nazi concentration camps. Plato was right to suggest that art is dangerous, but perhaps that's exactly what art should be—something that pricks the bubble of illusion, that exposes pain and injustice, that challenges us to think about old things in new ways.

Art is often most dangerous when it creates an experience for us that defies what is considered politically and morally "correct." That's why one of the first acts of dictatorial regimes is to imprison a country's writers. Or why police shut down exhibitions of "offensive" paintings and photographs. Or why some governments issue death threats against artists who have allegedly committed crimes against the state.

Yet those who want to create art, and not propaganda, will always affirm their right to see with their own eyes, to speak in their own voice. Their messages may indeed be subversive. But we soon forget books or paintings or music or films or plays that merely entertain us. We remember instead those that have astonished or disturbed, moved or changed us. They're part of who we are.

Issue 1

SERIOUS PLEASURE: THE ROLE OF THE ARTS

Clive Cockerton

*I*n many people's eyes, the arts are the toy department of life—occasionally amusing perhaps but in the long run a waste of time for men and women of action and purpose. The Greek philosopher Plato (427–347 B.C.) argued that art was a distraction we would be better off without. According to Plato, art was a distraction for the following reasons:

1. Art deals with images not truth; it doesn't advance knowledge, it doesn't discover anything, it only seems to understand.

2. Art imitates reality; to learn about reality it is much better to study reality itself rather than a pale imitation.

3. Art is sensual and distracts us from the more important quests (such as moral or spiritual quests). In its arousal of basic instincts, in its stimulation/simulation of violence and lust, it is anarchic, a force for disorder in the community.

In short, empty, imitative and corrupting.

Since Plato, many moralists have branched off from these arguments and urged us to consider that bright colour and decoration were immoral because they call attention to the self instead of singing the praises of God, or that "realistic" novels were too shocking for the delicate sensibilities of young women, or that rock 'n' roll would corrupt and deprave youth with its primitive rhythms. At a much less passionate level, many business people are skeptical of the arts, except where they can be trained to serve the purpose of promoting consumption of goods and services in advertising. Politicians frequently see the arts as "frills," and in a time of recession the artistic community is the first to feel the cuts of government support. All of these views, whether held by philosophers, moralists, business people or politicians, have in common the conviction that art is not serious.

This doesn't mean that the effects of art can't be serious. Plato was concerned that literature and art were disruptive and corrupting. Stories need sinners to be interesting. Tales of people who always do the right thing are predictable, preachy and boring. Yet stories that embrace all that is human, the sinners as well as the saints, compel us to accept the humanity of those who lie, cheat, betray, of those who are greedy, lustful and cruel. Not just accept the humanity of others, but also recognize those very qualities in ourselves. Moralists worry that this recognition and acceptance are subversive and undermining of moral authority. Whenever we encounter an argument that says that a certain film or type of music will inflame or deprave, or that violence on TV will lead to violent children, we are dealing with an offshoot of Plato's original concern.

Aristotle, a student of Plato's, developed a counter-argument that suggested that the symbolic experience of violence in the arts was actually helpful, and worked like a safety valve for our violent sides. Through the emotion raised in watching a story unfold, we achieve catharsis, a cleansing and purging of destructive emotion in a safe and contained way. For Aristotle, nothing was to be gained from denying our destructive urges. Indeed, the opportunity to face our sometimes violent and immoral nature in a story lessened the threat of our urges becoming reality. In other words, in watching a violent and terrifying story, we rehearse the emotion along with the actors and are released from having to act it out. However, recent psychological tests on children who were exposed to violent television suggest that some harmful results do occur. There's no simple, mechanical process whereby children watch violent acts and then always re-enact them. It's a more subtle process of shifting the atmosphere, of weakening the inhibition to violence that over time can result in changed behaviour. However, Aristotle couldn't predict Saturday morning TV and its impact on children. His insights were an attempt to describe adult responses to serious drama and remain useful as reflections on how the adult mind responds. Even adults have terrors and nightmares, and the arts enable us to both face what horrifies us and move beyond it as well.

But can art have a harmful impact on sane, responsible adults? Recently, the Canadian legal system seemed to be saying that citizens needed to be protected from their own reactions when it seized paintings by Eli Langer of children in potentially sexual positions. This action was curiously directed at the paintings themselves rather than at the painter. The clear suggestion is that some subject matter cannot be explored, a suggestion that most artists would resist. Society clearly has interests at stake, and probably should find ways to protect itself from exploitation of sensational subject matter, but there is a great deal of difference between the sleazy exploitation of the pornographer and the serious exploration of the artist. The courts, however, have not found a reliable way of measuring that difference. Should the failure of the courts and the anxieties of moralists shut us off from discussing certain controversial subject matter? Is the danger from the arts real? As Plato writes:

> Much is at stake, more than most people suppose; it is a choice between becoming a good man or a bad; poetry, no more than wealth or power or honours, poetry can tempt us to be careless of justice and virtue. (*The Republic*)

Although Plato refers to poetry here, this fear of temptation would apply equally to other arts, because the seductive power of all arts threatens the rule of reason. Elsewhere, Plato argued that drama:

> waters the growth of passions which should be allowed to wither away and sets them up in control although the goodness and happiness of our lives depend on their being held in subjection.

This idea may seem exaggerated and extreme to a modern audience, but for Plato our happiness depended on leading a good life, and a good life depended on control of the emotions by reason.

Plato's second objection, that art imitates reality, reflects his concern that we could be deceived by the distortions and exaggerations of the story-telling process. Put crudely, a film such as *Disclosure* which presents the story of a man who is sexually harassed by his female employer, however worthwhile the story may be in artistic terms, could lead the viewer to gross misperceptions about the nature of sexual harassment and power in the workplace. Clearly, the social reality has been that men have been the dominant gender in terms of business power and are far more likely to harass employees than women. Yet the fictional story may be compelling because it touches our emotions, or thrills us and we may be tempted to think of the film as a realistic and likely representation of what really goes on in business. The reality becomes apparent when we think about it, but for Plato we are always in danger when we succumb to the pleasurable pull of a story that could lead us down a rhetorical path to error. Of course, we are all aware and a little bit wary of the common lies of film—the couple overcoming all obstacles to their love and riding off into the sunset and the hero triumphing against seemingly impossible odds. However, the creators of these stories could defend their stories by saying that they don't have to be likely, just plausible, and that the preference for heroic triumph over dismal failure is an understandable and universal audience choice.

My favourite distortion is the glaring omission that very few characters in film worry about who pays, and no screen time is consumed with the practical issues of getting and saving money that takes up so much time in the actual world. Writers and filmmakers could respond that all stories must necessarily involve compression, and that compression involves eliminating superfluous detail, leaving the essential story to stand out boldly, without being submerged in the minute and tedious chores of everyday life. I'm just not sure that our relationship to money is always so inessential.

Perhaps Plato's intellectually most interesting objection is the first one—that art involves an inevitable illusion. What we see in film is not reality; when we read fiction we enter a world that is entirely made up. For Plato, the fact that we see images and enter into fantasy worlds means that we are turning away from truth. After reading a novel, can we say we know anything about the real world? We may think we know something of the human situation focused on in the plot of the novel, but have we acquired any verifiable concepts that we might have if we had read a psychology textbook instead?

Well, perhaps not verifiable in the same controlled, scientific, experimental way, and maybe not full-blown concepts, but I would argue that yes, novels provide us with genuine insights into human behaviour and situations. And these insights are verifiable, at least in a comparative way. When we finish a novel, we compare the truth of what we have read with our experience of the truth. In this way, every reading is some kind of experiment, some kind of verification. The fact that Hamlet or Falstaff are made-up characters in Shakespeare's plays does not prevent us from learning a great deal about ourselves and other people from them. They may be literally non-existent but it makes no sense to refer to them in this way as their creation enriches our understanding of the real. So too does the imaginative testing of possibilities involved in any serious novel. And since every testing of fictional possibilities is verified or rejected by every reader, novels that are read and endorsed by many readers probably have a lot to say to us. Perhaps novels are the most insightful artistic medium, but surely the same comparative experience operates with certain kinds of realistic film. With *Reality Bites*, for instance, the film clearly tries to capture something of the mood of young people today. The film follows the characters played by Winona Ryder and Ethan Hawke and their struggles with money, ambition and love. The audience naturally compares their own attitudes to the attitudes to money, work and romance presented in the film and almost immediately looks for answers to some interesting questions. Is the film credible? Does it fit with my own experience or is it at least plausible given the fictional characters and situation? When we see a film that affects us, we reflect on what we have seen, we search for verification in our own lives.

We experience stories as we experience the world—from a perspective, a point of view that is both emotional and rational. Plato was wary of our emotional natures; he believed that they were not to be denied perhaps, but kept in strict control. In our day, despite the enormous success of science, we generally don't experience life as detached observers. Indeed, detachment seems too clinical, and the perspective of the scientist lacks the engagement with experience that a fulfilled life seems to require. Instead we grope about through our lives, using bits of knowledge and lots of emotion in a constantly shifting understanding—as we do in novels. We discover that emotion can be as reliable a guide to right conduct and behaviour as ideas and concepts. Some actions just don't feel right. Others, despite what we might have been taught to believe, feel liberating and joyful. Literature helps us to feel more acutely and generously as it guides us through an ever-expanding repertoire of human situations contained in its pages. It involves a passionate way of knowing, different from, but not inferior to, the relentless rationality of the philosopher or the precise observation of the scientist.

Still, literature is the most intellectual art form. Ideas are undeniably present in great works, even if they are never talked at you, or talked about, they hover in the background. The consequences of ideas are revealed, are shown to be valuable or not, but not directly in argument form. Ideas are produced by scientists, philosophers, academics, by all of us. It is in literature that ideas are given flesh, tested not in debate, but in a re-creation of life. The cold, abstract and theoretical position is abandoned and replaced with a vantage point that is passionately considered and grounded in particular lives. As the philosopher, Lorraine Code, writes:

> The claim that literature is a source of knowledge rests upon a belief in the value of understanding the particular. It implies that a minute and inward understanding of particulars has the capacity to go beyond itself, to show something more general...(*Epistemic Responsibility*)

Why do some particular characters' lives seem to speak to all of us, when clearly not all of our lives resemble the particular character? The writer creates an image of human complexity that draws us into the fictional world, convinces us of its reality and at the same time throws light on to the real world. Theoretical understanding may be an essential element to knowledge, but without being grounded in the particular, theoretical understanding seems bloodless. Think of *Dances with Wolves* and its fictional presentation of ecological and human tragedy in the period following the U.S. Civil War. The presentation of the personal experience of a young cavalry officer and a band of Sioux enrich our understanding of history by making it intimate. And it is precisely this intimate knowledge that might elude a purely historical perspective.

The great American poet, Wallace Stevens, wrote a poem whose title, "Not Ideas about the Thing, but the Thing Itself," contains the ambition most writers have to deliver directly an intimate understanding of the world. For this intimacy to be achieved, characters can't just be mouthpieces of ideas or virtues, but instead must convince us of their full individuality and their real humanity. Our lives are shaped by diverse combinations of ideas and experience, whether we are conscious of them or not. Fiction provides a means of becoming more conscious, of constantly examining and testing these ideas and experience. Through this fictional process, we learn which ideas are useful, not just as ideas but as guiding principles.

When we read a novel, we may come to know a situation or a character very well; indeed, we may know all the significant details about a person's life (thoughts as well as actions). It's possible to know fictional characters better than our close friends. By providing us with all the information we need and by coming to a conclusion, novels present a complete vision. This completeness necessarily lacks some of life's random quality. Novels conclude, life goes on. By concluding, novels ask us to stop and think. By focusing on some of the most fundamental issues (growth, independence, love, pain, death) that we encounter in the real world, novels ask us to reflect on our own lives. But they don't just ask, they seduce us with pleasure, with worlds spun from word-magic. They extend the promise of intimacy, they leave us with insight.

Whenever it occurs, the combination of pleasure, beauty and insight is life-affirming. While pleasure and beauty are frequently found on the shimmering surface of art, in the form of delight in a turn of phrase or in intensity of vision, the insight cuts to the heart of issues, towards a deeper understanding of people and human experience. The answer to Plato's desire to rid his world of art lies in the value of pleasure and insight to the individual reader and viewer. Rather than being opposed to the quest for a rational life, perhaps the arts are complementary, providing a testing board for the different ideas that call out to us. At any rate, art's value doesn't stop with beneficial experiences for the individual, but extends to a community. Indeed, the shared experience of art helps to create a sense of community. Many cold winds blow through an individual's life, but the arts tell you that you're not alone, that others have cried as hard, laughed as loud, and loved as deeply. There's pleasure in that—in the community with others that the arts magically bring to us. Serious pleasure.

THE STORY OF STORIES

Sarah Sheard

Narrating, according to the *Oxford English Dictionary*, is the act of telling a story, of giving a full and detailed account of the facts of the matter. Or is it a *fiction* of the matter? An Ashanti African storyteller traditionally begins a tale with the warning: "I do not mean, I do not really mean, that what I am going to say is true." Similarly a Sudanese storyteller traditionally opens his or her sessions with an exchange that goes something like this:

"I'm going to tell a story."
"Right!" the audience shouts back.
"It's a lie."
"Right!"
"But not everything in it is false."
"Right!"

The storyteller concludes the narration with the words: "I put the tale back where I found it."

So narration needs not only a storyteller but also an attentive listener who agrees to accept the conventions of the tale and its telling. Compare the African storytellers' approach to the disclaimer we usually find printed in the front matter of novels or after the credits have rolled in movies: "Any similarity between actual persons, places or events and those depicted here are purely coincidental." (Right!)

The telling of stories is crucial to our daily lives and has been so since birth. Whether awake or asleep, we are continuously swimming down an ancient river of narrative that began flowing the moment humans first mastered speech itself. The categories of narrative genres today include allegory, poetry, satire, novel, short story, epic, drama, legend, fable, history, biography, pamphlet and essay, but we could stretch our definition of narrative a little to include, say, dreams, daydreams, nightmares, chronicles, diaries, records, reports, lies, gossip, local news, confessions, plans, predictions, announcements, pronouncements, prophesies, fantasies, intentions, as well as dances, popular music, pantomimes, paintings, stained glass windows, movies, cartoons and combinations of any of the above.

"...narration needs not only a storyteller but also an attentive listener who agrees to accept the conventions of the tale and its telling."

Our well-being and sometimes our very survival can depend on the story we hear. A revised scrap of memory, a secret location disclosed, the winning number leaked, a name overheard, or a crucial detail omitted from someone's testimony in court can actually change the course of history.

Even if almost anything with words can be considered a kind of narrative, we still need to know more about what defines it. We already accept that a story requires both a teller and a listener, but what about length? A narrative can nestle inside a single sentence like, "People in glass houses shouldn't throw stones"—or can take a thousand and one nights in the telling, like *The Arabian Nights*.

According to Aristotle, a narrative should have a beginning, a middle and an ending. "The middles should develop in a linear way to connect beginnings with ends sequentially in order to produce unified and harmonious effects upon readers ... ." He also thought that middles, unlike highways and Canada Post, oughtn't to take the shortest track between two points. Pleasure was to be taken in the scenery along the way.

Everything in a narrative also has to take place through *time*. The separate elements of theme, characters, plots, events, relationships, imagery and symbols all need time in which to be developed.

Issue 1

If the story has been clearly told, with sufficient details, ordered in a coherent and memorable fashion, then the reader will accumulate a sense of the story's past.

Narrative also needs to convey a clear sense of *sequence*, in order of occurrence. The organisation of experience created by the writer is recreated in the reader's mind, although the events themselves need not be presented chronologically. Readers today are all comfortable with the flashback or the story that opens in the middle of the character's life in which we may discover a tremendous amount about the person's life (or death) before we are told the first things about his or her childhood. A well-crafted narrative conveys a feeling of rightness in its order of unfolding of the events. Aristotle felt that the order must be such "that repositioning or removal (of a section of narrative) would cause confusion or misshapenness."

With sequence comes *consequence*. Part of a reader's pleasure (and proof of a writer's skill) is in being able to anticipate a probable outcome to the story based on an understanding and recollection of the characters and events of that particular story-world. How many of us emerge blinking from the movie theatre lost in the predictions of possible futures for the characters with which we've come to identify?

Yet writers are the first to admit the chaotic impulses that go into creating narratives. Richard Ford, a contemporary American novelist, describes the process this way: "Stories and novels too—are makeshift things. They originate in strong disorderly impulses that are supplied by random accumulations of life-in-words and proceed in their creation by mischance, faulty memory, distorted understanding, weariness, deceit of almost every imaginable kind, by luck and by the stresses of increasingly inadequate vocabulary and waning imagination—with the result being a straining, barely containable object held in fierce and sometimes insufficient control."

These would seem unlikely conditions by which well-ordered, elegantly styled, realistic narratives such as Ford's are spun; yet, if he and other writers are to be believed, they are precisely the ones which seem to work best.

So what were the first narratives? Perhaps they were tales of exploits brought back from the hunt and told to the others around a flickering fire, accompanied by broad gestures and pantomime, some collaboration from other witnesses in recalling the details and inevitably a little embroidery. Mothers and elders captured the interest of children with cautionary tales and parables about human nature and the natural kingdom that both instructed and amused them passing on wisdom in a form that was both pleasant and memorable. Eventually, inside any community, artists of narrative naturally would have emerged to become the shamans, sages and entertainers. Stories eventually expanded as people became spiritually sophisticated to include those about the world of gods and superhuman creatures living above earth as well also those of subhumans dwelling below—myths that explained and illustrated the origins of a people and their beliefs. Stories told in songs and rhyming verse gave rise to epic poems of warriors or sailors on brave quests, of knights and the women they loved, the dragons they fought.

With the revolution of printing techniques and the rise of literacy, narrative could be written and bound into books. The reader no longer needed to depend on a storyteller, priest or shaman for stories and information and thus, the pursuit of reading as a private pleasure was born. Stories in book form could easily travel around the world, be translated, and exchanged with those of other cultures. Stories could also exist, independent of their storytellers. In oral cultures, both singer or orator and listener shared a common reality simply because they were both present at the same place and time and shared an understanding of the world around them. Now with literacy, narratives could enjoy a kind of word-perfect immortality. Fixed on the printed page and passed down from generation to generation, they became permanent—and increasingly more detailed—records of realities that otherwise tended to pass into oblivion or suffered alteration by the imperfect recollections and biases of those who repeated them.

The revolution of print brought the first pamphlets, forerunners of the newspaper, to the common reader, featuring short essays of fact and opinion which gave rise to longer accounts of factual experience—or experience that declared itself to be very similar to fact—like Daniel Defoe's *Robinson Crusoe*, published in serial form in 1719. There have always been people curious to know the thoughts and feelings of others and written narrative was the only art that could reveal that interior. Writing expanded into the larger picture of life called the novel and became the dominant form of literature for the next two hundred or so years—"a key that lets us into the hearts of men we have never seen and not infrequently opens our own to us," as Oscar Wilde put it.

The hearts, minds and experiences of women also found their way into printed record for the first time as women picked up pens and wrote their own stories (sometimes under a male pseudonym like Mary Ann Cross who used the name George Eliot). To think of the development of the novel is to think of the works of Jane Austen, the Bronte sisters, Virginia Woolf, Harriet Beecher Stowe, and others. Novels began, more and more, to depict the real lives of men and women.

Books are powerful symbols of freedom and truth, records of the knowledge and wisdom of people accumulated throughout time, available to anyone possessed of the skill to decipher words. Smashing the vessel that holds ideas does not, of course, destroy the ideas themselves, but throughout history the burning of books has occasionally been resorted to in times of purge and oppression and is almost universally viewed as an act of sacrilege against humanity, demoralizing to those forced to stand by and watch—from Savonarola's bonfire of the *Vanities* during the Renaissance to Krystalnacht, the infamous night of Nazi book-pyres to the *Fatwah*-incited burnings in Manhattan of Salman Rushdie's *Satanic Verses*.

Yet, the story of ourselves will survive! Narratives have been written on tiny scraps of paper and smuggled out of prisons, stuffed inside the tires of cars and driven across the borders, packed into rockets and shot into space, interred with mummies in pyramids, chiselled into cliff faces and scratched into biscuit lids at the North Pole. The technology of recording and displaying narrative inevitably grows ever more sophisticated but the basic recipe—and hunger—for stories has not changed since the first account given by the first teller to the first listener.

APPETIZER

Robert H. Abel

I'm fishing this beautiful stream in Alaska, catching salmon, char and steelhead, when this bear lumbers out of the woods and down to the stream bank. He fixes me with this half-amused, half-curious look which says: You are meat.

The bear's eyes are brown and his shiny golden fur is standing up in spikes, which shows me he has been fishing, too, perhaps where the stream curves behind the peninsula of woods he has just trudged through. He's not making any sound I can hear over the rumble of the water in the softball-sized rocks, but his presence is very loud.

I say "his" presence because temporarily I am not interested in or able to assess the creature's sex. I am looking at a head that is bigger around than my steering wheel, a pair of paws awash in river bubbles that could cover half my windshield. I am glad that I am wearing polarized fishing glasses so the bear cannot see the little teardrops of fear that have crept into the corner of my eyes. To assure him/her I am not the least bit intimidated, I make another cast.

Immediately I tie into a fat Chinook. The splashing of the fish in the stream engages the bear's attention, but he/she registers this for the moment only by shifting his/her glance. I play the fish smartly and when it comes gliding in, tired, pinksided, glittering and astonished, I pluck it out of the water by inserting a finger in its gill—something I normally wouldn't do in order not to injure the fish before I set it free, and I do exactly what you would do in the same situation—throw it to the bear.

The bear's eyes widen and she—for I can see now past her huge shoulder and powerful haunches that she is a she—turns and pounces on the fish with such speed and nimbleness that I am numbed. There is no chance in hell that I, in my insulated waders, am going to outrun her, dodge her blows, escape her jaws. While she is occupied devouring the fish—I can hear her teeth clacking together—I do what you or anyone else would do and cast again.

God answers my muttered prayer and I am blessed with the strike of another fat salmon, like the others on its way to spawning grounds upstream. I would like this fish to survive and release its eggs or sperm to perpetuate the salmon kingdom, but Ms. Bear has just licked her whiskers clean and has now moved knee-deep into the water and, to my consternation, leans against me rather like a large and friendly dog, although her ears are at the level of my shoulder and her back is broader than that of any horse I have ever seen. Ms. Bear is intensely interested in the progress of the salmon toward us, and her head twists and twitches as the fish circles, darts, takes line away, shakes head, rolls over, leaps.

With a bear at your side, it is not the simplest thing to play a fish properly, but the presence of this huge animal, and especially her long snout, thick as my thigh, wonderfully concentrates the mind. She smells like the forest floor, like crushed moss and damp leaves, and she is as warm as a radiator back in my Massachusetts home, the thought of which floods me with a terrible nostalgia. Now I debate whether I should just drift the salmon in under the bear's nose and let her take it that way, but I'm afraid she will break off my fly and leader and right now that fly—a Doctor Wilson number eight—is saving my life. So, with much anxiety, I pretend to take charge and bring the fish in on the side away from the bear, gill and quickly unhook it, turn away from the bear and toss the fish behind me to the bank.

The bear wheels and clambers upon it at once, leaving a vortex of water pouring into the vacuum of the space she has left, which almost topples me. As her teeth snack away, I quickly and furtively regard my poor Doctor Wilson, which is fish-mauled now, bedraggled, almost unrecognizable. But the present emergency compels me to zing it out once again. I walk a few paces downstream, hoping the bear will remember an appointment or become distracted and I can sneak away.

But a few seconds later she is leaning against me again, raptly watching the stream for any sign of a salmon splash. My luck holds, another fish smacks the withered Wilson, flings sunlight and water in silver jets as it dances its last dance. I implore the salmon's forgiveness: something I had once read revealed that this is the way of all primitive hunters, to take the life reluctantly and to pray for the victim's return. I think my prayer is as urgent as that of any Mashpee or Yoruban, or Tlingit or early Celt, for I not only want the salmon to thrive forever, I want a superabundance of them now, right now, to save my neck. I have an idea this hungry bear, bereft of fish, would waste little time in conducting any prayer ceremonies before she turned me into the main course my salmon were just the appetizer for. When I take up this fish, the bear practically rips it from my hand, and the sight of those teeth so close, and the truly persuasive power of those muscled, pink-rimmed jaws, cause a wave of fear in me so great that I nearly faint.

My vertigo subsides as Ms. Bear munches and destroys the salmon with hearty shakes of her head and I sneak a few more paces downstream, rapidly also with trembling fingers tie on a new Doctor Wilson, observing the utmost care (as you would do) in making my knots. I cast and stride downstream, wishing I could just plunge into the crystalline water and bowl away like a log. My hope and plan is to wade my way back to the narrow trail a few hundred yards ahead and, when Ms. Bear loses interest or is somehow distracted, make a heroic dash for my camper. I think of the thermos of hot coffee on the front seat, the six-pack of beer in the cooler, the thin rubber mattress with the blue sleeping bag adorning it, warm wool socks in a bag hanging from a window crank, and almost burst into tears, these simple things, given the presence of Ms. Hungry Bear, seem so miraculous, so emblematic of the life I love to live. I promise the gods—American, Indian, African, Oriental—that if I survive I will never complain again, not even if my teenage children leave the caps off the toothpaste tubes or their bicycles in the driveway at home.

"Oh, home," I think, and cast again.

Ms. Bear rejoins me. You may or may not believe me, and perhaps after all it was only my imagination worked up by terror, but two things happened which gave me a particle of hope. The first was that Ms. Bear actually belched—quite noisily and unapologetically, too, like a rude uncle at a Christmas dinner. She showed no signs of having committed any impropriety, and yet it was clear to me that a belching bear is probably also a bear with a pretty full belly. A few more salmon and perhaps Ms. Bear would wander off in search of a berry dessert.

Now the second thing she did, or that I imagined she did, was to begin—well, not *speaking* to me exactly, but communicating somehow. I know it sounds foolish, but if you were in my shoes—my waders, to be more precise—you might have learned bear talk pretty quickly, too. It's not as if the bear were speaking to me in complete sentences and English words such as "Get me another fish, pal, or you're on the menu," but in a much more indirect and subtle way, almost in the way a stream talks through its bubbling and burbling and rattling of rocks and gurgling along.

Believe me, I listened intently, more with my mind than with my ears, as if the bear were telepathizing—I know you're not going to believe this, but it's true, I am normally not what you would call an egomaniac with an inflated self-esteem such that I imagine that every bear which walks out of the woods falls in love with me—but I really did truly believe now that this Ms. Bear was expressing feelings of, well, *affection*. Really, I think she kinda liked me. True or not, the feeling made me less afraid. In fact, and I don't mean this in any erotic or perverse kind of way but, I had to admit, once my fear had passed, my feelings were kinda mutual. Like you might feel for an old pal of a dog. Or a favourite horse. I only wish she weren't such a big eater. I only wish she were not a carnivore, and I, carne.

Now she nudges me with her nose.

"All right, all right," I say. *"I'm doing the best I can."*

Cast in the glide behind that big boulder, the bear telepathizes me. *There is a couple of whoppers in there.*

I do as I'm told and wham! the bear is right! Instantly I'm tied into a granddaddy Chinook, a really burly fellow who has no intention of lying down on anybody's platter beneath a blanket of lemon slices and scallion shoots, let alone make his last wiggle down a bear's gullet. Even the bear is excited and begins shifting weight from paw to paw, a little motion for her that nevertheless has big consequences for me as her body slams against my hip, then slams again.

Partly because I don't want to lose the fish, but partly also because I want to use the fish as an excuse to move closer to my getaway trail, I stumble downstream. This fish has my rod bent into an upside-down *U* and I'm hoping my quick-tied knots are also strong enough to take this salmon's lurching and his intelligent, broadside swinging into the river current—a very smart fish! Ordinarily I might take a long time with a fish like this, baby it in, but now I'm putting on as much pressure as I dare. When the salmon flips into a little side pool, the bear takes matters into her own hands, clambers over the rocks, pounces, nabs the salmon smartly behind the head and lumbers immediately to the bank. My leader snaps at once and while Ms. Bear attends to the destruction of the fish, I tie on another fly and make some shambling headway downstream. Yes, I worry about the hook still in the fish, but only because I do not want this bear to be irritated by anything. I want her to be replete and smug and doze off in the sun. I try to telepathize as much. Please, Bear, sleep.

Inevitably, the fishing slows down, but Ms. Bear does not seem to mind. Again she belches. Myself, I am getting quite a headache and know that I am fighting exhaustion. On a normal morning of humping along in waders over these slippery softball-sized rocks, I would be tired in any case. The added emergency is foreclosing all my energy reserves. I even find myself getting a little angry, frustrated at least, and I marvel at the bear's persistence, her inexhaustible doggedness. And appetite: I catch fish, I toss them to her. At supermarket prices, I calculate she has eaten about six hundred dollars worth of fish. The calculating gives me something to think about besides my fear.

At last I am immediately across from the opening to the trail which twines back through the woods to where my camper rests in the dapple shade of mighty pines. Still, five hundred yards separate me from this imagined haven. I entertain the notion perhaps someone else will come along and frighten the bear away, maybe someone with a dog or a gun, but I have already spent many days here without seeing another soul, and in fact have chosen to return here for that very reason. I have told myself for many years that I really do love nature, love being among the animals, am restored by wilderness adventure. Considering that right now I would like nothing better than to be nestled beside my wife in front of a blazing fire, this seems to be a sentiment in need of some revision.

Now, as if in answer to my speculations, the bear turns beside me, her rump pushing me into water deeper than I want to be in, where my footing is shaky, and she stares into the woods, ears forward. She has heard something I cannot hear, or smelled something I cannot smell, and while I labour back to shallower water and surer footing, I hope some backpackers or some bear-poaching Indians are about to appear and send Ms. Bear a-galloping away. Automatically, I continue casting, but I also cannot help glancing over my shoulder in hopes of seeing what Ms. Bear sees. And in a moment I do.

It is another bear.

Unconsciously, I release a low moan, but my voice is lost in the guttural warning of Ms. Bear to the trespasser. The new arrival answers with a defiant cough. He—I believe it is a he—can afford to be defiant because he is half again as large as my companion. His fur seems longer and coarser, and though its substance is as golden as that of the bear beside me, the tips are black and this dark surface ripples and undulates over his massive frame. His nostrils are flared and he is staring with profound concentration at me.

Now I am truly confused and afraid. Would it be better to catch another salmon or not? I surely cannot provide for two of these beasts and in any case Mister Bear does not seem the type to be distracted by or made friendly by any measly salmon tribute. His whole bearing—pardon the expression—tells me my intrusion into this bear world is a personal affront to his bear honour. Only Ms. Bear stands between us and, after all, whose side is she really on? By bear standards, I am sure a rather regal and handsome fellow has made his appearance. Why should the fur-covered heart of furry Ms. Bear go out to me? How much love can a few hundred dollars worth of salmon buy? Most likely, this couple even have a history, know and have known each other from other seasons even though for the moment they prefer to pretend to regard each other as total strangers.

How disturbed I am is well illustrated by my next course of action. It is completely irrational, and I cannot account for it, or why it saved me—if indeed it did. I cranked in my line and lay my rod across some rocks, then began the arduous process of pulling myself out of my waders while trying to balance myself on those awkward rocks in that fast water. I tipped and swayed as I tugged at my boots, pushed my waders down, my arms in the foaming, frigid water, then the waders also filling, making it even more difficult to pull my feet free.

I emerged like a nymph from a cocoon, wet and trembling. The bears regarded me with clear stupefaction, as if one of them had casually stepped out of his or her fur. I drained what water I could from the waders, then dropped my fly rod into them, and held them before me. The damned rocks were brutal on my feet, but I marched toward the trail opening, lifting and dropping first one, then the other leg of my waders as if I were operating a giant puppet. The water still in the waders gave each footfall an impressive authority, and I was half thinking that, well, if the big one attacks, maybe he'll be fooled into chomping the waders first and I'll at least now be able to run. I did not relish the idea of pounding down the trail in my nearly bare feet, but it was a damn sight better way to argue with the bear than being sucked from my waders like a snail from its shell. Would you have done differently?

Who knows what the bears thought, but I tried to make myself look as much as possible like a camel or some other extreme and inedible form of four-footedness as I plodded along the trail. The bears looked at each other, then at me as I clomped by, the water in the waders making an odd gurgling sound, and me making an odd sound, too, on remembering just then how the Indians would, staring death in the eye, sing their death song. Having no such melody prepared, and never having been anything but a bathtub singer, I chanted forth the only song I ever committed to memory: "Jingle Bells."

Yes, "Jingle Bells," I sang, "jingle all the way," and I lifted first one, then the other wader leg and dropped it stomping down. "Oh what fun it is to ride in a one-horse open sleigh-ay!"

The exercise was to prove to me just how complicated and various is the nature of the bear. The male reared up, blotting out the sun, bellowed, then twisted on his haunches and crashed off into the woods. The female, head cocked in curiosity, followed at a slight distance, within what still might be called striking distance whether I was out of my waders or not. Truly, I did not appreciate her persistence. Hauling the waders half full of water before me was trying work and the superfluous thought struck me: suppose someone sees me now, plumping along like this, singing "Jingle Bells," a bear in attendance? Vanity, obviously, never sleeps. But as long as the bear kept her distance I saw no reason to change my *modus operandi.*

When I came within about one hundred feet of my camper, its white cap gleaming like a remnant of spring snow and beckoning me, I risked everything, dropped the waders and sped for the cab. The bear broke into a trot, too, I was sure, because although I couldn't see her, had my sights locked on the gleaming handle to the pickup door, I sure enough could hear those big feet slapping the ground behind me in a heavy rhythm, a terrible and elemental beat that sang to me of my own frailty, fragile bones and tender flesh. I plunged on like a madman, grabbed the camper door and hurled myself in.

I lay on the seat panting, curled like a child, shuddered when the bear slammed against the pickup's side. The bear pressed her nose to the window, then curiously, unceremoniously licked the glass with her tongue. I know (and you know) she could have shattered the glass with a single blow, and I tried to imagine what I should do if indeed she resorted to this simple expedient. Fisherman that I am, I had nothing in the cab of the truck to defend myself with except a tire iron, and that not readily accessible behind the seat I was cowering on. My best defense, obviously, was to start the pickup and drive away.

Just as I sat up to the steering wheel and inserted the key, however, Ms. Bear slammed her big paws on to the hood and hoisted herself aboard. The pickup shuddered with the weight of her, and suddenly the windshield was full of her golden fur. I beeped the horn loud and long numerous times, but this had about the same effect as my singing, only causing her to shake her huge head, which vibrated the truck terribly. She stomped around on the hood and then lay down, back against the windshield, which now appeared to have been covered by a huge shag rug.

Could I believe my eyes?

No, I could not believe my eyes. My truck was being smothered in bear. In a moment I also could not believe my ears—Ms. Bear had decided the camper hood was the perfect place for a nap, and she was snoring, snoring profoundly, her body twitching like a cat's. Finally, she had responded to my advice and desires, but at the most inappropriate time. I was trapped. Blinded by bear body!

My exhaustion had been doubled by my sprint for the camper, and now that I was not in such a desperate panic, I felt the cold of the water that had soaked my clothes and I began to tremble. It also crossed my mind that perhaps Mister Bear was still in the vicinity, and if Ms. Bear was not smart enough, or cruel enough, to smash my window to get at me, he just might be.

Therefore, I started the engine—which disturbed Ms. Bear not a whit—and rolled down the window enough to stick my head out and see down the rocky, limb-strewn trail. I figured a few jolts in those ruts and Ms. Bear would be off like a shot.

This proved a smug assumption. Ms. Bear did indeed awaken and bestir herself to a sitting position, a bit like an overgrown hood ornament, but quickly grew adept at balancing herself against the lurching and jolting of my truck, which, in fact, she seemed to enjoy. Just my luck, I growled, to find the first bear in Alaska who wanted a ride into town. I tried some quick braking and sharp turn maneuvers I thought might send her tumbling off, but her bulk was so massive, her paws so artfully spread, that she was just too stable an entity. She wanted a ride and there was nothing I could do about it.

When I came out of the woods to the gravel road known locally as the Dawson Artery, I had an inspiration. I didn't drive so fast that if Ms. Bear decided to clamber down she would be hurt, but I did head for the main road which led to Buckville and the Buckville Cannery. Ms. Bear swayed happily along the whole ten miles to that intersection and seemed not to bat any eye when first one big logging truck, then another plummeted by. I pulled out onto the highway, and for the safety of both of us—those logging trucks have dubious brakes and their drivers get paid by the trip—I had to accelerate considerably.

I couldn't see much of Ms. Bear except her back and rump as I had to concentrate on the road, some of which is pretty curvy in that coastal area, shadowed also by the giant pines. But from the attitude expressed by her posture, I'd say she was having a whale, or should I say a salmon of a time. I saw a few cars and pickups veering out of the oncoming lane onto the shoulder as we swept by, but I didn't have time, really, to appreciate the astonishment of their drivers. In this way, my head out the window, Ms. Bear perched on the hood, I drove to the Buckville Cannery and turned into the long driveway.

Ms. Bear knew right away something good was ahead for she rose on all fours now and stuck her nose straight out like a bird dog on a pheasant. Her legs quivered with nervous anticipation as we approached, and as soon as I came out of the trees into the parking area, she went over the front of the camper like someone plunging into a pool.

Don't tell me you would have done any differently. I stopped right there and watched Ms. Bear march down between the rows of cars and right up the truck ramp into the cannery itself. She was not the least bit intimidated by all the noise of the machines and the grinders and stampers in there, or the shouting of the workers.

Now the Buckville Cannery isn't that big—I imagine about two dozen people work there on any given day—and since it is so remote, has no hurricane fence around it, and no security guard. After all, what's anybody going to steal out of there besides a few cases of canned salmon or some bags of frozen fish parts that will soon become some company's cat food? The main building is up on a little hill and conveyors run down from there to the docks where the salmon boats pull in—the sea is another half mile away—and unload their catch.

I would say that in about three minutes after Ms. Bear walked into the cannery, twenty of the twenty-four workers were climbing out down the conveyors, dropping from open windows, or charging out the doors. The other four just hadn't got wind of the event yet, but in a little while they came bounding out, too, one fellow pulling up his trousers as he ran. They all assembled on the semicircular drive before the main office and had a union meeting of some vigor.

Myself, I was too tired to participate, and in any case did not want to be held liable for the disturbance at the Buckville Cannery, and so I made a U-turn and drove on into Buckville itself where I took a room above the Buckville Tavern and had a hot shower and a really nice nap. That night in the Tap and Lounge I got to hear many an excited story about the she-bear who freeloaded at the cannery for a couple of hours before she was driven off by blowing, ironically enough, the lunch whistle loud and long. I didn't think it was the right time or place to testify to my part in that historical event, and for once kept my mouth shut. You don't like trouble any more than I do, and I'm sure you would have done about the same.

THE GREENHOUSE EFFECT

Sarah Sheard

What, exactly is the point of art? Why, for instance, have I lined whole rooms in my house with shelves of the novels, plays, art books and poetry that I've been collecting since childhood, together with cassettes, as well as those supposedly indestructible CDs, of everything from Ghanaian talking drum music to my brother's annual Christmas compositions? Visitors have asked me, why do I invest so much time and space *and money* in this stuff of art?

If it's a stranger asking and I'm feeling a little shy I might go the rational route and quote the humanist psychologist Carl Rogers. Our society, he says, is not particularly encouraging of creative, individualistic thinking. Just look, he might say to my questioner, at what we're wearing right now for example. What did we eat for breakfast; what route did we take to school or work; what endearing words did we murmur to our lovers on the phone, our cat on the chair? How far does any of us stray from a repetition of the comfortingly familiar? In order to survive, Rogers says, humans need to respond to their rapidly changing world with creativity and imagination — to anticipate the future before it all too swiftly becomes the past. Reading novels, listening to music, looking at paintings and photographs keeps our imaginations stimulated, nourishes the playful parts of ourselves. Even polar bears have been known to take time out from the serious business of survival to frolic with husky dogs. We humans need to frolic too and the arts are perhaps the highest form of that.

This kind of response satisfies the casual questioner but for my close friends I reveal a second, more intimate reason for my lifelong indulgence in books, art and music: because of the pure, raw *pleasure* they give me. The arts are medicinal. I put on my Ghanaian drum chants because I crave the excitement they pump into my bones, the chemistry they stir up in my blood, the delicious tension they arouse in my muscles, until soon I'm shaking and shimmying off a week's worth of traffic jams and cobwebs, my body remembering once again how much it loves moving to music until the sweat flies off my hair.

On the other hand, highway driving was made for opera. I prefer German these days to Italian and devotional choral music in minor keys from almost any culture, all of which I find emotionally moving but never distracting. The sound of voices singing in a language I can't understand provides companionship, strengthens my concentration and, I've been told, significantly smoothes my moves through heavy traffic.

In general, whenever I find myself emotionally blunted by the repetitious aspects of life and love in the big city, I use music to sharpen myself back to normal, amplify whatever is going on inside me so that I can feel it better –even the blues. Sometimes a hurtin' country and western song or a blast of Miles Davis' trumpet is exactly what the doctor ordered.

One snapping cold day in February, when the downtown sky matched the colour of the salt-caked concrete below, my whole being began to ache for the bright splash of tulips and the smell of warm earth. Walking into the Art Gallery that afternoon was like entering a greenhouse. I floated through rooms hung with paintings like windows onto English landscapes, Paris cafes, gardens where nobles lounged against trees with their ladies. There were Classical Greek sculptures of incredibly graceful men and women, story paintings of heroes battling giants, whales capsizing ships, then two rooms of contemporary photographs, huge framed shots of streets around the world. I stared down the length of a winding Tokyo thoroughfare, stood before the Winter Palace in St. Petersburg, a meadow outside Hamburg, a bustling marketplace in Rome. Around the corner I found myself staring into the weary eyes of a saint. Beyond him, those of a nymph, crinkled with pleasure as she tugged her lover's beard, his big ears flushed with passion. On the wall opposite, a Madonna shielded her child with a fold of cloth painted so skilfully, the fabric glowed like a candle through milk. I crept closer to search for brush strokes, for the technique behind the magic and then noticed the date. The hand that had applied those brush strokes, over 500 years ago, had long since turned to dust. I shivered, feeling a thrill of pleasure at being alive to enjoy my bleak February afternoon.

When I stepped back outside, it was even colder and almost dark now but I felt warmed and awake again to the scene around me, my sense of scale restored. I'd been given a holiday from myself and my world by experiencing the countless, gorgeous visions of others.

"Art is a resuscitator, eye candy, soul food."

Books and films, music, plays, photographs, all these provide almost instant relief from feelings of staleness and boredom with myself. They help me "kickstart" my own forgotten playfulness and joy whenever my brain gets flooded with the six o'clock news, the afternoon mail, the stacked-up phone calls, the looming deadlines, the unkept promises. Art is a resuscitator, eye candy, soul food. It can bring on for a moment the taste of a second childhood, restore something of our own innate creativity and remind us that life need not be an entirely grey affair.

Issue 1

ON PHOTOGRAPHY

Susan Sontag

*R*ecently, photography has become almost as widely practised an amusement as sex and dancing—which means that, like every mass art form, photography is not practised by most people as an art. It is mainly a social rite, a defense against anxiety, and a tool of power.

Memorializing the achievements of individuals considered as members of families (as well as of other groups) is the earliest popular use of photography. For at least a century, the wedding photograph has been as much a part of the ceremony as the prescribed verbal formulas. Cameras go with family life. According to a sociological study done in France, most households have a camera, but a household with children is twice as likely to have at least one camera as a household in which there are no children. Not to take pictures of one's children, particularly when they are small, is a sign of parental indifference, just as not turning up for one's graduation picture is a gesture of adolescent rebellion.

Through photographs, each family constructs a portrait-chronicle of itself—a portable kit of images that bears witness to its connectedness. It hardly matters what activities are photographed so long as photographs get taken and are cherished. Photography becomes a rite of family life just when, in the industrializing countries of Europe and America, the very institution of the family starts undergoing radical surgery. As that claustrophobic unit, the nuclear family, was being carved out of a much larger family aggregate, photography came along to memorialize, to restate symbolically, the imperiled continuity and vanishing extendedness of family life. Those ghostly traces, photographs, supply the token presence of the dispersed relatives. A family's photograph album is generally about the extended family—and, often, is all that remains of it.

As photographs give people an imaginary possession of a past that is unreal, they also help to take possession of space in which they are insecure. Thus, photography develops in tandem with one of the most characteristic of modern activities: tourism. For the first time in history, large numbers of people regularly travel out of their ha-

275

Issue 1

"...each family constructs a portrait-chronicle of itself."

bitual environments for short periods of time. It seems positively un-natural to travel for pleasure without taking a camera along. Photographs will offer indisputable evidence that the trip was made, that the program was carried out, that fun was had. Photographs document sequences of consumption carried on outside the view of family, friends, neighbours. But dependence on the camera, as

Issue 1

the device that makes real what one is experiencing, doesn't fade when people travel more. Taking photographs fills the same need for the cosmopolitans accumulating photograph-trophies of their boat trip up the Albert Nile or their fourteen days in China as it does for lower-middle-class vacationers taking snapshots of the Eiffel Tower or Niagara Falls.

A way of certifying experience, taking photographs is also a way of refusing it—by limiting experience to a search for the photogenic, by converting experience into an image, a souvenir. Travel becomes a strategy for accumulating photographs. The very activity of taking pictures is soothing, and assuages general feelings of disorientation that are likely to be exacerbated by travel. Most tourists feel compelled to put the camera between themselves and whatever is remarkable that they encounter. Unsure of other responses, they take a picture. This gives shape to experience: stop, take a photograph, and move on. The method especially appeals to people handicapped by a ruthless work ethic—Germans, Japanese, and Americans. Using a camera appeases the anxiety which the work-driven feel about not working when they are on vacation and supposed to be having fun. They have something to do that is like a friendly imitation of work: they can take pictures.

People robbed of their past seem to make the most fervent picture takers, at home and abroad. Everyone who lives in an industrialized society is obliged gradually to give up the past, but in certain countries, such as the United States and Japan, the break with the past has been particularly traumatic. In the early 1970s, the fable of the brash American tourist of the 1950s and 1960s, rich with dollars and Babbittry, was replaced by the mystery of the group-minded Japanese tourist, newly released from his island prison by the miracle of overvalued yen, who is generally armed with two cameras, one on each hip.

❖

Photography has become one of the principal devices for experiencing something, for giving an appearance of participation. One full-page ad shows a small group of people standing pressed together, peering out of the photograph, all but one looking stunned, excited, upset. The one who wears a different expression holds a camera to his eye; he seems self-possessed, is almost smiling. While

"Taking photographs has set up a chronic voyeuristic relation to the world."

the others are passive, clearly alarmed spectators, having a camera has transformed one person into something active, a voyeur: only he has mastered the situation. What do these people see? We don't know. And it doesn't matter. It is an Event: something worth seeing—and therefore worth photographing. The ad copy, white letters across the dark lower third of the photograph like news coming over a teletype machine, consists of just six words: ". . . Prague . . . Woodstock . . . Vietnam . . . Sapporo . . . Londonderry . . . LEICA." Crushed hopes, youth antics, colonial wars, and winter sports are alike—are equalized by the camera. Taking photographs has set up a chronic voyeuristic relation to the world which levels the meaning of all events.

A photograph is not just the result of an encounter between an event and a photographer; picture-taking is an event in itself, and one with even more peremptory rights—to interfere with, to invade, or to ignore whatever is going on. Our very sense of situation is now articulated by the camera's interventions. The omnipresence of cameras persuasively suggests that time consists of interesting events, events worth photographing. This, in turn, makes it easy to feel that any event, once underway, and whatever its moral character, should be allowed to complete itself—so that something else can be brought into the world, the photograph. After the event has ended, the picture will still exist, conferring on the event a kind of immortality (and importance) it would never otherwise have enjoyed. While real people are out there killing themselves or other real people, the photographer stays behind his or her camera, creating a tiny element of another world: the image-world that bids to outlast us all.

Photographing is essentially an act of non-intervention ... how plausible it has become, in situations where the photographer has the choice between a photograph and a life, to choose the photograph. The person who intervenes cannot record; the person who is recording cannot intervene. ... Dziga Vertov's great film, *Man with a Movie Camera* (1929), gives the ideal image of the photographer as someone in perpetual movement, someone moving through a panorama of disparate events with such agility and speed that any intervention is out of the question. Hitchcock's *Rear Window* (1954) gives the complementary image: the photographer played by James Stewart has an intensified relation to one event, through his camera, precisely because he has a broken leg and is confined to a wheelchair; being temporarily immobilized prevents him from acting on what he sees, and makes it even more important to take pictures. Even if incompatible with intervention in a physical sense, using a camera is still a form of participation. Although the camera is an observation station, the act of photographing is more than passive observing. Like sexual voyeurism, it is a way of at least tacitly, often explicitly, encouraging whatever is going on to keep on happening. To take a picture is to have an interest in things as they are, in the status quo remaining unchanged (at least for as long as it takes to get a "good" picture), to be in complicity with whatever makes a subject interesting, worth photographing—including, when that is the interest, another person's pain or misfortune.

Review

On Photography

In this thoughtful essay, the author studies the cameras and the role the related practice of photography plays in our lives.

As Sontag suggests, photographs are regarded as such an accurate representation of what lies "out there" that they are commonly admissible as evidence in a court of law. We "take" wedding, baby and other pictures to chronicle important events.

And we use the camera, Sontag argues, as a defense against our anxieties and fears, to make us feel comfortable in foreign spaces. "Most tourists feel compelled to put the camera between themselves and whatever is remarkable that they encounter," she observes. "Unsure of other responses, they take a picture."

So, when encountering amazing works of nature or humans, like Niagara Falls or the Great Wall of China, the Grand Canyon or the Parthenon, the tourist aims, frames and clicks the shutter. The camera shapes the experience and by default establishes a passive role for the tourist, who by seeing the world through a viewfinder becomes a chronic voyeur, a spectator, an observer instead of a participant. The tourist denies his own awe and sense of wonder, capturing though diluting the power of the moment.

According to Sontag, the camera, and thereby the person using it, takes a morally neutral position towards the photographic subject. Taking a photograph, she writes, is "an act of non-intervention." The media show astonishing, even shocking photographs related to natural and human-made disasters and tragedies, floods, famines, assassinations and other events focusing on human suffering that are repetitiously the central component. By snapping the picture, the photographer preserves the unfortunate situation on film before attempting to improve it. And so, says Sontag, the picture taker may end up prolonging the suffering for as long as it takes to get a "good" picture.

FILM: CULTURE OR COMMERCE

Jean-Claude Carriere

This essay by Jean-Claude Carriere describes the attempt by the United States to seek a worldwide monopoly in film and TV production. To promote this campaign, Americans vigorously oppose any effort by foreign countries to protect and support their own production of images and stories. In France, film is considered an art form; in the U.S., motion pictures are big business. Big business wants free trade; art, particularly in countries with a small potential audience, needs government protection and support. Is it possible for countries like France, Great Britain and Canada to resist being swamped with American stories and perspectives? Jean-Claude Carriere asks, "Is the ability to tell our own stories with the most modern means, to study ourselves in our own mirror, merely a way of enhancing life, or is it vital to life itself?" His clear response is that it is vital to see your world from a perspective grounded in your own culture. Otherwise, the whole world is destined to view the problems of growing up, finding a mate, facing danger and growing old through the filter of California eyes. Carriere makes it clear that he doesn't want to ban American film and TV, but only to make a place for other voices. His essay has a special resonance for Canadians, who often find themselves trying to protect their cultural products from the aggressive actions of American commerce.

The following essay is an excerpt from Jean-Claude Carriere's book, The Secret Language of Film. *Carriere is president of FEMIS, France's only film school, and his screenwriting credits include* The Tin Drum, The Unbearable Lightness of Being, The Return of Martin Guerre, Cyrano de Bergerac *and* Belle de Jour.

*F*ilm (they say) is a popular art form that now seems restricted to a dwindling audience of filmmakers and filmgoers. No one can really say why. Perhaps because, in television, the cinema has met an even more popular challenger. But this is not certain. Nor, I believe, is the game over.

In most countries, particularly in the Third World (with the exception of India, China, and Iran), it is getting harder, chiefly for economic reasons, to make films. The North American audiovisual industry has launched an all–out war. It seeks worldwide monopoly. Many countries didn't wake up to this in time and failed to protect themselves. Today, despite its vast potential market, starting a film company in a country like Brazil is an almost inevitable prelude to heroic failure.

American films, or rather American audiovisual products, movies and TV combined, are spreading across the globe and slowly annihilating local production.

This conquest is in fact a reconquest. In the early 1920s Hollywood enjoyed a near-monopoly on the manufacture of motion pictures, accounting for some eighty percent of world production. This percentage dropped in the following decades with the rise of foreign motion picture industries and the outbreak of the Second World War, which cut a large swath of territories off from American distribution.

Film: global culture or global commerce?

Issue 1

In 1945 the reconquest began. Its aims were clear and openly acknowledged. Its promoters consider film a consumer product like any other, of no particular cultural importance. They pursue their massive program of reconquest with every weapon that comes to hand. They have even been known to give certain television series to Brazilian and Russian networks, virtually free of charge.

It is a rational enterprise aimed at depriving all other countries, across the board, of their cinematic voice. "Movies are us," runs the American message, clear–eyed and uncompromising. "Why don't you make something else?"

Perhaps to skirt the kind of name–calling trap that sees Americans routinely stigmatized as "imperialists" and the French as "chauvinists," we should recall that our opposing viewpoints, which clashed along a broad front during the recent **GATT** talks, are rooted in separate but parallel traditions.

GATT—General Agreement on Tariff and Trade

The Anglo–Saxon tradition is the older of the two. It goes back to an early eighteenth-century edict of Queen Anne's, which gave printers the right to run off copy (or copyright). It allowed publishers and printers to buy a work from an author and do what they wanted with it. For nearly three centuries, with occasional ups and downs, the tradition has flourished in northern Europe and more recently in the United States.

A contrary tradition, born in late eighteenth–century France with Beaumarchais, holds that the author of the work remains its owner, with financial and moral rights to the work. This conception, considerably developed by Victor Hugo, has gained wide acceptance. It led, at the end of the nineteenth century, to the signing of the Berne Convention, which today is subscribed to by nearly a hundred countries across the world.

This fundamental contradiction between the two traditions explains why American film, never considered an art, has for so long been the work of producers. In Europe, on the other hand (and particularly in France), the idea that film is a form of artistic expression (and even an art in its own right) has taken root and matured. Like the directors and critics who launched the New Wave, the author or authors of films, insisting on the personal nature of their work by the Berne Convention, considered themselves artists on a par with painters and writers.

Issue 1

With this immediate consequence: if film is indeed an art, a legitimate form of cultural expression, it deserves to be given official support, even perhaps to be protected. In France this support comes from the Ministry of Culture; since 1947 it has taken different forms, chief among them a tax on cinema box–office receipts which goes to finance future film production.

The various issues that divided us during the GATT talks in no way diminish our old and lasting admiration for the enormous achievements of the American cinema. It is absurd to claim that Europe wants to shut itself off from American production, given that American images occupy seventy percent of our movie and television screens. Indeed, film seems to be part of the very flesh and blood of America. We could no more imagine America without film than we could imagine living (as the Iranians must) deprived of American film.

In fact, the whole quarrel is based on a misunderstanding. Once we have set it aside it becomes obvious that our two traditions, which have always coexisted, most often in total harmony, cannot possibly be amalgamated. It would be like asking a soccer team and an American football team to take the field together. Clearly impossible.

Nor can either tradition replace the other. They must go on co-existing. In the world ahead any kind of monopoly on the visual image would be unjust for some and dangerous for everyone.

In the discussions surrounding GATT or the North American Free Trade Agreement, the constant watch–word of American negotiators was "free competition." Unfortunately, the term doesn't mean the same thing everywhere. Could we call Mali and California "free" to compete with each other? That would clearly be meaningless. The term is a nineteenth-century formulation that masks boundless economic greed. Or, as someone put it: "A free fox in a free henhouse."

What the most ferocious measures of dictatorial regimes have historically failed to achieve—the silencing of the voice of nations—a simple trading clause could still bring about. In many countries, in fact, this has already happened. In the name of "liberalizing the market" (and not always foreseeing the danger), producers and authors have lowered their guard. And the fox has come in through the front door, bringing with him basketfuls of images and sounds, but also a whole gamut of products—clothes, drinks, cereals, vehicles, cigarettes, right down to the most basic items of everyday life—all represented and often glorified by those same images.

We know too that we have embraced these moving images as a universal language. But it is a language not every people gets to speak. Or more accurately, has the means to speak.

So at a deeper level we must ask whether the cinematographic image is necessary to nations. Is the ability to tell ourselves our own stories with the most modern means, to study ourselves in our own mirror, merely a way of enhancing life, or is it vital to life itself?

I believe it is vital to life. America's distributors say the opposite: what matter if Africans, Brazilians, even Europeans can no longer make films? We'll do it for them.

Africans are already condemned to an exclusive television diet of thrillers and romances made under alien skies, images which never speak to Africans about Africans.

The same danger threatens us.

The French production system—probably the world's most sophisticated, since it permits a mix of public and private money—represents the last square of resistance to the American invasion. If it collapses, not only French cinemas will disappear, but with it the last vestiges of European cinema: farewell Wim Wenders, Andrzej Wajda, Pedro Almodovar, Theo Angelopoulos, and so many others. And along with them every other maker of ambitious, poetic, innovative cinema (cinema still coproduced on the French model) across the world: farewell Kurosawa, Mikhailkov, Yi Mu, and Souleyman Cisse.

By defending ourselves we defend them too. Far from being "chauvinists," we are defending the right to exist of different concepts of film, wherever they may arise.

Two radically different conceptions are at war.

The two countries that invented cinema, the United States and France, once again face each other across the battle lines. What an enormous pity, particularly when you reflect that this commercial war is being waged in one direction only. No one in Europe seeks the disappearance of American film. That would be absurd and unreal. American film is and has long been massively represented on our screens, and we very much want it to stay. Ours is practically nonexistent in the USA.

Issue 1

MUSEE DES BEAUX ARTS

W.H. Auden

*A*bout suffering they were never wrong,
    The Old Masters: how well they understood
    Its human position; how it takes place
    While someone else is eating or opening a window or just
        walking dully along;
    How, when the aged are reverently, passionately waiting
    For the miraculous birth, there always must be
    Children who did not specially want it to happen, skating
    On a pond at the edge of the wood:
    They never forgot
    That even the dreadful martyrdom must run its course
    Anyhow in a corner, some untidy spot
    Where the dogs go on with their doggy life and the torturer's
        horse
    Scratches its innocent behind on a tree.

    In Brueghel's *Icarus*,[1] for instance: how everything turns away
    Quite leisurely from the disaster; the ploughman may
    Have heard the splash, the forsaken cry,
    But for him it was not an important failure; the sun shone
    As it had to on the white legs disappearing into the green
    Water; and the expensive delicate ship that must have seen
    Something amazing, a boy falling out of the sky,
    Had somewhere to get to and sailed calmly on.

---

[1] Icarus and his father, Daedalus, were characters in Greek mythology. According to the story, Daedalus, imprisoned on the island of Crete, made wings for himself and his son to escape their confinement. The wings were fastened to their body with wax, and Daedalus warned Icarus not to fly too close to the sun. Once they took off, however, Icarus became intoxicated with flight and climbed higher and higher despite his father's warnings. He soon reached a level too close to the sun, and the sun's rays caused the wax to melt, the wings to fall off and Icarius to plunge into the sea below as his father watched helplessly.

LOVE SONGS WITH NO TOMORROWS

Jon Pareles

*I*n the video clip for Boyz II Men's "I'll Make Love to You," a young man struggles over a love letter. Finally, he copies down some lyrics from a Boyz II Men CD. The object of his affection, who somehow doesn't recognize the song, nearly swoons over the letter; the words were all she wanted. Once again, a love song has provided the script for romance.

Pop songs have the perennial job of distilling emotions down to verses and choruses. The eternal human perplexity over love—with its ever-shifting proportions of lust and affection, of longtime partnership and immediate gratification, of friction and transcendence—has always been reflected in love songs, and pop provides bulletins on the current states of the heart. There are sentiments for all occasions, from "You Send Me" to "Hit the Road, Jack."

Some love-song scripts never change: vows of endless love, signals of desire. But these are complicated times for young lovers. Young pop fans are the children of a divorced generation, and they have come of age amid the AIDS epidemic. In some areas, feminism has changed the rules; on college campuses, especially, a new consciousness of date rape and sexual harassment, and sometimes new formal codes of sexual behaviour, are trying to reshape the mating game. Men feel threatened, women are admitting anger, pleasure is linked to danger, every connection seems temporary—and it all filters into the three-minute ditties about love that will be ubiquitous this Valentine's Day.

Love songs for the 1990's, like nearly every other cultural product, have grown more specialized. Some songwriters avoid them entirely; many others address love only when it's troubled or lost. For songwriters still willing to entertain the possibility of romance, the old American dichotomy, virgin or slut, still thrives. In current love songs, the gap seems to be widening, so that desire and devotion often seem to occupy separate spheres.

The double-entendres of flirtation, implying hope for a sustained romance, are far outnumbered by the single-entendres of come-ons expecting only a one-night stand. Those come-ons, sung by both sexes, often dispense with poetic ambiguity in favour of a bluntness that's just this side of phone sex. After all, they're competing for attention with Ricki Lake and Howard Stern.

Rock has always had brazen come-ons like Hank Ballard's "Work With Me, Annie," along with party songs that simply want to let the good times roll. But in past eras there were also plenty of songs, written with teenagers in mind, to capture the feeling that puppy love would last forever. As the 1960's began, the Shirelles agonized about going all the way, wondering, "Will You Still Love Me Tomorrow?", the Dixie Cups took their budding romance to the "Chapel Of Love,"

As they hoped and pledged, the old girl-group songs struggled to find socially acceptable frameworks for primal yearnings, and they came up with as much fantasy as reality. After all, plenty of young marriages ended in divorce. Now, in an era of candour, pop songwriters have dropped many of the euphemisms and stripped away romantic illusions. They assume that nothing lasts forever, and that there's no need to construe a proposition as a proposal.

A modern girl group like TLC, now in the top 10 with the album "Crazy Sexy Cool," presents its members as both agents and objects of desire. In the hit song "Creep," they two-time a cheating boyfriend, inverting the old double standards: "If he knew the things I did he couldn't handle it." In "Kick Your Game," they wait for a shy suitor to say "something more clever than just your name," while thinking, "I wanna take you home/ But you gotta show me that your game is on." They don't expect much from romance; although they sing "love lasts forever" in "Take Our Time," they're just asking for unhurried sex.

Increasing sexual frankness, even boastfulness, is taken for granted from dance music to country. But for different demographic groups, there are different stereotypes, reinforced by radio-station formats and recording-company expectations.

Outside of country music, straight white men are reluctant to admit affections; it's left to women and minorities to express anything beyond lust. Young blacks are allotted both the most explicit

"Some love-song scripts never change: vows of endless love, signals of desire."

sexual banter and the most old-fashioned protestations of lasting love. Most hip-hop details a battle of the sexes: predatory males versus gold-digging females, competing to score without any emotional involvement. Only a rare exception, like Salt-n-Pepa's "Whatta Man," admits that there might be some mutual enjoyment in the transaction.

Ballad singers take a friendlier line in songs designed as soundtracks, and sometimes instruction manuals, for seduction. They aim for Marvin Gaye's suavity and Prince's lasciviousness, slowing down the groove to suspend time. Albums like Jodeci's "Diary of a Mad Band" start with big promises—"You're the girl of my life"—and, just four songs later, get down to specifics in "Ride and Slide." The two women in Changing Faces ask, coyly, "Do you mind if I stroke you up?"

In Boyz II Men's current hit, the singers promise to get down "On Bended Knee" if an ex-lover will take them back; now that she's gone, they're thinking about commitment. But "I'll Make Love to You"—nominated for a Grammy as 1994's song of the year—gives no long-term assurances. With its silky harmonies, "I'll Make Love to You" sounds like a love song, but it has its eye exclusively on the bedroom. Friendship is for those under the age of consent, like

Issue 1

the 15-year-old Brandy, whose hit "I Wanna Be Down" offers "a shoulder to cry on."

Young white men tend to avoid love entirely, snarling about apocalypse or whining about boredom. For hard rockers, sexuality is tied to aggression; Stone Temple Pilots' show stopper is "Sex Type Thing," a rapist's monologue. Nine Inch Nails' 1994 hit "Closer" is aghast at the intimacy of sex—"you let me violate you/you let me desecrate you"——but driven by lust, wanting sex "like an animal."

Collegiate rockers allow for the possibility of romance, but they're wary, prepared to see it collapse like everything else. "I'm no one you can trust," Lou Barlow warns in Sebadoh's "Rebound," even as he's hoping that he has found "maybe perfect love by chance." Across the Atlantic, English rockers prefer to sow gender-bending confusion: "Love in the 90's is paranoid," Blur observed in "Girls and Boys": "Looking for girls who want boys who like boys who do girls who do boys like they're girls who do girls like they're boys. Always should be someone you really love."

Female performers once sang almost exclusively about love; even now, they still spend more time on the subject than their male peers. But they are gradually freeing themselves from their old roles as yearners, sirens or earth mothers. For every group like the Cranberries—whose Dolores O'Riordan spends a lot of time pining and simpering because, as one song puts it, "I can't be with you"—there are women who can take love or leave it, skewering male egos or hurling accusations. "I love him so much it just turns to hate," Courtney Love sings in Hole's "Doll Parts."

Others, like P.J. Harvey, treat love and desire as uncontrollable, elemental forces, capable of exaltation and devastation at nearly the same moment. Love is no longer a panacea. Even Madonna, who despite her image sang some of the most monogamous love songs of the 1980's, doesn't spend all her time catering to her partners anymore; "Happiness lies in your own hand," she declares on "Bedtime Stories."

Perhaps love songs have grown more stratified by age. For frisky youngsters, there are tales of desire and infatuation; for young adults, who know a lot about risks and pitfalls, there are love songs of ambivalence and uncertainty. It's up to older performers to put love in long-term perspective.

They're not shocked or surprised by the facts of life any more, so they don't need to boast; they've also tested romantic ideals against experience. While they sometimes turn out narcissistic—like Tom Petty, informing his intended, "You don't know how it feels to be me"—older songwriters may also have ideas about what to do after infatuation wears off. They are the ones still singing old-fashioned valentines.

Performers like Bonnie Raitt can flirt without flaunting it in a song like "Something to Talk About." Chrissie Hynde, leading the Pretenders, vows, " I'll Stand by You." And Melissa Etheridge puts both body and soul on the line to hold on to a lover who's threatening to stray, as she insists, "I'm the only one who'd drown in my desire for you."

Songs like "I'm the Only One" are strong chart contenders alongside commitment-shy come-ons. They are scripts that listeners—and lovers—still want to hear. When today's young couples look back on "our song," will it be "Creep" or "Stroke You Up"? Or will it be "I'll Stand by You"?

OBJECTIVE VS. SUBJECTIVE RESPONSES TO ART

The whole of art is an appeal to a reality which is not without us but in our minds.

Desmond MacCarthy

Art is ruled uniquely by the imagination. Images are its only wealth. It does not classify objects, it does not pronounce them real or imaginary, does not qualify them, does not define them; it feels and presents them—nothing more.

Benedetto Croce

A work of art has no importance whatever to society. It is only important to the individual, and only the individual reader is important to me.

Vladimir Nabokov

Art is the imposing of a pattern on experience, and our aesthetic enjoyment is recognition of the pattern.

Alfred North Whitehead

OBJECTIVITY AND SUBJECTIVITY

Clive Cockerton

*W*hen we attempt to choose a movie for Saturday night, we might begin by poring over the newspaper, scanning the listings, reading the reviews. We might weigh and balance the fact that Costner is "one prince of a thief" in *Robin Hood*, whereas Anthony Hopkins' performance is "chilling and brilliant" in *Silence of the Lambs. Jungle Fever* is mercilessly funny while *Thelma and Louise* is one of the best films of the year. This film is an "absolute delight," that film is "irresistible," this one "touching and sensitive." Choices, choices. How does one sort the good from the bad from such a list? Add to the questions of the intrinsic worth of the film the problem of the individual's mood. Sometimes "touching and sensitive" just doesn't stand a chance against "frivolous and fun."

In fact, most of the decisions regarding choosing a film are subjective. After all, how can one effectively compare a musical to a thriller except on the basis of how one feels at the moment? In choosing a film we make decisions based on content that is suitable to our mood and a faith that the form of the film will measure up to its content. Once we have seen the film, however, we usually wish to weigh the success of our choice. Our conclusions usually fall into two categories:

1. "I really like the film because ..."
2. "That is a good film because ..."

These statements are really very different from each other, with the first statement recording a subjective preference while the second attempts an objective evaluation. Preference tends to be more content-oriented as in "I really liked the ending," or "It was a great love story," while attempts to prove the worth of the film tend to be more form-oriented as in, "The photography was beautiful" or "The pace was exciting."

For must of us, whether or not we like a film is much more important than whether the film is any good. As well, it is clearly possible to like a film we know we cannot defend as a good film. Our preference may be formed because of the presence of a favourite actor, a locale such as Africa or New York that fascinates us, or moments such as steamy love scenes or violent car chases that we find irresistible. The presence of these elements in no way forms a criterion for excellence, and the absence of these elements does not indicate a bad film. Indeed, our preference for these elements declares a lot about ourselves and our own feelings but says virtually nothing about the film. As well, it is quite possible to dislike a film that we know to fulfill all the requirements of a good film, again for strictly personal reasons such as the fact that the film reminds us of unpleasant or painful moments in our own lives.

Although there is clearly no possibility of argument or contradiction about personal feelings on an art object (they just simply are what they are), it is also clear that we can change our minds about works of art. A painting can look shapeless and disorganized to us until someone more expert reveals a previously overlooked organizing principle. A novel can sometimes seem obscure and difficult until we become familiar with its language and world view. We might condemn a film as confusing and subsequently read an interview with the director where he states that he wants his audience to feel confused. If the film achieves its aim, how can we condemn it? These examples happen frequently and point to the fact that proper artistic evaluation is more than just a subjective statement about our perspective at the moment. It is not simply a case of thinking one thing on Monday and another on Friday. We replace the first view with the second because we think that the second view more accurately and objectively describes the art. It is as if at first glance we perceive a frog, but after consultation with experts we begin to discern the prince hiding within. Of course, there are many more frogs than princes, and we are more frequently deceived by art works that initially seem good but over time don't stand up to close examination.

Experts attempt to engage our minds in the task of analyzing the aesthetic emotion. They teach us to analyze the art work, to look separately at its elements, and to establish standards or criteria to evaluate the elements. The use of this largely mental process can help us to understand more about the art work independent from our own subjective bias. Aristotle identified three criteria based on his study of Greek poetry and drama: unity, clarity, and integrity. Unity (of mood, of time and place among others) as a criterion didn't have the longevity of the other two: Aristotle couldn't anticipate the successful mixing of comic and tragic mood that would take place in Shakespeare's plays and other later works. However, clarity of expression seems as useful a standard by which to judge as any. Integrity, in the relationship of the parts of the play/poem to the whole and in the relationship of the whole to reality, forms the basis of much critical judgment. If we substitute simplicity of design, or perhaps more appropriately, focus for the concept of unity, we have a starting point in our discussions of criteria.

However, in our search for objective criteria by which to judge art objects, it must be admitted that no criteria work universally for all art objects. We praise the playful fantasy in the paintings of Henri Rousseau yet we do not condemn the paintings of Eduoard Munch for lacking that quality; indeed we praise Munch for his graphic rendering of inner torment. We appreciate one novel's realistic depiction of character and delight in another's cartoon-like parodies. We appreciate the grim honesty of films like *Full Metal Jacket* and at the same time are charmed by the simple beauty of films like *The Black Stallion*. Yet on occasion films displaying "simple beauty" or "grim honesty" lack other qualities and we find them unsatisfactory. The fact that no one criterion or element guarantees a work's value makes the job of appraisal that much more difficult. One thing is clear: on different occasions we judge by different criteria. Moreover, the skilled and open-minded consumer of art lets the individual work of art dictate by which criteria it is to be judged.

Some contemporary critics suggest that in a modern consumer society we are so overwhelmed with artistic experiences and images that the task of sorting them into piles of good and bad is a hopeless one. These critics see a rough equality of banality in all objects, and find that wit and beauty come from the perspective of the audience, and are not necessarily contained in the art. It is how you see a TV program, for instance, not the TV program itself that makes the experience lively and intelligent or dull and stupid. Some of these critics would go so far as to say that a book has no meaning by itself, that an unread book is a vacuum, and that the reader is the one who provides the meaning. Since every reader's experience is shaped by their gender, their class and cultural background, there can be no universal objective meaning, only a collection of diverse and subjective impressions. As one recent critic, Frank Lentricchia, has written of his relationship to literature:

> I come to the text with specific hangups, obsessions, worries, and I remake the text, in a sense, for me, for my times. ... The moment you start talking about it, you have injected interpretation. The text is not speaking; you are speaking for the text. You activate the text.

Still other critics focus on the possibility of consensus (among informed observers) operating as a kind of objectivity. This agreement by experts operates as a kind of "rough guide" to truth. However, these "agreements by experts" do not always have the shelf life that one would expect. It is clear that some art work does not seem to travel well from one historical period to the next. The novels of Sir Walter Scott (*Ivanhoe, The Heart of Midlothian*) were extremely popular in the nineteenth century, and are hardly read today. In our own twentieth century, the literacy reputation of Ernest Hemingway was extraordinarily high in the '20s and '30s but today Hemingway is more often seen as an interesting but minor writer.

One historical period may form an aesthetic preference for certain artistic qualities, preferring, for instance, clean and simple elegance to the previous generation's taste for exuberant and stylized decoration. When watching old films on television, we can be initially struck by what now seems bizarre fashion and style. Our experience of these films can be even more seriously undermined by outmoded attitudes, particularly sexist and racist ones. Everything that has happened to form our present consciousness stands as an obstacle to the appreciation of these films.

Even within an historical period critics sometimes disagree about the value of an individual work. Recently, films such as *The Prince of Tides, Pretty Woman,* and *Gandhi* have received very diverse reviews. All the critics may agree for instance, that pace in editing and structure is a very important element in a film's success. They may all agree that pace is a problem in a film such as *Gandhi.* But some critics will find that the other elements of the film compensate for the weakness in pace and will give the film an overall high evaluation. Some of the disagreement can be explained by the fact that, despite agreement in theory on the importance of pace, in practice many critics habitually weigh some criteria more than others. Therefore

Issue 2

those critics who regard editing as the most essential creative act in film will habitually favour films that possess skilful editing in spite of other problems that may exist in the film. Other critics may habitually value elements of script, acting or cinematography more highly than editing and refuse to accept that the obvious virtues in editing make up for the perceived weakness in acting. When a preference is habitual, we can be pretty sure that its origin is rooted deeply in our own personality and experience.

In spite of the effort of art critics to focus on the art rather than themselves, to analyze and evaluate the elements of art rather than narrate and describe their own experiences, it remains obvious that elements of personality can't always be overcome or transcended. Perhaps the relationship between art and our experience of art is circular. The more we possess the inner experience, the more we grow curious about that external art object. The more we learn about art, the more we learn about what makes us who we are. That moment on Saturday night when the theatre goes dark, we watch the slowly brightening screen and wonder what this film world will be like. At the end of the film, if we have been moved by the film, the natural instinct is to be quiet, to digest our own experience before surfacing to the workaday world. But watching movies is a social activity, and it's irresistible to turn to our friends and ask, "What do you think? Wasn't it good? I really liked the part where ..." We share our delight, and we compare experiences. Our view becomes larger.

❖

Ultimately, the question is much larger than whether our statements about art are objective or not. The question applies not only to art. It's about the world. It's just that art is a convenient place to begin the argument. If we cannot agree on the meaning of a single art object, with its known borders, its beginnings, middle and end, with its human author, how can we make statements about a limitless universe—a universe not divided into neat stages of development, ending in closure, but a universe (caused/uncaused) constantly evolving, stretching out to infinity and a universe whose author is either unknown or not available to interview.

Is the external world totally independent of us or as the Greek philosopher Protagoras held, is it us, and our perceptions that are the measure of all things? Even if we grant the existence of the external world, it doesn't seem possible to get beyond our perceptions of it. Scientists have their protocol, the scientific method, that is meant to banish subjective interpretation. In the search for the underlying principles of things as they are (remember Tom Olien's article), science took over from religion the chief role of establishing truth. And what a magnificent job science has done. In revealing the structure of sub-atomic particles, in predicting the location and timing of an earthquake or volcano, in isolating a deadly virus and developing vaccines and in improving the quality of life for millions, science can lay claim to being humanity's must successful enterprise.

Think of the surgeon holding a human heart in his or her hands, repairing a faulty valve and placing it back into the person's chest, giving them twenty years more of life. All of the knowledge, the complex theory and practical skill that go into a successful operation rest on a physician's informed judgment that an operation is called for. That judgment is fallible, as are all human judgments. For the history of science is full of examples of misreadings, of scientists finding only what they were looking for, and not finding what they weren't, of finding solutions to problems that not only fit the hypothesis but also the prevailing ideology. Ultimately, scientists too must depend on their very fallible senses (or their high tech extensions) to draw conclusions. As well the role of the scientist confers no immunity to normal human pressures, the ego needs, the economic necessity to succeed, the political compulsion to research in certain directions. Scientists may be the most objective amongst us, but even in this highly trained class of people, subjective considerations colour many perceptions.

The truth about the world, the final objective Truth, is getting harder to find, yet meaning, subjective meaning is everywhere. A single rational explanation for the universe and all it contains may no longer be possible. Our knowledge (scientific and otherwise) has grown and grown until it has reached a point beyond where any one individual can comprehend the whole. To see the whole domain of our knowledge we need to climb a very high mountain; we haven't found the mountain yet (although on several occasions we thought we had) and are beginning to doubt if it exists.

Instead of the overview from the mountain, what we have is the micro-view of the specialist. What we have are fragments of the whole, knowledge and insight from the physicist, the philosopher, the biologist, the historian, the psychologist, the literary critic, the political economist. The fragments don't cohere into one magnificent interpretation of the universe. They exist as beams of light that illuminate the darkness for a certain time, as probes that reveal something about the world, and as a point of view.

We both rely on and are suspicious of experts. We rely on them, for their fragmentary understanding of the world is the best insight that we've got. But in a deeper sense we know them to be fallible. No political thinker predicted the collapse of communism in Eastern Europe, yet we continue to tune into the TV to hear what they have to say. Young parents read everything they can get their hands on about child rearing, yet are highly selective in what ideas they apply to their own children. We may listen with interest to the reasoned arguments of the nuclear power experts, but when they tell us that we have nothing to fear the shadow of Chernobyl falls over the discussion.

Every discipline of study is currently racked with conflict, with dissenting voices. If even the experts can't agree, are the rest of us just gambling on what and who we choose to believe? It becomes so difficult to judge the worth of arguments that quickly threaten to go beyond our expertise. The difficulty causes many of us to give up the task of sifting through the ideas, adopting instead a weary and cynical assumption that all views are equal. Many of us come from school systems that value self-expression as the highest good. It doesn't so much matter what gets expressed (all views are roughly equal anyway); just so long as a view gets expressed, the system will applaud. This emphasis involves a radical turning away from the searching after truth that has so long inspired our education. If there's no truth to search for, why struggle so hard?

If there's no truth, then what we have left is competing views, subjective perceptions. My view becomes as valuable as yours because there's no way to successfully weigh and measure them against each other. On the surface, there's an increase in tolerance as we all recognize that what may be true for me may not be true for you. But beneath the surface lurks the urge for dominance, the recognition that the prevailing view belongs to the loudest, most powerful voice.

Issue 2

And so we have the competition of interests and perspectives: Quebec, the West, free trade, feminists, unionists, native peoples, blacks, environmentalists. The competition is healthy, the diversity of views enriching. But without truth as a goal, the contest of ideas has no referee; it's too easy for reason to become a weapon to beat your opponent, not a tool to dig for understanding. Still, we're in the middle of a huge process in our relationship to the world and each other. If fragmentation into competing perspectives and specialized bits of knowledge is the current mode, perhaps all we need to do is wait for the emergence of new and better ideas that might reconcile some of the conflicts and satisfy our yearning for something to believe in. The competition of ideas has been evident throughout this text: are we free or determined in Unit One; what changes and what remains the same in Unit Two; do we have the sense to co-operate with each other or are we doomed to conflict in Unit Three; can science provide the solutions to the problems it creates in Unit Four? Do we have to make a choice? Do we have to run to the comfort of certainty? Or do we have to learn to love the paradox—to see in contradiction the breathing in, the breathing out of ideas?

The arts, particularly narrative arts such as film and the novel, may have a role to play in helping us to reconcile apparent contradiction. By successfully creating a fictional world that re-creates the real world, the author/artist sets artificial boundaries to what is included in the story, how many characters, subplots and themes. Fictionalizing the world tells us everything we need to know; the author/artist creates a vision of life that is remarkable in its completeness. The sharing of this vision creates a sense of community between artist and audience and holds out the possibility of consensus. We are not alone; others see the same world, sometimes with great clarity and undeniable insight. It's as if the film or novel creates a fictional mountain, from which we can finally see the human truth stretched out below, in all its complexity and contradiction. It is just a glimpse, but reassuring. In the midst of the darkest night-time thunderstorm, the lightning can suddenly illuminate our world in a flash of brilliant light, letting us know that the world is still there, under the cover of darkness.

THE SEARCH FOR FORM

Clive Cockerton

*I*t is clear that the Canadian government, through its body of experts, believes that objective evaluations can be made about works of art and about what they can contribute to a culture. The experts reward the good art with government money and discourage the bad by withholding funding. Each of the experts from the different artistic areas brings criteria drawn from years of experience to judging art. As well as the criteria for good art, they also bring some sense of what might contribute to the broader Canadian culture, what might serve as Canadian cultural self-expression. The problem occurs when certain themes or styles become identified as officially Canadian, that is, promoting a standardized Canadian vision. It has been frequently said that our best Canadian film director, David Cronenberg, seems somehow un-Canadian. His stories of sophisticated people in urban settings confronted with physical horrors don't address the "official" themes of Canadian culture. His films may be about victims, but they are not victims of the cold or of loneliness. They do not endure long and hard trials; rather, they explode in intense and horrific ways. How un-Canadian. Yet he is a director who has lived all his life in Toronto and who has made all his films in Canada. If he is not Canadian, it is because we have an overly rigid expectation of what constitutes a Canadian vision. Organizations like the Canada Council naturally tend to promote works that express a coherent view of ourselves, but this coherence can sometimes become conformity, conformity to an official version of ourselves.

More fundamentally, many people have difficulty accepting the notion that a body of experts can come to valid conclusions about works of art. We can probably all recall moments when a teacher seemed to drone on about the monumental significance of a short story that made us ache with boredom, or the deeper levels of meaning in a poem whose message totally eluded us. It is always right to be skeptical about the experts, but our challenges to authority should also be matched by a willingness to apply the rules of evidence to any work of art. Just as we must always question the officially proclaimed ideas, we must also discover that some work is simply better than others.

Take the following two sentences, containing roughly the same content, and try to rank them according to merit.

Version 1: Generally speaking there are a lot more unhappy moments in life than there are happy ones.

Version 2: Happiness was but an occasional episode in a general drama of pain.

As subjectively attached as I am to Version 1 (I wrote it), it must be admitted that while it has a conversational matter-of-fact quality about its grim message, it lacks the complexity and power of Version 2. When we look at Version 2, we notice the precision of the language and the tightness of the structure. Notice how key words are twinned to heighten the contrast: occasional and general, episode and drama, and, most importantly, happiness and pain beginning and ending the sentence. You might also notice that the sounds of the first half of the sentence are softly melancholic, while the second half has a leaden heaviness and finality. No doubt about it, once you examine closely, it is easy to see that in Version 2 the content has found its clearest and most forceful expression.

Let's look at two versions of another grim sentiment.

Version A: Days go by one after the other in a monotonous way. This trivial parade of time ends in death. Life doesn't mean anything; it is just full of noise and anger, ultimately meaningless.

Version B: Tomorrow and tomorrow and tomorrow creep in this petty pace from day to day, lighting the way for fools to dusty death. Life is a tale told by an idiot, full of sound and fury, signifying nothing.

Version B is probably the most famous statement of thorough-going pessimism in the English language. It is full of wonderful images, days lighting the passage to ultimate darkness, the ranting idiot's tale, while Version A will never be read anywhere beyond these pages, and even then quickly forgotten.

In literary terms, having the right (write) stuff has its base in the author's ability to create magical effects with language. These effects can be achieved through precise use of words, through an ability to manipulate the sound and rhythm of language, and through an ability to create haunting images.

Issue 2

Look at the following paragraph and notice how it begins in re-laxed but precise observation of an ordinary occurrence. Where and how does it turn into something monstrous?

Four men were at the table next to mine. Their collars were open, their ties loose, and their jackets hung on the wall. One man poured dressing on the salad, another tossed the leaves. Another filled the plates and served. One tore bread, another poured wine, another ladled soup. The table was small and square. The men were cramped, but efficient nonetheless, ap-parently practised at eating here, this way, hunched over food, heads striking to suck at spoons, tear at forks, then pulling back into studious, invincible mastication. Their lower faces slid and chopped; they didn't talk once. All their eyes, like birds on a wire, perched on a horizontal line above the action. Swallowing muscles flickered in jaws and necks. Had I touched a shoulder and asked for the time, there would have been snarling, a flash of teeth.

D.H. Lawrence in his novel, *The Rainbow*, wrote the following de-scription of horses bunching around a woman walking in the fields. The woman has broken off with her fiancé and has subsequently discovered that she is pregnant. She walks the fields in extreme an-guish when she confronts a herd of horses.

But the horses had burst before her. In a sort of lightning of knowledge their movement travelled through her, the quiver and strain and thrust of their powerful flanks, as they burst before her and drew on, beyond.

She knew they had not gone, she knew they awaited her still. But she went on over the log bridge that their hoofs had churned and drummed, she went on, knowing things about them. She was aware of their breasts gripped, clenched nar-row in a hold that never relaxed, she was aware of their red nostrils flaming with long endurance, and of their haunches, so rounded, so massive, pressing, pressing, pressing to burst the grip upon their breasts, pressing forever till they went mad, running against the walls of time, and never bursting free. Their great haunches were smoothed and darkened with rain. But the darkness and wetness of rain could not put out the hard, urgent, massive fire that was locked within these flanks, never, never.

She went on, drawing near. She was aware of the great flash of hoofs, a bluish, iridescent flash surrounding a hollow of darkness. Large, large seemed the bluish, incandescent flash of the hoof-iron, large as a halo of lightning round the knotted darkness of the flanks. Like circles of lightning came the flash of hoofs from out of the powerful flanks.

Why the horses seem menacing is mysterious, but we're sure that we're seeing them with the eyes of Ursula, the heroine. Literature can often startle us with this kind of experience, with being inside the head of another (if fictional) person. But it's the *form* of the language that opens the door to this experience.

Michael Herr, in his book *Dispatches*, a chronicle of the Vietnam war, attempts to capture the emotional texture of combat in this paragraph.

Fear and motion, fear and standstill, no preferred cut there, no way even to be clear about which was really worse, the wait or the delivery. Combat spared far more men than it wasted, but everyone suffered the time between contact, especially when they were going out every day looking for it; bad going on foot, terrible in trucks and APC's, awful in helicopters, the worst, travelling so fast toward something so frightening. I can remember times when I went half dead with my fear of the motion, the speed and direction already fixed and pointed one way. It was painful enough just flying "safe" hops between firebases and lz's; if you were ever on a helicopter that had been hit by ground fire your deep, perpetual chopper anxiety was guaranteed. At least actual contact when it was happening would draw long ragged strands of energy out of you, it was juicy, fast and refining, and travelling toward it was hollow, dry, cold and steady, it never let you alone. All you could do was look around at the other people on board and see if they were as scared and numbed out as you were. If it looked like they weren't you thought they were insane, if it looked like they were it made you feel a lot worse.

This is a writer writing at the top of his game, taking the reader on a roller-coaster ride, using his craft to capture the subtle ways terror can grip.

❖

There is a deep satisfaction that comes from an appreciation of form. An arrangement of words, images, colours or notes can illuminate a moment, create powerful emotion, and so change our perceptions that we never look at life or art in quite the same way again. Art can be more than form, and to be sure it can be full of ideas, archetypes and moral discriminations. But while it can be more than form, without form it is nothing; it loses its magical hold on us.

Outside the realm of art, that perfect arrangement is harder to find in human relationships. Many of us find a sense of energy and harmony in nature, and discover a solace in contemplation of the beauties of nature. Perhaps this respect for nature explains our sense of the violation we experience when confronted with massive pollution, and explains why acid rain, the lead in the air, the depletion of ozone, the poisoning of our water, seem obscene. We have become so sensitive to this tampering with natural form that intentional pollution with toxic substances is now considered a criminal and not merely a civil offense. Companies such as Exxon become associated in the public mind with ecological disaster and do so at their peril. The public's tolerance of irresponsible and negligent behaviour on the part of private companies is slowly becoming a thing of the past, and the so-called "green movement" is emerging as a powerful political force.

In Unit IV Tom Olien talked of the search for an underlying principle as the great creative urge of scientists. Toby Fletcher's article in Unit III looks for a new world order to deal with global problems.

When we transcend sovereign nation thinking, we become citizens of the world. Global interdependence requires new definitions. Our personal and national interests can only be served through a more sophisticated, cooperative and collaborative relationship among nations.

Clearly, this relationship among nations can only be achieved by providing the institutions (the form) which will guarantee enough safety and security for sovereign nations to surrender some portion of their power to a world body.

This global view is evidenced in the way we look far beyond our national borders, the way we appreciate the inter-connectedness of nations. We listen with keen interest to reports from the former Soviet Union hoping for a better life for the average Russian and a more secure future for us all. If we accept the good things of interdependence, however, it is also true that we feel more keenly the tragic disappointment of hopes in China, as the tanks and boots of the army attempt to crush the democratic spirit of the young students. It is an event that takes place far away, yet it touches us because we share the same urge for freedom as the Chinese students—our freedom already won, theirs in the process of a fierce and bloody struggle with a repressive government.

Whenever new ideas clash with an existing form, there is some dislocation, something lost as well as gained. Unit II of this text looked at what happens when the old values are challenged by new technologies and new ideas. People cannot see what is happening to them and vainly try to deny the impact of the change. Some societies can be aware of the process of change in varying degrees, but the task of integrating new forms with old always challenges our best efforts.

Finally, it is in our own lives that form has the greatest significance, as we attempt to find shape and meaning in the daily flow of our existence. The facts, the contents of our lives, are distressingly similar, as a comparative glance at any number of résumés shows. We are born, go to school, make friends, take part-time jobs, go to college and then on to a career. Along the way, we may form romantic attachments, get married, have children, grow older, watch children leave us, retire from our jobs and grow older still. But this sameness doesn't tell the whole story. As the old jazz lyric goes: "It ain't what you do, but how you do it." Some people's lives are tragic, while others with the same observable facts seem heroic. After we bury some people, all we can hear, after our own tears subside, is the sound of their laughter. What makes this life comic and that life pathetic? Clearly, it has something to do with perception, the perception of the individual who lives it as he or she contemplates the moment and discovers the pattern in the flow of daily experience. These moments of perception are often struggled for, but sustain the idea of a conscious life. To be conscious, to understand what is happening to you, and to others, here and now, is a large part of the urgency and energy of human life.

Issue 2

THINKING AND WRITING SKILLS

Humanities is concerned with the issues and topics that have pre-occupied humankind throughout history. Because of the complexity of the issues, clarity of thought and expression are essential. It is obvious that certain thoughts require high levels of skill in language. The development of these high-level skills is achieved more efficiently when we attempt to grapple with challenging content. It is the purpose of this course to offer such content and to help the student develop the skills necessary to express his or her own thoughts about the content.

The following skills section will assist you in performing essential thinking and writing tasks such as summary, comparison and contrast, and evaluation.

TIPS ON WRITING AN ESSAY EXAM IN HUMANITIES

R. Chris Coleman

*H*ere is an actual question taken from a previous essay exam in Humanities. The answer had to be a minimum of 250 words and was worth 70 points. Fifty percent (35 points) was given for content and 50% for how well the sentences communicated ideas. How would you go about answering this question?

Question:

How does ONE of the four theories of personality explain human nature? For instance, why are we frequently in conflict with ourselves? How does our personality develop? Can we change our basic personality behaviour? Explain.

In answering an essay type question, it's important not to make the task any more difficult than it is already. Your instructor wants you to show (a) that you took notes during lectures, (b) that you read the assigned sections in the text, (c) that you understood and remember what was said, and (d) that you appreciate its relevance and significance.

Also, it is especially important to realize you are not expected to explore just your own thoughts, feelings and opinions. In the example above, for instance, it would be a mistake to write something like this:

In my opinion, our basic personality is already formed at birth as a result of our past-life experiences before we were born.

While some people may believe this theory, it is not one of the four theories of personality dealt with directly in the Humanities course material.

On an essay exam, you are expected to recall as much as you can of the course material. So, of course, it's a major advantage to know the material well before you write.

One of the challenges in writing an essay exam is that time is limited. Because of the lack of time to rewrite, planning and preparing become more important than usual.

One helpful tip is, *before you start actually composing your essay,* jot down in point form everything you can think of related to the question. Don't worry yet whether or not you will include every point in your final answer. Just make the list as long as you can. Having such a list helps you organize your material and keeps you on topic.

Useful Tip—Before you start actually composing your essay, jot down in point form everything you can think of related to the question.

To illustrate, suppose in answering the question above that you chose to explain the psychoanalytic school of personality theory. Somewhere in your list of points you would include these points, though probably not in this order:

Sigmund Freud (turn of century)

3 Aspects Of Personality:

1) **Id** = unconscious
- **eros** = instinct for life
- **thanatos** = death wish
- child-like

2) **Ego** = awareness of self
- thinks, deals with, reacts
- mediates between id & superego
- adult

3) **Superego** = conscience, shoulds
- *socialization* = internalize values
- parental

(etc.)

Of course, to be complete for the above question, your actual list would be much longer.

Your list might even include a quotation or two that you've memorized during study for the exam. Including memorized passages in an essay-type answer is fine, providing you fully understand what they mean and can explain them in your own words. Here's a quotation that would be useful in formulating a line of argument for the answer to the above question:

Appendix A

"Human personality emerges … by the interactive functions between *ego*, *superego*, and *id*." (*The Human Project*, p. 8-9).

Once your list is more or less complete, you are ready to *organize* the material. Usually the question itself not only will tell you what your instructor expects, but also will hint at how you should arrange the material.

Generally speaking, key words in the question like "**Define**, **Summarize**, **Compare**, **Contrast**, **Evaluate**" are cues as to how your instructor expects you to organize your answer. In the example we're working on, there are two key words, very closely related: "*explain* and *how*". You must explain how human personality emerges and develops, according to Freudian psychoanalytic theory.

Any essay is basically an *argument*. First you make a definite statement, called a **Thesis Statement**. Then you *support* or back up your thesis statement using specific points taken directly from the course material. Try to show, prove or demonstrate that there is sufficient evidence to support your thesis statement.

For many questions on essay exams, there is no single, absolutely right answer—just those answers that are adequately supported with specific points, and those answers which, unfortunately, are not. Therefore, it is advisable to use as much material from the text and lectures as you can.

In organizing your answer, you might find it helpful to construct an outline. Some people actually jot their outline down on paper. Others, to save time, merely keep their outline in their heads. It doesn't really matter, as long as you proceed according to some definite plan or strategy.

Don't make the mistake of just starting to write hoping something positive will magically happen.

For the question above, your outline might look something like this:

1. Thesis statement; Define 3 parts of personality: id, ego, superego.
2. Explain how they interact with each other.
3. Why we are frequently in conflict with ourselves.
4. How our personality develops.
5. How we can change.

Notice how similar the outline is to the question itself? It should be. Otherwise you may not be covering everything the question is asking for.

The average sentence in college level writing is about 15-20 words. Therefore, if you plan to write a short paragraph for each of the 5 points on your outline, with each paragraph containing 3-5 sentences, you should have no trouble meeting the requirement of a minimum of 250 words: (5 paragraphs) x (4 sentences) X (15 words) = 300 words. Of course, this is a very rough guide.

> **Useful Tip**—Usually the question itself not only will tell you what your instructor expects, but will also hint at how you should arrange the material.

With your list of points and your outline complete, you are ready to start composing your answer. One difference between an essay exam and a regular essay is that you already know that your audience is your own instructor. So imagine your instructor sitting directly opposite you, and proceed to talk to that person on paper the way you would if you were face to face.

Do not try to impress your instructor by using "big" words. On the other hand, you should avoid street language as well. Use precise vocabulary. *Write to express what you mean, clearly.*

> **Useful Tip**—Don't make the mistake of just starting to write hoping something positive will magically happen.

Another difference between an essay exam and a normal essay is that you are not expected to write a striking introduction, or a thoughtful conclusion. Simply start with your thesis statement. Very often the wording of your thesis statement will be quite similar to the question itself. For example, using the quotation you memorized, you might write something like this as a thesis statement:

> Sigmund Freud, who originated psychoanalytic theory at the turn of the century, suggested that "human personality emerges by the interactive functions between ego, superego, and id." (26 words)

The next step is to define terms. Compose sentences incorporating the points you jotted down on your list of points. *Try to be concise by combining as many specific points as you can into each sentence you write without being verbose.* It would be ridiculous to write something like this:

> In my opinion at this point in time it seems like what Freud was saying was that the id is the same as what we in this day and age in our society call the unconscious. (36 words)

Appendix A

Although this sentence is 36 words long, it would get only one or two marks for content. In fact, it might even lose a mark or two because it communicates the ideas so poorly. Think about it this way. If somebody were to write just seven such sentences, although they would be well over the 250-word minimum, their mark for content would be only 14 out of 35, or 40%.

A much better sentence might look something like this:

The id or unconscious, the most important aspect of personality, contains eros and thanatos, two instincts that govern all behaviour. (20 words)

This sentence is only twenty words long, yet it contains about seven valid points.

The id or unconscious (*point*) the most important (*point*) aspect of personality (*point*) contains eros (*point*) and thanatos (*point*), two instincts (*point*) that govern all behaviour (*point*).

Useful Tip—Compose sentences incorporating the points you jotted down on your list of points. Try to be concise by combining as many specific points as you can into each sentence you write without being verbose.

Now, if you could write 20 sentences, with each sentence containing only two valid points, you would have 40 points, well over the 35 points offered for content for this question. Of course, not all instructors will mark answers exactly this way, but this can be a useful guide for constructing your answers.

The next sentence in your answer might define eros and thanatos:

Eros is our drive for life, sex and pleasure, while thanatos is for death, aggression, hostility and destruction. (18 words)

Notice that there are more points included in this sentence than appeared on the original list of points. Obviously, it's a good idea to incorporate more points if they occur to you as you're writing.

Useful Tip—Try to give yourself enough time at the end of the exam to read your answer over a couple of times. Read first for your ideas. Then read to correct grammar, spelling and punctuation.

Following these three sentences might come a sentence defining ego, then another defining superego. Then you would have a five sentence paragraph defining the parts of personality according to psychoanalytic theory.

In the next paragraph, you might discuss how these parts interact with each other and what happens if one part gets repressed or has too much expression. This paragraph would naturally lead into a third paragraph that explains why we are frequently in conflict with ourselves. And so on.

As you go, you might want to give examples from your personal experience to illustrate your points. This is often a good idea, providing you have enough room to include all the course material as well, and providing your illustrations are very brief and concise:

> For example, when I want a donut, my id says, "Go for it!"; my superego says, "Don't. You're on a diet!"; and my adult ego says, "Let's have carrot sticks instead."

Often you can be more persuasive if you consider opposing views. Anticipate what someone might say, or already has said, to argue against you. Then show why you think your argument is more logical, consistent, justified or valid. In answering the question above, it might be useful to mention the other three theories of personality. In no more than a sentence for each, you might indicate how each differs from the theory you have chosen to explain more fully.

Some final tips. Although you will be trying to write fast, be careful not to write so quickly that your writing becomes illegible.

Also, try to give yourself enough time at the end of the exam to read your answer over a couple of times. Read first for your ideas. Then read to correct grammar, spelling and punctuation.

Good luck

Appendix A

COMPARISON AND CONTRAST

Clive Cockerton

*T*his course, like many other courses, will frequently ask you to compare and contrast two or more thinkers, issues and situations. When you are asked to compare and contrast, you are being asked to do more than just *describe* two things. You are being asked to do the work of finding the most significant points of similarity and difference. It is a complex task involving both analysis in detail (breaking up whatever is being compared into smaller parts) and synthesis (bringing the parts together in the new light shed by your comparison).

Many people, when asked to compare, for example, Freud and Skinner, would launch into an essay that would list everything about Freud followed by everything about Skinner and would look something like this:

Introductory Paragraph:
Topic Identified

Part A: Freud   Part B: Skinner

While this essay format can *describe* the ideas of the two men in a very sophisticated way, it doesn't really bring them together and compare them on the basis of some element (their attitude to the question of free will, for instance). A much better format would look like the diagram below.

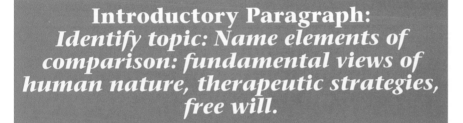

Introductory Paragraph:
Identify topic: Name elements of comparison: fundamental views of human nature, therapeutic strategies, free will.

Part A: Fundamental Views of Human Nature

Part B: Therapeutic Strategies

Part C: Free Will

Part D: Conclusion

Appendix A

Theories of Human Personality

Elements	Freud	Skinner	My Conclusion
View of human nature	We are largely unconscious of the interplay of powerful urges (eros and thanatos). Psyche divided into three areas: id, ego, superego.	We are extremely flexible beings whose behaviours are controlled and shaped by the environment and the effect of rewards and punishments.	
Therapeutic strategies	Talking with analyst. Attempts to make patients conscious of the forces that motivate them.	Behaviour modification. Change the behaviour by changing the consequences.	
Free will	No free will	No free will	

It should be clear from this format that the elements (the fundamental views of human nature, therapeutic strategies, and free will) are the main organizing elements of your comparison and must be carefully chosen to make an effective comparison.

Of course, we use this comparison technique outside of school all the time, whenever we need to make a choice, whether it be what car to buy or in which restaurant to have dinner. In both cases, we look for the most significant elements. In the instance of the car, the first step is to analyze the decision into its elements—such as cost, technological innovation, space, comfort, and safety. There may be many more elements but usually there are only one or two dominant ones such as cost and safety upon which we naturally concentrate most of our time. Similarly, the example of restaurants yields a number of factors such as cost, quality of food, decor and service. Again, there are priorities. Although decor and service may form a minor part of our decision, most often the choice will be made based on value and quality. When comparing thinkers and their ideas we analyze or break down the subject into elements as well. This is a critical phase and many writers like to use a grid, such as that above, so that they can chart their comparison in a more graphic way. As well you may wish to include space for your conclusion or decision on the relative merits of the competing theories.

As in the case of cars and restaurants, you may quickly decide that one or two elements are dominant with the others playing supporting but minor roles. You may wish to group all the minor elements into one paragraph, and plan to spend at least one paragraph on each of the major elements. It is useful to think about the rhetorical structures that can be helpful in comparison. Such structures might include:

1. *While* Freud emphasizes X, Skinner, *on the other hand,* suggests Y.
2. *Although* Freud and Skinner disagree about A, there seems to be some common ground on the subject of B.

In many cases, your consideration of the elements will lead you to decide that a particular thinker has an advantage in his explanation of the various elements, and you may wish to provide the reader with a sense of where you stand on the issue and which thinker you support.

When you have read the first selection in Unit Three, you might like to try filling out the following grid on the views of human nature of Hobbes, Locke, Marx, and Mill. Be sure to come to your own conclusion on each element. Ask yourself if there are any important elements of comparison left out of this grid. After completing the grid, think about how you would turn the elements into paragraphs.

Comparison and Contrast
When you are asked to compare and contrast, you are being asked to do more than just describe two things. You are being asked to do the work of finding the most significant points of similarity and difference.

Theories of Human Nature

Thinkers Elements	Hobbes	Locke	Marx	Mill
The nature of the individual				
Relationship of the individual to society				
The role of authority				
Importance of a fair contract				
Self-interest vs. altruism				

Appendix A

EVALUATION

Wayson Choy

"What's my life worth?" "What do I mean when I say 'I want to be happy'?" "What can I do about changing my life?"

These are questions every intelligent person comes to ask. There are, of course, no easy answers. However, in *The Human Project* text, the same questions are raised in challenging ways—and you are asked to take on the adventure of coming to some possible conclusions. You are asked to *evaluate* the knowledge presented to you in your readings, in the lectures and in the give-and-take of the seminar classes.

You are asked to *evaluate* ideas, theories, concepts, and feelings—to begin to understand how to take information and discover the differences between opinion and knowledge. If you're fortunate, you may also discover the differences between knowledge and wisdom, feelings and insights.

For example, most people assume that "one opinion is as good as another." In fact, most opinions are not to be trusted, however sincere the opinion-maker may be.

Naturally, if our life does not depend on the opinion, we may simply ignore it or politely nod our head. But, if your life depended on the opinion, "It's hot outside!"—because your rare blood disease will kill you at any temperature over 30 degrees—you would probably need to evaluate that opinion. You would depend, not on the opinion, "It's hot outside!"—but more wisely on the statement, "The official Canada Weather Thermometer Report reads 25 degrees Celsius…"

People's lives have actually depended upon these opinions:
"The bottom line is that you can't fight City Hall!"
"Russia is the Evil Empire."
"Only homosexuals get AIDS. That's God's punishment."
"That grenade is not defective."
"John knows a scientist who says smoking is harmless."

"Tell you the truth, all you need is money to be happy."
"You can't do anything about poor single mothers."
"If you fail this test, you're just stupid."
"People should have the right to carry guns."
"Any one gets raped, they asked for it!"
"You just have to work hard to succeed in life."
"Foreigners shouldn't take work away from Canadians."
"Women should stay home; it's more natural."
"A man should always stand and fight!"

Imagine accepting all of these opinions as if they were true; as if, indeed, we need only hear them and nod our heads and live our lives accordingly. Many people do just that regardless of how disturbed they may be when they hear the words spoken.

The process of education begins with that feeling of being disturbed: Education of any personal worth is often a process of disturbance—first, disturbance; then, evaluation.

You will hear startling things, discover that your world may be more complex than you ever realized. You will test modern social and psychological theories, use new ideas and new language to begin to understand your own life. You will refer to authorities, artists, writers, facts and figures, make judgments, use logic in your debate, think in new ways, and—perhaps reluctantly at first—you may even throw out some ideas you thought were true. There will be fresh ways to test your most sacred ideas, and, if you work hard, you will learn how to communicate your new insights more clearly to others.

You will begin to *evaluate.* It is, finally, your own life that you will evaluate.

EXERCISE

Take any *one* of the opinions above that disturbs you, and explain why you think it is "only an opinion" and *not* knowledge. Begin by defining what you mean by "opinion" ad "knowledge." Finally, discuss the steps which would help you logically challenge that particular opinion—and perhaps change the mind of those who believe the opinion to be true.

Appendix A

APPENDIX B

STUDYDESK:
A COMPUTERIZED
GUIDE FOR
THE HUMAN PROJECT

STUDYDESK

*T*o help you understand the many topics covered in *The Human Project*, we have included a computer study guide with the textbook. The StudyDesk program contains the following:

Glossary: definitions and commentary on over 100 terms and concepts.

Key Concepts: essential concepts you should understand on a unit by unit basis.

Quick Quiz: multiple-choice self-testing to review unit concepts.

Reading Room: a selection of representative works by authors mentioned in the textbook along with reference materials.

Reference Section: background information on over 60 historical figures

Textbook Summaries: point-form summaries of each textbook article.

StudyDesk is a Windows **hypertext** program. Hypertext means you control what you read by simply clicking the mouse on a hotword (words printed in green text) to activate a **jump** or a **popup**. When a jump occurs, new information will appear in place of what you were reading. When a popup occurs, new information appears above what you are reading. Unlike a book whose pages are read in order, with hypertext you use the mouse to call information instantly to the screen you are interested in reading.

StudyDesk also includes a number of **hypergraphics**. Hypergraphics work just like hypertext except the hotspots are graphics or multiple hotspots on a single graphic. When you place the cursor on a hypergraphic, it will change from a pointer to a hand just as happens when you place the cursor on a hotword. And when you click the mouse, either a popup or a jump will occur. Check out the hypergraphic for Freud's concept of the unconscious to see how hypergraphics work.

Throughout StudyDesk you will also find two navigational graphic hotspots:

 The StudyLamp icon links to key concepts or to related readings in the Reading Room

The Reading Room icon links to works by authors under discussion

The StudyDesk includes a number of navigational aids to help you keep oriented. When you first use the program, it would be a good idea to begin by clicking the Help button to read more about how StudyDesk is organized and its techniques. For example, you will certainly want to find out how to start a word processor and learn how to copy information from StudyDesk into your notes and essays.

How to Start StudyDesk

StudyDesk can be run directly from the disk that accompanies your textbook or, for the program to run faster, it can be loaded to a hard drive. Please consult your computer manual to learn how to create a directory, copy files to it, and to create a program icon.

Running StudyDesk from a Floppy Disk:

1) Insert StudyDesk in a external 3.5" drive. External drives are usually designated drive A:\ or drive B:\ depending on whether the computer has one or two external drives.

2) Click on **File** from the Program Manager menu bar. A dropdown menu will appear.

3) Click **Run** from the dropdown menu. A dialog box will appear.

4) In the dialog box, type the drive letter of the external drive and: studydsk.hlp

   for example: a:\studydsk.hlp

5) Click the **OK** button. StudyDesk will then start.

MINIMUM SYSTEM REQUIREMENTS

Computer: 386

RAM: 4mb

Disk space: 1mb

Operating System: Windows 3.1

CREDITS

Photography and Illustrations

LITERARY

5: Excerpt from *The Moon by Whalelight* by Diane Ackerman, reprinted with permission from Random House, Inc.

24: Excerpt from "Seeing the Blossom" by Dennis Potter, reprinted with permission from Faber and Faber.

45: Excerpt from *An Introduction to Modern Philosophy*, 5th edition, by Alburey Castell and Donald M. Borchert, reprinted with permission from MacMillan Publishing.

77: "Father Tells What It's Like for Black Kids in Metro" by Philip Mascoll, reprinted with permission from the Toronto Star Syndicate.

87: "Sex, Statistics and Wages," reprinted with permission, the *Globe and Mail*, January 21, 1993.

89: "Are Women's Salaries Behind Men's?" reprinted from the *Globe and Mail*, with permission from Nancy Riche.

102: Excerpt from *Jobshift: How to Prosper in a Workplace without Jobs*, William Bridges, reprinted with permission, Addison-Wesley Publishing Company, Inc.

112: "German Workers Like Time, Americans the Cash," by Daniel Benjamin and Tony Horwitz, reprinted with permission from the *Wall Street Journal*.

135: Excerpt from *Marat/Sade* by Peter Weiss, translated by Adrian Mitchell, reprinted with permission from Marion Boyars Publishers Ltd.

170, 286: "The Unknown Citizen" and "Musée des Beaux Arts," from *Collected Shorter Poems* by W. H. Auden, edited by Edward Mendelson, © 1940, 1968 by W. H. Auden; reprinted with permission of Random House, Inc.

174: "A Cosmopolitan among the True Believers," by Michael Ignatieff, excerpt from *Blood and Belonging*, reprinted with permission from Farrar, Straus & Giroux, Inc.

192: Excerpt from "A Killer's Tale," by John E. Burns, reprinted with permission from the *New York Times*.

243: Excerpt from "Cronenberg on Cronenberg," edited by Chris Rodley, reprinted with permission from Faber and Faber.

207: "The Matter Myth," Paul Davies, reprinted with permission.

224: "Limits of the Possible" by Douglas Shenson reprinted with permission from the *New York Times*.

262: "Appetizer," by Robert H. Abel is reprinted from *Ghost Traps* with permission of the University of Georgia Press.

275: Excerpt from *On Photography* by Susan Sontag, © 1973, 1974, 1977 by Susan Sontag; reprinted with permission of Farrar, Straus & Giroux, Inc.

281: "Film: Culture or Commerce," from *The Secret Language of Film*, Jean-Claude Carriere. Translation copyright © 1994 by Random House, Inc. Reprinted by permission, Pantheon Books, a division of Random House, Inc.

288: "Love Songs with No Tomorrows" by Jon Pareles, reprinted with permission from the *New York Times*.

306: "Eating Out," Leonard Michael, from *I Would Have Saved Them If I Could*, reprinted with permission from Farrar, Straus & Giroux, Inc.

307: Excerpt from "Dispatches" by Michael Herr, reprinted with permission from Alfred A. Knopf, Inc.

THE GOLDEN BOOK OF
ROME

ANCIENT ROME - THE VATICAN - THE RESTORED SISTINE CHAPEL
CHURCHES - MUSEUMS - MONUMENTS

BB
BONECHI

* * *

© Copyright 1995 by CASA EDITRICE BONECHI
via Cairoli 18/b - 50131 Firenze - Italia
Tel. 55/576841 - Telex 571323 CEB - Fax 55/5000766

Printed in Italy by Centro Stampa Editoriale Bonechi.

ISBN 88-7009-444-8

Texts by: Fabio Boldrini, Leonardo Castellucci, Stefano
Giuntoli and the editing staff
Maps: Michele Mancini and Studio Bellandi Giovannini
Mariani
Editing staff: Maurizio Martinelli
Graphics: Stefano Grisieti
English translation: Erika Pauli for Studio Comunicare,
Florence

*The photographs are the property of the Archives of Casa
Editrice Bonechi and were taken by:* Gaetano Barone, Nicolò
Orsi Battaglini, CISCU Lucca, Gianni Dagli Orti, Foto Musei
Vaticani, Foto Rev. da Fabbrica di San Pietro in Vaticano,
Paolo Giambone, Maurilio Mazzola, Pubbli Aer Foto,
Fabrizio Tempesti, Mario Tonini.

HISTORY

Rome began when groups of shepherds and farmers settled on the hill now known as the Palatine. Etymologically Roma *may mean the city of the river, or more probably the city of the Ruma, an old Etruscan family.*

After the semi-legendary period of the monarchy, the first authentic historical references date to the moment of transition from the monarchy to the republic (509 B.C.), when the Etruscan civilization, which had dominated Rome with the last kings, began its slow decline. The long period of the republic was marked by the formation of a real democracy governed by the consuls and the tribunes (the former represented the so-called plebeians), which went so far as to institute equal rights for patricians and plebs.

In the 4th century B.C. Rome already held sway over all of Latium and later extended its rule to many other regions in Italy, subjugating numerous Italic peoples and the great Etruscan civilization. Even the Gauls, and the Greeks in southern Italy, laid down their arms to Rome and by 270 B.C. the entire Italian peninsula had fallen under Roman domination. In the 3rd century B.C. this power began to spread out beyond the borders of the peninsula. Between 264 and 201 B.C. the entire Mediterranean (with the Punic wars) fell under Roman rule, and in the east, Rome extended its frontiers into Alexander the Great's kingdom, and in the west, subjugated the Gauls and the peoples of Spain. It is at this point that the republic became an empire, beginning with auspices of power and greatness under Augustus.

The empire, as it was conceived, was meant to be a balanced mixture of the various republican magistratures under the direct control of the senate and the will of the people. This was what it was meant to be, but in reality as time passed the empire took on an ever increasing dictatorial and militaristic aspect. With its far-flung frontiers, Rome found itself divided and split and as its authority began to wane, it went into a slow but inexorable decadence. The city was no longer the emperor's seat and the senate continued to lose its political identity. This decadence reached its zenith after the first barbarian invasions, but the city never lost its moral force, that awareness which for centuries had considered Rome the caput mundi, *a situation which was also abetted by the advent of Christianity which consecrated it as the seat of its Church.*

After the middle of the 6th century A.D., Rome became just another of the cities of the new Byzantine empire, with its capital in Ravenna. Even so, two centuries later, thanks to the presence of the Pope, it once more became a reference point for this empire and its history becomes inseparable from that of the Franco-Carolingian empire. Charlemagne chose to be crowned emperor in Rome and hereafter all emperors were to be consecrated as such in Rome.

The city proclaimed itself a free commune in 1144. In this period it was governed by the municipal powers, the papacy and the feudal nobility. The powers of the commune and those of the pope were often in open contrast and were marked by harsh struggles. At the beginning of the 14th century the papacy moved to Avignon and the popular forces were freer to govern. At the end of the 14th century and in the early 15th century the situation once more was reversed: the pope returned to Rome and managed to gain control of the city and recuperate most of the power the popular government had gained in the preceding century. The city flourished in this period, for it became the capital of the Papal State and was as splendid as ever, one of the most important crossroads for culture and art. In the centuries that followed, politically Rome tended towards an ever greater isolation: the Papal State kept at a distance from the various international contrasts and while this set limits on its importance from a political point of view it gave free rein to a development of trade and above all the arts and culture.

This situation continued up to the end of the 18th century when the revolutionary clime which struck Europe in those years also involved the Church in an unexpected crisis and the papal rule of the city passed to the Republic (Pius VI was exiled to France). Temporal power had a brief comeback with Pius VII, but only a few years later Napoleon once more revolutionized the situation, proclaiming Rome the second city of his empire. After varying vicissitudes in which the city returned to the pope (1814), came the period of the Risorgimento when, under the papacy of Pius IX, Rome was a ferment of patriotic and anticlerical ideals. In 1848 a real parliament was formed; the following year the Roman Republic was proclaimed and the government passed into the hands of a triumvirate headed by Giuseppe Mazzini until the intervention of the French army restored temporal power. In 1860 with the formation of the Kingdom of Italy, the pope's power was limited to Latium alone. Ten years later, with the famous episode of the breach at Porta Pia, the French troops protecting the papacy were driven out of the city, which was annexed to the Kingdom of Italy and became its capital. Dissension arose between the Papal State and the new Italian political reality which eventually led to the conciliation between the State and the Church in the Lateran Pact (Feb. 11, 1929). After World War II, when Italy passed from the monarchy to the republic, Rome became the seat of the Italian Parliament.

ARCHITECTURE

In the beginning Rome developed on the Palatine hill and gradually spread to the surrounding hills. The Servian walls *date to the 4th century B.C.. The circuit of* Aurelian walls *are later. The urban fabric changed almost radically during the felicitous period of the Republic and the city* expanded rapidly (the Cloaca Maxima and the Basilica Aemilia belong to this period). With the advent of the empire, the city expanded still further (marked by the imposing Imperial Fora, the Basilica Julia, the reliefs on Trajan's Column and on that of Marcus Aurelius, the reliefs on the Arch of Titus and those on the Arch of Septimius Severus, the Pantheon, the Colosseum, Nero's Domus Aurea and Trajan's Markets, the Baths of Caracalla and of Diocletian).

After the fires of A.D. 64 and 80, Rome was almost completely rebuilt on a more modern and rational plan. In the 2nd century A.D. the population of the city numbered about a million inhabitants, unusual for the times. The city began to decline in the 3rd century and a new circuit of walls went up. The haunting catacombs (brought to light in the 20th century) date to the 3rd and 4th centuries and the magnificent mosaics of S. Pudenziana and of SS. Cosma and Damiano are not much later. With the arrival of the Goths and then of the Lombards, Rome was practically deserted (50,000 inhabitants) and the development of the arts came to a standstill. Numerous churches, including those of Santa Maria Maggiore, Santa Sabina and San Clemente, were built in the early Christian period.

In the 9th century the city was demolished by the Saracens and then in 1084 by the Normans. In the 10th, 11th, and 12th centuries the cultural awakening of the city began (with the Romanesque churches of San Clemente, Santa Maria in Trastevere, San Crisogono). The Romanesque style was replaced by the Gothic style, which, however, left few signs in the city (Church of Santa Maria sopra Minerva, the ciboria Arnolfo di Cambio made for the Churches of San Paolo and Santa Cecilia). Not until the papacy returned to Rome after its period of exile in Avignon did Rome rapidly return to its role of being an exceedingly important crossroads for culture and trade.

During the 15th century, under the impulse of the Church, the city flourished once more. Many of the most illustrious artists worked for the Vatican. Works of art realized in this period include the bronze doors of St. Peter's by Filarete; the decoration of the Vatican Chapel by Fra Angelico; the bronze funeral monuments of Sixtus V and Innocent IV by Antonio del Pollaiolo; the Palazzo Venezia and the Palazzo della Cancelleria were built. With the arrival of the 16th century, Rome was once more its old self, the « caput mundi », and absolute masterpieces were created by the greatest artists of the time: Raphael, Michelangelo, Bramante, Giulio Romano, Baldassarre Peruzzi, the Sangallos, Vignola and many others who, one after the other, took turns in providing the city with unique masterpieces: churches, squares, fountains, palaces and roads of unequalled beauty came into being.

This felicitous period continued throughout the 17th and 18th centuries. The Carraccis (Farnese Gallery), Guido Reni, Guercino worked in Rome. But above all, Gian Lorenzo Bernini, who laid out St. Peter's square and revealed himself as a peerless sculptor (works in the Museo Borghese). In the 19th and 20th centuries the city grew prodigiously in size and new districts, new roads and new social realities were intertwined with the old urban fabric.

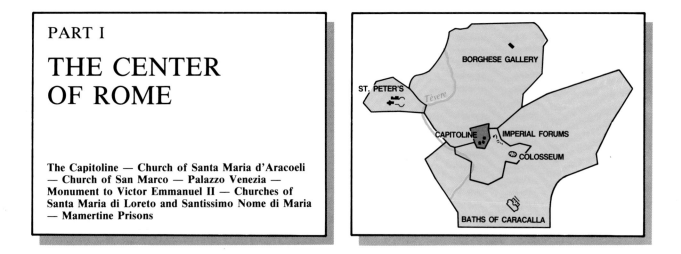

PART I

THE CENTER OF ROME

The Capitoline — Church of Santa Maria d'Aracoeli — Church of San Marco — Palazzo Venezia — Monument to Victor Emmanuel II — Churches of Santa Maria di Loreto and Santissimo Nome di Maria — Mamertine Prisons

THE CAPITOLINE

From earliest times on, the Capitoline hill (or Campidoglio) was the center of the political, social, and religious life of Rome. In addition to the old *asylum*, this was the site of the great Italic temple dedicated to the Capitoline Jupiter, and the name of *Capitolium* was used almost exclusively to designate the temple rather than the entire site. Among others the *arx*, with the Temple of Iuno Moneta (the Admonisher) and the temple of the Virtus, also stood on the northern tip of the two knolls which comprised the height. The *clivus capitolinus* was the carriage road which led to the hill of the forum; there was also a flight of stairs which led to the arx alone and from which, near the Mamertine Prisons, the famous *Scalae Gemoniae* branched off.

The staircase of the Capitoline with the statue of the Dioscuri and the Palazzo Senatorio.

Piazza del Campidoglio, with Marcus Aurelius surrounded by the Palazzo dei Conservatori, Palazzo Senatorio and Palazzo Nuovo. Opposite: the equestrian statue of Marcus Aurelius.

The most sacred of the hills of Rome (even though the smallest) has continued to be the seat of power throughout the centuries. Michelangelo's **Piazza del Campidoglio** now stands on its summit, defined by illustrious palaces and magnificently decorated by the **statue of Marcus Aurelius**, set at the center of the intriguing interplay of elipses and volutes Michelangelo himself designed on the gray pavement of the square. Formerly in the Lateran square, the Marcus Aurelius was moved to the Capitoline in 1538 and had not apparently been previously taken into consideration by Michelangelo as decoration for the square.

The Palazzo Senatorio, the Palazzo Nuovo (or of the Capitoline Museum) and the Palazzo de'Conservatori define the limits of this first plateau of modern Rome. Both the **Palazzo Nuovo** and the **Palazzo dei Conservatori** were designed as twins by Michelangelo and built respectively by Girolamo Rainaldi (under Innocent X) and Giacomo della Porta (after 1563). Both of Michelangelo's palaces are characterized by an architectural layout sustained by large Corinthian pilasters, and are crowned by an attic with a balustrade supporting large statues.

The **Palazzo Senatorio**, however, with a facade that is attributed to Rainaldi and Della Porta (although there was an earlier project by Michelangelo) stands on the histori-cal site of the *Tabularium* and is distinguished by its converging flights of stairs, designed by Michelangelo and built while the artist was still alive. Inside is a series of famous rooms, including the *Sala delle Bandiere*, that of the *Carroccio* (or *Chariot*), the *Green Room*, the *Yellow Room*, and the large *Council Hall* where the Senate Tribune met. The Palazzo Nuovo contains the **Capitoline Museum**, which is well known both for the wealth of material and for the fact that it is the oldest museum collection in the world. Begun by Sixtus V, in 1471, it was enriched by popes Pius V, Clement XII (who opened it to the public), Benedict XIV, Clement XIII and Pius VI. Installed on two floors, the collection of the Capitoline Museum occupies practically all the rooms on the ground floor, as well as those on the upper floor, including the hall. Note should be taken on the first floor of the *Egyptian Collection* and, in the *Hall of Oriental Cults*, of an impressive series of statues, inscriptions, and reliefs. Treasures of classic art are contained in the other rooms on the ground floor (to the right of the atrium) and on the upper floor. In particular the monuments in the *Hall of Columns* and the *Hall of Emperors* (with *65 busts of Roman emperors*) come to mind as well as the *Hall of Philosophers*, the *Hall of the Faun*, and the famous *Hall of the Dying Gaul* (also called the *Dying Gladiator*).

IMP·CAESARI·DIVI·ANTONINI·F·DIVI·HADRIANI
NEPOTI·DIVI·TRAIANI·PARTHICI·PRONEPOTI·DIVI
NERVAE·ABNEPOTI·M·AVRELIO·ANTONIO·PIO
AVG·GERM·SARM·PONT·MAX·TRIB·POT·XXVII
IMP·VI·COS·III·P·P·S·P·Q·R

The simple facade of the Church of Santa Maria d'Aracoeli.

CHURCH OF SANTA MARIA D'ARACOELI

Mention of the church appears as early as the 7th century. In the 10th century it became a Benedictine Abbey and then passed to the Friars Minor, who saw to its reconstruction around 1320. A place for associative life as well as a place of worship, the church continued in this unique calling into the 16th century and the civic victory of Marcantonio Colonna after the victory of Lepanto (1571) was celebrated here.

The **exterior** has a gabled roof and three doorways under three windows. A sort of vestibule is set against the central portal. Renaissance elements of some importance in the austere 14th-century facade are the reliefs with *Saints Matthew and John* over the two smaller portals.

The **interior**, a typical basilica, has a nave separated from the two side aisles by 22 reused antique columns. The *Cappella Bufalini* (in the right aisle) contains frescoes by Pinturicchio that are considered his masterpieces.

CHURCH OF SAN MARCO

Opening onto the Piazza San Marco, the church has to all extents been incorporated by Palazzo Venezia, even though its foundations can be traced back to the 4th century when it was founded by Pope Mark, later sanctified and eponymous with the church. Its destiny is part and parcel of the palace of which it is now a part. Rebuilt by Pope Paul II Barbo, around the middle of the 18th century it was given a Baroque face-lifting, especially in the interior.

The **exterior** is marked by its facade and three-arch porch and an elegant loggia which bears the mark of Giuliano da Maiano.

The basilical **interior** with a nave and two aisles is richly decorated and frescoed, in line with the 18th-century project of Filippo Barigioni. Of particular note in the apse are the mosaics in the conch which date to the period of Pope Gregory IV (first half of the 9th cent.).

PALAZZO VENEZIA

Outstanding monuments and historical buildings overlook the Piazza Venezia. The most important, on the west side of the square, is the **Palazzo Venezia**, the design for which is attributed to Leon Battista Alberti, while the actual building was carried out under Bernardo Rossellino. Commissioned by Pietro Barbo (future Pope Paul II) and terminated by Marco Barbo, Pietro's nephew, the building was the headquarters of the Venetian embassy in Rome, and, as Venetian territory, even belonged to the Austrians until 1916. More recently it was the representative seat of Mussolini's government and the dictator had his cabinet meetings here (in the *Sala del Mappamondo*).

Above: the facade of Palazzo Venezia. Below: the wooden statue of St. Anne, the Virgin and Child, German school, 16th cent., Museo di Palazzo Venezia.

Ever since 1944 it has been the home of the Museum of Palazzo Venezia, a particularly privileged exhibition site. The main facade of the palace faces onto the Piazza Venezia and is distinguished by a tripartite architectural layout and large cross windows on the *piano nobile*. Of note on the doorway are the *Barbo coats of arms* and, on the facade on the Via del Plebiscito, the other *portal* decorated by Giovanni il Dalmata. Inside, on the other side of the atrium, is the *courtyard* partially defined by Giuliano da Maiano's incompleted *portico*.

Inside Palazzo Venezia, the **Museo di Palazzo Venezia** is installed in the rooms of *Paul II's Apartment* and in the adjacent *Cybo Apartment* (as well as in part of the *Palazzetto di Venezia*). Characterized by the variety of material on exhibition (in part due to the varied tastes of the popes-collector), the collections of Palazzo Venezia occupy a series of rooms: the *Sala Regia*, with the collections of arms and tapestries, the *Sala delle Battaglie* or *of the Concistoro*, the famous *Sala del Mappamondo*, the *Hall of the Labors of Hercules*, which contains wooden sculpture, and another six rooms full of fine collections of silver and ceramics.

MONUMENT TO VICTOR EMMANUEL II

After an extenuating competition, the realization of the monument was entrusted to Giuseppe Sacconi and was

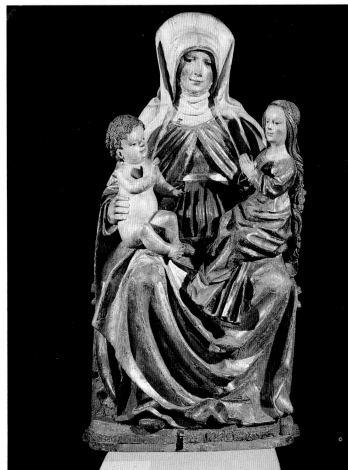

Above: monument to Victor Emmanuel II with the « altare della patria ». Below: the twin churches of Santa Maria di Loreto and the Santissimo Nome di Maria.

begun in 1885, to be finished and inaugurated in 1911. Its intentions were those of celebrating the splendor of the nation after the Unification of Italy, and with this in mind Sacconi envisioned it in imposing classicistic forms that would mirror the emotional and patriotic heart of the monument, the **Altar to the Homeland**, which was in turn envisioned as architecture within architecture with the solemn statue of *Rome* keeping watch over the **Tomb of the Unknown Soldier**. Note should also be taken of the **equestrian statue of Victor Emmanuel II**, for it is an integral part of the monument, also decidedly classicistic in style, as well as the fateful words from the Bulletin of Victory of Nov. 4, 1918.

CHURCHES OF SANTA MARIA DI LORETO AND SANTISSIMO NOME DI MARIA

These two churches, both on the Largo del Foro Traiano, have the same central plan although the former, dedicated to the **Madonna of Loreto**, was founded at the beginning of the 16th century (1501) while the latter was built between 1736 and 1738 after plans by Antonio Derizet. The plans for the robust square building block and the cupola which rises up over it, as well as the corresponding

Above: view of the Roman Forum with the columns of the Temple of Saturn, the Curia and the Arch of Septimius Severus. Below: the interior of the Mamertine prisons with the column Saints Peter and Paul were traditionally bound to.

octagon in the interior, to be found in Santa Maria di Loreto, have been attributed to artists as prestigious as Bramante and Antonio da Sangallo the Younger.

Despite their external resemblance, the interior of the **Church of the Santissimo Nome di Maria** is on an elliptical plan with seven sumptuous chapels opening off the perimeter.

MAMERTINE PRISONS

Under the Church of S. Giuseppe dei Falegnami, on the slopes of the Capitoline hill, north of the Temple of Concord, are the « prisons » known in medieval times as « Mamertine ». The travertine facade of the building can be dated from the inscription referring to the consuls Gaius Vibius Rufinus and Marcus Cocceius Nerva who were consuls between 39 and 42 A.D.. A modern entrance leads into a trapezoidal chamber built in blocks of tufa, dating to the middle of the 2nd century B.C.. A door which is now walled up led into the other rooms of the prison called « *latomie* » because they were adapted from the tufa quarries. A circular opening in the pavement of this room was originally the only entrance to an underground chamber where those condemned to death and enemies of the State were tortured and killed, generally by strangulation. It only appears to be a later legend that St. Peter was kept prisoner here.

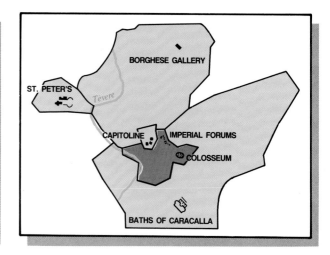

IMPERIAL FORUMS

Although the Imperial Forums built near the precedent Forum of republican times, the underlying concept was more rational and grand. These enormous public squares (80-90,000 sq. meters) were enclosed by porticoes and an equestrian statue of the emperor was often to be found at the center while the square was shut off at the back by an imposing temple. The Imperial Forums were created with theope of enhancing the prestige of the city and providing the citizens with a place for their markets, from which they could listen to harangues, and where they could participate in religious ceremonies. The first forum built was the **Forum Iulium** *(54-56 B.C.), under the auspices of Caesar himself. Next came the* **Forum of Augustus** *(31-32 B.C.), the* **Forum of Vespasian** *or of Peace (71-75),* **Nerva's Forum** *(A.D. 98) and lastly* **Trajan's Forum** *(113). After the 6th century, the Forums were com-*

Below: Trajan's Column. Opposite: two stretches of the Via dei Fori Imperiali.

A section of the colonnade in Trajan's Forum with, in the background, Trajan's Markets.

pletely neglected and began gradually to be destroyed. During the Middle Ages a tiny portion was recuperated and a small district came into being which blended with the other Roman ruins. Most of it however became a mud-field and was rebaptized the zone of the « Pantani » or bogs, and the splendid buildings of Imperial times were destroyed or gravely damaged. Forgotten for centuries, the area was partially urbanized in the Renaissance but not until the 19th century and above all the 20th were the remains of this once magnificent architecture brought to light and the Via dei Fori Imperiali created.

TRAJAN'S FORUM

Trajan's Forum extends northwards from Caesar's Forum and is oriented in the same direction. It is perpendicular to the forum of Augustus with which it borders on the west. The last and most imposing of the Imperial forums in Rome, it is the most important public work carried out by the emperor Trajan and his architect Apollodorus of Damascus. This imposing complex (300 m. long and 185 m. wide) was built between 106 and 113 A.D., financed by the proceeds of the Dacian war that had just been concluded.

The **Basilica Ulpia** which closed off the back of the square has also been excavated only in part. This is the largest basilica ever built in Rome, 17 meters long and almost 60 meters wide, taking its name from the family name of the emperor.

Trajan's Column stands in Trajan's Forum, between the two libraries, behind the Basilica Ulpia and in front of the temple of Divus Trajanus. Dedicated in A.D. 113, it is Doric; altogether it is almost 40 meters high, and at the top there was a statue of Trajan which was lost and replaced by one of St. Peter by Pope Sixtus V in 1587. The column was meant to serve as the tomb of the emperor and the entrance in the base leads to an antechamber and then a large room which contained a golden urn with Trajan's ashes. The same door on the right leads to a spiral staircase of 185 steps, cut in the marble, which rises to the top of the column.

A continuous frieze moves around the shaft of the column. About 200 meters long and varying in height from 90 to 125 centimeters, it represents Trajan's two victorious *Dacian campaigns* of A.D. 101-102 and 105-106, separated in the narration by a figure of *Victory* writing on a shield.

The **Temple of the Divus Trajanus** and of the Diva Plotina terminates the Forum to the northeast. It was built in A.D. 121 by Hadrian after Trajan's death. Not much is known about this temple which stood on the present site of the Church of S. Maria di Loreto and which must have been of colossal size with eight Corinthian columns on the front and eight on each side, over 20 meters high.

Right: the statue of Trajan placed in the Imperial Forums in modern times. Below: the hemicycle of Trajan's Markets.

*Above: Trajan's Markets with the Loggia of the Knights of Rhodes.
Below: a view of the Markets with the Torre delle Milizie in the
background.*

TRAJAN'S MARKETS

The construction of Trajan's Forum required the
removal of part of the Quirinal hill, and the architect,
Apollodorus of Damascus (who built the Forum as well),
brilliantly made use of the slopes to realize a unified
structural complex.

The front of the markets consists of a large hemicycle in
brick behind the eastern exedra of Trajan's Forum, echo-
ing its shape and separated from it by a road paved with
large irregular polygonal blocks of lava which had been
polished. A series of *tabernae* open in the bottom floors;
on the upper floor another row of shops are set against
the rock of the cut on the hillside. On the ground floor,
at the sides of the tabernae, are two large semi-circular
halls, with windows and covered by half domes, that may
have been used for schools.

The third level of the complex is a road that rises steeply
and which was called « Via Biberatica » in the Middle
Ages, (*biber* = beverage or *piper* = spices). What with
the addition of a basilica, shops and offices, the entire
complex consisted of six separate floors.

Above: the ruins of the Temple of Mars Ultor in the Forum of Augustus. Below: a modern statue of Augustus erected in the Imperial Forums.

THE FORUM OF AUGUSTUS

The **Forum of Augustus** lies between the Forum of Caesar on the west and the *Subura* district to the east. It was later enclosed on the north by the Forum of Trajan and to the south by the Forum Transitorium. It was constructed after costly expropriations on the part of the emperor so that he could free the area which was occupied by private dwellings. The entrance side, to the southwest, adjacent to the eastern side of Caesar's forum, is now under the Via dei Fori Imperiali as is the case with the front part of the square and the colonnades. There were also two secondary entrances at the back of the forum. The **Temple of Mars Ultor** consisted of a cella on a tall podium faced in marble, access to which was via a staircase with an altar at the center and two fountains at its outer edges. It had eight Corinthian columns over seventeen meters high on the front and eight on the long sides while the back was without (*peripteros sine postico*). The inside also had seven columns in two rows along the walls and at the back an apse with the cult statues of *Venus*, *Mars* and the *Divus Iulius*.

Above: Caesar's Forum and, at the side, a portrait of Caesar now in the Museo della Civiltà Romana.

THE FORUM OF CAESAR

The **Forum of Caesar**, the first of the great imperial forums, lies northeast of the republican Roman Forum, along the Clivus Argentarius.

The project was planned as an elongated esplanade, 160x75 meters, with porticoes on three sides and the large Temple of Venus Genetrix in the back, a temple which Caesar had vowed before the battle of Pharsalus against Pompey in 48 B.C..

The **Temple of Venus Genetrix** had a single cella on a high podium with a flight of stairs on each side. There were eight Corinthian columns on the front and nine at the sides, in line with the formula of the *peripteros sine postico*. Two square fountains were set in front of the podium. The interior wall of the cella was articulated by six columns on either side. In the back was an apse with the cult statue of Venus Genetrix but the cella also contained other works of art such as paintings by Timomachus of Byzantium. The temple decoration as we know it now dates to Trajan's period.

THE FORUM TRANSITORIUM OR NERVA'S FORUM

This **Forum** takes its name from the fact that it lies between the republican Roman Forum, the Forum of Augustus, the Forum of Caesar, and Vespasian's Temple (or Forum) of Peace. It is superposed on a stretch of the old road of the Argiletum and the long narrow shape (m. 120x45) was dictated by the limited space available, which also explains the absence of an internal portico and the illusionistic device of setting up a row of columns a short distance from the outer wall. Above them was an attic with reliefs illustrating *Myths* connected with Minerva and a frieze with *Scenes of feminine occupations*. On the south side a stretch of the outer wall in blocks of *peperino* and two Corinthian columns, the so-called « *Colonnacce* », are still standing. In the frieze is the *Myth of Arachne* and on the attic a figure of *Minerva*. The short entrance side was curved, while the pronaos of the **Temple of Minerva**, a Corinthian hexastyle on a podium with a tripartite apsed cella, projected from the back.

Right: detail of the remains of the portico of Nerva's Forum, known as « Le Colonnacce ». Below: remains of buildings in Nerva's Forum.

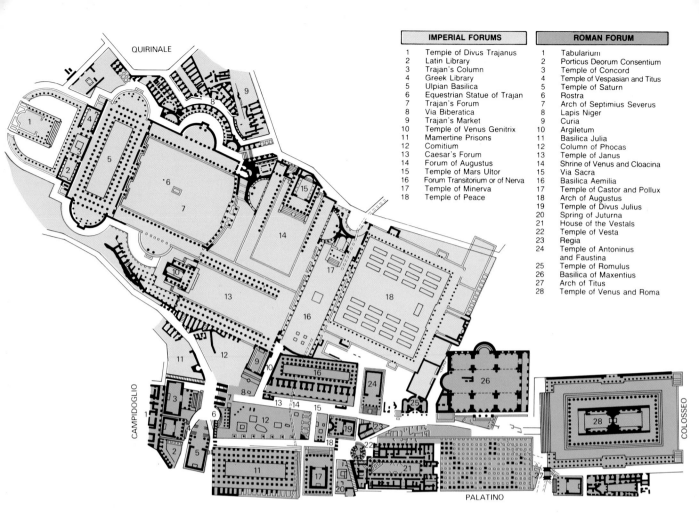

IMPERIAL FORUMS		ROMAN FORUM	
1	Temple of Divus Trajanus	1	Tabularium
2	Latin Library	2	Porticus Deorum Consentium
3	Trajan's Column	3	Temple of Concord
4	Greek Library	4	Temple of Vespasian and Titus
5	Ulpian Basilica	5	Temple of Saturn
6	Equestrian Statue of Trajan	6	Rostra
7	Trajan's Forum	7	Arch of Septimius Severus
8	Via Biberatica	8	Lapis Niger
9	Trajan's Market	9	Curia
10	Temple of Venus Genitrix	10	Argiletum
11	Mamertine Prisons	11	Basilica Julia
12	Comitium	12	Column of Phocas
13	Caesar's Forum	13	Temple of Janus
14	Forum of Augustus	14	Shrine of Venus and Cloacina
15	Temple of Mars Ultor	15	Via Sacra
16	Forum Transitorium or of Nerva	16	Basilica Aemilia
17	Temple of Minerva	17	Temple of Castor and Pollux
18	Temple of Peace	18	Arch of Augustus
		19	Temple of Divus Julius
		20	Spring of Juturna
		21	House of the Vestals
		22	Temple of Vesta
		23	Regia
		24	Temple of Antoninus and Faustina
		25	Temple of Romulus
		26	Basilica of Maxentius
		27	Arch of Titus
		28	Temple of Venus and Roma

Above: the Roman Forum. Overleaf and following page: part of the large model of ancient Rome in the Museo della Civiltà Romana showing the Forums, the Colosseum, the Palatine and the Circus Maximus.

ROMAN FORUM

HISTORY

Situated in a valley between the Palatine, the Capitoline and the Esquiline hills, the area was originally a most inhospitable zone, swampy and unhealthy, until surprisingly modern reclamation work was carried out by the king Tarquinius Priscus, who provided the area with a highly developed drainage system (Cloaca Maxima). Once this complex reclamation work was finished, the Roman forum became a place for trade and barter. Numerous shops and a large square known as the market square were built and a zone was set apart for public ceremonies. It was here that the magistrates were elected, the traditional religious holidays were kept and those charged with various crimes were judged by a real court organization. After the Punic wars, thanks to the extraordinary development of the city, the urban fabric of the Forum took on a new look. As early as the 2nd century B.C., various basilicas — Porcia, Sempronia, and Aemilia — were built, the temples of the Castors and of Concordia were rebuilt, and the network of roads connecting the Forum to the quarters of the city continued to grow. After various transformations under the emperor Augustus, the Roman Forum became so large as to be considered the secular, religious, and commercial center of the city. Af-

ter a period in which secular and political interests centered on other parts of the city, the Roman Forum reacquired its original prestige under Maxentius and Constantine who ordered the construction of the Temple of Romulus and the great Basilica of Constantine. With the decadence of the Roman Empire, the splendid venerable structures of the Forum were severely damaged by the Barbarian invasions, especially the Goths (A.D. 410) and the Vandals (A.D. 455). The Roman Forum meanwhile became a place of worship for the early Christians who built the Churches of SS. Sergio e Bacco (on the Via Sacra), of S. Adriano (on the Curia), SS. Cosma e Damiano (Temple of Peace).

As time passed, the Forum was completely abandoned. What was left of the antique monuments was used by the people or demolished. During the Middle Ages the Forum became a pasture for sheep and cattle (hence its name of Campo Vaccino). For many centuries the prestige of the Roman Forum was a thing of the past. Not until the early 20th century was there a systematic re-evaluation of the area with excavation campaigns which lasted for various decades and which brought back to light the splendid evidence of the Rome of the kings as well as that of the republic and of the empire.

On this page, above: a stretch of the Via Sacra with the remains of the Basilica Aemilia with the Curia (to the left) and the Temple of Antoninus and Faustina (to the right). Below: the remains of the Basilica Aemilia with, in the background, the Temple of Antoninus and Faustina. Opposite: two details of the remains of the Basilica Aemilia.

THE BASILICA AEMILIA

The Basilica Aemilia comprises the long side of the square of the Roman Forum and is fronted to the west by the road of the Argiletum.

The Basilica Aemilia consists of a large hall (m. 70x29) divided into aisles by rows of columns. The nave, about twelve meters wide, is flanked by one aisle on the south and two aisles on the north. There are remains of paving in colored marble. On the side towards the square of the Forum the building was preceded by a two-story portico with sixteen arches on piers. The three columns still standing belong to the reconstruction after A.D. 410. Behind the portico is a series of *tabernae* for bankers, built to take the place of the *tabernae novae*, wiped out in the construction of the basilica. The three entrances that led to the hall are set between them.

Fragments of slabs in marble which belonged to a figured frieze that ran along the architrave of the first interior order have been found in the basilica. The subject matter was concerned with stories relating to the origins of Rome: the *Childhood of Romulus and Remus with Acca Larenzia*, the *Founding of the city*, the *Rape of the Sabines*, the *Killing of Tarpeas* and others.

The Temple of Antoninus and Faustina on the structures of which the Church of San Lorenzo in Miranda was built.

THE TEMPLE OF ANTONINUS AND FAUSTINA

The temple faces onto the Via Sacra, in front of the north side of the Regia to the east of the Basilica Aemilia.
The building has reached us in good condition because the church of S. Lorenzo in Miranda was built inside in the early Middle Ages. The temple, imposing in its size, consists of a cella originally faced with cipolin marble, and placed on a podium, access to which is by a modern staircase, with a brick altar in the center. The pronaos consists of six Corinthian columns on the front and two on each side, in cipolin marble and seventeen meters high, on some of which images of gods are engraved. The frieze has confronting griffins and plant designs.

THE VIA SACRA

Various ancient sources have provided detailed information on the Via Sacra but the entire route followed by this course, which changed along with the history of the city of Rome, has not yet been completely identified. There are various hypotheses regarding the use of the term « Sacra ». Varro tells us it depended on the fact that it was the route taken by the sacred processions while Festus adds the mythical episode of the sacred pact between Romulus and Titus Tatius which tradition locates here. In any case it seems likely that a decisive element in the acquisition of the name is the fact that the oldest and most important places of worship were situated along this route.

Above: a stretch of the Via Sacra with the Arch of Septimius Severus and, beyond, the remains of the Tabularium. Right: a marble fragment with an inscription of the Antonine period.

The square building of the Curia, built entirely in brick.

THE CURIA

The building touches on the southwest side of Caesar's forum of which it is in a sense an adjunct, between the road of the Argiletum and the Comitium.

It represents the seat of the Roman Senate. Tradition attributes the founding of the first permanent Curia to king Hostilius from which it took the name *Curia Hostilia*. It was rebuilt and enlarged in 80 B.C. by Silla but in 52 B.C. it was destroyed in a fire provoked by incidents connected with the funeral of the tribune Clodius. It was then moved from its original site by Caesar who built his Forum there and who began to rebuild the Curia in its present site.

His death in 44 B.C. interrupted work and the new Curia, rebaptised by decree of the Senate *Curia Iulia*, was not finished until 29 B.C. by Augustus, who also erected a portico known as *Chalcidicum*.

After the fire of A.D. 64 it was restored by Domitian in A.D. 94, but it had to be restored once more by Diocletian after the fire of Carinus in A.D. 283 and it was then rededicated in A.D. 303.

The ground plan as we have it now dates to this phase even if Honorius I transformed the building in A.D. 630 into the Church of S. Adriano, and it was frequently remodelled and finally torn down between 1930 and 1936 in order to bring to light the important archaeological site.

The building has a rectangular ground plan with four large buttress piers at the external corners, in line with the facades. The main facade has an entrance door and three large windows which illuminate the hall which is 21 meters high, 27 meters long and 18 meters wide, its proportions respecting the Vitruvian canon for curias. It had a flat timber roof and the present one is obviously

One side of the base of the column commemorating the decennial games of A.D. 303, set in front of the Curia, with a scene of sacrifice.

modern.

Two reliefs known as the *Plutei of Trajan* and found in the central area of the Forum in 1872 are to be seen inside the Curia. They are sculptured on both sides and must have belonged to some unknown monument, perhaps the enclosure of the *Ficus Ruminalis* or the Rostra Anziati. Both panels have a pig, a sheep and a bull, for the « *suovetaurile* » sacrifice, on one side. The other two sides have two historical friezes which refer to moments in Trajan's reign.

One panel shows Trajan, on the left, escorted by lictors, haranguing the crowd from the Rostra Aziaci in front of the Temple of the Divus Julius. Various monuments in the Forum can be recognized in the background: the Arch of Augustus, the Temple of Castor and Pollux and, beyond the *Vicus Tuscus*, the Basilica Julia, and then the *Ficus Ruminalis* and the statue of *Marsyas*. Near the

center of the relief, the emperor appears once more on a pedestal, seated and flanked by the personifications of *Italia* with a child in her arms, perhaps a statue placed in the square of the Forum to celebrate the liberal imperial measures.

The scene on the other panel illustrates the cancelling of the outstanding debts of the citizens: archive officials bring the registers with the outstanding debts and burn them in the presence of the emperor, in the Forum. Spatially and conceptually this scene is a continuation of the preceding relief, as also shown by the buildings on the same side of the Forum represented in the background. From the left are repeated the *Ficus Ruminalis* and the statue of *Minerva*, then the rest of the eastern side of the Basilica Julia, the *Vicus Iugarius*, the Temple of Saturn, the Temple of Vespasian and Titus, to end up with the Rostra Anziati.

Above: the south side of the Arch of Septimius Severus. Left: detail of the north side with the Arch of Titus in the background.

Detail of the model of ancient Rome in the Museo della Civiltà
Romana which reproduces the Forum as it was 2000 years ago.

THE ARCH OF SEPTIMIUS SEVERUS

The arch is situated between the Rostra and the Curia and faces onto the square of the Roman Forum on the northeast. It was built in A.D. 203 to celebrate Septimius Severus' two Parthian campaigns of 195 and 197.

The arch is about 20 meters high, 25 meters wide and over 11 meters deep and has three passageways, a large one in the center and two smaller ones at the sides with short flights of steps leading up to them. On top is a tall attic with a monumental inscription which dedicates it to Septimius Severus and his son Caracalla. Representations of the monument on antique coins show that there was once a bronze quadriga with the emperors on the summit.

The arch is built of travertine and brick faced with marble. On the front are four columns standing on tall plinths decorated with reliefs of Roman soldiers and Parthian prisoners. The decoration includes two *Victories*, above *Genii of the Seasons*, which frame the central opening, and *Personifications of Rivers* for the side openings, with a small frieze with the *Triumphal Procession of the emperors* above. Gods are represented in the keystones: *Mars* twice for the principal arch and two female figures and two male figures, one of whom is *Hercules*, on the lesser arches.

But the most interesting part of the decoration is the series of four panels (m. 3.92x4.72) set above the side open-

ings. The story of the two *Parthian campaigns* unfolds in a series of significant episodes. Each panel should be read from the bottom to the top, beginning with the left-hand panel on the side towards the Forum. Here are represented the phases of the first war, with the departure of the army from an encampment, a *Battle between Romans and Parthians* and the *Freeing of the city of Nisibis* to which the Parthians had laid siege, with the flight of their king Vologases and terminating with a scene of the *Emperor delivering a speech* to his army.

The second panel presents events from the second war: in the lower register the *Roman attack on Edessa* using war machines, including a large battering ram, and the *City opening its gates to surrender*; in the central band *Abgar*, king of Osrhoene, makes the *Act of submission to Septimius Severus* who harangues the army; in the upper tier is shown an imperial *Council of war* in a *castrum* and the *Departure* for enemy territory.

The third panel shows the *Attack on Seleucia*, a city on the Tigris, with the *Fleeing Parthians on horseback*, the *Submission of enemies* to the emperor and his *Entrance into the conquered city*.

And lastly the fourth panel shows the *Siege of the capital, Ctesiphon*, with war machines, and the flight from the city of the Parthian king Vologases and, in conclusion, the *Emperor's speech* before the conquered city.

The remains of the front of the Temple of Saturn and, in the background, the Roman Forum.

THE TEMPLE OF SATURN

The temple was pseudoperipteral with Ionic columns on a high podium, situated southwest of the Rostra, on the slopes of the Capitoline hill.

It was one of the oldest temples in Rome and was erected in 497 B.C. but was completely rebuilt in 42 B.C. by the aedile L. Munazius Plancus. The large podium entirely faced in travertine, 40 meters long, 22.50 meters wide and 9 meters high, which is still extant dates to this phase. As indicated by the inscription on the architrave the temple was once more restored in A.D. 238 after a fire.

An avant-corps in front of the base consisted of two podia separated by a flight of stairs which led to the temple. One of these must have contained the headquarters of the Roman State Treasury. The threshold is still to be seen on the side facing the Forum.

The cella of the temple contained the statue of the god which was carried in procession for triumphal rites.

When this temple was built, Rome was passing through a particularly critical period due to extensive famines, epidemics and a severe economic and commercial crisis which characterized the years subsequent to the fall of the

Above: a reconstruction of the Roman Forum with the Colosseum in the background. Right: the Column of Phocas, erected in A.D. 608 for the Byzantine emperor after whom it is named.

monarchy.

Evidence of the sense of distress which took hold of the Roman people is the erection in these years of a number of temples: to Saturn in 497 B.C.; to Mercury, protector of commerce, in 495 B.C.; to Ceres, goddess of the earth and fertility, in 493 B.C.. The building of the Temple to Saturn must also be seen in this light for the god, before being identified with the Greek Cronos, was venerated for a particular characteristic known as « *Lua Saturni* », in other words the possibility of freeing the city from its afflictions.

Above: a view of the Roman Forum with, on the right, the remains of the Basilica Julia. Below, and opposite: two details of the basilica.

THE BASILICA JULIA

The basilica comprises the long south side of the Forum and it is bordered on the west by the *Vicus Iugarius* and on the east by the *Vicus Tuscus*, which separate it respectively from the Temple of Saturn and the Temple of the Castors. Work on the building was begun in 54 B.C. by Julius Caesar, from whom it took its name, and it was dedicated in 46 B.C.. The area was previously occupied by the *tabernae veteres* (market shops) and the Basilica Sempronia, built in 169 B.C. by Tiberius Sempronius Gracchus, father of the plebeian tribunes Tiberius and Gaius. At that time the house of Scipio Africanus as well as various shops had had to be torn down.

The Basilica Julia was finished by Augustus but was destroyed in a fire of 14 B.C. and reconstructed by Augustus who dedicated it in A.D. 12 to his adopted sons Gaius and Lucius. The fire of Carinus in A.D. 283 caused considerable damage and Diocletian saw to the restoration. It was once more partially destroyed when Alaric sacked Rome in A.D. 410 and it was reconstructed in A.D. 416 by the prefect of the city, Gabinius Vettius Probianus. The court of the *Centumviri* was held in the Basilica and

The Basilica Julia with, in the foreground, the remains of the piers; in the background, to the left, the columns of the Temple of Castor and Pollux with a section of the entablature.

it also served as a meeting place for those who frequented the Forum. The building, imposing in size (m. 96x48), was composed of a large central space (m. 82x18) with four aisles around it which were meant to serve as corridors. They were vaulted and set on two stories with arches framed by engaged columns.

The large central hall must have been divided into four parts by wooden partitions or curtains, so that four courts could carry on business at the same time, although in particularly important cases it was used in its entirety. The only part of the building still extant is the stepped podium, while the brick piers are a modern additon.

Still in place are various pedestals for statues, with inscriptions, three of which name Polykleitos, Praxitiles and Timarchus as sculptors. Various « gaming boards » (*tabulae lusoriae*) had been scratched into the pavement and steps, probably by the idlers who hung around the Forum. There are also *graffiti* sketches of some of the statues which seem to have been nearby.

THE TEMPLE OF CASTOR AND POLLUX

Facing on the square of the Roman Forum to the west of the Arch of Augustus, the temple is separated from the *Vicus Tuscus* by the east side of the Basilica of Gaius and Lucius. The temple was first built here in 484 B.C. and frequently rebuilt and enlarged. Its present aspect is that given to it by Tiberius in A.D. 6. The building was peripteral with eight Corinthian columns on its short sides and eleven on its long sides and with a cella on a concrete base (opus caementicium) (m. 50x30x7) which was originally faced with tufa blocks which were removed in modern times and reused.

The podium we now see dates to the restoration carried out by Metellius in 117 B.C., as do the stretches of black and white mosaic on the paving of the cella.

During the republican period, senate meetings were also held in the temple and after the middle of the 2nd century B.C. the podium also became a tribune for magistrates and orators in the legislative meetings that took place in this part of the forum square. It was from here that Caesar proposed his agrarian reforms. The building also became the headquarters for the office of weights and measures and during the period of the Empire part of the treasury of the tax office was kept in rooms in the long sides.

The remains of the colonnade of the Temple of Castor and Pollux with a section of entablature.

The podium of the Temple of Divus Julius, with the exedra commemorating Julius Caesar.

THE TEMPLE OF DIVUS JULIUS

The temple is at the eastern end of the Piazza del Foro with the Basilica Aemilia to the north, the Temple of the Castors to the south and the Regia to the east.

It was built in 29 B.C. by Augustus as part of his project for the restructuring of the area of the Roman Forum, in the intent of giving the square a new disposition. This building closed off the square on its short east side and thus excluded once and for all the archaic monuments such as the Regia and the Temple of Vesta.

The temple is dedicated to the deified Julius Caesar (it is the first example in Rome) and stands on the site of his cremation after his body had been brought near the Regia, his official residence as Pontefix Maximus. A marble column was erected here in memory of the « father of the country », as stated in the inscription, replaced by a semi-circular exedra with an altar, which opens at the center of the temple podium, on the facade.

The Temple of Divus Julius, of which only the base is still extant, consisted of a cella on a podium, access to which was provided by a flight of stairs on either side. The pronaos had six Corinthian columns on the front and two at the sides and, except for the facade, it was surrounded by a colonnade, to be identified as the *Porticus Iulia*. The

rosters taken from the ships of Antony and Cleopatra in the battle of Actium in 31 B.C. seem not, as formerly believed, to have decorated the podium, but were on the front of an orator's tribune which stood in front of the temple.

The building is connected to the Basilica Aemilia by the portico dedicated to Gaius and Lucius, Augustus' grandsons, and to the temple of the Castors (the brothers Tiberius and Drusus) by the Augustan arch of the victory of Actium which was replaced in 19 B.C. by the one of the « Parthian » victory. It therefore belongs to a real propagandistic program in which the emperor's aim was to have the whole square echo with the name of the *Gens Iulia*.

THE TEMPLE OF VESTA

The temple, which is one of the oldest in Rome, is situated to the south of the Via Sacra in front of the Regia. Its present appearance dates to A.D. 191, when it was restored (the last of many restorations) by Giulia Domna, wife of Septimius Severus. This was where the fire sacred to Vesta, the goddess of the household hearth, had to be kept perennially burning, for disaster threatened if the flame were to go out. This obviously meant the building was frequently in danger of fire.

The cult of Vesta goes back to the earliest days of Rome. According to tradition the mother of Romulus and Remus was a vestal virgin, and Livy refers that Numa Pompilius founded the order of the vestal priestesses charged with the care of the temple, establishing a retribution paid by the State and particular privileges.

The building is circular and consists of a cella surrounded by twenty Corinthian columns set on a podium 15 meters in diameter faced with marble and with a staircase leading up to it on the east. The roof was conical with an opening for the smoke. The cella, which was articulated externally by engaged columns, contained no cult statue but only the hearth that was sacred to the goddess.

THE HOUSE OF THE VESTALS

The *Atrium Vestae*, on the south side of the Via Sacra, was a complex consisting of the Temple of Vesta and the house where the vestal virgins lived. As priestesses of the cult of Vesta, they were the custodians of the sacred hearth and were charged with performing the various rites involved. The only femine body of priests in Rome, the six vestal virgins were chosen among the children of

Right: the Temple of Vesta in the typical circular form. Below: the remains of the House of the Vestals with the statues of the senior members of this religious order.

Above: two statues of the Vestals inside the house of the priestesses. Opposite: the Temple of Divus Romulus with its original bronze doors.

patrician family between six and ten years old. They were required to stay in the order for thirty years, respecting a vow of chastity. On the other hand they enjoyed important privileges: they were subtracted from parental authority and the *patria potestas* passed to the Pontefix Maximus, they could travel in the city in a wagon (which was forbidden to women), they had reserved seats at the spectacles and ceremonies and could do as they best saw fit with a sort of stipend they received from the State.

The entrance to the House of the Vestals is to the west, flanked by an aedicula which probably served as a lararium. It leads into a large rectangular central courtyard around which is a colonnade with eighteen columns on the long sides and six on the short sides, arranged in two orders.

The porticoes originally housed the statues which represented the *Virgines Vestales Maximae* (the senior members of the order), many of which have been found in the courtyard together with bases naming them in inscriptions which all date from the time of Septimius Severus on. Sone of the statues have been left here, arbitrarily arranged and on pedestals which do not belong to them.

The central part of the east side of the complex is comprised of the so-called « *tablinum* », a spacious hall that was originally vaulted, from which six rooms open off. They were also vaulted and are all about the same size (m. 4.15x3.50) which would lead one to think they were the rooms of the six vestal virgins. This group of rooms is generally thought to be the sanctuary of the Lares and is also where the *statue of Numa Pompilius* which has come down to us may originally have stood.

On the ground floor the south side has a series of service rooms set along a corridor — an oven, a mill, a kitchen, etc. Upstairs are the rooms of the vestals with baths. There must also have been a third floor.

A view of the Basilica of Maxentius with, on the right, the Church of Santa Francesca Romana.

THE TEMPLE OF DIVUS ROMULUS

The building faces onto the Via Sacra between the area occupied by the archaic burial grounds and the Basilica of Maxentius. It appears not to have been a temple dedicated to Romulus, deified son of Maxentius, for the building is of Constantinian date and was probably the temple to the Penates which we know originally stood in the area occupied at the beginning of the 4th century A.D. by the Basilica of Maxentius and then transferred to an adjacent site. The building is circular in plan and built in brick. The entrance with its original bronze portal opens at the center of the curved facade. It is framed by two porphyry columns with bases in travertine and marble capitals which support a marble architrave. Four niches for statues are on either side the entrance and two elongated apsed rooms flank the temple. They are preceded by two columns in cipolin marble and must have housed the statues of the Penates.

In the 6th century A.D. the temple became the atrium of the church of SS. Cosma and Damian, originally a large room of the Forum of Peace that lay behind it. One hypothesis identifies this temple with that of Jupiter Stator which has never been localized but which was mentioned in literary sources of Constantinian date together with other buildings on the left of the Via Sacra, whereas no mention is made of the Temple of Divus Romulus.

THE BASILICA OF MAXENTIUS

Access to the Basilica of Maxentius, which stands outside the current archaeological zone of the Roman Forum, is from the Via dei Fori Imperiali. The building was begun in A.D. 308 by Maxentius and finished by Constantine, who modified the internal layout, shifting the entrance from the east to the south side, on the Via Sacra.

The imposing arches of the Basilica of Maxentius.

The building stands on a platform which is in part a sub-structure and which is superimposed on storerooms of considerable size, occupying an area of 100 by 65 meters. The entrance in the first plan, which Constantine also retained, opened into a narrow elongated atrium from which three openings led into the large central area, oriented east-west, 80 meters long, 25 meters wide and 35 meters high, covered by three cross vaults supported by eight columns in proconnesian marble, 14.50 meters high, set against piers (none of which are still *in situ*). At the back, right across from Maxentius' entrance, there was a semi-circular apse which contained an enormous acrolithic statue of Constantine (with the uncovered parts of the body in marble and the rest probably in gilded bronze), the head of which, 2.60 meters high, and a foot, two meters long, were found in 1487.

The aisles on either side of the nave were divided into three communicating bays with transversal coffered and stuccoed barrel vaults. Constantine's new project shifted the axis of the basilica from east-west to north-south, maintaining the tripartite division, with an entrance on the south side with four tall porphyry columns and a flight of steps which led from the Via Sacra to the floor of the building which was partly encased in the Velian hill. Across from this entrance a new semi-circular apse was set into the wall at the center of the north aisle, preceded by two columns and with niches for statues framed by small columns on corbels.

The nave was illuminated by a series of large windows in the clerestory while the side aisles had two tiers of arched windows.

The ground plan and dimensions of the building were inspired by the imposing halls of the imperial baths, which were also called « *basilicas* ».

The Church of Santa Francesca Romana with its bell tower.

CHURCH OF SANTA FRANCESCA ROMANA

Built in the second half of the 10th century, the church was remodelled more than once in the course of time. The profiled white **facade** in travertine dates to the early 17th century and is by Carlo Lombardi who was extremely active in Rome at the time. The gabled facade is crowned by statues and has two orders of paired pilasters set on high stylobates. Above there is a large balcony and a porch with three arches.

The single nave **interior** has a fine coffered ceiling and a very old square of Cosmatesque mosaic in the pavement. At the back of the nave is an arch known as the Holy Arch, with a *Confessio* in polychrome marble by Bernini and a shrine with four columns which contains a fine marble group of *Saint Francesca Romana and an Angel* by Giosue Meli (1866). On the back wall of the right transept are two blocks of basalt, protected by a gate, with two imprints which tradition says were made by Saint Peter when he knelt to pray here. On the left wall is the lovely *Funeral Monument of Gregory XI* by Olivieri. The apse is covered with mosaics depicting the *Madonna and Child with Saints Peter and Andrew*; on the high altar is the reputedly miraculous image of the *Madonna and Child* (12th cent.). Descending into the **crypt** we find the mortal remains of the saint at the altar and right across, a fine relief medallion of *Saint Francesca and an angel* by the school of Bernini. Lastly the, **Sacristy** houses rather fine paintings, including the panel of *Santa Maria Nova* (or the *Madonna del Conforto*) dating to the 5th century; a *Madonna Enthroned* by Sinibaldo Ibi from Perugia (1524); an imposing altarpiece, the *Miracle of St. Benedict*, by Subleyras, and various fine paintings by the school of Caravaggio. The adjacent **Convent** is the seat of the **Antiquarium Forense**.

The eastern side of the Arch of Titus.

THE ARCH OF TITUS

The arch rises in the eastern zone of the forums, south of the Temple of Venus and Roma.

The inscription on the side towards the Colosseum tells us that it was dedicated to the emperor Titus probably after his death in A.D. 81 by his brother and successor Domitian to commemorate the victory in the Judaic campaign of A.D. 70.

The arch has a single passageway, and is 5.40 meters high, 13.50 meters wide and 4.75 meters deep, faced with pentelic marble (with piers in travertine restored by Valadier in 1822) and on the front and back it has four engaged columns with composite capitals. The decorative sculpture on the outside includes two figures of *Victories on globes and with banners* above the archivolt, the *Goddess Roma* and the *Genius of the Roman people*, on the

The remains of the Temple of Venus and Roma with, on the left, the Arch of Titus.

keystones and a frieze in very high relief in the architrave with the *Triumph of Vespasian and Titus over the Jews*. Inside the arch a panel at the center of the coffered vault contains a relief with the *Apotheosis of Titus*. The panel on the north depicts a procession in which *Bearers of the lictor's fasces* precede the *Emperor who is being crowned by a Figure of Victory*; on the south side the *procession* as it passes through the *porta triumphalis* which is represented in a perspective view.

THE TEMPLE OF VENUS AND ROMA

Begun in A.D. 121 and inaugurated in 135, the Temple of Venus and Roma was designed by Hadrian himself. The building was set within an enclosing double colonnade which left the two principal facades free and which had two entrance propylaea at the center of the long sides. The dimensions (m. 145x100) of the entire ensemble are imposing.

The temple itself had ten columns on the front and nineteen on the sides; it lacked the traditional podium of Roman temples but stood on a stylobate with four steps and consisted of two cellae which were set back to back. Entrance to the cella was via two porches with four columns between the antae. Originally neither cella was apsed and they were covered with a flat timber roof. Their present aspect is the result of restoration effected by Maxentius in A.D. 307, after a fire. The cellae were given apses at the back which contained the cult statues of Venus and of the Goddess Roma while coffered and stuccoed barrel vaults replaced the original ceiling.

THE PALATINE

This is the most famous of Rome's hills and it retains the earliest memories of the old city. In fact the first groups of huts of the square city were built on the Palatine, before they spread over to the adjacent hills. Important public buildings, large temples and many private dwellings such as those of Cicero, Crassus and Tiberius Graccus went up here. Later the hill became the residence of the emperors of Rome who had their sumptuous palaces built here, including the **Domus Augustana**, the **Domus Flavia**, the **Domus Transitorio**, the **Domus Aurea**, and the **Domus Tiberiana**, of which considerable remains are still extant. The Palatine was then the residence of the Gothic kings and of many popes and emperors of the Western Empire; in the Middle Ages convents and churches were built. Finally in the 16th century most of the hill was occupied by the immense structures of **Villa Farnese** and the **Orti Farnesiani** (the first real botanical gardens). Archaeological excavation was begun in the 18th century and evidence of Rome's past was brought to light, including remnants of the **Domus Augustana**, the splendid paintings of republican period and the remains of the first dwellings that stood on the hill, as well as the imposing 16th-century entrance portal to the Orti Farnesiani.

At the side and below: two stretches of the so-called Stadium of the Domus Augustana on the Palatine.

On the two preceding pages. Left: an aerial view of the Colosseum and the Forums. Right: the Colosseum as it is and as it once was.

THE COLOSSEUM

The largest amphitheater ever built in Rome and a symbol for Romanism was the work of the Flavian emperors and was therefore called « *Amphiteatrum Flavium* ». The name Colosseum first came to be used in the Middle Ages and can be traced to the nearby colossal bronze statue of Nero as the sun god which rose up from the site of the vestibule of the *Domus Aurea*.

The emperor Vespasian began the construction of the Colosseum in the valley between the Caelian, Palatine and Esquiline hills, on the site of the artificial lake around which Nero's royal residence was centered and which had been drained for the purpose. Vespasian's intentions were to restore to the Roman people what Nero had tyrannically deprived them of, as well as that of providing Rome with a large permanent amphiteater in place of the amphiteater of Taurus in the Campus Martius, a contemporary wooden structure erected by Nero after the fire of A.D. 64 but which was no longer large enough.

Work began in the early years of Vespasian's reign and

Opposite and above: the Colosseum as it is and as it was.

in A.D. 79 the building, which had gone up only to the first two exterior orders with the first three tiers of steps inside, was dedicated. The fourth and fifth tiers were completed by Titus and it was inaugurated in A.D. 80 with imposing spectacles and games which lasted a hundred days. Under Domitian the amphitheater assumed its present aspect and size. According to the sources he added « *ad clipea* », in other words he placed the bronze shields which decorated the attic, adding the *maenianum summum*, the third internal order made of wooden tiers. Moreover he also had the subterraneans of the arena built, after which the *naumachie* (naval battles for which the arena had to be flooded) could no longer be held in the Colosseum, as we know from the sources. Additional work was carried out by Nerva, Trajan and Antoninus Pius. Alexander Severus restored the building after it had been damaged by a fire caused by lightning in A.D. 217. Further restoration was carried out by Gordian III and later by Decius, after the Colosseum had once more been struck by lightning in A.D. 250. Other

Opposite: the entrance to the Colosseum. Above: the interior of the arena with the cavea.

works of renovation were necessary after the earthquakes of A.D. 429 and 443. Odoacer had the lower tiers rebuilt, as witnessed by the inscriptions which we can read with the names of the senators dating from between 476 and 483 A.D. The last attempt at restoration was by Theodoric, after which the building was totally abandoned.

In the Middle Ages it became a fortress for the Frangipane and further earthquakes led to the material being used for new constructions. From the 15th century on then it was transformed into a quarry for blocks of travertine until it was consecrated by Pope Benedict XV in the middle of the 18th century.

The building is elliptical in form and measures 188x156 meters at the perimeter and 86x54 meters inside, while it is almost 49 meters high. The external facade is completely of travertine and built in four stories. The three lower stories have 80 arches each, supported on piers and framed by attached three-quarter columns, Doric on the first floor, Ionic on the second and Corinthian on the third. They are crowned by an attic which functions as a fourth story, articulated by Corinthian pilasters set alternately between walls with a square window and an empty space which once contained the gilded shields. The beams which supported the large canopy (*velatium*) to protect the spectators from the sun were fitted into a row of holes between corbels. The canopies were unfurled by a crew of sailors from Misenum. The arches of the ground floor level were numbered to indicate the entrance to the various tiers of seats in the *cavea*. The four entrances of honor were situated at the ends of the principal axes of the building and were unnumbered, reserved for upper class persons of rank such as magistrates, members of religious colleges, the Vestal Virgins. The entrance on the north side was preceded by a porch (a small two-columned portico) which led to the imperial tribune through a corridor decorated with stuccoes.

Above and left: stretches of the cavea with the connecting corridors.

The external arcades led to a twin set of circular corridors from which stairs led to the aisles (*vomitoria*) of the *cavea*; the second floor had a similar double ambulatory, and so did the third, but lower than the other two, while two single corridors were set one over the other at the height of the attic.

Inside, the *cavea* was separated from the arena by a podium almost four meters high behind which were the posts of honor. It was horizontally divided into three orders (*maenianum*) separated by walls in masonry (*baltei*). The first two *maeniana* (the second subdivided once more into upper and lower) had marble seats and were vertically articulated by the entrance aisles (*vomitoria*) and stairs. The result are circular sectors called *cunei*. It was therefore possible for the seats to be identified by the number of the tier, the cuneo and the seat. The third *maenianum* (or *maenianum summum*) had wooden tiers and was separated from the *maenianum secundum* below by a high wall. There was a colonnade with a gallery reserved

Above and right: the vaulted passageways inside the Colosseum.

for the women, above which a terrace served for the lower classes who had standing room only.

Access to seats in the *cavea* was based on social class, the higher up the seat the less important the person. The emperor's box was at the south end of the minor axis and this was also where consuls and Vestal Virgins sat. The box at the extremity was for the prefect of the city (« *praefectus Urbis* ») together with other magistrates. The tiers closest to the arena were reserved for senators. The inscriptions to be read on some of the extant tiers inform us that they were reserved for specific categories of citizens.

The arena was originally covered with wooden flooring which could be removed as required. In the case of hunts of ferocious animals the spectators in the *cavea* were protected by a metal grating surmounted by elephant tusks and with horizontally placed rotating cylinders so that it was impossible for the wild animals to climb up using their claws.

The area below the arena floor contained all the structures necessary for the presentation of the spectacles: cages for the animals, scenographic devices, storerooms for the gladiators' weapons, machines, etc. They were arranged in three annular walkways with openings that permitted the areas to be functionally connected with each other. A series of thirty niches in the outer wall was apparently used for elevators which took gladiators and beasts, up to the level of the arena.

The artificial basin created for the lake of the Domus Aurea was rationally exploited in the construction of the Colosseum, saving an enormous amount of excavation work. Once drained, the foundations were cast and travertine piers were set into a large elliptical concrete platform, forming a framework up to the third floor with radial walls in blocks of tufa and brick set between them. It was thus possible to work on the lower and upper parts at the same time, so that the building was subdivided into four sectors in which four different construction yards were engaged simultaneously.

Left, above: the model in the Museo della Civiltà Romana with the cross-section of the arena of the Colosseum, showing the cages and the underground passageways for the wild animals. Below: a terra-cotta panel from the Roman period reproducing the arena and a scene of the hunt.

Right: two details of the mosaics of Tusculum in the Museo Borghese (3rd cent. A.D.) depicting a venatio *(above) and a duel between gladiators (below).*

PVRPVREVS ENTINVS ~ BACCIBVS

Various types of spectacles were given in the Colosseum: the *munera* or contests between gladiators, the *venationes*, or hunts of wild beasts and the previously cited *naumachie* which were soon transferred elsewheres because of the difficulty of flooding the arena of the amphitheater. Titus' reconstruction of the naval battle between Corinth and Corcyra in which 3000 men were employed was famous.

The gladiator contests took place in the form of a duel between opposing sides, generally until the death of one or the other. In the *venationes* those condemned to various penalties had to fight wild beasts and they were often unarmed. Records of the bloody outcome of these spectacles is to be found in the writings of ancient authors with reference to 10,000 gladiators and 11,000 wild beasts employed by Trajan on the occasion of his triumph over the Dacians or the impressive number of beasts in the hunts organized by Probus for his triumph.

Christians may or may not have been martyrized in the Colosseum. In A.D. 397 Honorius emanated an edict which prohibited gladiatorial games, but they were renewed under Valentinianus III. From A.D. 438 on, only hunts were allowed, which gradually diminished in importance until the last hunt held in A.D. 523 under Theodoric. A final point to consider is the number of spectators the Colosseum was capable of containing: opinions vary but the figure must have been around 50,000.

Left: a stretch of the pavement of the road in front of the Colosseum. Below: a view of the Flavian Amphitheater. Opposite: the Arch of Constantine.

CONSTANTINE'S ARCH

The largest of the arches erected in Rome is on the route which the triumphal processions took in antiquity, between the Caelian and the Palatine hills. It is 21 meters high, almost 26 meters wide and over 7 meters deep, with three passageways, the central one of which is larger. It was built in A.D. 315 by decree of the Senate and the Roman people to celebrate the 10th anniversary of Constantine's ascent to the throne and his victory over Maxentius in the battle of Ponte Milvio in A.D. 312. The decoration of the arch employed a number of reliefs and sculpture from other monuments. The four detached marble columns on each of the principal sides, surmounted by eight statues of Dacians, are in *pavonazzetto* marble (white with purple veining, from Asia Minor) and date to Trajan's time. Eight tondos about two meters in diameter of Hadrian's period are set in pairs over the side passageways, inserted into porphyry slabs. Four *Scenes of the hunt* are represented, and four *Sacrificial scenes*. The figure of Hadrian appears in each scene, even though his head has been replaced by that of Constantine. On the attic, on either side of the inscription which is repeated both on the front and the back of the monument, are eight reliefs from the period of Marcus Aurelius, also set in pairs, which probably came from an honorary arch. They form a cycle which celebrates the *Return of the emperor* in A.D. 173 after his campaigns against the Marcomanni and the Quadi, in a series of exemplary episodes which correspond to scenes presented in the Aurelian column. A large marble frieze from Trajan's time has also been reused. It has been cut into four parts, two of which are on the short sides of the attic and two on the interior of the central passage. The scenes represented have to do with Trajan's two *Dacian campaigns* (A.D. 101-102 and 105-106). The decorative parts which date to the building of the arch comprise the reliefs at the bases of the columns, the keystones of the arches and, on the short sides, medallions with the *Sun God* and the *Goddess of the Moon* on a chariot. The most important part of Constantine's decoration is however the large historical frieze set above the lesser openings, and which continues on the short sides of the arch with episodes from the *Military Deeds* of Constantine.

Above: the Circus Maximus as it is now. Left: a relief of the 1st cent. A.D. in the Museo della Civiltà Romana with a charioteer, winner of the races.

THE CIRCUS MAXIMUS

Now only the lay of the land, much higher than the original arena, betrays the form of the original structure. For a long time it was built entirely of wood. In 329 B.C. the *carceres* or stalls for the horses and chariots were built in painted wood, as well as the *spina* in the center which covered and channeled the stream which ran through the valley and around which the race was run.

In 174 B.C. the censors Fulvius Flaccus and Postumius Albinus had the *carceres* built in masonry, and placed seven stone eggs along the spina as markers for the number of circuits the chariots had run. In 33 B.C. Agrippa had bronze dolphins set up for the same scope. Caesar also used the Circus for hunts. On the side towards the Palatine, Augustus had the *pulvinar*, a sacred box reserved for the tutelary gods of the games, set up and in 10 B.C. he had the obelisk of Ramsetes II taken at Heliopolis placed on the spina. The obelisk, 23.70 meters high, was transferred to Piazza del Popolo by Pope Sixtus V in 1587.

Above: the reconstruction of the Circus Maximus at the Museo della Civiltà Romana, which also houses the relief on the right (2nd cent. A.D.) with a phase of the races in the Circus Maximus.

Claudius took a hand in the restoration after a fire in A.D. 36. He had the *carceres* rebuilt in marble and had the *metae* (the goals, conical extremes of the *spina*) covered in gilded bronze. The Circus was once more destroyed in the fire of A.D. 64. Nero rebuilt it and increased the number of seats. Another fire under Domitian ravaged the building and reconstruction was finished by Trajan.

Constantine restored it and Constantius II embellished the *spina* with a second obelisk of Tuthmosis II, which came from Thebes and was even higher than the other one (32.50 m.) and which Pope Sixtus V had placed in Piazza San Giovanni in Laterano in 1587.

The Circus measured 600x200 meters and had a capacity of 320,000 spectators who watched the chariot races that were held there. The most important were those of the *Ludi Romani* the first week of September, which opened with a religious procession in which the highest religious and civil authorities of the city took part.

CHURCH OF SANTA MARIA IN COSMEDIN

In the 6th century the Church of Santa Maria in Cosmedin was built near the temples of Hercules and of Ceres on the remains of a large porticoed hall dating to the Flavian period. The name derives from the Greek, for it had been turned over to Greeks who had escaped the iconoclastic persecution and who probably decorated it (the word « Cosmedin » could refer to these « ornaments »). The *Schola Graeca*, as the church was also called, was then restored by Nicholas I, Gelasius II and Calixtus II, respectively, in the 9th and 12th centuries, when the women's galleries were walled up and lost, although the church acquired a new porch with a central vestibule. In the 18th century Giuseppe Sardi decorated the **facade** richly, but the restorations Giovenale carried out at the end of the 19th century restored the church to its original state, bringing it into line with the tall Romanesque **bell tower**. The **interior**, which had also frequently been remodelled in the course of the centuries, was also restored to the original 8th-century forms with a few concessions to the 12th-century style. What we have then is a typical basilican ground plan with a nave and two aisles, divided by piers and reused antique columns, and terminating in three apses. The **Chapel of the Choir** and the **Sacristy**, access to which is from the right aisle, were then added to the actual basilica. The architectural decoration, also strictly in keeping with the original style, includes the paschal candlestick, the bishop's cathedra, the baldachin over the high altar, the monolithic altar in red granite. The **crypt**, which consists of three rooms and a small apse, was obtained from the foundations of the Flavian hall. Only a part of all this is still original for most of what we see is the result of restoration.

Opposite, above: Santa Maria in Cosmedin and the Bocca della Verità. Below: the Forum Boarium. Right: the temple of Fortuna Virilis (above) and the one known as the « temple of Vesta » below.

Above: part of the structures of the Theater of Marcellus. Left: the Synagogue.

THEATER OF MARCELLUS

The project for the so-called theater of Marcellus dates to Caesar's time, but the building was finished in 13 B.C. by Augustus who officially dedicated it in the name of his nephew Marcellus, his first designated heir, who died early in 23 B.C.

In the 13th century the building was occupied by the noble Savelli family; in the 18th century it passed to the Orsini. The fine Renaissance palace that occupies the third floor of the exterior facade of the *cavea* is the work of the architect Baldassarre Peruzzi.

The theater must have been built on powerful substructures, and the front was provided with a facade of 41 arches, framed by engaged columns, on three floors. The first two floors are Doric and Ionic orders, the third, of which nothing remains, must have been an attic closed by Corinthian pilasters. It was originally 32.60 m. high. It has been calculated that the *cavea* (diam. 129.80 m.) could hold between 15 and 20,000 spectators, making it the largest theater in Rome as far as audience capacity was concerned. Beyond the orchestra (diam. m. 37) was the stage, of which nothing remains. On either side were apsed halls, of which a pier and a column of one are still standing. Behind the stage was a large semi-circular exedra with two small temples. The building was also noticeable for its rich decoration, still visible in the Doric frieze on the lower order.

The Isola Tiberina and the Ponte Rotto.

SYNAGOGUE

The **Synagogue**, or Israelite Temple, stands on the Via del Portico di Ottavia, along the Tiber. Like other Italian synagogues, it is characterized by a style that can be classified as exotic revival, in this case Assyro-babylonian. The building terminates in a large alluminum dome, which marks it as belonging to the early twentieth century. In fact the Synagogue dates to 1904 and was designed by the architects Armanni and Costa.

ISOLA TIBERINA

According to an old written tradition, the small island in the Tiber now known as Isola Tiberina was formed when the grain that had been harvested in the Campus Martius (private property of the Tarquins) was thrown into the river after the expulsion of the Etruscan kings from Rome.

The first important building erected on the island dates to 291 B.C.. This was the temple of Aesculapius.

Nothing remains today of the original building but the site is probably that of the 17th-century **Church of S. Bartolomeo**, and the well that still exists near the altar could correspond to the sacred fount. The porticoes of the sanctuary of Aesculapius were a real hospital. Numerous inscriptions preserved mention miraculous healings or dedications to the god. In the Middle Ages the island continued to be set aside as a hospital, thanks in part to its being isolated from the inhabited areas, and it is still used as such with the **Hospital of the Fatebenefratelli**, adjacent to the small **Church of S. Giovanni Calibita**.

In antiquity the island was also joined to the city by two bridges. The one which still today connects it to the left bank, near the theater of Marcellus, is the ancient **Pons Fabricius**.

The Pons Fabricius is 62 m. long and 5.50 m. wide; the two large slightly flattened arches have a span of 24.50 m. and spring from a massive central pier, which is pierced by a small arch that serves to relieve the pressure of the water on the structure during floods.

The other bridge which joins the island to Trastevere is no longer the original one. The Pons Cestius was torn down between 1888 and 1892. It had been built in the first century B.C., perhaps by the praetor of 44 B.C., the same C. Cestius to whom the famous funeral monument in the shape of a pyramid is dedicated. In A.D. 370 it was restored by emperor Valentinian I.

The unique form of the Isola Tiberina in the shape of an elongated boat, together with the remembrance of the ship which had brought the serpent of Aesculapius to Rome, gave rise to an odd architectural adaptation of the site which probably dates to the first century. The easternmost point of the island was turned into the prow of a trireme.

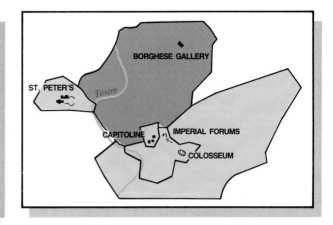

PIAZZA NAVONA

The most famous square of Baroque Rome stands on the site of Domitian's stadium and the name seems to derive from a popular corruption of the term for the competitive games « *in agone* » which were held here. From the times of Domitian on, the place was used almost exclusively for sports events, including the famous August regatta in which the participants wore the colors of the nobles and the civic clergy. Even now the feast of the *Befana* (the Italian version of Santa Claus who arrives on January 6th) is celebrated there in January with a typical market. But the real attraction of the square is the famous **Fountain of the Four Rivers** by Gian Lorenzo Bernini, dated 1651, and thanks to which the artist gained the admiration and protection of the pope then in office, Innocent X. The rivers represented in the fountain are the Danube, the Ganges, the Nile, the Rio de la Plata. They are arranged on a steep rocky reef from which a Roman obelisk taken from the Circus of Maxentius daringly rises up into the air. In line with the Fountain of the Four Rivers are the **Fountain of the Moor**, in front of the **Palazzo Pamphili**, and the **Fountain of Neptune**, formerly of the *Calderari*, at the northern end of the square.

Below: the Fountain of the Four Rivers in Piazza Navona. Opposite: the square with the Church of Sant'Agnese in Agone.

Above: the front of the Pantheon and, on the left, a view of the interior and the dome.

PANTHEON

The first building was erected in 27 B.C. by Marcus Vipsanius Agrippa, the faithful advisor of Augustus.

In Trajan's time, the temple was completely rebuilt by Hadrian between 118 and 128, in the form we still see today. The inscription on the frieze of the porch, *M(arcus) Agrippa L(uci) f(ilius) co(n)s(ul) tertrium fecit*, was therefore placed there by Hadrian who never put his own name on any of the monuments he built.

Hadrian's reconstruction profoundly modified the original building. The facade was set facing north, the porch was set on the site occupied by the original temple and the large rotunda coincided with the open area in front. Still today the large columned porch has a facade composed of eight columns in grey granite. Two red granite columns each are set behind the first, third, sixth, and eighth column of the facade, thus forming three aisles. The central aisle, which is the widest, leads to the entrance. The side aisles end in two large niches destined for the statues of Agrippa and Augustus. The tympanum was decorated with a crowned eagle in bronze of which only the fix-holes still remain. The ceiling of the porch was also decorated in bronze but this was removed by Pope Urban VIII Barberini (which lies at the root of the famous pasquinade: « *quod non fecerunt barbari, fecerunt Barberini* »).

Behind the porch is a massive construction in brick,

Left: the Column of Marcus Aurelius. Right: the elephant with the obelisk in Piazza della Minerva.

which joins it to the Rotonda, a gigantic cylinder with a wall that is six meters thick, divided into three superposed sectors, marked externally by cornices. The wall gets lighter as it rises, and the thickness of the walls, with brick vaulting in various places, is not always completely solid. The height of the Rotonda to the top of the dome is precisely that of its diameter (m. 43.30) so that the interior space is a perfect sphere. The dome is a masterpiece of engineering: it is the largest dome ever covered by masonry and it was cast in a single operation on an imposing wooden centering.

The interior of the building has six distyle niches at the sides and a semicircular exedra at the back, with eight small aedicules in between which have alternating arched and triangular pediments. The dome is decorated with five tiers of lacunar coffering except for a smooth band near the oculus, the circular opening (9 m. diam.) which illuminates the interior.

COLUMN OF MARCUS AURELIUS

Set at the center of Piazza Colonna, it was named after the emperor Marcus Aurelius, who had it erected between 189 and 196 in honor of his victories over the Marcomanni, the Quadi and the Sarmatians. Almost 30 meters high,

the shaft is enveloped by a bas-relief spiral, which, like the one on Trajan's Column, narrates the events of the Germanic and Sarmatian wars. The statue of *Saint Paul* on the top was set there by Domenico Fontana in 1588 and replaced the one of Marcus Aurelius once there.

The site was originally in the heart of the imperial Rome of the Antonines, between the Temple of Marcus Aurelius and the Temple of Hadrian.

Now the column rises in Piazza Colonna with a base restored by Fontana who, as shown by the inscription, erroneously thought it had been dedicated to Antoninus Pius. The interior of the column is hollow and a spiral staircase of 190 steps leads to the top.

ELEPHANT OF PIAZZA DELLA MINERVA

Considered one of Bernini's most delightful inventions, the *elephant* serves as the support for the Egyptian *obelisk* dating to the 6th century B.C., formerly set up in the nearby Isaeum Campense or Temple of Isis. Sculptured by Ercole Ferrata in 1667, it is relatively so small that it is popularly known as « Minerva's chick », even though the inscription on the base transforms it into the symbol of a robust intellect capable of supporting great wisdom, by which the obelisk is meant.

Above and left: two views of the Trevi Fountain.

TREVI FOUNTAIN

It may or may not be the most beautiful fountain in Rome but it is without doubt the most famous. The imaginative concept, the theatrical composition, the sober and imposing beauty of the sculptured marble figures make it a true masterpiece both of sculpture and of architecture. Pietro da Cortona and above all Bernini, who began the undertaking, both had a hand in the project. The death of Pope Urban VIII brought work to a standstill and it was not until about a hundred years later that Clement XII entrusted the work to Nicola Salvi, who finished the undertaking between 1732 and 1751.

The fountain is highly symbolic with intellectual connotations. A tall and sober *Arch of Triumph* (the palace of Neptune) dominates the scene from on high. It is comprised of an order of four Corinthian columns and is surmounted by an attic with statues and a balustrade. A large niche at the center of the arch lends balance and symmetry to the whole ensemble. A smaller niche to the left contains the statue of *Abundance* by F. Valle, and above this is a fine relief depicting *Agrippa approving the plans for the Aqueduct* by Andrea Bergondi. The niche on the right contains the figure of *Salubrity*, also by F. Valle, with a relief above of the *Virgin showing soldiers the Way*, by G. B. Grossi.

The central niche seems to impart movement to the imposing figure of *Neptune* who firmly guides a chariot drawn by sea horses, known as the « *agitated* » horse and the « *placid horse* », names obviously derived from the way in which the two animals have been represented. As they gallop over the water, the horses are guided in their course by fine figures of *tritons* which emerge from the water and which were sculptured by P. Bracci in 1762. The setting all around consists of rocks.

Right: detail of one of the tritons guiding the horses of Neptune (below).

Two views of the Palazzo del Quirinale. Opposite, right: the Triton Fountain. Below: Via Veneto.

PALAZZO DEL QUIRINALE AND PALAZZO DELLA CONSULTA

These two palaces, the former dating to the second half of the 16th century and the latter to the 18th century, face onto the Piazza del Quirinale.

Among the architects who worked on the **Palazzo del Quirinale** were Martino Longhi, Domenico Fontana, Carlo Maderno, Gian Lorenzo Bernini and Ferdinando Fuga who was also the architect for the Palazzo della Consulta between 1732 and 1734. The Quirinale was the seat of the papacy from Clement XII to 1870, the year in which it was chosen as the palace for the kings of United Italy, and then after 1947 as official residence of the Italian President.

The exterior has a monumental facade in two stories with a large gabled portal by Maderna, topped with statues. The facade of the **Palazzo della Consulta** is just as imposing. The name derives from the fact that the Court of the Sacra Consulta had its seat here until 1870 when it became the ministerial headquarters of the Kingdom. It now houses the Constitutional Court. As mentioned, the well balanced facade articulated with pilaster strips and decorated with statues by Filippo Valle was by Ferdinando Fuga.

TRITON FOUNTAIN

Still another fascinating famous fountain by Gian Lorenzo Bernini is set in the center of the Piazza Barberini. Dating to 1643 it is characterized by the apparent lack of any kind of architectural support for the statue of the *Triton* from which the fountain takes its name. He is supported by a scallop shell which in turn rests on the arched tails of four dolphins. The water, which endows the whole ensemble with life, is naturalistically blown upwards by the Triton through a conch.

VIA VENETO

An important element in the town-planning projects of Rome at the beginning of the 20th century and the building up of the Ludovisi District, the Via Vittorio Veneto goes from the Piazza Barberini to the Porta Pinciana and is lined with outstanding works of architecture as well as with hotels, shops and universally famous rendezvous. Various periods of history are represented: the **Fountain of the Alps** by Bernini, the **Church of Santa Maria della Concezione** by Antonio Casoni, the **Church of Sant'Isidoro** (all 17th cent.) to the 20th-century **palaces** of the **Ministry of Industry and Trade** by Marcello Piacentini and Giuseppe Vaccaro, and the **Banca Nazionale del Lavoro**, also by Piacentini, as well as the **Palazzo Boncompagni-Ludovisi**, then **Margherita**, a late 19th-century work signed by Gaetano Koch.

PIAZZA DI SPAGNA AND TRINITÀ DEI MONTI

One of the most characteristic squares in the city, the Piazza di Spagna, stretches out for over 270 meters, divided into two triangular areas. It is surrounded by outstanding buildings, such as the **Palazzo di Propaganda Fide**, seat of the *Congregation of Propaganda Fide* instituted by Pope Gregory XV in 1622. The facade on the square is by Bernini (1644) and is articulated in three floors. The sober, elegant design is in brick. The more complex facade at the side however is by Borromini (1665) and is concave in the center. It is articulated by pilaster strips which reach up to the first floor where unique concave windows are set off by columns and pilasters. The large portal leads to the vestibule with, nearby, Borromini's **Church of the Magi** (dei Re Magi) (1666). The restrained luminous interior has a fine *Adoration of the Magi* by Giacinto Gemignani (1643). Another noteworthy complex is the **Palazzo di Spagna** built by A. Del Grande in 1647 which has an important facade with lovely portals tied together by severe rustication. The square is centered on the **Barcaccia Fountain**, by Pietro Bernini (1627-1629), an ingenious and lively representation of a large boat which is sinking and spouting water from both stern and prow. Piazza di Spagna is where the famous **Spanish Steps (Scalinata di Trinità dei Monti)** begin. Built entirely in travertine by Francesco De Sanctis (1723-1726) the twelve flights of steps of varying widths branch off into various blocks as they move upward towards the Piazza Trinità dei Monti. At the center of the square is the *Sallustian Obelisk* which comes from the Sallustian Gardens. The square is dominated by the powerful structures of the **Church of Trinità dei Monti**, one of the most imposing Franciscan churches in the city. Begun in 1503 at the request of Louis XII, the church has been remodelled at various times. The sober facade, by Carlo Maderno, with a single order of pilasters and a broad portal with columns and a large balustrade, is preceded by a staircase by Domenico Fontana that is decorated with capitals and antique bas-reliefs. The interior has a single large nave and contains fine works of art including a lovely fresco with *Stories of St. John the Baptist* by Naldini, in the first chapel on the right; Daniele da Volterra's famous and brilliant *Assumption*, in the third chapel on the right. The second chapel on the left contains the *Deposition*, another masterpiece by Daniele da Volterra, and in the sixth chapel on the left, Perin del Vaga's *Assumption* and *Isaiah and Daniel* (on the front of the tomb), Taddeo Zuccari's *Death of Maria* and the *Assumption* by Federico and Taddeo Zuccari. Another outstanding work by Federico Zuccari, the *Coronation of the Virgin*, is in the chapel to the left of the presbytery. The **Cloister** contains frescoes by various artists with *Stories from the life of Saint Francis of Paola*.

Above: the Palazzo di Giustizia. Left: the Mausoleum of Augustus.

PALAZZO DI GIUSTIZIA

Built between 1889 and 1910 to designs by Guglielmo Calderini, the court building is characterized by the fact that the central block is higher than those on either side (3 floors), as well as by its imposing dimensions. The architecture is also accompanied by typical examples of monumental sculpture, such as the large *Quadriga* by Ettore Ximenes which crowns the principal block, the enormous statues (almost the equivalent of antique colossi) of the *Jurists* on the entrance ramps, the group with *Justice*, *Force* and the *Law* on the central portal.

MAUSOLEUM OF AUGUSTUS

The dynastic tomb of the first emperor of Rome is a circular structure consisting of a series of concentric walls in tufa connected by radiating walls. The first accessible chamber was at the end of the long entrance corridor (*dromos*). Two entrances in this wall lead to the annular corridor which rings the circular cella.
At the center is a pier inside which is a square chamber. The tomb of Augustus was here, in corrispondence to the bronze statue of the emperor which was at the top of the pier. The three niches of the cella contained other tombs of important members of the Julio-Claudian dynasty.

Above: Piazza del Popolo. Right: the water clock in the Pincio.

PIAZZA DEL POPOLO

Piazza del Popolo, one of the most characteristic areas of neoclassical Rome, is the child of Giuseppe Valadier's creative genius in the field of town planning and architecture, a project he began work on in 1793.

It is distinguished by the low exedras which define the boundaries of the square and which are topped by statues of the *Four Seasons*, while the center is emphasized by the two fountains, *Neptune and the Tritons* and *Rome between the Tiber and the Aniene River*. All the sculpture mentioned above dates to the first half of the 19th century and was made respectively by Gnaccarini, Laboureur, Stocchi, Baini, Ceccarini.

PINCIO

The public gardens of the Pincio stretch out on the slope beyond the exedra to the right of the Piazza del Popolo. Like the Piazza, they too were laid out by Giuseppe Valadier between 1810 and 1818. Already famous in antiquity, the site was occupied by the Gardens (*horti*) of Lucullus, the Acilia family, the Domizi, and finally the Pinci after whom the site, and then the park, was named. In line with a typically Italian type of garden architecture, *busts* of men famous in the world of art and history are scattered throughout the Pincio.

Above: the Casino Borghese. Left: the Temple of Aesculapius in Villa Borghese.

VILLA BORGHESE

First created for Cardinal Caffarelli Borghese early in the 17th century, the park was completely renewed at the end of the 18th century by the architects Asprucci and the painter Unterberger, but what we see now was the work of Luigi Canina at the beginning of the 19th century.

Generously donated to the city of Rome in 1902 by Umberto I, King of Italy, it was supposed to have been called after him. However, notwithstanding official names, it is still known as Villa Borghese in honor of the man who founded it.

This is the largest park in Rome with a perimeter of six kilometers and it is also the loveliest with a wealth of trees and charming paths. Entrance is from the overpass of the Viale dell'Obelisco, but also from the Porta Pinciana, Piazzale Flaminio and other minor entrances.

Above: the Emperors Gallery in the Museo Borghese. Right: the
bust of Cardinal Scipione Borghese by Bernini.

MUSEO AND GALLERIA BORGHESE

One of the most prestigious collections of sculpture and
painting in the world is housed in the fine building known
as the Casino Borghese, built for Cardinal Scipione Borghese by Giovanni Vasanzio (1613-1615). The Museum is
installed on the ground floor and the itinerary leads
through a portico, the Salone, and eight rooms, with various masterpieces by Bernini and Canova as well as examples of marble sculpture from Roman times. The Gallery,
installed on the upper floor, has a spacious vestibule and
twelve rooms and a selection of paintings which are truly
priceless. A brief survey of the two famous collections
follows.

Museo Borghese: **Portico**: sculpture from the Roman
period and two panels of sarcophagi which depict the
Muses. **Salone**: twelve *busts* in colored marble by G. B.
della Porta (16th cent.) are in the niches; the vaults were
frescoed by Martino Rossi in the second half of the 18th
century (*Camillus breaking off negotiations with Brennus*
and the *Allegory of Glory*); the pavement contains five
fragments of third-century mosaics (scenes of gladiators
and the hunt). From the left, various pieces of antique
sculpture (*Isis*, the *Satyr*, *Augustus*, a *Faun*, *Hadrian*,

79

Bacchus, Antoninus Pius); **Room I** (Sala della Paolina): the decoration on the vault and walls (*Judgement of Paris* and *Stories of Aeneas*) by D. De Angelis; the highlight at the center of the room is *Pauline Borghese as Venus Victrix (1805)* by Canova, strikingly beautiful in its softly modeled forms and dominated by a subtle tempting sensuousness. *Room II* (of David): the frescoes in the vault are by Caccianiga (*Fall of Phaethon*); the five niches in the room contain five late Roman *busts*; but what most strikes the eye is the dynamic sculpture of *David*, an early work by Gian Lorenzo Bernini (1623-1624), at the center of the room. Around it are various Roman *statues*. **Room III** (of Apollo and Daphne). The fresco in the vault depicts the *Death of Daphne* by Pietro Angeletti. At the center is Bernini's wonderful sculpture of *Apollo and Daphne*, a bold and innovative work of 1624; the surrounding statues are Roman. **Chapel**: the walls are lined with *frescoes* by Deruet and Lanfranco; particularly noteworthy is a *female head with serpents* dating to the 5th century B.C. **Emperors' Gallery** (Room IV) with eighteen *Busts of Emperors* in porphyry and alabaster (17th cent.). The *Story of Galathea* is represented in the

vault, at the center is the *Rape of Proserpine*, another example of Bernini's complex sculpture (1622); of particular note otherwise are the statues of *Dionysius* and the *Marine Venus*. **Room V** (of the Hermaphrodite): in the vault *Hermaphrodite and Salmace* by Buonvicini; the Roman mosaic in the pavement has fishing scenes; of note the statue of the *Sleeping Hermaphrodite*, a reproduction of a Hellenistic original. **Room VI** (of Aeneas and Anchises): in the vault: the *Council of the Gods*, by Pacheux; at the center the marble group of *Aeneas and Anchises* by Gian Lorenzo and Pietro Bernini. The most striking piece on one side, among other Roman works, is *Truth unveiled by Time*, another important work by Bernini (1652). **Room VII** (Egyptian room): in the vault *frescoes* by T. Conca, in the pavement three Roman *mosaics*; the most striking of the other Roman statues is the *Youth on a Dolphin*, a copy of a Hellenistic original. **Room VIII** (of the Dancing Faun): in the vault, the *Sacrifice to Silenus* by T. Conca and, at the center, the *Dancing Faun*, a Roman copy of a Hellenistic original.

Galleria Borghese: **Vestibule**: housed here are the *Three Ages of Man*, painted by Sassoferrato, as well as works

Opposite: the Rape of Proserpine and the Apollo and Daphne by Bernini. This page, above: Pauline Borghese by Canova, and, below, Bernini's David.

by Luca Cambiaso and Rutilio Manetti. **Room IX**: in the vault the *Stories of Aeneas* by A. De Maron (1786), particularly of note among the other works are the *Deposition*, one of Raphael's Roman masterpieces; the *Portrait of a Man* and the *Portrait of a Lady with a Unicorn*, also by Raphael; the crystalline *Madonna and Child, the young Saint John and Angels* by Botticelli; the imposing *Holy Family* by Fra Bartolomeo, Perugino's *Madonna* and other works by Andrea del Sarto, Lorenzo di Credi, Santi di Tito, Mariotto Albertinelli, Pinturicchio. **Room X**: striking are the *Madonna and Child with the young St. John* by Andrea del Sarto, and Bronzino's dramatic *St. John the Baptist*; also works by Luca Cranach, Berreguete, Sodoma and Rosso Fiorentino. **Room XI**, with Lorenzo Lotto's *Madonna and Child with Saints* and his *Self Portrait*; of particular note, as well as works by Savoldo, Palma il Vecchio, and Bernini. **Room XII**: contains works by Annibale Carracci, Domenichino, Pietro da Cortona. **Room XIII**: contains works by Giulio Romano, Puligo, Scipione Pulzone, Franciabigio. **Room XIV**: in the vault the *Council of the Gods* by Lanfranco. Particular mention among the works exhibited goes to

Above, left: Youth with Fruit, by Caravaggio. Right: Botticelli's
tondo with the Madonna and Child, the young Saint John and
Saints. Below: Madonna and Child with Saint by Lorenzo Lotto.

Opposite, above, left: St. John the Baptist Preaching, by Veronese.
Right: Holy Family by Sodoma. Below, left: Portrait of a Young
Man by Ghirlandaio; right: Portrait of a Courtesan by Carpaccio.

the *David with the head of Goliath*, the *Madonna of the Serpent* (painted for the Palafrenieri), and *St. John the Baptist in the Desert*, three sublime paintings by Caravaggio; there are also works by A. Carracci, Guercino, and some realistic sculpture by Bernini. **Room XV**: in the vault, *Allegory of Aurora* by D. Corvi. **Room XVI**: in the ceiling, *Flora* by G. B. Marchetti; the room is almost completely dedicated to the works of Iacopo Bassano. **Room XVII**: in the vault, *Story of Walter of Angers* by G. Cades; as well as works by Dossi, Garofalo, Scarsellino, Francia. **Room XVIII**: in the vault, *Jupiter and Antiope* by G. Gagneraux; outstanding are many paintings by Rubens, his famous *Susannah and the Elders* and the *Deposed Christ*. **Room XIX**: among the many works exhibited in this room mention must be made of Correggio's touching and intimate *Danae*. **Room XX**: here are some of Titian's masterpieces, such as *Sacred and Profane Love*, *Venus Blindfolding Cupid*, and *St. Domenic*; Antonello da Messina's profoundly introspective *Portrait of a Man* and works by Veronese, Bellini and Carpaccio.

CASTEL S. ANGELO

Castel S. Angelo, whose imposing mass still dominates the panorama of Rome, and which is known as the *Mole Adriana*, was not originally built for defensive purposes but as the funeral monument of the emperors. A new bridge (called Pons Aelius from the *nomen* of the emperor) which still exists as **Ponte S. Angelo** was built to put the monument in communication with the Campus Martius. This bridge flanks Nero's bridge, further downstream. It consisted of three large central arches and two inclined ramps supported by three smaller arches on the right bank and two on the left bank.

Most of the structural parts of the Mausoleum, which was incorporated into Castel S. Angelo in the Middle Ages, have been preserved. The building consisted of an enormous quadrangular basement, 89 m. per side and 15 m. high. On top was a cylindrical drum (diam. 64 m., height 21 m.) flanked by radial walls. A tumulus of earth planted with trees rose up over the drum. Along the edges were decorative marble statues and at the center, raised even higher up, was a podium with columns on top of which was a bronze quadriga with the statue of Hadrian. The exterior of the enclosure was faced with Luna marble and with inscriptions of the *tituli* of the personages buried in the monument; engaged pilasters were set at the corners and the upper part was decorated with a frieze of garlands and bucrania (fragments are preserved in the Museo del Castello). The drum was faced on the outside with travertine and fluted pilaster strips. The entire monument was enclosed in a wall with bronze gates, decorated with peacocks (two are in the Vatican), perhaps a funerary symbol.

The original entrance to the tomb, with three openings, was on the side of the base that faces the river. The current entrance is at least three meters higher up. From here a corridor (*dromos*) led to a square vestibule with a semicircular alcove on the back wall, faced with yellow Numidian marble. The helicoidal gallery which rises ten meters and leads to the funeral chamber begins to the right of the vestibule. The vault of this corridor, with four vertical light wells, is in rubblework; the pavement still retains traces of its original mosaic decoration while the walls were covered with marble to a height of three meters. The funeral chamber, right at the center of the massive drum, is square (3 m. per side) with three rectangular niches; illumination is from two oblique windows in the vault. The cinerary urns of the emperors were placed in this room. Above the funerary chamber were two superposed cellae which by means of an annular corridor led to the top of the monument.

As early as A.D. 403 the emperor Honorius may have incorporated the building in an outpost bastion of the Aurelian walls. In 537, when it was already a fortress, it was attacked by Vitiges and his Goths. In the 10th century it was transformed into a castle. Its appearance today is that of a massive fortress on a square base and with circular **towers** at the four corners (known as the towers of **St. Matthew**, **St. John**, **St. Mark**, and **St. Luke**) onto which a circular body has been grafted. This was built following the lines of the Imperial mausoleum under Benedict IX. Further work was ordered by Alexander VI and by Julius II who had the south loggia above the papal apartments added.

At the summit is the panoramic terrace, watched over by the *Angel* about to fly off, which seems to be why the building is called as it is, for the winged messenger is said to have saved Rome from a terrible plague at the time of Gregory the Great.

Inside the castle-fortress are the rooms of the **Museo Nazionale Militare** and of **Art**.

Opposite: Castel Sant'Angelo. Right and below: two views of the Ponte Sant'Angelo over the Tiber river.

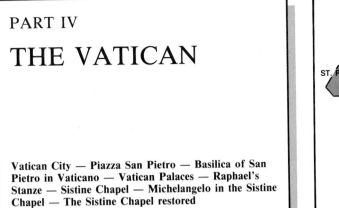

PART IV
THE VATICAN

Vatican City — Piazza San Pietro — Basilica of San Pietro in Vaticano — Vatican Palaces — Raphael's Stanze — Sistine Chapel — Michelangelo in the Sistine Chapel — The Sistine Chapel restored

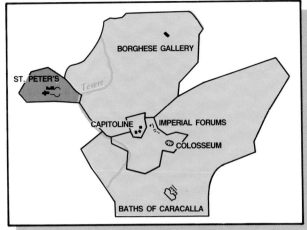

VATICAN CITY

HISTORICAL SKETCH

Vatican City spreads out to the right of the Tiber and lies between Monte Mario to the north and the Janiculum to the south. Of old the area now covered by the small Vatican State was called Ager Vaticanus and it was occupied by a circus and Nero's gardens. Since 1929, the year in which the Lateran Treaty was stipulated between the Holy See and the Italian State, the Vatican City has been an independent sovereign state and it contains exceedingly important examples of art and architecture. The boundaries of this state, whose residents can be numbered in the hundreds, is defined by the Via Porta Angelica, Piazza del Risorgimento, Via Leone IV, the Viale Vaticano, Via della Sagrestia, and the Piazza San Pietro. The Pope, in addition to being the head of the Apostolic Roman Catholic Church, has full legislative, executive and judiciary powers. The Vatican State is completely independent of the Italian state, even though they maintain extremely friendly relations. The Vatican prints its own stamps, has its own railroad station, and a well-known newspaper, the Osservatore Romano, which is distributed throughout Italy. The city also has its own police force (once called Pontifical Gendarmes) and a real police service as represented by the famous « Swiss Guards » which, from the early 16th century, protected the person of the pope and still today wear uniforms that were probably designed by Michelangelo.

Opposite and above: two views of the Via della Conciliazione with
the Basilica of Saint Peter's in the background.

PIAZZA SAN PIETRO

The fact, alone, that the great and truly unique Basilica of St. Peter's in Vatican faces out on this square would make it perhaps the most widely known of Roman piazzas. But above and beyond this, the space itself merits attention for its size (an enormous ellipse whose greatest diameter measures 240 m.) and the brilliant project by Gian Lorenzo Bernini whose scope was that of singling out this square from all others through the use of the imposing porticoes.

These porticoes are arranged in semicircles along the short sides of the square and consist of four parallel rows of Tuscan-Doric columns which provide a choice of three paths. Above the canonic entablature are 140 colossal statues of *Saints*, as well as the insignia of the patron pope, Alexander VII. At the center of the square, the plain obelisk, flanked by two fountains, stands at the crossing of the two diameters of the ellipse. Termed « aguglia » (needle) in the Middle Ages, the *obelisk* came from Heliopolis and was brought to Rome by the emperor Caligula, and set on the spina of Nero's Circus,

which is where St. Peter's in Vatican now stands. Throughout the various phases of restoration, destruction, and reconstruction, the « aguglia » stayed next to the Basilica and was not set up at the center of the square until 1586 by Domenico Fontana, who also saw to the engineering aspect of the undertaking. The other architect, Carlo Fontana, designed the left-hand *fountain* in Piazza San Pietro, built in 1677 as a *pendant* to the one on the right designed by Carlo Maderno about fifty years earlier. A curious fact concerning the obelisk mentioned above is that it was used, or was believed to have been used in the Middle Ages, as a reliquary for the ashes of Caesar, and then (up to now) for a fragment of the Holy Cross.

BASILICA OF SAN PIETRO IN VATICANO

In the classical period the site was occupied by Nero's Circus, between the Tiber, the Janiculum, and the Vatican hill, and St. Peter, the Prince of the Apostles, was

Above: a view of Piazza San Pietro. Left: one of the fountains in the square with the Pope's window in the background.

martyred and then buried here. Pope Anacletus had already had a small basilica, *ad corpus*, or a simple shrine built here. In 324 the emperor Constantine replaced the presumably modest shrine with a basilica of Constantinian type, in line with the other churches built in Rome in that period. Finished in 349 by Constantius, son of Constantine, the original St. Peter's was enriched throughout the centuries by donations and updatings by the popes and munificent princes. It was in Constantine's basilica that Charlemagne received the crown from the hands of Leo III in 800 and after him Lothair, Louis II, and Frederick III were crowned emperors. Even so, a thousand years after its foundation St. Peter's was falling into ruin and it was Nicholas V, on the advice of Leon Battista Alberti and with a plan by Bernardo Rossellino, who began to renovate and enlarge the Basilica. Various parts of the building were torn down, and work on the new tribune was started but soon came to a halt when Nicholas V died. Work was not resumed until 1506 when Julius II della Rovere was pope. Most of the original church was dismantled by Bramante (who earned himself the title of

The facade of the Basilica of Saint Peter's.

« maestro ruinante »), with the intention of building ex novo a « modern » building in the classic style: a Greek-cross plan inspired by the Pantheon. Various supervisors succeeded each other until about the middle of the century: Fra Giocondo, Raphael, Giuliano da Sangallo, Baldassarre Peruzzi, Antonio da Sangallo the Younger, and, finally, Michelangelo, who needless to say interpreted Bramante's plan, modifying it in part, and envisioned the great dome (originally hemispherical) which crowned the renovated basilica. Michelangelo was succeeded by Vignola, Pirro Ligorio, Giacomo Della Porta, Domenico Fontana, all of whom interpreted his ideas quite faithfully. Then under Paul V, it was decided to reinstate the basilica plan, and return to the Latin-cross idea. With this in mind, the architect Carlo Maderno added three chapels to each side of the building and brought the nave as far as the present facade, the building of which was entrusted to him when he won an important competition. Work was begun in November of 1607 and terminated in 1612, after having « employed mountains of travertine from Tivoli ».

The **facade**, which is truly imposing in its proportions, is based on the use of the giant Corinthian order, which articulates the front of the building with columns and pilasters. On the ground floor these frame a large central porch, with an arch on either side (the one on the left, the so-called Arch of the Bells, leads to Vatican City), and, above, a row of nine balconies. The crowning element is a canonic attic surmounted by a balustrade which supports thirteen enormous statues, representing all the *Apostles*, except for St. Peter, as well as Christ and St. John the Baptist. Above all looms Michelangelo's imposing **dome** with its strong ribbing, and, emerging from the front but to the side, the « minor » domes of the Gregoriana and the Clementina chapels by Giacomo Barozzi da Vignola. After the death of Carlo Maderno in 1629, the next director of works, Gian Lorenzo Bernini, left his unmistakeable mark. The prevalently Baroque character the building now displays was his doing. It is sufficient to mention the decorative transformation of the nave and the aisles, the erection of the justly famous bronze *baldacchino* (begun in 1624 and inaugurated on St. Peter's

Above and opposite: the interior of Saint Peter's. Left: the
Monument to John XXIII by Emilio Greco.

day in 1633), the decoration of the piers of the dome with
four large statues, the installment at the back of the apse
of the *Throne of St. Peter*, one of Bernini's most sumptuous inventions, a truly marvelous machine, built around
the old wooden chair which a pious tradition says was
used by the apostle Peter. The organization of St. Peter's
square, once more by Bernini, also dates to the papacy of
Alexander VII (who financed the works for the throne),
while under Clement X the architect designed and built
the small round temple which comprises the shrine of the
Chapel of the Sacrament.

There are any number of chapels, all splendid in one way
or the other, set along the perimeter of St. Peter's basilica, to begin with the **Chapel of the Pietà**, named after
Michelangelo's famous marble sculpture of the *Pietà*
which the young artist made between 1499 and 1500 for

SEPULCRUM
SANCTI PETRI APOSTOLI

Above: the Tomb of Saint Peter. Opposite: Michelangelo's Pietà.

cardinal Jean de Bilheres. After the **Chapel of Saint Sebastian** (which contains Francesco Messina's *Monument to Pope Pius XII)* is the better known **Chapel of the Holy Sacrament** with Bernini's *ciborium* mentioned above and the bronze railing designed by Borromini; next is the **Gregoriana Chapel**, a late 16th-century work finished by Giacomo della Porta and heavily decorated with *mosaics* and precious marbles; the **Chapel of the Column** with the astounding marble altarpiece depicting the *Encounter between St. Leo and Attila* by Algardi, and with the *sepulchers* of the many popes named Leo — the II, III, IV, XII; the **Clementina Chapel**, named after Pope Clement VII, built for him by Giacomo della Porta, which houses the mortal remains of St. Gregory the Great; and, also by Della Porta, the sumptuous **Chapel of the Choir** decorated with gilded stuccoes; finally the **Chapel of the Presentation** with the recent *Monument to Pope John XXIII*, by Emilio Greco.

The Basilica of St. Peter's in Vatican also contains a whole collection of famous monuments, from Michelangelo's *Pietà* to the venerated *effigy of St. Peter* shown in the act of blessing, which dates to the 13th century; Bernini's *Funeral Monument for Pope Urban VIII*, and the analogous *Funeral Complex for Paul III* by Guglielmo Della Porta, the *bronze Tomb* created by Antonio Pollaiolo for Pope Innocent VIII, which was part of the original St. Peter's, and the neoclassic *Monument to the Stuarts* by Canova. Brief mention must also be made of the *baptismal font*, in porphyry, once part of a classical sarcophagus (and then used as the sepulcher for Otho II), transformed into a baptismal font by Carlo Fontana.

The imposing **Sacristy** lies before the left transept. Large as a church, it was conceived of as an independent building, and consists of the **Sagrestia Comune** on an octagonal central plan, the so-called **Sacristy of the Canons**, and the **Chapter Hall**. It was all designed by the Roman Carlo Marchionni at the behest of Pius VI, who laid the first stone in 1776.

Annexed to the Basilica is the **Museo della Fabbrica di San Pietro**, or Historical Artistic Museum, which includes the *Treasury of St. Peter's*. It was designed by Giovan Battista Giovenale and contains the remains of the enormous patrimony of the church which was repeatedly scattered and carried off by the Saracens, the Sack of Rome in 1527, the Napoleonic confiscations.

VATICAN PALACES

One of the most sumptuous and articulated monumental complexes in the world is without doubt that of the Vatican Palaces, which began to be built in the 14th century so as to house as befitted their rank the popes who had finally « returned » from their stay in Avignon, and who had previously resided in the Lateran. The first pope to take up permanent abode in the Vatican was Gregory XI and his successors later enlarged and beautified the complex. In 1410 Alexander V had the communication « corridor » built between the palace and Castel Sant'Angelo. But the greatest impetus to the building and organization of the sumptuous complex was provided by Nicholas V. The heart of the complex is the square palace which encloses the famous **Cortile del Pappagallo**, and on which Leon Battista Alberti and Bernardo Rossellino as well as others worked. The **Chapel of Nicholas V** is dedicated to Saints Stephen and Laurence and is decorated with *frescoes* by Fra Angelico.

The world-famous **Sistine Chapel** was created between 1473 and 1480, under Sixtus IV, when Giovanni de' Dolci reconstructed what was originally the Palatine Chapel. Innocent VIII even went so far as to have himself a Palazzetto built on the highest point of the Belvedere. The building appears in Andrea Mantegna's paintings, but was then lost with Bramante's reorganization and a still later construction of the Museo Pio Clementino under Pope Pius VI. When Alexander VI once more took up residence in the square **Palace of Nicholas V**, his enlargement was terminated by the erection of the **Borgia Tower** (named after the pope's family).

The maecenas pope, Julius II, sponsored a reorganization which could fall under the heading of town planning when he entrusted Bramante with finding the solution of how to connect the Palace of Nicholas V with that of Innocent VII: the result was, as is known, the **Courtyard of the Belvedere** with the *niche* by Pirro Ligorio (1560) at one end, in turn derived from the transformation of Bramante's exedra with its twin flight of stairs. Bramante was also responsible for the elevation of the **Loggias of the Courtyard of Saint Damasus**, finished and decorated with frescoes by Raphael. Thanks to this expansion, the Pope's Palace could now face out on Piazza San Pietro. Between 1509 and 1512 Michelangelo frescoed the vault of the Sistine Chapel for Julius II, and in 1508 Raphael began to decorate the Stanze, which were finished in 1524. After the disastrous sack of Rome, which to some extent brought the grand papal project of the *Instauratio Urbis* to a halt, work on the Vatican Palace continued under Paul III, who entrusted Antonio da Sangallo the *Younger with the building of the* **Cappella Paolina**, the **Sala Ducale**, and the **Sala Regia**, entrusting the decoration of the Cappella Paolina and the termination of the frescoes in the Sistine to Michelangelo. The highlight of

Above: the statue of Laocoon in the Vatican Museums. Below: the Belvedere Apollo in the Octagonal Courtyard.

The Disputation on the Holy Sacrament, by Raphael, in the
Stanza della Segnatura.

the Baroque in the Vatican Palace coincides with the papacy of Sixtus V and the architect Domenico Fontana, who designed the present papal residence and « cut » the Belvedere with the **Cortile trasversale** (now seat of the **Sistine Hall** of the Library).

In the 17th century, Urban VIII had the **Scala Regia** begun on designs by Bernini, as well as the **Pauline Rooms** in the Library and the Archives. In the following century the transformation into museums of part of the great complex was begun: the **Christian Museum (Museo Sacro)** and the **Profane Museum (Museo Profano)** (connected to the **Library**) were joined by the **Pio-Clementine Museum**, planned and installed by Michelangelo Simonetti and Giuseppe Camporese (1771-1793); by the **Chiaramonti Sculpture Gallery** bound to the name of Antonio Canova (1806-1810); the so-called **Braccio Nuovo** or **New Wing** designed by Raffaele Stern for Pius VII. Lastly, in the 20th century, Pope Pius XII initiated archaeological excavations under the Basilica of St. Peter's, while John XXIII turned his attention to the construction of new rooms which could better house the museum collections of the Lateran Palace.

RAPHAEL'S STANZE

The rooms known as Raphael's Stanze because they contain so many of the painter's masterpieces, were built under the papacy of Nicholas V. Their decoration was initially entrusted to Andrea del Castagno, Benedetto Bonfigli and Piero della Francesca. Afterwards, under Julius II, the undertaking passed to Lorenzo Lotto, Perugino, Sodoma, Baldassarre Peruzzi, and Bramantino. Only in the last phase, upon Bramante's advice, did Julius call in Raphael, who was already famous. The painter was also flanked by a choice team of « advisors ». Chronologically the first Stanza to be frescoed, or rather the vault, was the **Stanza della Segnatura**, so-called because this was where the court of the Segnatura met. Here Raphael painted the *Disputa* or *Disputation on the Sacrament*, which was thus his first pictorial work in Rome and which depicts the exaltation of the glory of the Eucharist rather than a « dispute ». Even more famous is the fresco on the wall across from the Disputa, the so-called *School of Athens*, which gathers the wise men and philosophers of antiquity together with the « contemporary » artists

and lords, in other words the protagonists of the Renaissance, in an imposing architectural setting where they are all assembled around the great ancients, Plato and Aristotle. The composition of *Parnassus*, which decorates the wall of the window overlooking the Belvedere, is dated 1511 (the year is on the lintel of the window). The vault of the same Stanza has medallions which contain symbolic representations of *Philosophy*, *Justice*, *Poetry*, *Theology*, and panels with the *Fall of man*, *The Judgement of Solomon*, *Apollo and Marsyas*, *Astronomy*.

Next, chronologically speaking, is the **Stanza di Eliodoro**, which furnishes an example of what might be called historical painting, for Raphael had proposed various miraculous events which were decisive in the story of the Church, perhaps suggested by Julius II. These included *Leo I repulsing Attila*, the *Mass of Bolsena*, the *Expulsion of Heliodorus*, the *Liberation of St. Peter*. These date to the years 1512-1514, while the vault was presumably frescoed by De Marcillat, who most likely continued Raphael's ideas.

The decoration of the **Stanza dell'Incendio** however dates to 1514-1517. The name derives from the leading fresco which depicts the event of 847 when the *Fire in the Borgo* was miraculously stopped when Leo IV made the sign of the cross. An interesting detail in the fresco shows us the main facade of old St. Peter's, which had not yet been torn down when the picture was painted.

The last of the Stanze is the **Sala di Costantino**, which cannot really be said to be by Raphael for the work was carried out almost entirely by Giulio Romano after the Master's death, although the plans were certainly his. It was finished in 1525. The decoration depicts episodes — famous and less famous — in the life of the emperor Constantine: from the *Baptism* (on the entrance wall), to the *Battle against Maxentius* (on the facing wall), the *Apparition of the Cross*, the mythical *Donation*. Raffaellino Del Colle and, above all, Francesco Penni were Giulio Romano's collaborators.

Above: The Expulsion of Heliodorus from the Temple, by Raphael, in the Stanza di Eliodoro.

*General view of the Sistine Chapel before restoration.
On the back wall, Michelangelo's great fresco of
the Last Judgement.*

SISTINE CHAPEL

Between 1475 and 1481, under the pontificate of Sixtus IV Della Rovere, Giovannino de' Dolci, on a plan by Baccio Pontelli, built what may be called the Chapel of Chapels. Architecturally the Sistine Chapel is a spacious rectangular hall with a barrel vault, divided into two unequal parts by a splendid marble *transenna* or screen by Mino da Fiesole together with Giovanni il Dalmata and Andrea Bregno. The same artists also made the *choir loft.*

But the chief attractions of the Sistine Chapel are of course its frescoes, particularly those by Michelangelo, on the walls and vault. Michelangelo's marvelous paintings, however, came after others, which had been painted under the pontificate of Sixtus IV between 1481 and 1483, and which cover the wall facing the altar and the two side walls (these include paintings by Perugino, Pin-

turicchio, Luca Signorelli, Cosimo Rosselli, Domenico Ghirlandaio, Botticelli). The vault was blue and scattered with stars until Julius II commissioned Michelangelo to redecorate the vast surface.

Michelangelo worked on the ceiling from 1508 to 1512 and created a powerful architectural framework for the well known figures of the *Sibyls* and the *Prophets*, the elegant bold *Ignudi*, the nine *Stories from Genesis*, including the universally famous *Creation of Man.*

Twenty-five years later, between 1536 and 1541, Michelangelo returned to the Sistine Chapel, this time under the papacy of Paul III Farnese. The new great fresco of the *Last Judgement* covers the whole back wall of the Sistine Chapel and it was so large that two of Perugino's frescoes had to be destroyed and two large arched windows had to be walled up.

Facing page, above: The Creation of Adam, by
Michelangelo, in the Sistine Chapel, and, below, a detail;
above: the Original Sin and The Expulsion from the
Earthly Paradise.

The photos on these and the following pages were taken
after recent restoration had revealed the original splendor
of the colors of Michelangelo's famous frescoes in the
Sistine Chapel.

MICHELANGELO IN THE SISTINE CHAPEL

*Michelangelo, the famed master of the Sistine Chapel,
completed his frescoes in two phases: the period between
1508 and 1512 was employed in painting the vaults under
commission of Pope Julius II, whereas his other masterpiece, the Last Judgement, was commissioned by Pope
Clement VII for the back wall of the chapel nearly a
quarter of a century later. These two frescoes, which
cover a surface of approximately 800 square meters,
represent perhaps the greatest artistic achievement of all
time. Beginning from the back, of the left-hand, side of
the vault we can see:* Jeremiah in meditation, *the* Persian
Sibyl reading, Ezekiel holding a papyrus as he listens to
an angel, *the* Eritrean Sibyl consulting a book, Joel reading a papyrus, Zachariah consulting a book, *the* Delphic
Sibyl unwinding a papyrus, Isiah in meditation with a
book in his hand, *the* Cumaean Sibyl opening a book,
Daniel writing, *the* Libyan Sibyl turning to pick up a
book *and last* Jonah in ecstasy at the moment of his exit
from the whale's belly. *Above these twelve figures, softly*

*rendered nude figures support festoons and medallions.
In the center, nine pictures reproduce the stories of the
Genesis: beginning from the one above the altar we find:*
God separating light from darkness, God creating the
Sun, the Moon, and the plants on Earth, God separating
the waters and creating fish and birds, *followed by the
well-known* Creation of Adam, *the* Creation of Eve from
Adam's rib, *the* Original sin *and the* Expulsion of Adam
and Eve from the garden of Eden, *the* Flood, *and* Noah's
drunkenness. *The vault is also crowned by numerous triangular sections depicting other stories from the Old
Testament:* Judith and Holofernes, David and Goliath,
Ahasuerus, Esther and Haman, *and the* Bronze serpent.
*The lunettes of the windows, and above them the vault
sections, contain equally splendid frescoes depicting
Christ's ancestors. An impressive pictorial composition
representing the* Last Judgement *rotates around the com-
manding figures of Christ who, with an expressive and
dramatic gesture, condems sinners.*

The Original Sin, by Michelangelo, the restored fresco.

The Expulsion from Paradise, by Michelangelo, restored fresco.

Above and on the preceding page: two restored lunettes with Prophets and Sibyls.

Following pages: the vault of the Sistine Chapel after its skillful restoration.

THE RESTORED SISTINE CHAPEL

The restoration of Michelangelo's great frescoes on the vault of the Sistine Chapel and of the Last Judgement has finally been terminated. Merit goes above all to the contribution of the Nippon Television Network Corporation which employed sophisticated technological means in the television filming of each detail.

Begun in 1981 and shown to the public in the spring of 1994, the restored works took scholars by surprise and in part opened up new questions regarding the literature on the master's oeuvre which, up to that time had centered around

Michelangelo's somber hues and his introspective approach to color. As the work of restoration progressed, layers of candle smoke, damage due to atmospheric agents and other causes were removed and the authentic colors gradually emerged. The frescoes can once more be seen in their original glowing light-toned hues, unquestionably more shocking and modern than those that preceded them.

A «rediscovered» Michelangelo, the painter of the Sistine Chapel, who continues to amaze us even after almost five centuries.

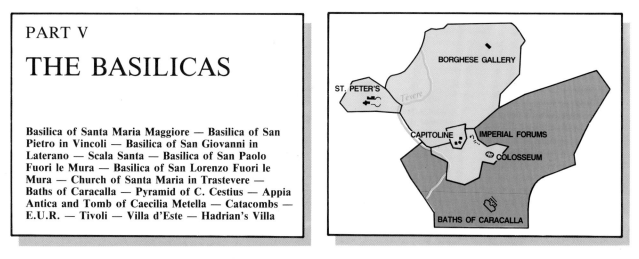

PART V
THE BASILICAS

Basilica of Santa Maria Maggiore — Basilica of San Pietro in Vincoli — Basilica of San Giovanni in Laterano — Scala Santa — Basilica of San Paolo Fuori le Mura — Basilica of San Lorenzo Fuori le Mura — Church of Santa Maria in Trastevere — Baths of Caracalla — Pyramid of C. Cestius — Appia Antica and Tomb of Caecilia Metella — Catacombs — E.U.R. — Tivoli — Villa d'Este — Hadrian's Villa

BASILICA OF SANTA MARIA MAGGIORE

In the 4th century a church, which was the ancestor of the present Basilica, was built on the hill of the Esquiline. The church was popularly called Santa Maria della Neve because Pope Liberius had drawn the perimeter in the snow which had miraculously fallen in the summer of 352. The present Church of Santa Maria Maggiore was completely rebuilt by Sixtus III (432-440) after the Council of Ephesus (and the holy arch does indeed bear the dedicatory inscription « XYSTUS.EPISCOPUS. PLE-BI. DEI »). The Basilica stayed as it was up to the 13th century when Eugene III had a portico built for the principal elevation, much like those still extant for example in San Lorenzo fuori le Mura or in San Giorgio al Velabro. At the end of that century, Nicholas IV promoted the renovation of the apse and not until the 18th century, after having demolished the original portico, did Clement X entrust the creation of a new facade to Ferdinando Fuga.

Below: the Basilica of Santa Maria Maggiore. Opposite, above: the mosaics of the apse conch and, below, the imposing interior of the basilica.

This **facade** almost seems to be squeezed between two tall palaces (dating to the 17th and 18th centuries), and sits at the top of a spacious flight of steps. There is a portico with an architrave on the ground floor and a loggia with arches above, the whole crowned by a balustrade which curiously extends on either side of the facade to include the twin palaces at the sides. A rich sculptural decoration runs along the front and under the portico, while the loggia of the upper floor still preserves the mosaic decoration of the old 13th-century facade.

The **interior** is on a tripartite basilican plan with forty Ionic columns supporting a trabeation with a mosaic frieze. The flat *ceiling* is commonly attributed to Giuliano da Sangallo, while, as to be expected, the *pavement* is in Cosmatesque work although much of it was restored under Benedict XIV. An old tradition says that the rich gold decoration of the ceiling was made with the first gold that came from America, given to the Basilica by the Kings of Spain who were the illustrious protectors.

The chapels that branch off from the aisles mostly date to the 16th century. Of particular note are the **Sistine Chapel**, a Greek-cross plan with a cupola, by Domenico Fontana, and the **Paolina Chapel**, like the former in plan, by Flaminio Ponzio. Lastly, of importance in the right aisle is the Baptistery, also designed by Flaminio Ponzio, into which Valadier set a porphyry *baptismal font*.

BASILICA OF SAN PIETRO IN VINCOLI

This basilica stands on the slope of the Esquiline hill, overlooking the plain where the Capitoline, Palatine, and Caelian hills run together. The name of the church derives from a legend about Eudocia, wife of the emperor of the Eastern Empire, Theodosius II. During a pilgrimage to Jerusalem, she is said to have found the chains which had been used to bind the apostle Peter. Part of these chains remained in Constantinople, but some of the links were sent to Rome to Eudocia minore who in turn presented them to the pope. And then came the miracle. While Leo the Great was holding them, the links were miraculously welded together with other links said to come from the same holy chain and already venerated in Rome. Be that as it may San Pietro does not appear to have been consecrated by Leo the Great but by his predecessor, Sixtus III, who was pope from 432 to 440. Moreover the present building, the one which was consecrated, was preceded by another church of a different name. Excavations have revealed the remains of an apsed hall with a single nave and a « pierced » presbytery, dating to the third century and enclosed in the area of the church built in the middle of the 5th century by Philip, who however tended to a« modern » solution, replacing the simple straight hall with a tripartite structure with a transept. Perhaps the best known and most incisive restorations of the Basilica are the so-called Roverian restorations, promulgated by Cardinal Francesco Della Rover (later Pope Sixtus IV) and above all Cardinal Giuliano Della Rovere, who became titular of St. Pietro in Vincoli in December 1471. These restora-

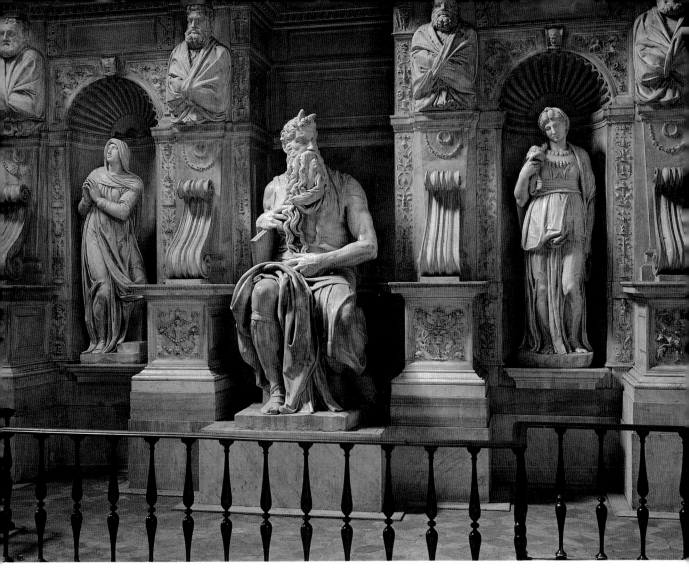

Opposite, above: the entrance to the Basilica of San Pietro in Vincoli; below: the chains with which the apostle Peter was supposedly bound. Above: Michelangelo's Moses between Rachel and Leah.

tions, which were finished in 1475 (for the Jubilee) or at the latest in 1483, seem to have been planned and directed by the architect Baccio Pontelli, who appears also to have prepared the project for the renovation of the palace annexed to the Basilica and the adjoining Cloister, which were however not finished until Julius II.

The *tomb of Julius II* was set up around 1540 after numberless vicissitudes. The contract that Michelangelo signed with the executors of the Pope's will is dated May 6, 1513, and stipulated for twenty-eight figures and three reliefs, all to be set in a suitable architectural setting. The entire project was to be finished in seven years at a total cost of 16,500 gold ducats. But as time went by, the project kept shrinking and the successive stages of the project are witnessed by contracts of 1516 and 1532. Ultimately the final agreement between the artist and the heirs provided for only three statues by Michelangelo and three by Raffaelo da Montelupo. All that now remains in San Pietro in Vincoli is the famous Moses, seated between *Rachel* (or the *Contemplative Life*) and *Leah* (or

the *Active Life*), while the mortal remains of Julius II were wretchedly lost during the ill-omened sack of Rome in 1527. In the second half of the 16th century, still further modifications were carried out on the old Early Christian Basilica which had already been so heavily restored. An additional structure was added above the portico, which ended up by concealing the old openings so that new ones had to be put in. In 1705 Francesco Fontana, son of Carlo, was charged by Giovan Battista Pamphili with the screening off of the open trussed timber beams of the roof by means of a large wooden vault, while the framing of the portal on the interior by an aedicule dates to sixty years later. This was also when the Basilica was repaved in brick, altering the original level by raising the floor about ten centimeters. The last change was made by Vespignani and is mentioned here because it is an important element in the present aspect of the church. Vespignani worked on the area of the presbytery and replaced the Baroque altar with a typical open *ciborium* preceded by the confessio.

BASILICA OF SAN GIOVANNI IN LATERANO

Built by Constantine, plundered by the Vandals of Genseric, frequently sacked, damaged by the earthquake of 896 and various fires, the Basilica of St. John Lateran was continuously being rebuilt and restored, with the participation of Giovanni di Stefano, of Francesco Borromini, who brought it up to date for Innocent X, and Alessandro Galilei, who redid the facade in 1735. **Outside**, the Cathedral of Rome is characterized by the monumental architectonic structure of the giant Corinthian order used by Galilei, and it is enlivened by the jutting central part and the balustrade, above the attic, and the colossal statues of *Christ*, *Saints John the Baptist* and *John the Evangelist* and the *Doctors of the Church*. There are five entrances (the last to the right is known as « Porta Santa » and is opened only for the Holy Year or jubilee), surmounted by five loggias.

The imposing **interior** is a Latin cross with a nave and two aisles on either side. The antique columns were encased in robust piers, while grooved pilasters support a rich trabeation and above, a sumptuous ceiling, said to have been designed by Pirro Ligorio. Along the walls are ranged the figures of *Prophets*, *Saints*, and *Apostles* designed by Borromini but executed by his followers in the 18th century. At the crossing, the visitor unexpectedly finds himself at the Gothic heart of the Basilica: the *tabernacle* by Giovanni di Stefano, an airy slender silhouette against the gilded grates which enclose the precious relics of the heads of Saints Peter and Paul. Another of St. Peter's relics, the rough wooden altar table on which the apostle is said to have celebrated mass in the catacombs, is preserved in the papal altar. A double flight of stairs leads to the subterranean burial of Martin V, with its well-known *tomb slab* by Simone Ghini, probably under Donatello's supervision. The great conch of the apse at the back of the Basilica is covered with mosaics which date to different periods. Some are 4th century, some 6th and some 13th century (note in particular the figures of the *Apostles*, signed by Jacopo Torriti). Above the organ, the large 19th-century frescoes by Francesco Grandi depicting episodes, both ancient and modern, concerning the *Founding and construction of the Basilica*. The decoration which entirely covers the transept also deals with this subject (including the *Conversion of Constantine*) and was completely restored under the papacy of Clement VIII by the architect Giovanni della Porta and the painter known as Cavalier d'Arpino. Right under Cavalier d'Arpino's fresco of the *Ascension of Christ* is the *gable* in gilded bronze and supported by antique bronze columns which protects the *Altar of the Sacrament*, designed for Clement VIII by Pietro Paolo Olivieri and holding a precious *ciborium* like a small classic temple. Among the chapels which were built in various periods as further decoration for the Basilica, note should be taken of the so-called **Cappella del Coro**, by Girolamo Rainaldi (1570-1655); the **Cappella del** **Crocifisso**, which preserves a fragment of the presumed *Funeral Monument of Nicholas IV*, attributed to Adeodato di Cosma (13th century); the **Cappella Massimo**, by Giacomo della Porta; the **Cappella Torlonia**, unlike the precedent, splendidly decorated in neo-Renaissance style by the architect Raimondi (1850); the **Cappella Corsini**, architecturally completely self sufficient, on a Greekcross plan, by Alessandro Galilei for Clement XII. A corridor leads to the **Old Sacristy**, with the *Annunciation* by Venusti, and a *St. John the Evangelist* by Cavalier d'Arpino, and to the **New Sacristy**, with the 15th-century *Annunciation* of Tuscan school.

SCALA SANTA

The **Palazzo** owes its name to the fact that it was originally built to contain, or incorporate, the **Pope's Chapel** or *Sancta Sanctorum*. Pope Sixtus V commissioned the palace from the architect Domenico Fontana in 1585-1590. The Chapel was originally part of a building known as « Patriarchio » (7th-8th century), when it housed the papal court. The name **Scala Santa** derives from an erroneous identification of one of the staircases of the Patriarchio with a flight of stairs that was part of Pilate's *Praetorium* and which therefore would have been ascended by Christ when he was judged by Pilate. Nowadays the *Sancta Sanctorum* is used to indicate the **Chapel of Saint Laurence**, overflowing with relics and at the same time a true jewel of Cosmatesque art.

Opposite: the facade and interior of San Giovanni in Laterano. Below: the Scala Santa.

BASILICA OF SAN PAOLO FUORI LE MURA

Built by Constantine on the tomb of the apostle Paul, the church remained standing until July 15, 1823, when it was gutted by fire, not to be reconsecrated until 1854. On the **exterior**, St. Paul's now has an imposing quadriporticus in front of the main facade (on the side towards the Tiber) with 146 granite columns which define a space that is dominated by the statue of the *Apostle Paul*, by Pietro Canonica. The facade, which rises over the quadriporticus is richly decorated with mosaics both in the gable (the *Blessing Christ between Saints Peter and Paul*) and in the frieze (an *Agnus Dei* on a hill that rises up symbolically between the two holy cities of Jerusalem and Bethlehem) and the four large *Symbols of the Prophets*, which alternate with the three windows of the facade. The **interior** is just as richly decorated and is divided into a nave with two aisles on either side, separated by eighty columns in granite from Baveno. A continuous frieze runs along the crossing and the aisles with *Portraits of the 263 popes successors of Saint Peter*. On the walls, Corinthian pilasters rhythmically alternate with large windows with alabaster panes (which replace those destroyed in the explosion of 1893). The coffered ceiling has large gilded panels which stand out against the white ground.

Left: the facade of San Paolo fuori le Mura and, below, the interior of the basilica.

Two imposing statues of *Saints Peter and Paul* overlook the raised transept with the sumptuous *triumphal arch*, called the *Arch of Galla Placidia*, which dates to the time of Leo the Great, framing the apse which was already decorated with mosaics in the 5th century. In the 13th century the mosaics were renewed by Honorius III, using Venetian craftsmen who were sent for the purpose to the pope by the doge of Venice. The mosaics depict a *Blessing Christ between Saints Peter, Paul, Andrew, and Luke*, while Honorius, significantly in much smaller proportions, kisses the foot of the Savior. The *Redeemer* is also set on the gold-ground mosaic in the triumphal arch, this time flanked by two *Adoring Angels* and the *Symbols of the Evangelists*, dominating the two rows of the *Elders of the Apocalypse* with the slightly off-center figures of *Saint Peter and Saint Paul* on either side on a blue ground. Objects housed in the Basilica include the *tabernacle* Arnolfo di Cambio made in 1285 in collaboration with a certain « Petro », identified by some as Pietro Cavallini, also thought to have executed the *mosaics* (of which only fragments remain) decorating the back side of the arch of triumph and which once adorned the exterior of the Basilica. Under the fine canopy of Arnolfo's tabernacle is the altar beneath which is the *tomb of Saint Paul* with the inevitable *fenestrella confessionis* (confessional window) through which can be seen the epigraph incised on the stone « *Paulo Apostolo Mart.* », dating to the 4th century.

Right and below: two sections of the elegant cloister of San Paolo fuori le Mura.

BASILICA OF SAN LORENZO FUORI LE MURA

Built on the tomb of the deacon Laurence during Constantinian's time, the basilica was enlarged in 1210 and between 1848 and 1864. The main **facade** is now preceded by a hexastyle narthex on antique columns (the capitals are of more recent date) which support a simple trabeation with mosaic decoration, while the **interior** of the portico repeats the decoration of a feigned curtain wall in red and white. Three entrances lead into the **interior** which is characterized by an evident lack of homogeneity: a typical basilica with a nave and two aisles, ending in a triumphal arch (the *Honorian Basilica*, known also as « western ») and a second lower structure, not in line with the former, with columns on three sides and a women's gallery (which is the Pelagian Basilica, known also as « eastern »). The « eastern » Basilica also contains the *Tomb of St. Laurence* in the nave, in correspondence to the ciborium (dated 1148) by the Roman marble artisans Giovanni, Pietro, Angelo, and Sasso, sons of Paolo. Lastly the Pelagian mosaic on the central arch depicts the *Blessing Christ* with an astylar cross, *between Saints Peter, Paul, Laurence and Stephen*, and at either end, *Hippolitus* and *Pelagius II*, who as to be expected offers the Saviour a model of the renewed church.

CHURCH OF SANTA MARIA IN TRASTEVERE

Founded as early as the 3rd century by Saint Calixtus and terminated under St. Julius, Santa Maria in Trastevere basically maintained its original aspect, notwithstanding various restorations in the course of the centuries (as was the case with other churches of more or less this period), until the 18th century, when Pope Clement VII had the architect Carlo Fontana add on a portico.

The **facade** therefore has a large crowning gable, and is divided by three large arched openings which correspond to the three richly decorated portals under the portico.

The **interior** is, as to be expected, a tripartite basilica with columns of various diameters and orders (Ionic and Corinthian), with a presbytery, and an apse that is decorated with *mosaics* by Pietro Cavallini as well as other mosaics (in the upper zone) that date to the middle of the 12th century.

Various chapels are scattered along the perimeter of the church, the most outstanding of which (due also to their position on either side of the apse) are the so-called **Winter Choir** and the richly decorated **Altemps Chapel** by Martino Longhi the Elder. Lastly, next to the Basilica is the fine Romanesque **campanile** which has an ancient bell over the roof.

Opposite, above: the Baths of Caracalla; below: a fresco from the Roman period
with a scene of life in the baths. Above: the pyramid of Cestius near Porta San Paolo.

BATHS OF CARACALLA

The Baths of Caracalla are the most imposing and best preserved example of thermae from the Imperial period still extant. They were built by Caracalla beginning in A.D. 212. In the 16th century excavations carried out in the enormous building brought to light various works of art including the *Farnese Bull* and the *Hercules*, now in the National Museum of Naples. *Mosaics with athletes*, which decorated the hemicycles of the large side courtyards of the thermae, were discovered in 1824 (Vatican Museums).

In their ground plan the Baths of Caracalla clearly distinguished between the actual bath sector and the surroundings where all the accessory non-bathing services were located.

At present the central building is accessible and the itinerary is quite like that followed in antiquity by the bathers. The vestibule leads on the right into a square chamber, flanked by two small rooms on either side, covered with barrel vaults. This was the *apodyterium* (dressing-room). Next came one of the two large palaestrae from where the bathing itinerary generally started after various sports and exercises had been done in the palaestra. From here one went to a *laconicum* (turkish bath), the imposing *calidarium* (hot bath) and the *tepidarium* (temperate bath), a more modest rectangular chamber flanked by two pools. Next came the large central hall, the *frigidari-*
um. The *natatio*, which could also be reached from the *frigidarium*, was uncovered. It has a fine front elevation with groups of niches between columns, once meant to contain statues.

PYRAMID OF C. CESTIUS

The funeral building dating to the early imperial period was obviously inspired by Egyptian models, of the Ptolemaic rather than Pharaonic period, fashionable in Rome after the conquest of Egypt (30 B.C.). The base measures 29.50 m. on each side and the pyramid is 36.40 m. high. On the west side is a small door that leads into the funeral chamber, a hollow in the concrete core which has a rectangular ground plan (m. 5,85x4) and is covered with a barrel vault and faced with *opus latericium*, a facing of brick. The wall was then plastered and richly painted in the so-called third Pompeian style. Interest has centered on the building ever since the Middle Ages when it was called « *Meta Remi* ». An inscription placed on the monument records the fact that in 1660 Pope Alexander VII authorized the excavation. Four antique inscriptions, one on the east side, one on the west, and two engraved on the pedestals which supported the bronze statues of the deceased (in the Capitoline Museums), document the public offices and the heirs of the man for whom the tomb was made.

APPIA ANTICA AND TOMB OF CAECILIA METELLA

The most important of the Roman consular roads, known as *Regina Viarum* (the queen of roads), begins at Porta San Sebastiano and winds towards the interior bordered with ancient monuments and others that are not so old. Miraculous events such as the famous « *Domine quo vadis?* » are thought to have taken place here.

The **Tomb of Caecilia Metella** lies on the Via Appia Antica. This sumptuous mausoleum, a typical example, was originally built for Caecilia, wife of Crassus and daughter of Quintus Metellus, conqueror of Crete. It belongs to the late republican period and was modified in 1302 by the Caetani who adapted it as a tower to defend their neighboring castle. Even so the tomb chamber of the ancient tomb with its conical cover can still be identified.

CATACOMBS

These deep galleries were once quarries for travertine and pozzolana. Situated at the periphery of Rome, they became meeting places for the early Christians and shortly thereafter were also used as cemeteries (1st-4th cent.). Mention will be made of those of Domitilla, Saint Calixtus, Saint Sebastian, Saint Agnes and Priscilla. In the 16th century they were rediscovered and reappraised after centuries of abandon.

The **Catacombs of Saint Domitilla**, known also as catacombs of SS. Achilleus and Nereus, are the largest in Rome and traditionally developed from a simple family burial ground that belonged to Domitilla, wife or niece of the consul Flavius Clemente put to death by Domitian. The catacombs contain the remains of the Basilica of SS. Nereus and Achilleus, behind the apse of which is a cubicle with the fresco of the *Deceased Veneranda invoking St. Petronilla*. The ancient burial grounds of the Aurelian Flavians lie near the basilica. In another part of the catacombs, named after the *Good Shepherd* because the earliest representation of this subject was found here, paintings from the 2nd century are to be found in the vault. Lastly, in the area of later date there are fine depictions of the grain market, scenes of daily life and work (3rd-4th cent.).

The **Catacombs of Saint Calixtus** are just as famous and extend for twenty kilometers. They were developed by Pope Calixtus III and became the official burial grounds for the bishops of Rome. They are excavated on four levels and contain the *Crypt of the Popes*, in which several of the early popes were buried. They contain interesting decorations as well as epigraphs of Pontianus Lucius Eutychianus and Sixtus II. The *Cubiculum of Saint Cecilia*, where the remains of this Christian martyr were found, is decorated with painting from the 7th and and 8th centuries. After this comes the *Gallery of the Sepulchers*, again with interesting paintings, the fine *Crypt of Pope Eusebius* and the *Crypt of Lucina*. The most remote parts of the necropolis (2nd cent. A.D.) are decorated with paintings of fish and symbols of the Eucharist.

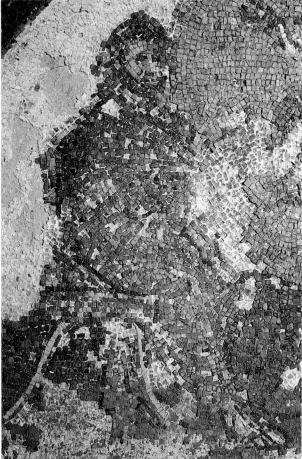

Above: a marble sarcophagus in the catacombs. Left: the mosaic depicting St. Peter, 4th cent. A.D., in the Catacombs of Saint Domitilla.

The **Catacombs of Saint Sebastian** are also excavated on four levels: the first has been partially destroyed but still has an austere chapel where St. Philip Neri used to go to pray; on the second floor is an intimate crypt, known as the *Crypt of Saint Sebastian*, with a *Bust of the saint* attributed to Bernini. An underground passage leads to three tombs with decorations and stuccoes dating to the 1st century A.D.

At the side: a room with loculi in the catacombs. Below, left: the statue of the Good Shepherd (4th cent. A.D.) from the Catacombs of Saint Domitilla. One of the rooms is shown on the right.

E.U.R.

This famous district, at one and the same time the most recent and the most historical, was originally created for the Esposizione Universale di Rome (World Fair of Rome) to be held in 1942. Designed by a group of famous architects (Pagano, Piccinato, Vietti, and Rossi) coordinated and directed by Marcello Piacentini, it covers an area of 420 hectares in the shape of a pentagon.

The formative concept was that of monumentality and it was built with a view to the future expansion of Rome towards the Tyrrhenian Sea. Included among its significant paradigms of Italian architecture of the first half of the 20th century are the **Palazzo della Civiltà del Lavoro**, as well as the sites of the **Museo Preistorico ed Etnografico Pigorini**, the **Museo dell'Alto Medioevo (Early Middle Ages)**, the **Museo delle Arti e Tradizioni Popolari** and the **Museo della Civiltà Romana**.

Opposite, above: the Palazzo della Civiltà
del Lavoro and, below: the Palazzo
dell'ENI, in the quarter of E.U.R. Above:
Villa d'Este in Tivoli.

TIVOLI

VILLA D'ESTE

Right outside Rome, Tivoli, the ancient *Tibur*, was already a favorite holiday resort for the Romans as well as a place for the worship of local divinities. It is now the site of the **Villa Gregoriana**, a fine **Cathedral**, the renowned **Rocca Pia**, and, above all, the **Villa d'Este**, with an Italian garden deservedly famous for its magic atmosphere.

Built on the ruins of a Roman villa, it was first a Benedictine convent and then the Governor's Palace, and as such was magnificently restored by Pirro Ligorio on commission of the governor at the time, Ippolito d'Este, around 1550. After various vicissitudes it became the property of Austria, was returned to the Italians in 1918, then restored before the monumental part and the immense park were opened to the public. Of note on the grounds is the **Loggia** by Pirro Ligorio, which is the finest part of the main facade which faces the city and the mountains.

The **Italian gardens**, with their geometric compartmentalization, the five hundred fountains, the age and rarity of the trees, is certainly one of the finest gardens to be found both in and outside Italy. No visit is complete without a stop at the *Grotto of Diana*, richly stuccoed with mythological scenes, the so-called « *Rometta* » or little Rome, with reproductions in an allusive key of parts of the city (the Isola Tiberina, the ruins), the various *Fountains of Bacchus*, the *Organ Fountain* (the water organ was designed by Claudio Vernard), the *fountains of Proserpine, of the Dragons* (signed by Ligorio), *of the « Mete »*, *of the Eagles*, and so on, up to the romantic *Cypress Rotonda*, considered one of the most enchanting elements in both garden and villa. Even in this end of the garden signs of antiquity are present, as witnessed by the ruins of a **Roman villa** to the right of the Cypress Rotonda.

HADRIAN'S VILLA

Tivoli is also the site of an imposing architectural complex dating to Hadrian's time. This emperor's gifts as an architect can be seen in the series of palaces, baths, theaters, etc. which he had built there between 118 and 134,

On this page: three of the many fountains of Villa d'Este in Tivoli.

and which were meant to remind him, here in Italy, of the places he most loved in Greece and the Near East.
Mentioned for the first time in literature by Flavio Biondo, the Villa, or rather what was left of it, was visited and studied by famous persons (Pope Pius II, Pirro Ligorio) and excavations were carried out particularly in the 18th century (Piranesi made engravings of some parts). Bought by the Italian government in 1870 from the Braschi family which had owned it since the beginning of the 19th century, the villa was restored, while many of the works of art (especially sculpture) from the site can now be seen in the rooms of the Museo Nazionale Romano. Mention will be made only of some of the best known and important places in the complex. For an idea of the entire set-up (and as orientation) a study of the model at the entrance, even though it is more a matter of hypothesis, can be useful. The monuments include the **Stoà Poikile** (commonly called Pecile) and the **Naval Theater**, the **Small Thermae** and the **Great Thermae**, the **Canopus** (with obvious reference to the sanctuary in Egypt), the **Museum** (with the precious objects found in the excavations, including a copy of the *Amazon* by Phidias), and lastly the **Emperor's Palace** subdivided into three blocks and aptly described as a « city in the shape of a palace ».

Above and at the side: two sections of the
Canopus on the grounds of Hadrian's Villa
in Tivoli.

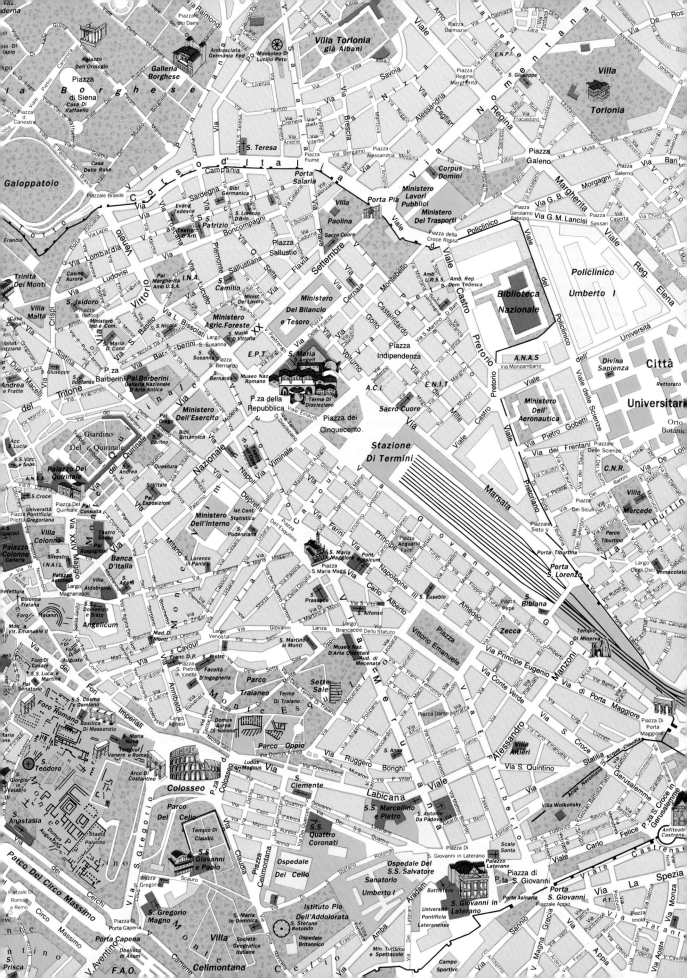

INDEX